WILLS, TRUSTS, AND ESTATE ADMINISTRATION

FOR

PARALEGALS

MARK A. STEWART, J.D.

UNIVERSITY OF CALIFORNIA, LOS ANGELES

MEMBER, STATE BAR OF CALIFORNIA

SOUTH-WESTERN PUBLISHING CO.

1 2 3 4 5 6 7 8 9 0 D 03 02 01 00 99 98 97 96 95 94

Printed in the United States of America

Acquisitions Editor:	Betty Schechter
Production Manager:	Carol Sturzenberger
Managing Editor:	Bob Lewis
Coordinating Editor:	Barry Corrado
Production Editor:	June Davidson
Designer:	James DeSollar
Production Artist:	Sophia Renieris
Associate Photo Editor/Stylist:	Michael O'Donnell
Marketing Manager:	Colleen Thomas

PHOTO CREDITS

p. 165 H. Armstrong Roberts
p. 249 STOCK-BOSTON
p. 277 STOCK-BOSTON
p. 305 H. Armstrong Roberts

Library of Congress Cataloging-in-Publication Data

Stewart, Mark A. (Mark Alan), 1957-
     Wills, trusts, and estate administration for paralegals / Mark A.
Stewart.
          p.   cm.
     Includes index.
     ISBN 0-538-70935-9
     1. Probate law and practice—United States.   2. Inheritance and
succession—United States.   3. Executors and administrators—United
States. 4. Legal assistants—United States—Handbooks, manuals,
etc.   I. Title.
  KF765.S74   1995
  346.7305'2—dc20
  [347.30652]
                                                              93-8745
                                                              CIP

PREFACE

ABOUT THIS TEXTBOOK

Wills, Trusts, and Estate Administration for Paralegals is a practice-oriented textbook for the probate paralegal. It serves both as an ideal primary resource in a formal course of study *and* as a general resource and reference at the workplace. *Wills, Trusts, and Estate Administration for Paralegals* is truly comprehensive in scope—in addition to encompassing all topics one would expect to find under its title, it also includes an in-depth treatment of *protective proceedings* (guardianships and conservatorships) as well as *ethical problems* specific to the working probate paralegal. *Wills, Trusts, and Estate Administration for Paralegals* is written for use in all jurisdictions. Statutes and U.P.C. provisions are included throughout the text for illustration, clarification, and interest. While comprehensive in scope, *Wills, Trusts, and Estate Administration for Paralegals* is not intended as the sole resource in a course of study. The student should also examine the relevant statutes and local court rules in the jurisdiction in which he or she intends to work, as well as consult the federal tax laws and appropriate publications and instructions of the Internal Revenue Service to supplement the tax materials in this text.

The Case-Study Approach

Although *Wills, Trusts, and Estate Administration for Paralegals* provides a solid theoretical foundation for the probate paralegal, its primary concern is with the paralegal's practical, everyday functions. The text immediately brings the student into the law-firm setting by way of two hypothetical case studies. The student follows the text's primary case—the *Estate of Irene Parker*—through the entire process of formal decedents' estate administration, from the initial probate interview to closing the estate. The second case study—involving a married couple named *Walter and Betty Taylor*—serves as a catalyst for exploring the estate-planning process, including the use of *inter vivos* trusts, durable powers of attorney, living wills, and other estate-planning tools and techniques.

Each chapter (except for the final chapter) begins with a *Paralegal Assignment* involving one of the two case studies; the textual materials then provide the student with the knowledge required to carry out the job assignment. References to the appropriate case-file "exhibits" are inserted throughout the text. This format enables the student to examine the textual materials and illustrative forms and legal documents side by side.

ORGANIZATION AND SEQUENCE OF TOPICS

The first chapter includes an overview and a survey of the various forms of property ownership, with particular emphasis on joint ownership between spouses. Chapter 2 begins by examining the laws of intestate succession as a backdrop for a complete discussion of wills in Chapters 2 and 3. The focus of the text shifts to postmortem concerns in Chapter 4, which explores alternatives to formal estate administration and which serves as a prelude to the "main event" in this course of study—formal decedents' estate administration (Chapters 5 through 8).

Chapters 5 through 8 lead the student chronologically through the process of formal estate administration. Chapter 7 is devoted entirely to the important subjects of estate and gift taxation; the central concern of Chapter 7 is the preparation of the federal estate-tax return (IRS Form 706).

With Chapters 5 through 8 in mind, the student will then appreciate the significance and advantages of implementing a comprehensive estate plan, as discussed in Chapter 9. This chapter includes an overview of both the tax and nontax aspects of estate planning. The subject of planning for incapacity is postponed until Chapter 11, which also includes the subject of protective proceedings (guardianships and conservatorships). The procedural aspects of estate planning, with particular emphasis on the implementation and administration of *inter vivos* trusts, are considered in Chapter 10. The final chapter (Chapter 12) offers a unique and provocative look at various issues of professional responsibility that the probate paralegal will confront at the workplace.

Special Format-Related Features

To aid both the student and the instructor in assimilating the textual materials, the following iconic symbols are shown in the left-hand margin throughout the text:

PRACTICE TIP: The materials elaborate on certain procedural issues discussed immediately preceding the symbol. Practice Tips include procedural shortcuts and practical advice that the working probate paralegal would otherwise learn only through experience.

FOCUS: An issue or procedural matter of particular significance is either repeated or summarized for emphasis.

PARKER ESTATE: The textual materials immediately preceding the symbol are examined in the specific context of the *Estate of Irene Parker*.

TAYLOR TRUST: The textual materials immediately preceding the symbol are examined in the specific context of the estate-planning matter of *Walter and Betty Taylor*.

Most of the figures and tables included in the text are intended to convey ideas rather than to show sample forms and legal documents. A figure or table might summarize a chapter section, clarify an abstract idea, provide a classification scheme of some sort, or quote a statute or section of the Uniform Probate Code. Sample forms and legal documents are included in the Resource Manual

Examples are included in the textual materials wherever it is likely that the student will require immediate clarification or illustration of an idea or procedure. Each example presents a realistic hypothetical scenario followed by a *Result.* The text includes examples sparingly. Additional examples are included in the Resource Manual as study questions and, in lesser number, as multiple-choice questions.

ABOUT THE RESOURCE MANUAL

The Resource Manual that accompanies this text is not merely a supplement but is actually an essential and integral component of the course of study. The Resource Manual includes the Parker File and the Taylor File, which contain all of the sample forms, legal documents, and correspondence for the Parker and Taylor case studies. The Resource Manual also includes a generous number of study questions and objective questions for each chapter to reinforce and illustrate the textual materials.

ABOUT THE INSTRUCTOR'S MANUAL

The Instructor's Manual includes numerous features designed with the busy instructor in mind. A detailed annotated outline, suitable for lecturing, is provided for each chapter. Additionally, test questions of varying types are provided for each chapter. These test questions are comparable in style and difficulty level to the study questions and objective questions included in the Resource Manual.

ABOUT THE AUTHOR

Mark A. Stewart earned his Juris Doctor degree from the University of California at Los Angeles in 1984, joining the State Bar of California as an active member in November of that year. He has taught courses in Wills, Trusts, and Estates at the Santa Barbara College of Law and at the Ventura College of Law and has also served as adjunct professor at California Polytechnic State University, San Luis Obispo. He brings to this publication his commitment to excellence, his love of teaching, and his cumulative experience as a practicing attorney, educator, and published author. Mr. Stewart currently resides and works in Santa Barbara, California.

ACKNOWLEDGMENTS

I wish to thank the following members of South-Western Publishing Co. for their editorial and production assistance: Betty Schechter, Mark Linton, Barry Corrado, and June Davidson. I also gratefully acknowledge the assistance of Cat Skintik and of numerous independent reviewers for their editorial contributions. Finally, I extend my special thanks to Mark McCormick, not only for his editorial assistance but also for his continual encouragement and support.

In fondness, I dedicate this book to Darthy Vader.

Mark Alan Stewart

SUMMARY OF CONTENTS

CONTENTS

1 THE FIELD OF PROBATE LAW

Paralegal Assignment 1

Able, Berman & Cargis is a medium-sized law firm located in your community. The firm has recently established a separate probate department, which currently includes two attorneys, two secretaries, and one paralegal. The firm has decided to hire you as a second probate paralegal in this department to assist in establishing office forms and procedures and to accommodate the increasing volume of business. You will be supervised by Elaine Cargis, a partner of the firm. Ms. Cargis has scheduled an orientation session for you on Friday afternoon, during which you will meet with her and the other probate paralegal.

Ms. Cargis has suggested that as your first task you familiarize yourself with some concepts and terminology fundamental to a probate law practice prior to your orientation on Friday afternoon. She is particularly concerned that you become familiar with the various forms of shared ownership in property, because these concepts are central to a probate law practice and because you will be dealing with them on a daily basis. Ms. Cargis has given you the following materials to review before your orientation. She also has assured you that after your orientation (that is, beginning with Chapter 2), subsequent assignments will relate directly to actual client matters.

WILLS, TRUSTS, AND ESTATE ADMINISTRATION: A BIRD'S EYE VIEW

Wills, trusts, and estate administration deal primarily with the methods and processes of transferring a person's wealth, also referred to as the person's

estate, at death. A deceased person is referred to in the law as a **decedent**. A decedent who fails to provide a method of transferring his or her property upon death is said to have died **intestate**; this death is said to result in **intestacy**. The disposition of intestate property is governed by the laws of **intestate succession**, which generally provide for distribution to the decedent's closest living family member or members. An alternative distribution scheme may be provided for through proper planning, as discussed below.

Estate Planning

Estate planning involves developing a plan for building and preserving one's estate during one's lifetime and for transferring the estate after death. Lawyers, as well as other professional advisers such as financial planners, accountants, and stockbrokers, each serve their own respective function in the estate-planning process. The lawyer's role involves the legal aspects of estate planning, especially as they relate to the protection, proper management, and orderly distribution of an estate upon a person's incapacity or death. The lawyer employs a variety of planning tools to achieve these ends.

The most common estate-planning tool is the **will**. The primary purpose of the will is to provide for the disposition of a person's property after death in accordance with the person's wishes. A person who has died leaving a valid will is said to have died **testate** and is referred to after death as the **testator** of the will. These two terms are derived from the word **testament**, which is a synonym for the term *will*. A will has no legal effect until the person making the will has died; accordingly, a person is free to modify or revoke a will in any way prior to death.

A person may also avoid intestacy by using a trust. A **trust** is a legal entity created generally by a trust agreement executed either during a person's lifetime or after death for the purpose of management and control of the person's property. All trusts involve three essential parties:

1. The *settlor* (also referred to as the *trustor* or *grantor*), who transfers title in certain property to another person
2. The *trustee*, who is given legal title to the property, but must manage and distribute the trust property for the benefit of another person
3. The *beneficiary*, who is entitled to the benefits of the trust (according to its provisions)

Trusts are typically used to delay distribution to the beneficiary, although they may serve several other purposes as well. A **testamentary trust** is established under the terms of a will. Thus, this type of trust is not established and has no legal effect until after the trustor's death. In contrast, an *inter vivos* **trust** is established and is effective during the settlor's lifetime. The Latin term *inter vivos* means "among or between the living." One of the primary purposes of an *inter vivos* trust is to circumvent formal estate administration (see *Administration of Decedents' Estates and Trust Estates*). Property placed in trust during the settlor's lifetime is not generally subject to estate administration after the settlor's death. Instead, such property is managed and distributed, both during and after the settlor's lifetime, by the trustee according to the trustor's instructions. In this sense, an *inter vivos* trust serves as a substitute for a will.

Other common methods of transferring property at death include using the joint-tenancy form of property ownership (see *Forms of Property Ownership*), using certain types of accounts at financial institutions, as well as exercising various options under insurance policies and employee benefit plans. Like *inter vivos* trusts, these methods serve as will substitutes—for example, joint tenancy property passes automatically and directly to the surviving joint tenant(s), while insurance proceeds and employee death benefits pass to the designated beneficiaries, without passing through formal estate administration.

FOCUS: Decedent's estate administration may be circumvented through the use of an *inter vivos* trust, joint-tenancy form of ownership, or death-beneficiary designations for insurance plans and financial accounts. However, estate administration will not be avoided through the use of a simple will or testamentary trust.

Administration of Decedents' Estates and Trust Estates

The laws relating to wills and the disposition of property under a will are shaped by the important underlying notion that persons should have control over how their property will be distributed upon death. The court-supervised process of **decedent's estate administration** ensures the proper and orderly distribution of the decedent's estate. The court must be satisfied that all of the decedent's assets are accounted for, that legitimate claims of the decedent's creditors have been satisfied, and that the proposed distribution is proper. Additionally, the decedent's surviving spouse or children are generally entitled to various forms of protection against creditors and impoverishment prior to distribution of the decedent's property to other parties. All property disposed of under the terms of a will, as well as all intestate property, is subject to estate administration. Figure 1-1 shows the process of decedent's estate administration as part of the overall life cycle of a person's estate.

The person in charge of collecting these assets, paying the decedent's debts, and distributing the remaining property is referred to as the **administrator** of the estate. A will typically nominates someone to serve as administrator; this nominee, if appointed, is called the **executor** of the will. In some states, the administrator of an estate or executor is referred to instead as the **personal representative** of the estate (throughout this book, the term *executor* is used where appropriate; otherwise, the term *personal representative* will be used). Estate administration is also commonly referred to as **probate**, although the term *probate* technically refers to the process of proving and deciding the validity of a will, which is only the first step in the administration of an estate where the decedent died leaving a valid will.

FIGURE 1-1   THE LIFE CYCLE OF AN ESTATE

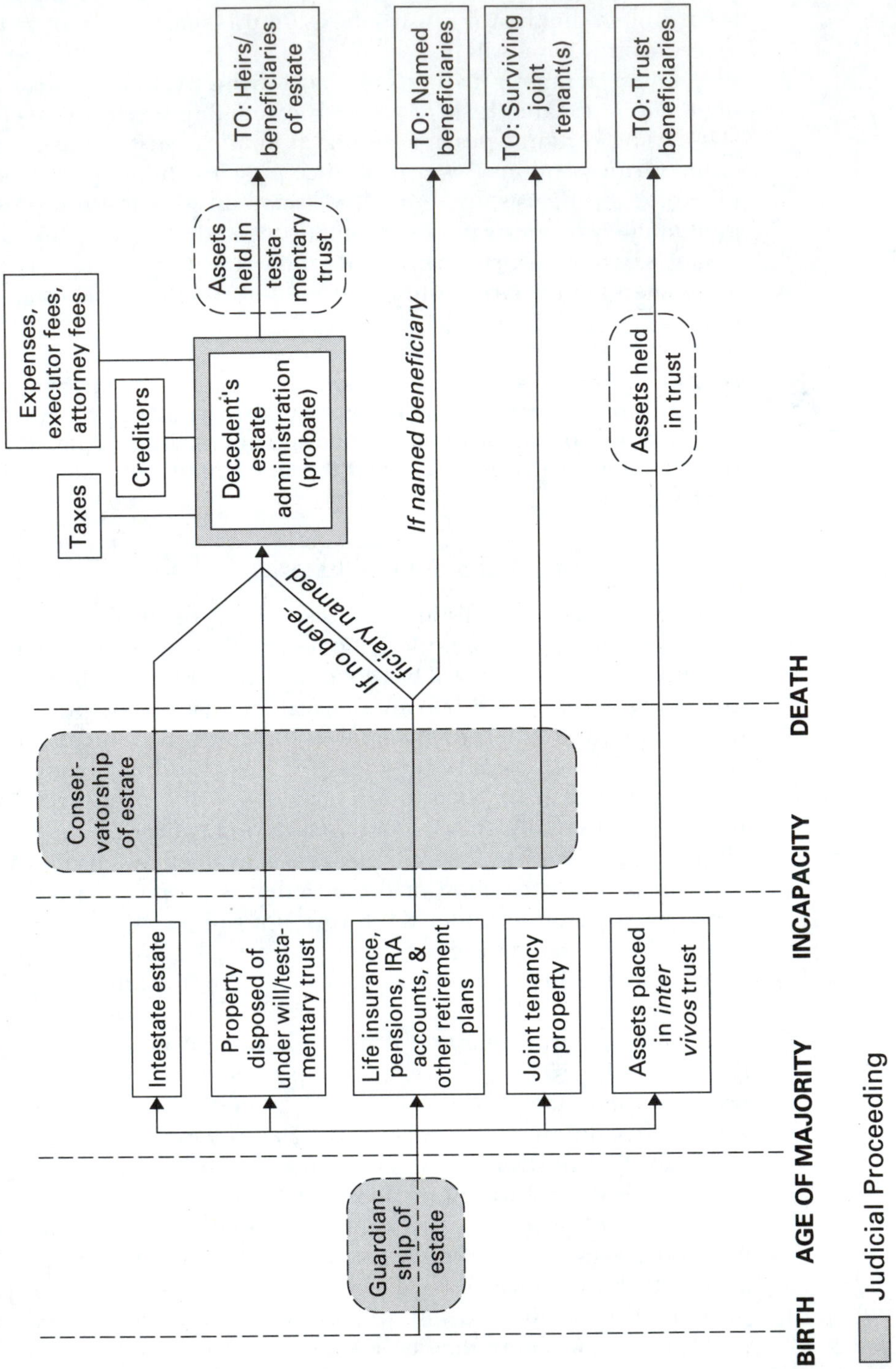

BIRTH   AGE OF MAJORITY   INCAPACITY   DEATH

Guardian-ship of estate

Conser-vatorship of estate

Intestate estate

Property disposed of under will/testa-mentary trust

Life insurance, pensions, IRA accounts, & other retirement plans

Joint tenancy property

Assets placed in *inter vivos* trust

If no bene-ficiary named

If named beneficiary

Taxes

Creditors

Expenses, executor fees, attorney fees

Decedent's estate administration (probate)

Assets held in testa-mentary trust

Assets held in trust

TO: Heirs/beneficiaries of estate

TO: Named beneficiaries

TO: Surviving joint tenant(s)

TO: Trust beneficiaries

Judicial Proceeding

The process of managing and distributing property placed in trust, or the *trust estate*, is referred to as **trust administration**. Trustees face a variety of decisions in the course of managing a trust and distributing trust assets to the beneficiaries of the trust. Many of these decisions require the trustee to understand its legal powers as trustee as well as its legal duties to the beneficiaries.

Personal representatives of decedents' estates and trustees are two types of *fiduciaries*. A **fiduciary** is a person who holds a position of high trust and confidence, thereby owing the highest possible legal duties of diligence and loyalty to those whose interests they represent. The personal representative in the case of a decedent's estate represents the interests of the decedent as a fiduciary, while a trustee stands as a fiduciary in relation to the beneficiaries of the trust.

Protective Proceedings

A *guardian* is another example of a fiduciary. A guardian represents the interests of another living person, referred to as the *ward*, who is legally incapable of handling his or her own affairs. In some states, the guardian of an adult is referred to as a *conservator*, while the adult ward is referred to as the *conservatee*. As in the case of a decedent, a formal court process is generally required in order to ensure that the interests of the ward (in a guardianship) or conservatee (in a conservatorship) are properly protected. Guardianship proceedings for the benefit of a minor terminate when the minor reaches the age of majority (generally 18). In the case of an adult, the guardianship (or conservatorship) continues until the ward (or conservatee) is once again able to handle his or her own affairs or until his or her death. Because guardianships resemble decedents' estates in so many important legal aspects, they are considered together as part of the same field of law. Figure 1-1 shows where a guardianship or conservatorship proceeding might occur during the life cycle of an estate.

FOCUS: Trustees, guardians, conservators, and personal representatives of decedents' estates are all fiduciaries, thereby owing the highest duty of diligence and loyalty to those whose interests they represent.

SOURCES OF LAW

The concept of individual ownership in property distinct from ownership by a family or clan can be traced back to ancient times. Our modern laws of succession to property and testamentary disposition of property are derived more directly from English common law.

Under the early feudal system in England, although testamentary rights regarding personal property were recognized, real property was owned exclusively by a small number of lords, and ownership could pass only to certain surviving family members of these lords. The laws respecting real property were created and administered by the king's courts. These laws slowly evolved, over a period of several centuries, to allow testamentary disposition of real property to persons outside the lord's family.

The laws of succession to personal property were developed and administered independently in England by the ecclesiastical courts—that is, by the church. Intestacy was viewed as shameful, and testamentary expressions shortly before death were considered confessional in nature and part of the cleansing of the soul. Ecclesiastical laws in feudal England varied widely according to local custom until late in the seventeenth century. The Statute of Distributions (1670) and the Statute of Frauds (1677) established uniform laws regarding the passage of personal property. The former is the precursor of our modern intestate succession statutes, and the latter, dealing with formal requirements of wills, is an essential part today of the law of wills in all 50 states. Eventually, the laws of succession and testamentary disposition of real and personal property merged, and today, both in England and in the United States, only a few traces remain in the law of the dual system.

The prevailing view among legal scholars in this country is that there is no constitutional right of succession to property, by either will or intestacy. According to this view, such rights are statutory in nature, and the U.S. Constitution does not forbid any state legislature to limit, condition, or even abolish these powers within its own state. Indeed, in many ways, state legislatures have placed significant restrictions on rights of succession. For example, the modern trend in this country is toward narrowing the class of relatives entitled to succeed to intestate property, thereby increasing the cases where such property will pass instead to the state (see Chapter 2). Also, certain surviving family members are generally protected from disinheritance under state laws (see Chapter 4).

The law of wills, trusts, and estate administration is governed, then, primarily by state law. Much of this law has been codified—that is, it has been enacted into statute by state legislatures. In most states, this body of statutory law is referred to as the state's *probate code* (another imprecise use of the term *probate*). Because the laws of the states are not entirely uniform, the probate paralegal must be cognizant of potential conflict-of-laws issues—that is, questions as to which state's laws should be applied, especially in the case of the mobile client. In addition, various questions of *jurisdiction* and *venue*—that is, which court is the proper one—also commonly arise where the decedent moved from place to place or owned property in more than one state.

About one-third of the states have adopted substantially all of the **Uniform Probate Code** (U.P.C.), a model set of laws drafted by a committee of legal scholars to be used as a guide for state legislatures. All states have been strongly influenced by the U.P.C., while the drafters of the U.P.C. are conversely influenced by trends in modern judicial decisions and legislation at the state level.

Although the law of wills, trusts, and estates is determined at the state level, a variety of federal tax issues also arise in estate planning and in estate and trust administration. Of particular significance are the Internal Revenue Code provisions for gift and estate taxation. Finally, local courts invariably develop their own procedural rules of court relating to estate administration. It is essential that the probate paralegal have a thorough working knowledge of local rules as well as state law.

TYPES OF PROPERTY: AN OVERVIEW

Because this text deals with the subject of estates, it is necessary to understand what constitutes a person's estate. A person's estate refers collectively to the person's property; property includes anything that is subject to ownership. The various types of property are classified in Figure 1-2. The following discussion refers to this classification scheme and is intended only as an overview, because this subject is treated more thoroughly in texts dealing specifically with the law of property.

Personal Property

Personal property includes all movable property—that is, everything that can be owned other than real estate. Personal property may be either *tangible* or *intangible*. Tangible personal property includes all personal property that exists physically, such as vehicles, household furnishings, clothing, and jewelry. Intangible personal property includes personal property that does not exist physically but that nevertheless exists in the sense that it can be owned. Examples of intangible personal property include cash, bank accounts, shares of corporate stock, corporate and government bonds, life insurance, contract rights, pension and profit-sharing plans, and intellectual property (copyrights, patents, and trademarks).

Real Property

Real property includes all interests in real estate. An interest in real property may be either *possessory* or *nonpossessory*. Possessory interests give the holder the right to possession. Possessory interests in real property may be classified further as either *present* interests or *future* interests. Present interests give the holder the right to present possession, while future interests give the holder the right to or possibility of future possession.

Present possessory interests may be classified as either *freehold* interests or *leasehold* interests. The distinction between a freehold and a leasehold interest relates to the time frame by which the interest is measured. A freehold estate is either potentially infinite in duration (referred to as a fee estate) or is measured by the owner's lifetime (referred to as a life estate). All other possessory estates in real property are referred to as leasehold estates. There are four types of leasehold estates:

1. Tenancy for years (continuing through a fixed period of time)
2. Periodic tenancy (continuing for successive periods, such as monthly or yearly)

FIGURE 1-2   FORMS OF PROPERTY OWNERSHIP AND TYPES OF PROPERTY INTERESTS

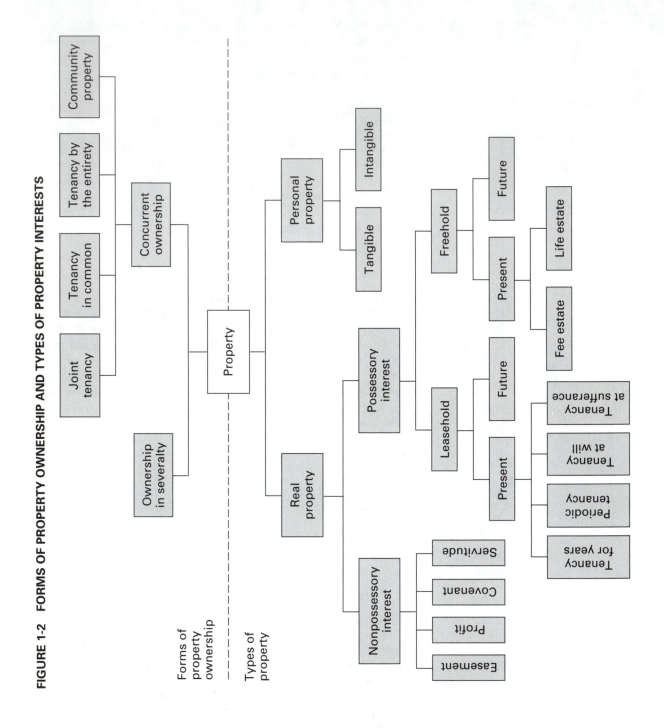

Forms of property ownership

Types of property

3. Tenancy at will (terminable at will of either landlord or tenant)
4. Tenancy at sufferance (arising when a tenant wrongfully remains in possession after expiration of a lawful tenancy)

One does not normally think about a lease agreement with a landlord as creating an ownership interest in real property for the tenant; however, the law views all leasehold estates as such, although the rights of the leasehold owner are limited in scope and duration. Nonpossessory interests in real property create a right to use land possessed by someone else and include easements, profits, covenants, and servitudes.

Most real-property interests transferred at death involve fee estates. Leasehold estates eventually revert back to the landlord, or fee owner, while life estates, by definition, terminate at the death of the owner of the life estate, either reverting back to the fee owner or passing to a remainderman. Although the owner of a fee interest in certain property may create a leasehold estate or life estate (along with a future interest) in that property under the terms of a will, this type of distribution scheme is relatively uncommon today.

FORMS OF PROPERTY OWNERSHIP

A person may own property either solely or concurrently with one or more co-owners. The various forms of ownership in property, which are of vital concern to the probate paralegal, are discussed in the materials that follow.

Ownership in Severalty and Concurrent Ownership

In order to determine the proper disposition of any particular property interest of a decedent, one must first determine the extent of the decedent's ownership interest in that asset. Figure 1-2 illustrates the various forms of property ownership. Exclusive and absolute ownership in property is referred to in form as **ownership in severalty** or, more commonly, simply as individual ownership. Ownership in severalty is by far the most common form of property ownership. Multiple or shared ownership in property is referred to generally as **concurrent ownership**. Concurrent ownership in property may take a variety of forms. The form will often determine the proper disposition of the decedent's interest after death (see Table 1-1).

Generally speaking, concurrent ownership in property may take one of four distinct forms:

- Joint tenancy
- Tenancy in common
- Tenancy by the entirety
- Community property

It is important to remember that all of these forms are mutually exclusive of one another; that is, shared ownership may take one and only one of these four forms. The last two forms involve shared ownership between spouses

TABLE 1-1   FORMS OF CONCURRENT PROPERTY OWNERSHIP

Form of Co-Ownership	Co-Owners	Nature of Interest	Effect of Transfer by Co-Owner during Lifetime	Effect of Co-Owner's Death	Where Available
Joint tenancy	Any two or more persons	Equal and undivided	Joint tenancy severed, transferee is tenant in common vis-à-vis other co-owners	Deceased co-owner's share passes automatically to surviving joint tenants	All states
Tenancy in common	Any two or more persons	Undivided	Other co-owners continue to own same proportionate interest	Deceased co-owner's interest passes to his/her heirs or beneficiaries; no effect on other co-owners	All states
Tenancy by the entirety	Spouses only	Equal and undivided	Tenancy by entirety severed (spouses must agree to transfer)	To surviving spouse	Minority of common-law states (not available in community property states)
Community property	Spouses only	Equal and undivided	Form transmuted to tenancy in common (spouses *may* have to agree to transfer)	To decedent's beneficiaries or heirs (subject to rights of surviving spouse)	Community-property states only

only. Property held in one of these two forms is referred to as **marital property**. No state provides for both forms of marital property. States that provide for the community-property form are referred to in this context as **community-property states**, while all other states are referred to as **common-law states** or **separate-property states**. There are eight community-property states: Arizona, California, Idaho, Louisiana, Nevada, New Mexico, Texas, and Washington. Wisconsin has adopted a similar system, with modest modifications in substance and terminology.

 FOCUS: The four forms of concurrent property ownership are mutually exclusive; that is, concurrent owners must hold title in one and only one of these four forms.

Under all of these forms of concurrent ownership, each co-owner is said to own an *undivided* interest in the property. This means that the property cannot be divided physically for the purpose of identifying each owner's interest but rather is treated as one indivisible unit. It is important to distinguish the concept of concurrent ownership from other forms of shared control of property. For example, two individuals who each own 50 percent of the stock in a corporation are not concurrent owners of stock; even though they may share in the ownership and control of the corporation, each person is the sole owner of his or her respective shares of stock. Also, two persons who are partners in a business are not concurrent owners; each partner owns a portion of the partnership as his or her sole property, which in turn gives him or her certain rights as to the control of the partnership business.

Joint Tenancy and Tenancy in Common

Under the **joint-tenancy** form of ownership, all joint tenants are said to own equal and undivided interests in the joint-tenancy property with the right of survivorship; that is, upon the death of one joint tenant, the deceased joint tenant's interest immediately and automatically vests equally among the surviving joint tenants. The result is that all surviving joint tenants continue to own equal (although larger) interests in the property (see Figure 1-3). During a joint tenant's lifetime, however, the joint tenant is free to transfer the joint-tenancy interest to another joint tenant or to some other party. When the transfer is to a party other than the other original joint tenants, the joint-tenancy relationship is automatically severed as between the interest transferred and all other interests, and a tenancy in common (see below) is created as between the transferee and all other concurrent owners.

FIGURE 1-3   COMPARISON OF JOINT-TENANCY AND TENANCY-IN-COMMON FORMS OF PROPERTY OWNERSHIP

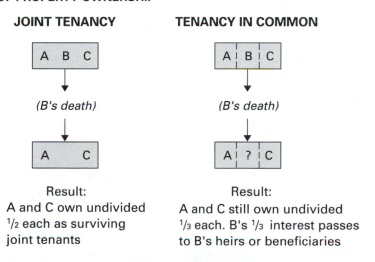

JOINT TENANCY	TENANCY IN COMMON
A B C	A ¦ B ¦ C
(B's death)	(B's death)
A C	A ¦ ? ¦ C
Result: A and C own undivided ¹/₂ each as surviving joint tenants	Result: A and C still own undivided ¹/₃ each. B's ¹/₃ interest passes to B's heirs or beneficiaries

A conveyance to two or more persons as joint tenants requires express intent—for example, ''to A and B, as joint tenants.'' In some states, intent must be more clearly expressed by indicating a right of survivorship—for example, ''to A and B, as joint tenants with right of survivorship.'' Absent express intent, a conveyance to two or more persons is presumed to create a **tenancy in common** (except in the case of a husband and wife under a community-property system; see *Community Property*). Under the tenancy-in-common form of shared ownership, the co-owners' interests may, but need not, be equal, and there is no automatic right of survivorship. Thus, it is possible for two people to own one-third and two-thirds interests, respectively, in a particular asset as *tenants in common*, and for each co-owner to transfer his or her respective ownership interest at death (or during his or her lifetime) to someone other than the other co-owner (see Figure 1-3).

*EXAMPLE: Alvarez, Blanco, and Chang own Blackacre as joint tenants. Alvarez transfers her interest during her lifetime to Davis. **Result:** Blanco and Chang now share an undivided two-thirds interest in Blackacre as joint tenants. Davis owns an undivided one-third interest in the form of tenancy in common.*

*EXAMPLE: Alvarez, Blanco, and Chang share an undivided one-half interest in Blackacre as joint tenants. Davis owns a one-half undivided interest. Alvarez dies. **Result:** Blanco and Chang now share an undivided one-half interest in Blackacre as joint tenants. Because Davis' interest was unequal to the interests of Alvarez and Blanco, Davis' undivided one-half interest was as a tenant in common, and Davis continues to own an undivided one-half interest in this form.*

*EXAMPLE: Alvarez, Blanco, and Chang own Blackacre as joint tenants. Alvarez transfers his interest during his lifetime "to Alvarez." **Result:** Alvarez has severed the joint tenancy with Blanco and Chang. Alvarez now owns a one-third interest in Blackacre in the form of tenancy in common. Blanco and Chang now share an undivided two-thirds interest in Blackacre as joint tenants.*

Tenancy by the Entirety

As noted earlier, the **tenancy-by-the-entirety** form of property ownership is restricted to ownership between spouses. Similar to joint tenancy, the spouses' interests are equal and undivided, although during the spouses' joint lifetimes the ownership interest of a spouse may be terminated by joint action only. In other words, one spouse cannot transfer his or her one-half interest in such property to a third party without the other spouse's consent. At divorce, the spouses will become tenants in common, unless otherwise agreed upon under the terms of the divorce settlement. At death, all property owned in the form of tenancy by the entirety passes to the surviving spouse.

In common-law states, unless a tenancy by the entirety is expressly indicated as the form of ownership, the asset must be owned entirely by only one spouse. As to which spouse actually owns a particular asset, generally speaking, if the asset is accompanied by a document of title (such as a deed for real property), certificate of ownership (such as a corporation's stock certificate or automobile ownership certificate), or signature card for a bank account, the form of title indicated on the document dictates which spouse owns the asset. With respect to other assets, the husband is generally presumed to own the asset.

Community Property

Several states have adopted a system of property ownership between spouses known as the **community-property system**. A thorough examination of the law of community property is beyond the scope of this discussion and is more central to a family law practice, because these issues arise most often in situations involving marital dissolutions. However, the laws of community property also come into play in the area of decedent's estates. Specifically, in determining the proper distribution of a decedent's estate, community property is treated differently than separate property. Also, regardless of where you work as a probate paralegal, you must have a basic understanding of what constitutes community property, because a portion of the estate of a decedent who resided in a separate property state may very well be characterized as community property if the decedent formerly resided in a community-property state.

Under the community-property system, each spouse in a marriage is entitled to a one-half ownership interest in each and every asset acquired during the marriage, regardless of whether the asset is attributable to the husband or to the wife. In addition, all assets that can be traced to community property—that is, all assets acquired with community-property funds—are also community property, and any increase in value of a community asset is also community property. The most notable exception to this basic community-property rule involves inheritances from relatives by one and only one spouse, which remain the **separate property** of the inheriting spouse.

It is important to note that these basic rules are rules of *presumption* only; that is, they hold true for a particular asset unless a spouse can provide sufficient evidence that the asset is actually the separate property of one spouse. One example of such evidence would be a contract between the spouses which explicitly states that some or all of their assets that would otherwise be characterized as community property should instead be treated as separate property.

 FOCUS: All property acquired by a married person while residing in a community-property state (except for inheritances by one spouse only) is presumed to be the community property of both spouses.

The community-property concept is a product primarily of sociological changes that have occurred in our culture, especially since the 1970s. Although our society has traditionally viewed the husband as the primary if not the sole contributor to the financial well-being and success of the family unit, changing attitudes and life-styles have influenced some legislatures to view the contributions of the husband and wife as equal, regardless of whether the spouse's efforts are rewarded tangibly—that is, regardless of which spouse actually makes more money. Under a community-property system, then, a marriage is treated as an equal partnership, each spouse contributing equally to the family unit and each spouse sharing equally in the profit or loss of the partnership.

Legal Issues Inherent to Community-Property Systems. A community-property system inherently raises numerous legal issues. One of the most common such issues involves the use of community-property funds to contribute to the purchase or improvement of a separate-property asset or, conversely, the use of separate-property funds to contribute toward the purchase or improvement of a community asset. For example, assume that an unmarried woman purchases a home, makes a down payment, and begins making monthly mortgage payments. If she later marries, and if her husband contributes to subsequent mortgage payments as well as permanent improvements, to what would the husband be entitled if they divorce or if the wife dies? The answer to this question would depend on the laws of the particular community-property state. Generally speaking, three views are possible:

1. The husband has acquired an ownership interest in the home.
2. The husband is entitled to reimbursement for his contribution.
3. The husband has made a gift and is entitled neither to reimbursement nor to an ownership interest.

Another common issue involves characterizing a business interest which, although initially the separate property of one spouse, increases in value during the marriage as the result of the spouses' labor. According to the general principles of community property, appreciation in value of a separate-property asset should also be treated as separate property. But isn't the family-business scenario quite different from that of a passive investment, such as shares of stock? Again, different states have responded to this question in different ways. Some statutes provide for a community interest in the business to reflect the contributing spouse's labor, while some statutes also give either a right of reimbursement or a community interest to the noncontributing spouse, particularly when the lion's share of the business's growth occurs during the marriage.

A myriad of other issues also arise under a community-property system, including the following:

■ The characterization of assets that are very personal in nature to one spouse only, such as education or training, personal-injury recovery, disability pay or worker's compensation, and business and professional goodwill
■ The characterization of property where the spouses take title in joint and equal form but contribute in a disproportionate manner to the purchase price
■ The characterization of property acquired with commingled funds—that is, with funds that have been combined over time to the extent that it is difficult to tell which funds are community and which are separate
■ The responsibility of one spouse for the financial obligations and debts of the other spouse
■ The rights of a spouse to the management and control of community property

Through statutes and judicial decisions, each community-property state has developed its own rules to resolve the various issues that arise under a community-property system.

Marital Property and the Mobile Client. If people never moved from state to state, your job as a probate paralegal would be rather straightforward—you would need to consider only the system (either community or common-law) that your particular state has adopted. However, because families often move their place of residence from a community-property state to a common-law state, and vice versa, the question arises as to how the property acquired in the first state should be characterized once the family has relocated.

The most fundamental point to keep in mind is that all property acquired by either spouse while residing in a community-property state is community property, while all property acquired by either spouse while residing in a common-law state is the separate property of the acquiring spouse. This general rule holds true even for real property that is located in a state other than the spouses' state of residence. For example, assume that either a husband or a wife, while residing in Texas (a community-property state), acquires with community-property funds a parcel of real estate located in Oklahoma (a common-law state). The Oklahoma real estate is community property, even though it is located in a common-law state. Assuming instead that the husband and wife reside in Oklahoma, while the real property acquired by one spouse with separate-property funds is located in Texas, then the Texas property will be characterized as the separate property of one spouse, even though the property is situated in a community-property state.

Moving from a Community-Property State to a Common-Law State How should spouses' assets be characterized when they change their state of residence from a community-property state to a common-law state? The basic rule to remember is that all property will retain its former character (see Figure 1-4). However, all property acquired by either spouse *after* they have moved to a common-law state will be characterized as separate property (and all property acquired with separate-property funds will be similarly characterized).

EXAMPLE: *H and W are married and reside in California (a community-property state) during the first several years of their marriage. During this time they purchase a home with community funds. After five years of marriage, H accepts a new job in Michigan (a common-law state). H and W sell their home in California and apply the proceeds toward the purchase of a home in Michigan. Mortgage payments for the Michigan home are subsequently made with the husband's income from his job in Michigan.*

Will the Michigan home be characterized as community property or separate property? Since the home in California was clearly a community asset, the proceeds from the sale of that home are community funds, and any asset acquired with these community funds (in this case, the Michigan home) will also be treated as community property. Thus, at the time the Michigan home was purchased, the initial equity is the community property of H and W.

FIGURE 1-4   MARITAL PROPERTY AND THE MOBILE CLIENT

However, H's subsequent payments from his separate-property income create a separate-property ownership interest for H. H's total ownership share will grow (and W's percentage ownership will shrink) as H continues to make more payments toward the purchase of the Michigan home from his separate-property income.

Moving from a Common-Law State to a Community-Property State When spouses change their place of residence from a common-law state to a community-property state, all property will retain its former character, except under the laws of two community-property states—California and Idaho (see Figure 1-4). In these two states, the rules depend on the context in which the property is being characterized. In the context of divorce, the rule is simple: All property acquired during the marriage will be treated as community property. Effectively, then, the spouse's separate property acquired during marriage and while residing in a common-law state is transformed into community property for the purpose of property settlement at divorce. This transformed property is referred to as **quasi-community property**.

The same rule applies in the context of the death of a spouse, with the notable exception of real property situated in a common-law state and acquired as separate property by a spouse. Such property will retain its separate character, even after the spouses move to a community-property state. Consider the following scenario:

SCENARIO: H and W are married and reside initially in Colorado (a common-law state), during which time W purchases a home as her separate property and H purchases two automobiles as his separate property. H and W later move to California (a community-property state that recognizes the concept of quasi-community property). While residing in California and using funds acquired since their move to California, they purchase an investment property located in Michigan.

In this scenario, at H's death, before his estate is distributed, we must determine what constitutes his estate. First, H has no ownership interest in the Colorado home—because the property is situated in a common-law state, it remains W's separate property, even after H and W move to California. Second, H owns a one-half community interest in the investment property in Michigan, even though the property is situated in a common-law state, because it was acquired with community funds. Third, since the two automobiles are personal rather than real property, they are quasi-community property, and W and H have equal ownership interests in them. Assuming instead that H and W are divorced while residing in the state of California, the Michigan home initially acquired by W during the marriage would also be quasi-community property, and H and W would each own an equal ownership interest in all of the assets mentioned above.

THE ROLE OF THE PROBATE PARALEGAL

It is Friday afternoon, and although Monday will be your first day of work, you are meeting briefly this afternoon with your supervising attorney and with the other paralegal in the department to discuss your job responsibilities as well as to determine which specific client matters you will begin handling on Monday. Ms. Cargis, your supervising attorney, describes your job and the knowledge and skills you will need to perform your duties.

The Business of Probate Law: A Team Approach

"The practice of probate law is a profession, but it is also a business. Accordingly, your function as a probate paralegal is twofold; you must direct your efforts both toward providing the highest quality legal services and toward the financial success of this department. Both objectives require a team approach among the attorney, paralegal, and other staff.

"In order to provide the highest possible quality of legal services as efficiently (and thus as profitably) as possible, all members of the team must devote their attention to their own particular functions. For example, I can provide the highest quality of service to the client as an attorney only by devoting my full attention to the practice of law, while delegating all other responsibilities to the paralegals and other staff. As a probate paralegal, you may be required to perform a wide variety of tasks in order to allow me more time for the practice of law. These tasks may include interviewing clients, gathering information, preparing documents and petitions, performing legal research, maintaining a library, and informing me of new developments in the law. Also, because the success of any team depends also on coordination and communication among the team members, you will perform a critical role as liaison between me and clients, staff, other attorneys, and the probate court. In order for you to perform your function as a probate paralegal in a competent and efficient manner, you must in turn delegate clerical tasks in order to devote as much time and attention as possible to those functions that you are uniquely trained and qualified as a paralegal to perform.

"To help you appreciate the integral role that the probate paralegal plays as a team member in determining the financial success of this business, you must understand the manner in which our department is compensated for its legal services. As compensation for handling the administration of a decedent's estate, guardianship, or conservatorship, the law firm is generally paid a percentage of the gross value of the estate. The law firm may also be entitled to additional compensation on an hourly basis for extraordinary services performed by both the attorney and paralegal in handling the administration of the estate. Because compensation is to a large extent fixed, the level of the law firm's efficiency bears directly on its profitability. The probate paralegal plays a vital role, then, in contributing to the firm's profitability by developing and maintaining efficient systems and procedures for handling estates, which I will discuss in more detail shortly.

"Most deaths in the United States result in either formal or informal estate administration. Thus, this area has traditionally been the primary source of business for our department and for most probate attorneys. However, because the courts are becoming overburdened, state legislatures are providing more methods of transferring property at death without the necessity of judicial proceedings. Avoiding these proceedings, however, requires proper planning. Thus, the estate-planning aspects of a probate-law practice are providing an increasingly significant source of business for our department. Generally, we charge clients for our estate-planning services on a fixed basis rather than an hourly basis. There are two primary reasons why we prefer to charge a fixed amount for estate-planning services. First, most clients prefer this method because they can determine at the outset the total cost for the services. Second, fixed compensation better reflects the value of the attorney's experience, knowledge, and judgment where the end result is a product, such as a will or trust, rather than a settlement or judgment (as in litigation or negotiation). The amount of compensation depends upon the complexity of the estate plan and the number and type of documents produced in order to establish the plan. Just as in estate administration, because our compensation for estate-planning services is fixed, profitability depends on efficiency. Also as in estate administration, it is your function as a probate paralegal to ensure maximum efficiency in processing estate-planning matters.

Specific Duties of the Probate Paralegal

"As you know, our department serves our firm's clients in the specialized area of law commonly referred to as probate. Now that you are familiar with your general function as a probate paralegal, allow me to explain what our practice encompasses and what your specific duties will entail as a paralegal in this department. Each task you perform will relate to one of four general types of legal matters: estate planning; decedent's estate administration, or probate, as we refer to it; conservatorship and guardianship proceedings; and trust administration. Let's look more closely at each of these four functions in the context of our firm's law practice. Don't be concerned if you don't fully understand the terminology and concepts right away. Instead, just try for now to get a sense of a typical workday as a paralegal in our department.

"With respect to estate planning, you are no doubt familiar with the concept of the simple will as an estate-planning device. Although we prepare simple wills for some clients, estate planning usually involves the use of a trust instead of a will. A simple will is just not sufficient to meet most clients' objectives, although initially the client may not understand this. A big part of our job, then, is to educate the client, especially the elderly client who may resist the idea of using any planning device other than a simple will. Even though I spend at least an hour with most clients in order to explain the purpose of each document we are preparing for them, many clients remain somewhat confused and have a lot of questions. You will be following up with many of these clients, so I expect you to be familiar with my clients' estate plans and to have a good understanding of the principles of estate planning and the purposes of various estate-planning documents.

"After you have become more experienced as a probate paralegal, I may ask you to assist in preparing initial drafts of will and trust provisions. All of the general provisions and clauses included in our wills and trusts are stored in our computer, but most clients have specific ideas that require special provisions or revisions of one or more general clauses. At times, I will request that you sit in for an estate-planning interview so that you can get a clear picture of the client's plan and the drafting that will be required. In fact, plan on joining me on Monday afternoon at 2:00 for a meeting with Walter and Betty Taylor, a husband and wife who have a fairly sizeable estate.

"In preparing trusts for our estate-planning clients, we generally assist in transferring many of the client's assets to the trust. You will be preparing and assisting the client in executing all of the various documents—such as deeds, bills of sale, and beneficiary designation forms—required to complete the transfer of assets to the client's trust. This task usually involves contact with banks and other financial institutions, title companies, stockbrokers, and county government recording offices. It can be frustrating to deal with these third parties because the paperwork often moves slowly; your own initiative is very important here, because you will be working independently to complete all necessary transfers to the client's trust as expeditiously as possible.

"In addition to your involvement in the estate-planning aspects of our law practice, you will also devote a substantial part of your time to probate matters. While one of our primary goals for our estate-planning clients is the avoidance of formal probate proceedings, many of our clients come to us after a relative has died without having taken the necessary steps to avoid these proceedings. We are currently handling about 25 active probate-estate files, and you should expect, as a paralegal, to become involved in many of these matters. A prospective client whose mother just passed away this week is coming in Monday morning at 10:00 to discuss her mother's estate. The mother's name is Irene Parker. I would like you to handle the administration of the estate from start to finish under my supervision. In fact, it would be a good idea for you to sit in on the interview and meet the daughter, whose name is Sharon Madson, because she will probably be serving as the administrator of the estate and will be working closely with you over the next several months.

''Our compensation for handling probate matters is to a large extent fixed, and we do not receive any fees until the estate is finally distributed; thus, we make every attempt to move our probate-estate matters toward final distribution as quickly as possible, without sacrificing quality of service. Efficiency and initiative on your part will contribute significantly toward this goal. You will be developing for your own use appropriate checklists, forms, and procedures for gathering all of the information necessary to process the paperwork involved in probate matters. The probate court will carefully examine all papers we file with the court to ensure that the paperwork is both complete and accurate; if it is not, delays are likely to result. You should also develop and use a tickler and calendar system to monitor probate matters closely; to avoid unnecessary delays, we should be ready for all regularly scheduled court hearings. To move the probate process along quickly, we should also be prepared to file all necessary papers with the court as soon as permissible under law—particularly relevant here are the petitions for appointment of personal representative and for final distribution, as well as the estate inventory and final account.

''Eventually, you should have a thorough knowledge of all probate procedural rules under state and local law, especially filing and notice requirements. Proper and timely notice of probate proceedings must be given to the decedent's beneficiaries and heirs. Certain rights of the decedent's surviving spouse and children may be exercised only upon appropriate filing and notice. Maximum protection against the decedent's creditors also requires strict compliance with notice requirements. A myriad of other procedural rules relate to handling creditor claims and to payment of the decedent's income and estate taxes. You must also become acquainted with many substantive rules of law, particularly those relating to the powers and duties of fiduciaries, the interpretation and construction of wills, and the grounds for contesting the validity of a will. Once you develop a working knowledge of the procedural and substantive rules, I expect you to work independently in determining the next task and in handling many of the problems as they occur along the way. However, you must also recognize problems that you either are not sufficiently experienced or are not authorized to solve independently; you must maintain continual communication with the attorney regarding these problems.

"Our department also handles legal problems arising in the course of trust administration. Trustees frequently encounter problems in the management and distribution of the trust estate that require legal advice or instruction by the court. Our firm occasionally advises and represents individual trustees in these matters, as well as representing trust beneficiaries who wish to challenge the actions and decisions of the trustee. When disputes between a trustee and the beneficiaries of a trust cannot be resolved by dialog and negotiation, the matter is referred to our litigation department.

"Finally, our department is also currently handling about a dozen conservatorship matters and three or four guardianship matters. Your duties with regard to these matters will include the preparation and filing of petitions as well as assisting the client in preparing periodic accountings as required by the probate court. Although guardianship matters are usually straightforward, conservatorship proceedings are often fraught with problems, many of which are not resolved until the conservatee's death. Family members are often in continual dispute regarding what course of action would best serve the interest of the conservatee. You can expect to spend a disproportionate amount of time with one particular conservator-client who is continually embattled with other family members and is not confident or secure enough to make all of the decisions for the conservatee without consulting us. Many of our conservator-clients simply need handholding, because they are going through a difficult time emotionally trying to take care of a parent or other loved one whose health is failing. In all but one of our conservatorship matters, we represent the conservator. However, in one rather unusual matter, we have agreed to represent a possible conservatee, a long-standing client whose son has petitioned the probate court to establish a conservatorship for our client without his consent.

"Although working in our department is probably not as stressful or unpredictable as working in litigation, dealing with people, especially with elderly clients, in this field of law holds its own unique challenges. The client's situation is almost invariably charged with emotion, because the client is forced to deal directly with the fact of human mortality and with the control and disposition of a lifetime's accumulation of material wealth. Your job as a probate paralegal will not only test your legal knowledge and organizational and communication skills, but will also require you to demonstrate patience, diplomacy, and compassion."

The Probate Paralegal's Workday

After your orientation meeting with Ms. Cargis, the other paralegal sits down with you to describe a typical workday for the probate paralegal.

"Perhaps the best way to explain to you what you will be doing from day to day here is to recount a typical workday for me. In fact, I'll tell you how I spent my time today here at the office. At 9:00 I met briefly with a client who is serving as executor of his brother's estate. The four-month period for creditors to file claims has expired, and we are ready to distribute the estate, except that we first must file a final accounting and petition the court for final distribution. This morning the client reviewed her books and records with me so that I can prepare and file the accounting and final inventory. I noticed a discrepancy between the initial and final inventory amounts, and I spent nearly an hour with the client looking for the source of the discrepancy and recomputing the figures.

"At about 10:00 I began reviewing a file for an estate-planning client who met with the attorney yesterday about establishing a living trust. I wanted to familiarize myself with the file to determine what assets we are going to transfer to the trust. I compiled a list of those assets from the attorney's client questionnaire, determined what information and documents the client still needs to provide to us, and called the client to discuss this. The client will be coming in on Monday with all of the information we need to get started on the transfers. I also drafted a special provision for this trust regarding the use of trust income and principal for the education of the beneficiaries. The client wants to restrict the trustee's discretion, and I spent about half an hour looking at some of our other trust forms as well as some legal form books to get some ideas about how to express the client's wishes. Since I was interrupted by several telephone calls, this project occupied my time for the remainder of the morning.

"After lunch I interviewed Sharon Madson, with whom you will be meeting on Monday morning to discuss her mother's estate. Sharon's brother Dennis Parker came in with her today; he's here from out of town for the funeral this weekend. I screen many of our clients before they meet with the attorney in order to make a preliminary assessment of those needs, to determine whether the matter is urgent, and to brief the attorney so that the attorney can be better prepared for the conference with the client.

"I spent the remainder of the afternoon today largely in gathering information to prepare the initial petition to establish a conservatorship, with occasional interruptions for telephone calls and for questions from our secretaries. At 4:00 I met with Ms. Cargis for our regular afternoon meeting to discuss the day's developments, to review files, and to coordinate our schedules for next week. I usually meet with Ms. Cargis every morning at 11:00 and every afternoon at 4:00. This morning, however, we didn't meet because her 10:00 conference with a client ran late.

"Monday is going to be a busy day as well. To help orient you to your new job and to our office procedures, on Monday you will be assisting me throughout the day. Let me show you my appointment book so that you know your schedule for Monday. [See Figure 1-5.]

"Be sure to pay close attention and take thorough notes during the meetings with Sharon Madson and the Taylors, because you will be following up on these matters yourself."

FIGURE 1-5   A PROBATE PARALEGAL'S TYPICAL WORKDAY

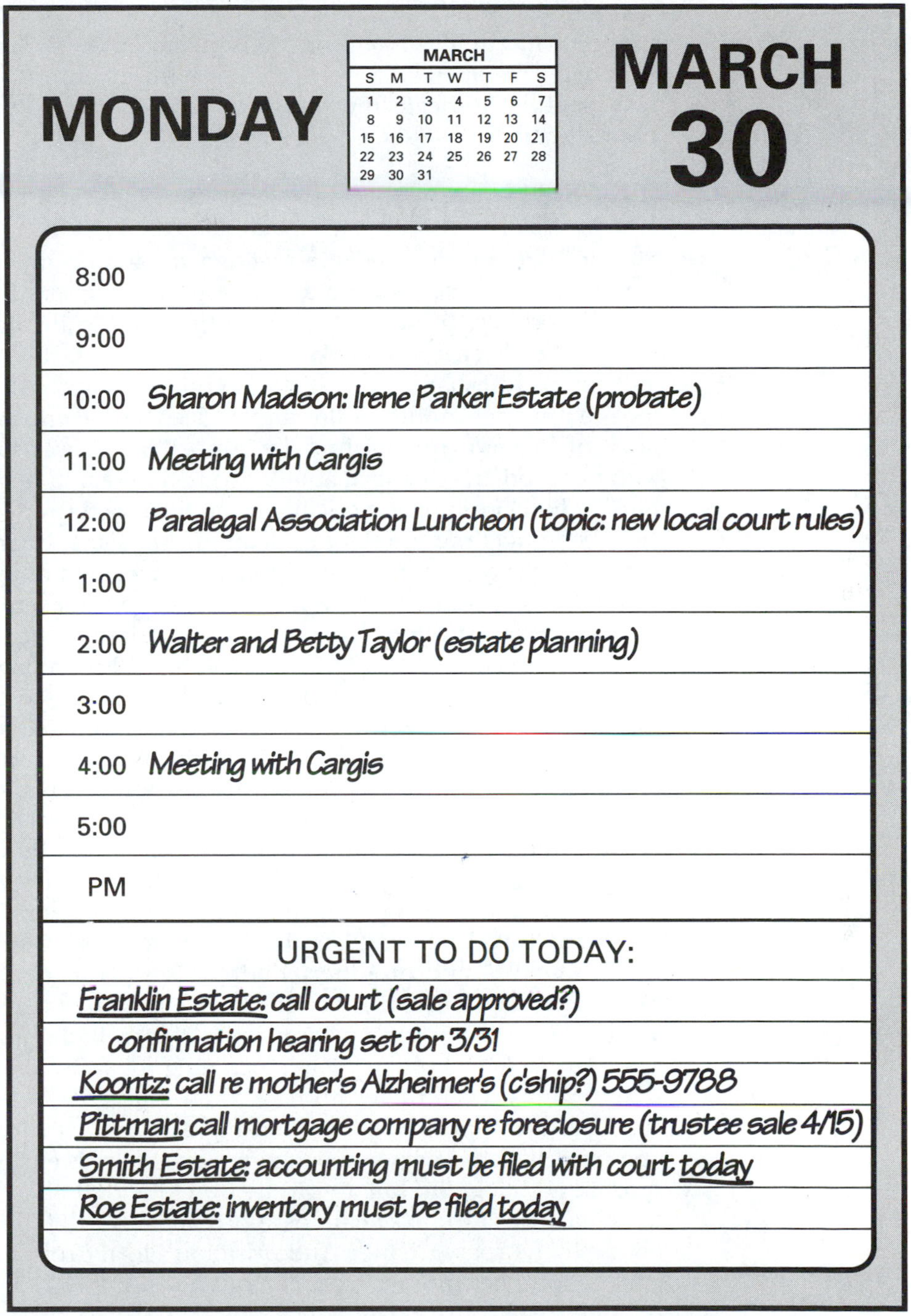

	MARCH						
	S	M	T	W	T	F	S
		1	2	3	4	5	6	7
	8	9	10	11	12	13	14
	15	16	17	18	19	20	21
	22	23	24	25	26	27	28
	29	30	31				

MONDAY

MARCH 30

8:00	
9:00	
10:00	Sharon Madson: Irene Parker Estate (probate)
11:00	Meeting with Cargis
12:00	Paralegal Association Luncheon (topic: new local court rules)
1:00	
2:00	Walter and Betty Taylor (estate planning)
3:00	
4:00	Meeting with Cargis
5:00	
PM	

URGENT TO DO TODAY:

Franklin Estate: call court (sale approved?)
    confirmation hearing set for 3/31
Koontz: call re mother's Alzheimer's (c'ship?) 555-9788
Pittman: call mortgage company re foreclosure (trustee sale 4/15)
Smith Estate: accounting must be filed with court today
Roe Estate: inventory must be filed today

TWO CASE STUDIES FOR THE PARALEGAL

It is Monday, your first day as a probate paralegal. As planned, you sit in on the 10:00 meeting with Sharon Madson and on the 2:00 meeting with Walter and Betty Taylor, taking notes during both meetings. Your notes from the two meetings indicate the following information about these clients and their situations.

Estate of Irene Parker

Sharon Madson attended the meeting today without her brother Dennis. Irene had died last weekend as the result of injuries sustained in a car accident. Tragically, Irene's other son John was also involved in the accident, and he died later in the week.

Irene's husband Fred died several years ago. Although Sharon had looked after her mother following Fred's death, Irene nevertheless handled most of her own financial affairs. Since Sharon was somewhat unfamiliar with her mother's financial affairs, she had to search her mother's house for bills and other important documents to try to determine her mother's financial situation at the time of her death. In so doing, Sharon found inside an envelope two typewritten wills, apparently executed ten years earlier, one by Irene and the other by her husband. In the same envelope, Sharon also found a letter written by Irene in her own handwriting, which also appears, at least in some respects, to be a will. The will nominates Irene's husband, Fred Parker, her sister, Ruth Adams, and her deceased son, John Parker, in that order, to serve alternately and successively as executor.

Dennis is very angry because, under the terms of the second will, it appears that he is not entitled to any portion of his mother's estate. After trying unsuccessfully over the weekend to convince Sharon to destroy Irene's second will, Dennis left town immediately after the funeral, indicating that he was going to discuss this matter with his own attorney.

Irene is survived by her daughter Sharon and son Dennis, as well as by her sister Ruth Adams. Sharon has two daughters—Cindy (age 11) and Deborah (age 6)—and no other children. John is survived by his wife Susan, who is pregnant with John's child, as well as by a 12-year-old stepson named Todd Burns from Susan's prior marriage. John had not adopted his stepson Todd. Irene left a modest estate, including the following: her residence, the title to which is still in her husband Fred's name; a small savings account; a certificate of deposit; a joint checking account with John; an automobile; and miscellaneous personal belongings, such as jewelry, clothing, and furniture. In addition, Sharon and Irene owned a joint checking account, which has a balance at Irene's death of approximately $1,000. Sharon also found a blank "Beneficiary Change Authorization" form from a life insurance company among her mother's papers, but has not found any other documents relating to a life insurance policy.

Irene's income was limited to Social Security benefits. Irene's only debts included mortgage payments for her residence, monthly bills for utilities, and insurance premiums and property taxes, which will be due shortly.

Walter and Betty Taylor

Walter and Betty Taylor have been married for about ten years. Walter is 57 years old, and Betty is 45 years old. Both have been married once before. Walter has three children by his previous marriage as well as six grandchildren. Betty has no children; her closest relatives include her two brothers and her sister. Walter's parents and Betty's parents are deceased.

Walter has built his own business as a general contractor over the past three decades, and the value of his business has recently been appraised at nearly half a million dollars. His son David has been working closely with him in the business over the last 15 years, and David has agreed to take over the business eventually. Walter owns a large home, which he built himself in an exclusive part of town. He also owns another house as an investment. Walter estimates the value of his estate, which also includes a life insurance policy, at approximately $900,000.

Betty's estate is more modest. She and her three siblings each own a one-fourth interest as joint tenants in a family ranch that was passed down to them by their parents. The total value of the property, which Betty and her siblings own free and clear, is about $400,000. Betty's brother lives at the ranch and makes quarterly payments as rent to the other three siblings. Betty's interest in the ranch is her only sizeable asset. She has been working as a real estate agent since shortly after her divorce from her former husband and is no longer receiving spousal-support payments from her former husband.

Although both Walter and Betty are concerned about establishing an estate plan that provides for the surviving spouse, Walter also wishes to help provide security for his children as well as a college education for his grandchildren.

The *Parker Estate*, the *Taylor Trust*, and the Rest of This Book

Throughout this book, you will be learning the law of wills, trusts, and estates and your role as a paralegal in this specialized field of law by following the estate of Irene Parker and the estate planning of Walter and Betty Taylor, completing job assignments as events in these two matters unfold. Complete client files for the estate of Irene Parker and for the Taylors are included in the Resource Manual as Appendixes A and B, respectively. Specific documents within these files are labeled as exhibits and are referred to as such throughout this book.

In reviewing your notes from the interview with Sharon Madson, perhaps you wondered whether the second will is valid and how the answer to this question would affect the distribution of Irene's estate. Did you ask yourself who has the legal right to assume control of Irene's assets, Sharon or Dennis? Perhaps you also wondered who is responsible, if anyone, for meeting

Irene's financial obligations. These and other similar issues will be explored in Chapters 2 through 8, which deal generally with the law of wills and substantive and procedural rules for administering and distributing a decedent's estate. You will discover in these chapters that Irene's lack of proper estate planning has created a variety of legal problems that must be resolved prior to the distribution of her estate, thereby leaving a legacy of potential delays, expense, and conflict for her family. In Chapters 4 and 9, you will learn that many of these problems, as well as the expense and delay involved with formal probate proceedings, could have been avoided had Irene used one or more "will substitutes."

In reviewing your notes from the interview with Walter and Betty Taylor, perhaps you began to think ahead to some of the problems that could arise among the families if a thoughtful plan is not established at this time. For example, would a large estate such as the Taylor estate be subject to one or more types of death taxes that might be minimized or avoided by careful planning? Also, if Betty inherits all or most of Walter's estate, what would prevent Betty from passing this inheritance entirely on to her own blood relatives (or to a friend or future spouse) to the total exclusion of Walter's children and grandchildren? Perhaps you anticipated that Walter and Betty may want to establish a trust in order to provide for the continued support of the surviving spouse and of Walter's children as well as for the education of Walter's grandchildren. If so, how could Walter and Betty ensure that the income and principal from the trust is distributed for these purposes, and what would constitute a fair distribution plan? These concerns and other similar issues are addressed in Chapters 9 and 10. Specifically, Chapter 9 will explore the various estate-planning objectives and strategies to achieve these objectives. Chapter 10 will focus on the powers and duties of the trustee and the various problems that a trustee encounters in managing and distributing the trust estate to the trust beneficiaries.

Chapter 11 will explore the realm of protective judicial proceedings (guardianships and conservatorships) as well as the various methods of planning for incapacity for the purpose of circumventing these proceedings. Finally, the focus of Chapter 12 will be the ABA Model Code of Professional Responsibility and Model Rules of Professional Conduct as they relate to the field of estate planning and probate and to the probate paralegal. You will discover that the Parker and Taylor matters present some potential ethical problems that the law firm must face and resolve in the course of its representation.

2 INTESTATE SUCCESSION AND AN INTRODUCTION TO WILLS

Paralegal Assignment 2

In the Parker matter, recall that Sharon Madson found among her mother Irene's personal effects an envelope containing a will prepared by a lawyer and executed several years ago while Irene's husband was living. Recall as well that the envelope also contained an undated letter written by Irene to Sharon which appears in some respects to be a second will. (The attested will and the holographic instrument are both included in the Parker File as part of Exhibit 7.) Ms. Cargis has pointed out to you that this letter is very important; if it is indeed a valid will, it may serve to revoke the prior attested will, at least in part, thereby altering dramatically the disposition of Irene's estate.

Ms. Cargis has asked you to

1. Assess the validity of the holographic instrument, researching the law as necessary
2. Determine what information Sharon Madson might provide to you that might be helpful here
3. Draft a letter to Sharon Madson explaining in layperson's terms the firm's opinion regarding this issue and soliciting any additional information that might help settle the issue

You may anticipate that your draft of the letter will be edited by Ms. Cargis and sent under her name.

INTESTATE SUCCESSION

The laws of intestate succession govern the disposition of a decedent's property not disposed of under the terms of a valid will or by some other method of transfer. The rules of intestate succession apply only to the decedent's intestate estate—that is, to those assets that are not otherwise disposed of through some other method, such as a will, trust, or joint-tenancy form of ownership. The disposition of property under the terms of a will or by other methods is governed by different rules and will be examined in later chapters.

Intestate Succession and the Probate Paralegal

The majority of deaths in the United States result in either total or partial intestacy. Thus, the probate law firm might actually handle more intestate estates than testate estates. A working knowledge of the rules of intestate succession is therefore essential to the probate paralegal, who must determine the identity of these heirs as well as their proportionate shares of the decedent's estate for the purpose of preparing and submitting a petition for final distribution to the court. Also, whether or not the decedent has died intestate, a decedent's heirs are generally entitled to certain notices during probate; thus, the paralegal must determine their identities for this purpose as well.

Terminology

Before examining the subject of succession to property, either under the laws of intestacy or otherwise, one should first be familiar with some basic terminology, beginning with certain genealogical terms. **Descendants**, also referred to as **issue**, include a person's children, grandchildren and so forth in the descending line. **Ascendants** or *lineal ascendants* are ancestors—parents, grandparents, and so on in the ascending line. **Collaterals** are relatives who are neither ascendants nor descendants but are related to a person through common ancestry; for example, a person's brother and uncle are both collaterals, the brother related through common parents and the uncle related through common grandparents. Relationship by blood is by **consanguinity**; relationship by marriage is by **affinity**.

As noted in Chapter 1, a decedent who fails to provide a method of transferring his or her property upon death has died *intestate*, in which event *intestacy* is said to have occurred. Where only a portion of the decedent's property is subject to the rules of intestate succession, **partial intestacy** is said to have resulted, in which event the decedent is said to have died *partially intestate*.

The law has used a variety of terms to describe the persons inheriting property from a decedent, to describe gifts under a will, and to describe the *act* of giving property under a will. The persons entitled to share in the decedent's intestate estate under the laws of intestate succession are referred to as the decedent's **heirs**. With respect to gifts under a will, under common law, the recipient of *real* property (real estate) was referred to as a **devisee**, while a gift of *personal* property under a will was referred to as a **bequest** or a **legacy**. Under common law, the terms **devise** and **bequeath** (respectively) referred to the act of giving real property or personal property under a will, while the terms **devisee** and **legatee** (respectively) referred to the person entitled to receive real property or personal property. Today, however, the terms *devise* and *gift* are used to describe *any* gift (either real property or personal property) under a will. The term *devisee* is now used to describe a person entitled to *any* type of gift under a will (and will be used in this manner throughout this text). The term *beneficiary* is also widely (and imprecisely) used for this purpose.

General Patterns of Intestate Succession

All states follow the same basic pattern of intestate succession, although there are some significant variations within this pattern that will be identified in the materials that follow. Figure 2-1 illustrates the intestate succession scheme provided for under the U.P.C. Because the laws of intestate succession do differ somewhat among the states, the rights of individuals may differ depending on which statutory scheme is applicable to a given estate. The law of the decedent's state of residence, or domicile, at death governs succession to personal property, while the law of the state where the property is situated governs the disposition of real property.

Share of the Spouse. The surviving spouse will be entitled to at least one-third, and possibly as much as all, of the decedent's intestate estate, sharing only with the decedent's surviving issue or parents. In most community-property states, separate property is treated differently than community property for the purpose of intestate succession. In a few community-property states, however, community property is treated the same as separate property. The U.P.C. reflects the former approach, requiring that the surviving spouse share the decedent's separate property with the decedent's issue or parent(s), while the spouse is entitled to 100 percent of the decedent's community property, regardless of whether the decedent leaves issue or parent(s).

Where the spouse must share with the decedent's issue or parents, statutes vary regarding the fractional share of the estate that the spouse takes. The general trend is toward ensuring adequate provision for the spouse at the expense of other heirs. The U.P.C. reflects this trend, entitling the spouse to the first $50,000 of the decedent's (separate-property) estate, as well as half of the remainder. The purpose of this rule is to provide for the spouse to the exclusion of other heirs in the event of a small estate. Under some statutes, the spouse's fractional share depends on the number of issue surviving the decedent, as in the Pennsylvania statute shown in Figure 2-2.

Shares of Descendants. Subject to the share of the surviving spouse, an intestate estate passes to the decedent's issue. Distribution among issue is generally governed by the common-law principle of *representation*. Under this

FIGURE 2-1 INTESTATE SUCCESSION UNDER THE U.P.C.

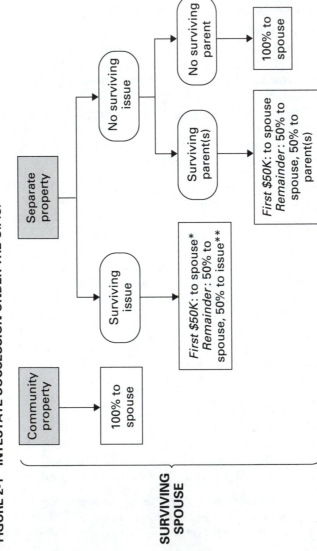

SURVIVING
SPOUSE

Community property → 100% to spouse

Separate property

Surviving issue → *First $50K:* to spouse* *Remainder:* 50% to spouse, 50% to issue**

No surviving issue

Surviving parent(s) → *First $50K:* to spouse *Remainder:* 50% to spouse, 50% to parent(s)

No surviving parent → 100% to spouse

* Unless one or more of decedent's issue
  is/are also issue of spouse.

** Per capita with right of representation.

FIGURE 2-1 CONTINUED

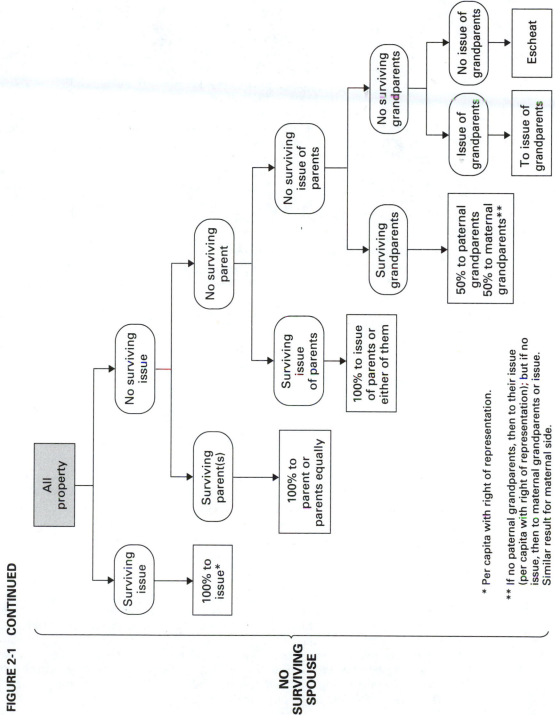

* Per capita with right of representation.

** If no paternal grandparents, then to their issue
(per capita with right of representation); but if no
issue, then to maternal grandparents or issue.
Similar result for maternal side.

FIGURE 2-2   PA. STAT. ANN. TIT. 20, SECTION 2102

The surviving spouse shall be entitled to the following share or shares:
(1) *More than one child.* One third if the decedent is survived by more than one child, or by one or more children and the issue of a deceased child or children, or by issue of more than one deceased child; or
(2) *One child.* One half if the decedent is survived by one child only, or by no child, but by the issue of one deceased child; or
(3) *No issue.* The first $20,000 in value and one-half of the balance of the estate, if the decedent is survived by no issue. In the case of partial intestacy, any amount received by the surviving spouse under the will shall satisfy pro tanto the $20,000 allowance; or
(4) *No issue or other designated person.* All of the estate if the decedent is survived by no issue, parent, brother, sister, child of a brother or sister, grandparent, uncle, or aunt.

principle, a person may inherit *through* a deceased parent; that is, a person may take what his or her parent would have inherited had the parent survived the decedent. A person who inherits through a deceased parent is said to inherit *per stirpes* (literally meaning "by the root") or by **right of representation**. Under the common-law principle of representation, the decedent's intestate estate (subject to the surviving spouse's share) is divided into as many shares as there are surviving children of the decedent and deceased children who left issue who survive the decedent. Each surviving child receives one share, and the share of each deceased child leaving issue is divided among the deceased child's issue in the same manner.

The common-law principle of representation looks to the decedent's children for the purpose of dividing the estate. The U.P.C. modifies the common-law principle of representation by instead looking to the first generation that includes at least one survivor, as well as providing for an equal (or *per capita*, literally meaning "by the head") distribution if all heirs are of the same generation (see U.P.C. §§ 2-103 and 106). Because this modified approach combines the *per stirpes* and *per capita* principles, it is often called *per capita* **with right of representation**. The distinction between the common-law principle of representation and the U.P.C. approach is illustrated by the three scenarios below, each of which involve the family of a hypothetical decedent named Michael (see Figures 2-3 and 2-4).

SCENARIO 1: *Michael's daughter Barbara fails to survive Michael. All of Michael's other issue survive Michael.* **Result (common law):** *Because Barbara left issue (Felicia), Michael's intestate estate is divided into three equal shares. Alan and Cathy will each receive an equal one-third share, while Felicia will take Barbara's one-third share by representation.* **Result (U.P.C.):** *Because at least one of Michael's children is alive, the estate will be divided into three shares (representing Michael's three children). Thus, the result will be the same as under the* per stirpes *approach.*

FIGURE 2-3   ISSUE OF HYPOTHETICAL DECEDENT

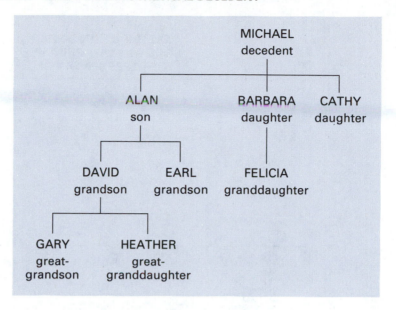

SCENARIO 2: Michael's children Alan, Barbara, and Cathy all fail to survive Michael. All of Michael's other issue survive Michael. **Result (common law):** Because Cathy left no issue surviving Michael, Michael's intestate estate will be divided into two equal shares (for Alan and Barbara). Felicia will take Barbara's one-half share by representation. David and Earl will take Alan's one-half share by representation, each taking one-fourth of the total estate. **Result (U.P.C.):** The initial division will be determined at the grandchildren's level rather than at the children's level. Accordingly, Michael's intestate estate will initially be divided into three equal shares for David, Earl, and Felicia, each of whom will take those shares as Michael's surviving heirs.

SCENARIO 3: Alan, Barbara, Cathy, and David all fail to survive Michael. All of Michael's other issue survive Michael. **Result (common law):** As in Scenario 2, because Cathy left no issue surviving Michael, Michael's intestate estate will be divided into two equal shares (for Alan and Barbara). Felicia will take Barbara's one-half share by representation. Earl will take one-half of Alan's share (one-fourth of Michael's intestate estate) by representation. Gary and Heather will take David's one-fourth share by representation, each taking one-eighth of the total estate. **Result (U.P.C.):** As in Scenario 2, the initial division will be determined at the grandchildren's level rather than at the children's level. Accordingly, Michael's intestate estate will initially be divided into three equal shares for David, Earl, and Felicia. Earl and Felicia will take their respective one-third shares, while Gary and Heather will share equally in David's one-third share, each taking one-sixth of the total estate.

 PARKER ESTATE: In the Parker matter, because Irene was not survived by a spouse, under applicable law, her entire intestate estate (if any) will be divided into three equal shares. Sharon and Dennis would each take their equal (one-

FIGURE 2-4   DISTRIBUTION OF INTESTATE ESTATE TO ISSUE

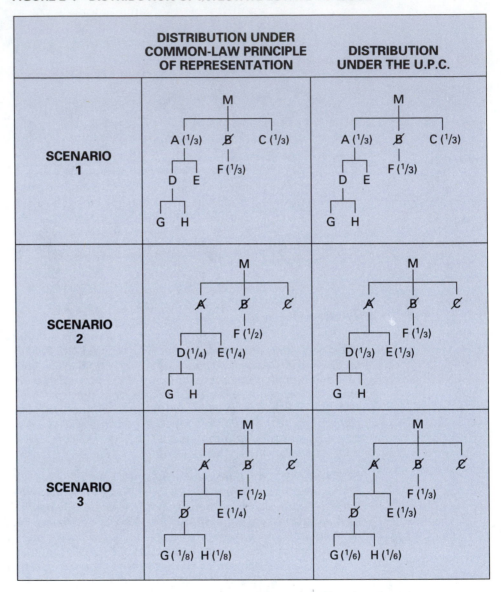

third) share. John failed to survive Irene by the minimum survivorship period established under applicable law (see *Problems of Definition and Status, Simultaneous Death*), and so John will be deemed to have predeceased Irene, and his one-third share will be distributed among his surviving issue, if any. Whether John's stepson Todd and his unborn child in gestation are considered heirs will be discussed later in this chapter.

Shares of Ascendants and Collateral Relatives. In nearly all states, where the decedent leaves no issue the intestate estate passes, subject to the surviving spouse's share, to the decedent's parent or parents equally. If the decedent is not survived by issue or parent, then the intestate estate passes to the issue of the parents or either of them by representation. The decedent's parent may have children by a relationship other than with the decedent's other parent; in this event, these issue would share as well.

Where the decedent is survived neither by issue, parent, nor issue of parent, most statutes provide for the estate to pass to the **next of kin**, although the definition of next of kin varies from state to state. The two most widely adopted methods of identifying next of kin are the **civil-law method** and the **modified civil-law method**. Both the civil-law method and the modified civil-law method involve counting the number of steps, one for each generation, from the decedent up to the nearest common ancestor of the decedent and the claimant, then counting the number of steps or degrees down from the common ancestor to the claimant. The total number of steps defines the proximity of relationship, or **degree of kinship**, between the decedent and the claimant. For example, a decedent's relationship to an uncle is of the third degree—two steps from the decedent up to a grandparent, who is the nearest common ancestor, and one step down from the grandparent to the uncle. The family member or members with the lowest total count take(s) the entire estate as next of kin to the exclusion of all other relatives. If the decedent is survived by two or more next of kin thus determined, under the civil-law method they would share equally as next of kin. In contrast, under the modified civil-law method, if two or more claimants stand in equal degree of kinship to the decedent but claim through different ancestors, those claiming through the ancestor nearest to the decedent will take to the exclusion of those who claim through a more remote ancestor.

The U.P.C. provides for the intestate estate to pass, if the decedent is survived neither by issue, parent, nor issue of parent, to the decedent's grandparents, half of the estate to the paternal grandparents and half to the maternal grandparents. The U.P.C. further provides that if both grandparents on a side predecease the decedent, then their issue take by right of representation, and that if there are no living grandparents or issue on a side, then the entire intestate estate passes to the other side (see Figure 2-1).

Shares of Relatives by Affinity. If the decedent is not survived by any blood relatives, most states provide for **escheat** of the intestate estate, which means that the intestate estate will pass to the state or some subdivision or agency thereof. However, in some states, if no blood relatives survive, the intestate estate passes to certain relatives by affinity—for example, a predeceased spouse's issue or parents. In a few states, the rights of the relatives by affinity extend even further. In California, for example, if the decedent is not survived by any member of the inner circle of relatives that includes the decedent's grandparents and their issue, then a predeceased spouse's issue and parents take to the exclusion of the decedent's next of kin.

In addition, some states provide an exception to the general rules of descent relating to certain property obtained by the decedent from a recently deceased spouse. These statutes typically provide for passage of such property to specified heirs of the previously deceased spouse ahead of all but the decedent's surviving spouse or issue. The purpose of such statutes is to acknowledge that, at least to a certain extent, the portion of the decedent's estate attributable to the predeceased spouse should more fairly be distributed to the family of the predeceased spouse rather than to the decedent's heirs.

Problems of Definition and Status

In addition to acquiring a working knowledge of the general pattern of intestate succession in his or her own state, the probate paralegal must also be able to resolve problems regarding the status of potential claimants under the intestate succession laws. Various problems of definition and status are addressed in the following materials.

Simultaneous Death. When two or more persons die in a common disaster, evidence of the order of death is sometimes lacking, which may create a problem in determining the proper distribution of the decedents' respective estates. For example, if two persons, X and Y, die simultaneously and it is presumed that Y survived X, then the portion of X's intestate estate that Y would otherwise take would pass to Y's estate. If it is presumed, on the other hand, that Y predeceased X, then that same portion would instead pass to X's other heirs. This problem must be resolved in favor of one of these two presumptions.

The Uniform Simultaneous Death Act, enacted in most states, provides generally that, absent a contrary provision in the decedent's will or other controlling instrument, such as a trust, where title to the property depends upon priority of death and there is no sufficient evidence that the persons have died other than simultaneously, the property of each person shall be disposed of as if that person had survived the other. By establishing a presumption of order of death, the Uniform Simultaneous Death Act prevents multiple estate administrations. The Act also makes it less likely that the property will pass to persons the decedent might not have chosen to share in the estate.

However, if it can be proven that the deaths were not simultaneous, the Uniform Simultaneous Death Act is inapplicable, even if the deaths occurred only a few hours or minutes apart. Thus, a few minutes of survivorship may have a dramatic effect on the identity of the decedent's respective heirs. To address this problem, the Uniform Probate Code requires that a would-be heir survive the decedent by 120 hours for the purpose of intestate succession (U.P.C. § 2-104).

PARKER ESTATE: In the Parker matter, the medical records pertaining to the deaths of Irene and John clearly establish that John's death occurred after the death of Irene. However, John failed to survive her by the minimum survivorship period established under applicable law. Accordingly, John will be deemed to have predeceased Irene for the purpose of intestate succession, and his one-third share of Irene's intestate estate (if any) will be distributed among his surviving issue (if any).

Adoption. Nearly all states have enacted statutes that create inheritance rights in adopted persons. Although such statutes initially tended to provide only for inheritance rights for adoptees *from* the adoptive parents, most statutes today have expanded the rights of adoptees to include inheritance *through* the adoptive parents from other members of the adoptive family as well. Under the U.P.C., adoption severs the relationship of the adopted child and the natural parents for the purpose of intestate succession—that is, the adopted child cannot inherit through or from the natural parents, who similarly cannot inherit through or from the natural child who has been adopted away, except in the case of an adoptive parent who is also the spouse of the natural parent (U.P.C. § 2-109[1]). Some statutes also allow the adopted child to inherit from and through natural parents if adoption occurred after the death of a natural parent (or both natural parents). In addition, some statutes allow certain specified members of the natural family, such as the adopted child's issue and whole-blood siblings (and their issue), to inherit from or through the adopted child.

Stepparents and Foster Parents. As a general rule, a stepparent or foster parent is not treated as the natural parent of the stepchild or foster child for the purpose of intestate succession. However, some states, either by statute or judicial decision, provide that such parents will be treated as adoptive parents under certain circumstances—for example, if the relationship began during the person's minority and continued throughout the parties' joint lifetimes and/or if the foster parent or stepparent would have adopted the person but for some legal barrier.

 PARKER ESTATE: It is not clear from the facts whether John's stepson Todd should be treated as an adopted child and thereby inherit from Irene through John (as well as directly from John). Because Todd is a minor, this question might turn on the particular circumstances surrounding John's relationship with Todd and the reasons that John did not adopt Todd.

Persons Born Out of Wedlock. In all states, children born out of wedlock, or so-called illegitimate children, are recognized as heirs of their mothers; that is, they can inherit from and through their mothers (and vice versa). In many states, however, the paternal relationship between an unmarried father and a child must be proved by adjudication in order to establish inheritance rights between the father and child (unless the natural parents participated in a marriage ceremony).

Half-Blood Relatives. Half-blood relatives include collateral relatives who are related through only one common ancestor. In most states, relatives of the half blood inherit equally with those of the whole blood. In those states that do not follow this rule, additional statutory provisions provide that whole-blood relatives either take a larger share or take prior to half-blood relatives.

Afterborn Heirs. Afterborn heirs, also referred to as *posthumous heirs*, include relatives conceived prior to but born after the decedent's death. All states have codified the common-law rule that relatives of the decedent conceived before the decedent's death but born thereafter inherit as if they had been born in the lifetime of the decedent.

 PARKER ESTATE: In the Parker matter, John's unborn child in gestation is clearly John's heir and is entitled to take a portion of Irene's intestate estate (if any) of his or her own right. The unborn child would take either one-sixth (if Todd is also considered issue of John) or one-third (if Todd is not considered issue of John) of Irene's intestate estate through John.

Persons Related to Decedent Through Two Lines. It is not uncommon for a person to be related to another in more than one manner. For example, a decedent's brother or sister may marry the spouse of a decedent and adopt a child of the former marriage. In this situation, the adopted child is related to the decedent's brother both as a child and as niece or nephew. Where parents are unable to care for their child, grandparents may adopt the child, in which case the child will be related to the grandparents as both a child and a grandchild. Under the U.P.C. and in most states, a person who is related to the decedent through two lines of relationship is entitled only to a single share based on the relationship that would entitle the person to the larger share.

Artificial Insemination. Where a husband is infertile, his wife may be artificially inseminated with sperm from a donor other than the husband for the purpose of providing a child for the husband and wife. Conversely, where a wife is unable to bear a child, a surrogate mother may be artificially inseminated with the sperm of the husband for the same purpose. The increasing use of artificial insemination complicates the matter of inheritance, as well as raises a variety of legal issues regarding child custody, child support, and constitutional rights.

Under the Uniform Parentage Act, which has been adopted by most states, if a wife is inseminated artificially under the supervision of a licensed physician and with the written consent of her husband, the husband, not the donor, will be treated as the natural father for the purpose of inheritance (as well for the purpose of child custody and support). If the U.P.A. requirements are not met, the rights of the parties involved are less certain. If the parties entered into a contractual agreement, then the terms of such an agreement would govern their respective rights. Also, most states have enacted statutes creating a rebuttable presumption that a husband of a woman at the time she gives birth is the father of the child. Generally, courts are very reluctant to give paternity rights to a sperm donor, particularly because such rights would also affect child-support obligations of the parties.

The provisions of the U.P.A. referred to above have consistently been held by the courts to apply only to sperm-donor situations (that is, where the husband is infertile) and not where a surrogate-mother is involved (that is, where the wife is infertile). In the latter situation, adoption away from the birth mother will sever that parent-child relationship and create a parent-child relationship between the adoptive mother and the child. Where the birth mother refuses to give up the child in violation of an agreement between the parties, the father may bring suit to establish paternity and thereby obtain custody of the child and allow adoption by his wife and away from the birth mother.

Nonmarital Relationships. Regarding the rights of unmarried persons with respect to their partner's estate, courts generally agree that an unmarried person will not be treated as a married person for the purpose of inheritance (as well as for the purpose of property settlement and spousal support upon separation of the couple). The courts have been reluctant to allow an unmarried person any such rights, particularly because this would invite a flood of litigation in an already overburdened judicial system. Marriages between two people of the same gender have not been recognized by the courts. Thus, these relationships are not as yet sufficient to establish inheritance rights.

Aliens. In most states, no person is disqualified to take as an heir because he or she (or a person through whom he or she claims) is not a citizen of the United States (U.P.C. § 2-112 reflects this general rule). A few states prohibit a nonresident alien from taking property by intestate succession or will unless, under the law of the country where the nonresident lives, there is a reciprocal right of American citizens to take property left them by citizens of that country. Also, a few states permit a court to impound property left to a nonresident alien if it is shown that such person will not have the benefit or use of the property if sent. The constitutionality of both types of statutes mentioned above, however, is currently in doubt.

Disqualification for Misconduct. Generally speaking, an heir's misconduct will not disqualify the heir from sharing in the intestate estate of a decedent. In a few states, however, adultery or desertion by a spouse or abandonment by a parent may disqualify the offender from inheriting from the offended spouse or child. In addition, although inheritance rights are generally unaffected by an heir's criminal conduct, nearly all states make exception, either by statute or judicial decision, in the case of homicide where the offender would otherwise inherit from the victim, either by will or inheritance as well as under the terms of a life insurance policy or survivorship provision of a deed (U.P.C. § 2-803 reflects this general rule).

Effect of Prior Transactions on Intestate Succession

Certain transactions between a decedent and a would-be heir prior to the decedent's death may affect the would-be heir's entitlement in the decedent's intestate estate, as discussed in the following materials.

Advancements. An **advancement** is an *inter vivos* gift by the decedent—that is, a gift made by the decedent during the decedent's lifetime—made with the intention that the gift is to be applied toward the donee's eventual inheritance. It is important to keep in mind that the doctrine of advancements comes into play only in the case of *total* intestacy. If the decedent left a will, even if partial intestacy results, it is assumed that the decedent took into consideration any prior gifts in determining the beneficiaries' shares under the will. Treatment of *inter vivos* gifts made after the will is governed by the related doctrine of *satisfaction*, which will be examined in Chapter 8.

An *inter vivos* gift will be treated as an advancement only if this was the decedent's intention. Under the U.P.C., the decedent's intention to make an advancement can be proven only by a contemporaneous written declaration by the decedent or subsequent written acknowledgment by the heir. Most statutes, however, do not impose these requirements. In most states, such intention may also be demonstrated by other written records, either formal or informal, as well as by the parties' oral declarations. Moreover, a substantial gift to a child (and to other descendants under common law in some states) is presumed to be an advancement; this presumption can be rebutted, but it is often unclear what evidence will serve to do so.

In many states, when the donee fails to survive the decedent, under either judicial decision or statute, the advancee's issue are charged with the amount of the advancement. In some states, however, as well as under the U.P.C., the advancee's issue are not so charged, unless a written declaration or acknowledgment provides otherwise.

The value of an advancement is determined under the U.P.C. as of the earlier of the time of the gift or the decedent's death. As a result, an *inter vivos* gift of property that appreciates in value between the time of the gift and the decedent's death will be valued as an advancement at the earlier (i.e., lower) value. However, under common law in many states, in the event the value of the property is stated in a contemporaneous written declaration by the decedent, that stated value is generally conclusive. In other states, the value of the advancement will in all cases be that of similar or "like" property as of the intestate's death.

In computing the heirs' intestate shares where an advancement has been made, before a donee-heir may share in the estate, the advancement must be brought into *hotchpot*. The principle of hotchpot requires that the value of the *inter vivos* gift be added back into the estate for purposes of computing the shares, and after the donee-heir's share is calculated, the *inter vivos* gift is deducted from it. Because the advancement is a gift rather than a loan, if the advancement exceeds the donee-heir's share of the estate, the donee-heir may refuse to come into hotchpot, keeping the gift without sharing in the estate.

*EXAMPLE: Victoria's estate at the time of her intestate death is $300,000. Her intestate heirs are her three children, Adrian, Benjamin, and Carmen. Adrian received an inter vivos advancement of $60,000. **Result:** To calculate Adrian's share of the estate, the $60,000 is brought into hotchpot, augmenting the estate to a total of $360,000. The shares of Adrian, Benjamin, and Carmen are then calculated as one-third each of the augmented estate, but Adrian's share is reduced by the amount of the inter vivos advancement. Thus, Adrian will receive $60,000, while Benjamin and Carmen will each receive $120,000.*

Releases and Assignments. Where a person, prior to a decedent's death, either relinquishes or assigns to another party all or a portion of an expected inheritance in the decedent's estate, whether that person will be bound by the release or assignment is a matter of common law rather than statute. Although this area is rather unsettled, generally speaking, the heir will be bound by the release or assignment only if the release or assignment is made for fair and adequate consideration. In addition, it has been held that the heir may also be so bound if the decedent refrained from executing a will in reliance upon such release or assignment.

Debts Owed to the Decedent. A debt owed to the decedent must be distinguished from an advancement; as noted earlier, an advancement is a gift rather than a loan, and the donee may keep the advancement if it exceeds the donee's share of the estate. However, a legal obligation to pay the decedent cannot be retained by the debtor-heir because it is not a gift. Thus, to the extent the amount of the debt exceeds the debtor-heir's intestate share, the debtor is legally obligated to repay the debt to the estate. However, if the debt does not exceed the debtor-heir's intestate share, then the practical effect of the debt will be the same as for an advancement. In either event, the debt will not be charged to any heir except the debtor. The debt is put into hotchpot before the estate is divided; then the debt is subtracted from the debtor's share.

 FOCUS: An advancement is a gift, and the donee-heir may elect to keep the gift (and forego sharing in the decedent's intestate estate). However, a debt owed to the decedent by an heir must be repaid to the estate.

DETERMINING THE VALIDITY OF A WILL

The remaining materials in this chapter will (1) examine the basic requirements for all valid wills, (2) describe the various specific types of wills that are authorized under the laws of most states, and (3) identify exactly what papers and other evidence are properly included as parts or components of a will. The probate paralegal must understand the basic rules in these areas in order to assist effectively in the preparation and the execution of wills, as well as to examine wills prepared by others and to prepare petitions to the court for probate of wills.

Applicable Law

In assessing the *validity* of a will (as well as in *interpreting* the will), the law at the time the will was executed governs. As to which state's laws apply for this purpose, the choice-of-law statute of the state where the will is offered to probate dictates this matter. At common law, the law of the decedent's domicile at the time of death determined a will's validity insofar as the will disposed of personal property, while the law of the state in which the real property was located governed the validity of the will insofar as it disposed of real property. Most statutes today extend the choice of law available to the probate court, thereby reducing the number of cases where total or partial intestacy results. The U.P.C. reflects this modern approach (see Figure 2-5).

FIGURE 2-5   DETERMINING THE VALIDITY OF A WILL: CHOICE OF LAW

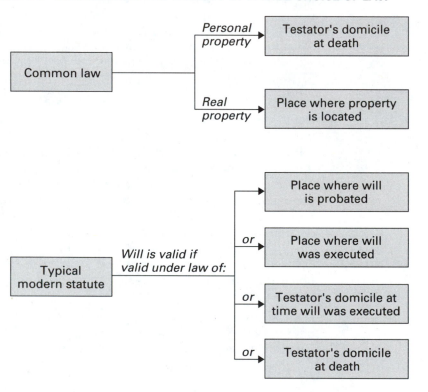

 PRACTICE TIP: It is possible that a will might eventually be offered for probate in any of the 50 states, which would seem to suggest that law-office procedure for execution of wills meet the requirements for valid wills in all 50 states. However, nearly all choice-of-law statutes include the law of the place where the will was executed as one choice of law. Thus, it is acceptable office procedure to meet only the minimum requirements of your state's laws for execution of wills.

Basic Requirements for a Valid Will

In order for a will to be valid, certain basic requirements must be met relating to its provisions as well as to the intent and mental capacity of the person making the will. In addition, certain formalities for execution are required. The following discussion examines these basic requirements.

Provisions Required for a Valid Will. To be admitted to probate, a will must either:

1. Dispose of property
2. Nominate one or more persons to serve as executor(s)
3. Revoke another instrument

A will cannot serve solely to disinherit an heir (for further discussion of disinheritance by will, see Chapter 3). Compare the following two examples:

*EXAMPLE: Theresa executes an instrument that states in its entirety, "I wish to exclude my son Frank from inheriting any portion of my estate, and I hereby disinherit him." **Result:** The instrument will be given no legal effect because it serves solely to disinherit Frank, even though it may satisfy all of the requirements for a duly executed will.*

*EXAMPLE: Theresa executes an instrument that states in its entirety, "I wish to exclude my son Frank from inheriting any portion of my estate, and I hereby disinherit him. Also, I leave to my daughter Julia my wedding ring." **Result:** The instrument might be a valid will, because it disposes of property.*

The Requirement of Testamentary Intent. A valid will requires **present testamentary intent**; that is, the testator must intend to make the particular instrument his or her will at the time he or she signs it. A written statement of intention to make a will in the future is not enough.

*EXAMPLE: Jonathan writes a letter to Renata stating, "I am going to make a will leaving all of my property to you." **Result:** This letter is not a will, even though it might satisfy all of the requirements for a duly executed will, because Jonathan does not intend to make a will now.*

Present testamentary intent may be proven by examining the instrument itself as well as the circumstances surrounding its execution. It is a universal practice among lawyers to include as the very first provision in a will an introductory clause, also referred to as an **exordium clause**, that clearly establishes the testator's present testamentary intent. Aside from whether the will includes such a clause, testamentary intent is strongly inferred if the instrument appears to meet all of the formal requirements for a valid will. However, it is possible that the instrument may have been made as a joke, and extrinsic evidence may be examined in order to determine whether this was the case.

A will (or a particular provision in a will) may be made expressly conditional upon the occurrence of a certain event. If so, and if the event does not occur, the will (or provision) will not be given effect. However, language that sounds like a condition might be interpreted as a declaration of motive for making the will rather than as a true condition which governs the will's effectiveness.

 PRACTICE TIP: Because of the potential difficulties in determining whether a will is conditional or merely states a motive, it is generally not recommended that conditional provisions be included in clients' wills. However, in situations where the client is adamant about conditioning a will (or a particular provision in a will) on the occurrence of an event, it is important to include a provision in the will which clarifies that the will is conditional (and not merely a declaration of motive) and that it is to be given legal effect only if the condition occurs.

The Requirement of Testamentary Capacity. Any person of legal age (generally 18) and of sound mind may make a valid will. A "sound mind" requires that the person know what property he or she owns and whom he or she wants to benefit from the will. The mental capacity required for execution of a will is less than that required for other legal instruments because the arm's length negotiations that may be necessary for other legal documents are not necessary for a will. An adult who has been adjudged legally incompetent by a court in a protective proceeding is not necessarily precluded from making a valid will.

Formalities for Due Execution of Wills. Certain formalities must be followed in order for a will to be valid. Generally, a valid will must be in writing, must be signed by the testator, and must be dated. In addition, unless the will is written in the testator's own handwriting, there must be at least two witnesses to the execution of the will. Each of these specific requirements will be examined in greater detail in Chapter 3.

SPECIFIC TYPES OF WILLS

In all states, a variety of specific types of wills are authorized, as discussed in the materials that follow.

Formal Attested (Witnessed) Wills

An **attested will** is simply a will whose execution (signing by the testator) is *witnessed*. A formal attested will must be in writing, must include the testator's signature, and must be executed in the presence of competent witnesses, who in turn must sign the will as witnesses. Each of these particular requirements will be examined in detail in Chapter 3.

Holographic Wills

A will in the testator's handwriting is referred to as a **holographic will**. A valid holographic will need not be witnessed. Statutes in nearly half the states (as well as the U.P.C.) authorize such wills. Although the law firm obviously does not assist clients in preparing holographic wills, it is important that the probate paralegal be familiar with the requirements for a valid holographic will and with the potential problems associated with them, because the paralegal will no doubt encounter such wills in probate matters where the decedent died leaving such a will.

The Requirement of Testamentary Intent. A valid holographic will, just like any other type of will, requires present testamentary intent. Determining whether this requirement is met can be particularly problematic with holographic wills, which often take the form of informal letters. As a general rule, where testamentary language appears in the context of a lengthy letter containing family news or other topics unrelated to testamentary concerns, it is unlikely that the letter will be probated as a valid will. However, if the content of the letter is largely testamentary in nature and direct and to the point, or if it can be shown that the letter was written in contemplation of death, it is much more likely that the letter will be admitted as a valid will.

Statement as to Date of Execution. Some statutes require that a holographic will include a statement as to the date of execution. Where a statute does not require such a statement, the absence of a date on the instrument might raise a problem if another will exists. If the date of execution of one or more of the instruments is not known, determining which instrument should be given effect may prove to be difficult. Generally, an undated holographic will is invalid to the extent it is inconsistent with another dated will, unless it can be shown that the holographic will was executed later than the dated will.

Testator's Handwriting. A minority of statutes authorizing holographic wills require that the will be *entirely* in the testator's handwriting. Under these statutes, where a purported will is written, for example, on stationery with preprinted words at the top or bottom of the paper, the purported will is invalid. However, most states authorizing holographic wills require that only the *material* provisions of the will appear in the testator's handwriting. Accordingly, a will written on preprinted stationery would be valid under most statutes. More problematic is the purported holographic will in which the testator has filled in the blanks of a preprinted will form. Most courts would deny probate of such an instrument as a holographic will, although the result may depend upon the extent to which the preprinted language constituted "material provisions."

Testator's Signature. A valid holographic will requires the signature of the testator. Signature by proxy is not permitted, as it is in the case of attested wills. The signature need not appear at the end of the will (except under a few statutes), as long as it is apparent that the testator's name was written with the intent that it serve as the testator's signature.

 PARKER ESTATE: Whether Irene's letter to Sharon constitutes a valid holographic will appears uncertain based on the foregoing discussion. The contents of the letter are indicated in Figure 2-6 (the actual handwritten letter is included in the Parker file, Appendix A of the Resource Manual, as part of Exhibit 7). Although undated, the letter will not fail as a valid holograph on this account, because applicable law does not require a statement as to the date of execution. The entire letter is clearly in Irene's handwriting. However, it is not clear whether the term "Your Mother" constitutes a signature as required under applicable law. In all probability, Irene intended that it serve as her signature, although research into the case law may be necessary to settle this issue. The letter also raises the issue of testamentary intent. Perhaps Irene's reference in the letter to "our wills" suggests Irene's intention that the attested will, but not the holograph, serve as her will. Are you persuaded by this argument? Consider this argument in light of the doctrines of integration and republication by codicil discussed later in this chapter, as well as in light of the discussion of revocation by subsequent instrument in Chapter 3.

FIGURE 2-6   HOLOGRAPHIC CODICIL OF IRENE PARKER

My dearest daughter Sharon,
    I am leaving this letter for you with our wills to make sure that you read it after I'm gone from this world. You have always been faithful to me, and so I want you to have the house. I'm going to put aside a few special things in your father's safe in the basement (the key is in the top right desk drawer) that I want my granddaughter to have. Do what you think is best with my other things.
    I adore my grandchildren, Sharon. Please make sure they are brought up right and go to college and make good in life.
    Your Mother

Joint Wills and Mutual Wills

A **joint will** is a single will executed by two or more persons and intended to serve as the will of each. **Mutual wills**, also referred to as **reciprocal wills**, are separate wills executed by two or more persons that contain substantially similar provisions. Although lawyers frequently use mutual (or reciprocal) wills, especially in the common situation where two spouses wish to leave their entire respective estates to each other, lawyers do not use *joint* wills because these wills present potential evidentiary and procedural problems—whether one or both wills have been revoked by physical act may be unclear, and the same original will must be admitted in two separate probate proceedings.

Oral Wills

Most states authorize at least one of two types of oral wills: (1) nuncupative wills and (2) soldiers' and sailors' wills. Statutes authorizing **nuncupative wills** permit a person in peril of death to dispose of limited amounts of personal property by oral statement. This type of will generally must be made during the testator's last illness, must be made before a certain number of witnesses at least one of whom was requested by the testator to serve as a witness to the will, and must be reduced promptly to writing. Statutes authorizing **soldiers' and sailors' wills** generally require that the testator be in active military service and that sailors be at sea. The U.P.C. does not provide for either type of oral will, because these wills are fraught with evidentiary problems and are sources of frequent litigation.

Statutory Wills

Many state legislatures have enacted statutes that provide a complete form for a valid will. Such a will is referred to as a **statutory will**. Compliance with the statutory form ensures validity of the will, at least with respect to form (although the will may nevertheless be executed improperly). Under a typical statute, the complete text of the will is provided, with the exception of variable information that is inserted by the testator by filling in blanks. Because these forms use a fill-in-the-blank approach, the possibilities for fraud and undue influence are much greater than with a customized will. For example, an elderly testator who is susceptible to undue influence may be pressured into signing such a will before all of the variable information has been inserted. As a result, many such statutes require that, in addition to being witnessed, the testator's signature be acknowledged before a notary public.

Where authorized, statutory wills are made available to the general public on preprinted legal forms through office supply stores. These forms are not typically used by law firms, because they afford very little flexibility, particularly with respect to dispositive provisions. However, statutory wills do serve an important function insofar as they provide a reliable means of preparing a will for individuals who either cannot afford to pay a lawyer or do not have enough time to prepare a customized will.

Preprinted Wills and Computer-Generated Wills

In addition to statutory wills, a variety of other preprinted will forms, including computer-generated forms, are widely available to the general public. Many such forms claim to be valid in all 50 states. The drawbacks in using these forms are the same as in using statutory will forms; in addition, however, it is very difficult for the layperson to determine by examining such a form if the form is intelligently and thoughtfully drafted—specifically, whether the provisions are clear and unambiguous, whether the form includes all of the most common and desirable provisions, and whether the form allows the user the most critical choices. Moreover, there is always an element of uncertainty as to whether the will is indeed valid in the state where the will is executed (or in any state).

Audio and Audio/Video Recorded Wills

Except where oral wills are authorized, all statutes require some form of writing. An audio or audio/video recording does not constitute a writing. However, in a few cases in those states that authorize oral wills, audio and audio/video recordings have been deemed valid as such where the speaker's

voice could be identified as that of the testator and where the other requirements for oral wills were met.

 PRACTICE TIP: It is not recommended that the law firm use audio or audio/
video recordings for clients as a substitute for written wills. The circumstances
under which such wills might be valid is still very much in question. However,
it has become increasingly common practice among law firms to record on
audio/video tape the execution and attestation of clients' wills. Although no
substitute for the presence of witnesses, an audio/video recording provides
additional evidence that the will was duly executed—it helps to prove (1) testamentary capacity; (2) testamentary intent; (3) the physical presence of witnesses; and (4) the absence of fraud, duress, and undue influence.

COMPONENTS OF A WILL

It is fundamental that only one will may be probated. If more than one
unrevoked will is found, the most recent dated will is generally determina-
tive in virtually all states (see Chapter 3). However, a single will may contain
many different components (see Figure 2-7). Papers present at the execution of the will may be *integrated* into the will, while other documents in
existence at the time of execution may be *incorporated by reference* into the will.
Testamentary instruments executed later may be included as *codicils* to the
will, while other independent events may be considered, under the doctrine
of *independent significance*, as part of the will for the purpose of interpreting
the will.

FIGURE 2-7   COMPONENTS OF A WILL

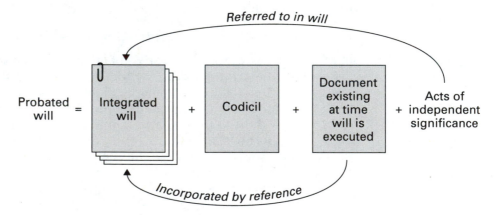

Integration

A will may, of course, consist of more than one piece of paper or writing, and
all of the pages are admitted to probate as a single testamentary instrument.
The problem of integration involves determining what the will consists of.
The basic rule to bear in mind is that a will consists of all papers or writings
(exclusive of codicils, incorporated documents, and independent events,

which will be discussed later) that were actually present at the time of execution and that the testator intended to constitute his or her will.

In most cases, integration is not a problem, especially in the case of wills prepared by the law firm. Pages are usually attached physically and/or numbered so that it is clear what pieces of paper the testator intended to comprise his or her will. Office procedure may require the testator, and possibly the witnesses as well, to initial each page of the will as an additional measure. Even where the pages are not numbered, attached, or initialed, the "pieces" of the will can often be "integrated" by noting the internal coherence of the provisions (for example, by the succession of numbered headings or by provisions running from one page to the next). In any case where integration is at issue, the courts also allow extrinsic evidence, such as the testimony of witnesses, to help the court determine which papers the testator intended to comprise the will.

Wills that do present integration problems are most often unwitnessed holographic wills where the pages are not attached or numbered and a coherent connection between the pages is lacking. Consider the surprisingly common scenario involving an envelope that has *Will* written on the front and contains several unattached pieces of paper. This scenario presents two questions: (1) whether all of the papers were present at the time of execution, and (2) whether any papers were removed or added (accidentally or intentionally by either the testator or by another person) after execution. Such scenarios are examined on a case-by-case basis, taking into account the coherence among the papers as well as extrinsic evidence such as statements made by the testator to others. Recent court decisions have been very liberal in construing several holographic documents, possibly made at different times, to be one will, as long as the testator intended the papers to be a single will.

 PARKER ESTATE: In the Parker matter, should the letter fail as a valid holographic will in itself, perhaps it could be given testamentary effect under the doctrine of integration. Although the holograph is not dated, its reference to "our wills" suggests that it was written after those wills were executed. Furthermore, Irene's expressed wishes in the holograph contradict those in her attested will, strongly suggesting that the two instruments were executed at different times and were not intended to be integrated as a single instrument. Accordingly, it is highly unlikely that the holograph may be given testamentary effect under the doctrine of integration. Consider as an alternative theory that the attested will was amended by the holographic instrument, just as other legal documents such as contracts may be amended. The discussion below concerning the subject of codicils suggests that such a theory may be plausible.

Codicils

A **codicil** is a testamentary instrument executed subsequent to the execution of a valid will. Codicils must be executed with the same formalities required for the execution of wills. Codicils are ordinarily intended to modify, alter, or expand a will, although a codicil may also serve to revoke a will or to revive a previously revoked will. A holographic codicil may relate to an attested will; similarly, an attested codicil may relate to a holographic will (a sample codicil and the effect of codicils on prior testamentary instruments will be examined in Chapter 3).

A codicil and the will to which it pertains are normally read together and treated as if they constitute a single testamentary instrument executed at the date of the codicil or of the last codicil. The will is deemed *reexecuted* with the codicil, so that the will is made to speak and is interpreted as of the date of the codicil. This rule is referred to as the doctrine of **republication by codicil**.

FOCUS: Codicils are subject to the same formal requirements as wills, although a holographic codicil may refer to a nonholographic will (and vice versa). A will is deemed reexecuted, and therefore is interpreted, as of the date the codicil referring to it is executed.

PARKER ESTATE: In the Parker matter, Irene's holograph may be given testamentary effect as a codicil if it meets the formal requirements for holographic wills. If it is a valid codicil, does the holograph raise any republication issues? Examine Irene's attested will (see Exhibit 7 in Appendix A) as to whether any gifts under that will would pass to different devisees, or whether the identification of certain property would differ, depending on when the will was deemed executed. Because the holograph is not dated, when should republication be deemed to have occurred? If the date that the codicil was executed cannot be determined, who is Irene's granddaughter for the purpose of the provision in the holograph disposing of certain items in the safe? Consider this question in light of the doctrine of independent significance, discussed later in this chapter.

Incorporation by Reference

Under the doctrine of **incorporation by reference**, a writing in existence at the time the will is executed may be made part of the will if the document is clearly identified in the will and if the language of the will manifests this intent. An invalid will may be incorporated by reference into a subsequently executed testamentary instrument. Nearly all states allow incorporation by reference, although a few states refuse to do so on the basis that incorporated writings lack sufficient safeguards against fraud. In most states authorizing holographic wills, a printed or typed instrument may be incorporated by reference into a holographic instrument.

Extrinsic evidence is not admissible to help identify the document or show the testator's intent to incorporate the document. Accordingly, it is essential that a provision in a will incorporating an existing document be properly drafted (see Figure 2-8). Some statutes also require that the will refer to the document as in existence (would the provision in Figure 2-8 meet the requirements of such a statute?).

FIGURE 2-8   SAMPLE WILL PROVISION—INCORPORATION BY REFERENCE

I leave to my brother ROBERT MURRAY a certain parcel of unimproved land located in the County of Skagit, State of Washington, the legal description of which is attached to the will, labeled as "Exhibit A," and by this reference made a part of the will.

EXAMPLE: Vincente's holographic will provides in part as follows: "Except for the gifts I have already mentioned, I want my estate to go to any one of several worthy organizations. I have attached a list of worthy charities to this will." Attached to the will is a typewritten list that includes several charitable organizations. ***Result:*** *Because the list is typewritten, it cannot be integrated into Vincente's holographic will. However, the list can be incorporated by the will's reference to it because (1) Vincente's intent that the list be made a part of the will seems clear, (2) the list existed at the time the will was executed, and (3) the list is sufficiently described to permit its identification.*

Events of Independent Significance

The precise identity of persons or property referred to in a will often can be determined only by looking outside the integrated will, as we have seen in cases where documents existing at the time the will is executed are incorporated by reference. Under the doctrine of **independent significance**, the court may interpret a will by referring to documents, acts, or events effectuated at any time during the testator's lifetime, as long as they have sufficient significance apart from their impact on the will. These documents, acts, or events are viewed as components of the will. Facts of independent significance typically help to identify either a beneficiary or a gift.

EXAMPLE: Fuji's will states, "I leave $5,000 to the person who is my housekeeper at the time of my death." ***Result:*** *In all probability, Fuji does not employ housekeepers primarily for the purpose of passing property to them upon her death. Thus, the identity of Fuji's housekeeper has sufficient significance apart from its impact on the will. Accordingly, the court may refer to this independent fact in order to determine the beneficiary's identity.*

EXAMPLE: Nancy's will states, "To my oldest grandson Mark I leave all automobiles that I own at the time of my death." ***Result:*** *It is highly unlikely that Nancy acquires automobiles solely for the purpose of making a testamentary gift. Thus, the identity of her automobiles at the time of her death has sufficient significance apart from its impact on the will, and the court may refer to this independent fact to determine the precise gift under the will.*

In some cases, whether the event referred to in the will holds sufficient independent significance is not so clear, as where the testator uses various containers such as boxes, drawers, or envelopes to effect a distribution plan of their contents.

EXAMPLE: Matthew's will states, "I leave to Susan the entire contents of the top drawer of my desk, and I leave to Lisa the entire contents of the bottom drawer of my desk." Result: Matthew's placing certain items in particular desk drawers may have a nontestamentary motive, such as organizing items or papers for ready access. However, in this example, if the gifts to Susan and Lisa were to be found instead in different envelopes in Matthew's desk, there would probably be no independent significance.

The doctrine of independent significance is also applicable to acts of other persons outside the control of the testator. Perhaps the most common such situation is where the testator directs that property be distributed in accordance with the will of another person. If the other person's will is in existence at the time the testator's will is executed, the other will may be incorporated by reference, as long as the other requirements for incorporation by reference are met. If the other person's will is not in existence at the time the testator's will is executed, then the doctrine of independent significance may be required in order to give effect to the dispositive provision in the testator's will.

 PARKER ESTATE: In the Parker matter, assuming Irene's holograph is a valid codicil, can the provision disposing of the "things" in Irene's safe be given testamentary effect? This problematic provision relies upon two external events or facts: (1) the identity of Irene's granddaughter, and (2) the contents of the safe. Regarding the former, the identity of Irene's granddaughter clearly has significance apart from the will; the more important issue regarding the identity of Irene's granddaughter involves the doctrine of republication (see *Codicils*). Regarding the second "event," whether Irene's act of placing certain "things" in the safe holds sufficient significance apart from its impact on the will may depend on the nature of these "things"—if they are irreplaceable and/or hold great monetary value, it would be reasonable to keep the items in a place that is secure from theft or fire, regardless of the testamentary intentions of the owner regarding the items.

Lists of Tangible Personal Property. In some cases, the event referred to in the will clearly has no significance apart from its impact on the will. The most common such scenario involves a list of items of tangible personal property (such as jewelry, kitchenware, or artwork) prepared and amended from time to time by the testator after execution of the will.

EXAMPLE: Miriam's will states, "I give various items of jewelry to those persons who I will list on a separate paper which I will keep with this will." Result: Because the list is not in existence at the time the will is executed, it cannot be incorporated by reference. Additionally, because the list has no significance apart from its testamentary impact, the doctrine of independent significance is inapplicable. Thus, the provision in Miriam's will is invalid (unless the list is a valid holographic instrument in itself).

One way of avoiding the result in the foregoing example would be to prepare the list prior to executing the will. However, after executing a will, the temptation is great for the testator to frequently change his or her mind about the disposition of certain items of tangible personal property. The doctrine of independent significance does not afford a way for the testator to make such frequent changes apart from executing a codicil, because lists are unlikely to have sufficient independent significance. The U.P.C. addresses this problem by creating an exception to the requirement of independent significance for such lists (Figure 2-9).

FIGURE 2-9   U.P.C. § 2-513 (SEPARATE WRITING IDENTIFYING BEQUEST OF TANGIBLE PROPERTY)

Whether or not the provisions relating to holographic wills apply, a will may refer to a written statement or list to dispose of items of tangible personal property not otherwise specifically disposed of by the will, other than money, evidences of indebtedness, documents of title, and securities, and property used in a trade or business. To be admissible under this section as evidence of the intended disposition, the writing must either be in the handwriting of the testator or be signed by him and must describe the items and the devises with reasonable certainty. The writing may be referred to as one to be in existence at the time of the testator's death; it may be prepared before or after the execution of the will; it may be altered by the testator after its preparation; and it may be a writing which has no significance apart from its effect upon the dispositions made by the will.

PRACTICE TIP: If your state does not have a statute similar to U.P.C. § 2-513, dealing with clients who continually change their mind about the disposition of particular items of property can be a problem. A partial solution is to instruct the testator, both at the time of execution and by follow-up letter, to refrain from making any changes without first consulting the law firm. An additional solution is to provide in the will for a list of items (incorporated by reference in the will) to pass to a group of beneficiaries equally as they agree or, if they fail to agree within a certain time period, as the personal representative determines. The client must, of course, consent to relinquish a certain amount of control over the disposition of these assets.

Testamentary Additions to *Inter Vivos* Trusts. The doctrine of independent significance is particularly relevant today in the context of pour-over wills and *inter vivos* trusts. *Inter vivos* trusts are usually made revocable, so that the settlor may amend or revoke the trust at any time. Along with the trust, the settlor typically executes a will which provides essentially that the settlor's property not placed in trust during the settlor's lifetime be given to the trustee of the *inter vivos* trust to hold under the terms of the trust instrument *as amended on the date of the settlor's death.*

Because the original *inter vivos* trust instrument is in existence at the time the pour-over will is executed, that instrument may be incorporated by reference into the will. However, the doctrine of incorporation by reference is not applicable where the testator has amended the trust (because the trust, as amended, was not in existence at the time the will was executed). Instead, the pour-over will must be given effect, if at all, by applying the doctrine of independent significance.

In the 1950s, when estate-planning lawyers first began using pour-over wills in conjunction with *inter vivos* trusts, the law was unclear as to the circumstances under which an *inter vivos* trust holds significance apart from the will plan. This issue has since been well settled, and the validity of pour-over provisions in a will is recognized today in nearly all states. In fact, most states have adopted by legislation the **Uniform Testamentary Additions to Trusts Act**, which permits the pour-over of estate assets into an *inter vivos* trust as amended on the testator's death "if the trust is identified in the testator's will and its terms are set forth in a written instrument (other than the will) executed before or concurrently with the execution of the testator's will or in the valid last will of a person who has predeceased the testator (regardless of the existence, size, or character of the corpus of the trust)." The Act is included in the U.P.C. (§ 2-511).

Paralegal Assignment 2

Recall that your second assignment for Ms. Cargis involves assessing the validity of the holographic instrument in the Parker matter and drafting a letter to Sharon Madson in layperson's terms explaining the firm's legal position on this issue and soliciting any additional information that might be helpful. Preliminary research on your part reveals case law strongly supporting the proposition that the words *Your Mother* at the close of Irene's letter constitute Irene's signature. Also, you have found no authority in the case law undermining Irene's testamentary intent by her reference in the letter to "our wills." Based upon the materials in this chapter, you are able to prepare the following draft of a letter to Sharon Madson (italicized portions were added by Ms. Cargis):

> As we discussed during our meeting on Monday of this week, before we submit to the court a petition for your appointment as administrator of your mother's estate, we must first determine what document or documents constitute your mother's last will. There is no question that your mother's original will is valid under the laws of this state. In addition, your mother's handwritten letter also appears to be valid as an amendment to the will. The laws of this state provide that if a will or an amendment to a will is not witnessed by two persons, the will or amendment must be written in the testator's handwriting and signed by the testator in order to be valid. Your mother's letter meets these requirements. *Should the court determine that the letter was written later in time than the execution of the original will, to the extent that the letter is inconsistent with the will, the provisions of the letter will become part of your mother's will instead of the provisions in the original will.*

Accordingly, we will be submitting both the original will and the letter amending the will to the court. The court will then make the final decision regarding the validity of these documents. Before our next meeting, please consider the following questions in order to help us prove that your mother's letter is part of her will:

1. Did your mother make any statements to you or to anyone else regarding the letter that would help to show that she intended the letter to be part of her will?

2. Did your mother make any statements regarding the letter that would help determine when the letter was written?

3. Can you identify with certainty that the letter was written by your mother in her own handwriting, or is there any possibility in your mind that the letter was forged?

4. *Since the original will was executed, have you made any statements or committed any acts that might possibly be construed by your brother Dennis or by any other person as unduly influencing or coercing your mother to write the letter?*

5. *Did your mother express any preference to you or to anyone else as to who should serve as executor of her estate?*

6. *Is there any evidence that your mother's mental faculties were impaired to the extent that she did not understand what she was doing or why when writing the letter?*

We should anticipate that your brother Dennis might object to the admission of the letter as part of the will. He may claim that the will does not meet the requirements for a valid will or that you unduly influenced your mother to write the letter. Although your brother is unlikely to prevail, your testimony may be required in court. Finally, your mother's letter presents some problems regarding the proper distribution of her estate. We will address these issues later, however, after the letter and the original will have been admitted to probate.

Finally, please assemble the additional information and documents which I indicated that we need in order to prepare the petition for probate of the will and to administer the estate. As soon as you have done so, please call our offices to arrange for an appointment with one of our firm's probate paralegals. We will then be able to complete the documentation needed for the petition and obtain your signature on the documents.

3 WILLS—PREPARATION, EXECUTION, AND OTHER MATTERS

Paralegal Assignment 3

Because the probate department at Able, Berman & Cargis is newly formed, many forms and procedures relating both to estate planning and to probate matters for use by all lawyers in the department have not yet been developed. Ms. Cargis has been anxious to create a series of standard form letters for use in common estate-planning situations. First priority on her list is a standard follow-up letter to clients who have just executed wills. Ms. Cargis has asked you to draft a form letter concerning the following subjects: (1) the safe-keeping of both the original will and photocopies; (2) making changes in the will; and (3) any events that might affect the will and that the client should be made aware of. In so doing, consider the materials in this chapter, together with the Practice Tip in Chapter 2 concerning lists of tangible personal property.

The first concern of this chapter is with the proper procedures for preparing and executing a valid attested (witnessed) will. Certain conventions are generally followed with respect to the organization, style, and overall appearance of wills, and formal requirements involving the signing and witnessing of attested wills must be strictly observed. The second concern of this chapter is what may happen to a valid will after it is executed. Once executed, what may otherwise appear to be a valid will will not necessarily be probated in its entirety. The will may have been revoked, either in whole or in part, by a subsequent testamentary instrument (as speculated in Chapter 2 regarding the effect of Irene Parker's letter to Sharon on Irene's attested will), as well as by a physical act performed upon the will or by the occurrence of certain events, such as marriage, divorce, or the birth of a child. Also, the execution of the will may have been tainted by undue influence, fraud, or mistake (in the Parker matter, for example, perhaps Sharon unduly influenced Irene to leave her entire estate to Sharon). Finally, certain restrictions upon the testator's power to dispose of his or her estate may come to bear—most significantly, the testator's spouse and children may be entitled to take a certain portion of the estate regardless of the terms of the will (in the Parker matter, for example, perhaps Sharon's brothers John and Dennis are entitled in any event to some portion of Irene's estate). All of these issues involve questions of both law and fact, and it is the responsibility of the probate paralegal through discovery to assist the lawyer in determining whether a particular instrument may be admitted to probate.

PREPARING AND EXECUTING A FORMAL ATTESTED WILL

Preparation and execution of attested (witnessed) wills is of vital concern to the probate paralegal for several reasons. First, the paralegal may assist in preparing wills and in ensuring that the wills prepared by the law firm are valid in form. Second, the paralegal typically assists in the execution of the will and so must ensure that the will is properly executed and witnessed. Third, the paralegal may make preliminary assessments as to both the validity and the components of wills prepared by others during intake for new estate-planning clients as well as for probate matters. Finally, a basic understanding of the rules discussed in the materials that follow is needed in order to assemble documents and to prepare petitions to the court for probate of wills.

Overall Length and Use of "Boiler-Plate" Provisions

A valid will may be very simple and brief indeed, as long as the will is executed with the necessary formalities. As a general guideline, though, a will should include no fewer and no more provisions than needed to reflect the precise intent and wishes of the testator. Wills prepared by lawyers on behalf of clients are usually several pages in length and rather comprehensive in coverage; a lawyer must strive to provide for all contingencies, which usually requires that the document be somewhat lengthy (except for codicils and certain types of wills such as pour-over wills).

Notwithstanding the customized nature of a will, wills prepared by lawyers invariably include certain standard or ''boiler-plate'' provisions. Boiler-plate provisions typically pertain to such matters as the powers of the executor and the definition of terms used in the will. Unless otherwise indicated in the will, the laws of the state where the will was executed dictate such matters; accordingly, many lawyers prefer to include a boiler-plate provision only if the testator's intent is contrary to what would otherwise result under the state's laws. However, if the client expresses a need to be absolutely certain about a particular matter, inclusion of the appropriate provision is recommended even though unnecessary. For example, assume a client with an adopted grandchild wishes to be certain that the grandchild is included in the client's distribution scheme equally with the client's natural grandchildren. Even though your state's law may be clear that an adopted child is included within the meaning of the term *issue* as used in a will (unless otherwise indicated in the will), the client may feel more secure if an appropriate definition of the term *issue* is included in the will.

Organization and Format

Wills prepared by lawyers are generally drafted in a certain conventional format and style. Although a valid will need not conform to these conventions, a will presented in a conventional format carries with it a certain dignity that reflects the legal import of the document. Also, a will that is conventional in its basic provisions and overall appearance may be reviewed and assimilated more quickly by the probate court, as well as by lawyers, paralegals, and others. Form books used by lawyers and paralegals for will drafting typically order and group the provisions of a will in a manner similar to the following:

1. Exordium (introductory) provisions
2. Funeral and burial instructions
3. Provision for payment for expenses of funeral and last illness
4. Dispository provisions
5. Provisions for the appointment and powers of the executor
6. General ("boiler-plate") provisions
7. Signatory clause and signature of testator
8. Attestation clause and signatures of witnesses

Will provisions are conventionally grouped under main headings, or "articles," to help locate particular provisions. Most lawyers also precede specific provisions by subheadings for the same purpose, although some lawyers prefer not to use subheadings. The contents of a will may be assimilated more quickly if headings and subheadings are employed. If headings are used, however, a provision should be included in the will which makes clear that headings are to be disregarded in construing the will.

Style and Appearance

Every lawyer and paralegal has his or her own style of writing that is usually reflected in all legal documents, including wills, drafted by that person. Nevertheless, because estate-planning clients are individuals (rather than corporations or other business entities) and usually without special legal training, the law firm should strive to adopt the use of plain English rather than legalese in its wills. Many of the form books still used by lawyers and paralegals today for drafting wills contain provisions that are verbose, that contain excessive legalese, and that use archaic language. The estate-planning client will be highly appreciative if the law firm makes an effort to prepare a will that is concise, contemporary in its use of language, and easily understood by the layperson.

A typeface style that is easily readable as text and appropriate for a legal document (e.g., Courier or Times Roman) should be used, and the size of the typeface should be large enough to be read without eyestrain. A client with poor vision may greatly appreciate a document printed in a larger point size. Some lawyers prefer to use single spacing in their wills, while others prefer double spacing.

The Testator's Signature

The testator must either sign the instrument or direct another to sign by proxy. If another person signs for the testator, as may be the case where the testator is physically incapable of signing, the proxy signing by the other person must be in the presence of the testator and must be at the testator's request or direction. The person signing for the testator may also sign his or her own name, and in some states must do so.

 PRACTICE TIP: Although there are no requirements as to the appearance—for example, printed as opposed to longhand—of the signature by proxy, it is generally recommended that the person signing for the testator do so in his or her own style of handwriting; printing the testator's name or attempting to emulate the testator's own signature makes it less clear who actually signed the instrument.

What Constitutes a Signature. The signature need not be the proper and full name of the testator. A signature is generally sufficient if it is the complete act intended by the testator to serve as his or her signature. Accordingly, a "signature" by initials, by nickname, or by mark is sufficient, as long as it is intended to serve as a completed signature.

 PRACTICE TIP: It is recommended that the testator (or the person signing by proxy) use the same name that the testator uses for signing other legal documents. This procedure avoids confusion over the identity of the testator.

Location of Signature. In most states, the testator's signature does not have to appear at the end of the will. It is recommended, however, that the testator sign the will at the end; a provision that follows the testator's signature (aside from an attestation clause and witnesses' signatures) might be deemed invalid, because its location suggests the possibility that the provision was added later, either by the testator or by another person. Also, in the minority of states that do require the testator's signature to be at the end of the will, such a provision would render the entire will invalid.

The Requirement of Witnesses

Witnesses are required for a valid will, unless the will is valid as a holograph. Procedural requirements and qualification of witnesses are examined in the materials that follow.

Procedural Requirements. Witnesses are required, unless the will is valid as a holograph. Statutes vary as to
1. The number of witnesses required
2. The particular act of the testator that must be witnessed
3. Whether the witnesses must be simultaneously present at the time of the specified act by the testator
4. The location and chronological order of the witnesses' signatures

Number of Witnesses The U.P.C. and most statutes require a minimum of two witnesses; some statutes require a minimum of three witnesses.

 PRACTICE TIP: In all states that require three witnesses, the choice-of-law statute authorizes application of the law of the place where the will is executed. Thus, if the law of your state requires only two witnesses, it is acceptable procedure to meet only this minimum requirement, despite the fact that some states require three witnesses (consider this point, however, in light of the discussion of *Qualification of Witnesses*).

Act That Must Be Witnessed Under U.P.C. § 2-502, the will "shall be signed by at least 2 persons each of whom witnessed either the signing or the testator's acknowledgment of the signature or of the will." The contents of the will need not be disclosed. The requirements in many states are more stringent than those of the U.P.C. In most states, the testator must sign the will in the presence of the witnesses; acknowledgment alone is insufficient. The term *acknowledgment* is used synonymously in § 2-502 with the term **publication**, which refers to a declaration made by the testator that the instrument is his or her will. Some states require publication of the will in the presence of the witnesses at the time the will is signed.

Simultaneous Presence The U.P.C. does not require simultaneous presence by all witnesses. Under the U.P.C., then, one person may witness the testator's signing the will, while a second person may later witness the testator's acknowledgment of either the will or the signature. Some statutes, however, require the simultaneous presence of all witnesses for the specified act.

Signatures of Witnesses In every state except Pennsylvania, witnesses are required to sign the will. Although not required under the U.P.C., in nearly all states witnesses must sign in the presence of the testator. Statutes vary as to (1) whether the witnesses must sign in each other's presence, (2) the permissible location of the witnesses' signatures, and (3) whether the witnesses must be requested to act as such by the testator. It is recommended that the witnesses sign the will later in time than the specific act of the testator (signing or acknowledgment), since the very nature of attestation suggests this order. However, some courts have held that the chronological order of signing is not crucial—that is, a witness may sign the will earlier in time than the testator—as long as all of the ceremonial requirements are met during the course of a single, continuous event.

PRACTICE TIP: In order to guard against charges of fraud in the area of witnesses' signatures, it is recommended that each witness print his or her name and address next to or below the signature. Even if a witness later moves, the information will help to verify the absence of fraud (as to the circumstances under which witnesses must later be located, see *Declarations of Witnesses*). At the time the will is offered for probate, if its validity is challenged and the signatures of the witnesses cannot be identified, the will might be denied probate under the rationale that fictitious names may have been used and thus the will might not have been witnessed at all.

Qualification of Witnesses. Under what circumstances is a person unqualified to serve as a witness to a will? If a witness is unqualified, is the will invalid as a result? The materials that follow address these and related questions.

Competency Any person generally competent to be a witness may act as a witness to a will. Generally speaking, a witness must be competent at the time of the witnessed act; the fact that the witness later becomes incompetent and thereby unable to testify in court regarding the execution of the will does not disqualify the witness. There is no requirement that a witness be an adult in order to be competent to serve as a witness. However, insofar as a person's maturity and memory bear on the credibility and reliability of a witness, it is generally recommended that minors not be selected for this purpose.

A witness who stands to benefit under the provisions of the will is referred to as an **interested witness**. At common law, interested witnesses were deemed incompetent; the rationale for this rule was that an interested witness is less likely to be truthful about the act of execution than is a disinterested witness. Accordingly, an interested witness was barred from testifying in court as to the acts of execution. Under common law, then, if two witnesses were required, and one of the two witnesses was beneficially interested in the will, the will could not be probated. This harsh rule has been abolished in nearly all states (as reflected in U.P.C. § 2-505).

PRACTICE TIP: If possible, young people should be used as subscribing witnesses to wills because they are more likely to be available if called upon to prove the will during a probate proceeding.

Entitlement of "Interested" Witnesses To what extent, and under what circumstances, is an interested witness entitled to benefits under the will? Under the U.P.C., the provision benefiting the witness is not made invalid as a result (U.P.C. § 2-505). Under most statutes, however, such entitlement may be affected if the interested witness is an *essential* witness—that is, if the number of disinterested witnesses fails to meet the statutory requirements for the total number of witnesses. However, if there are a sufficient number of disinterested witnesses, an interested witness is not essential, and his or her benefits under the will are not affected.

EXAMPLE: *Three persons—Ellen, Bill, and Joshua—serve as witnesses to a will. Ellen is a beneficiary under the will, although Bill and Joshua receive no* *benefits thereunder. Applicable law requires two witnesses to the signing of a will.* **Result:** *Because there are two other witnesses, both of whom are disinterested, Ellen is not an essential witness, and her beneficial interest will not be affected.*

In the example above, assume instead that the will is witnessed by only two persons—Ellen and Bill. Since Ellen would now be considered an essential witness, to what extent is she entitled to any benefits under the will? As noted earlier, under U.P.C. § 2-505, the provision benefiting the witness is not made invalid as a result. Another view, adopted by a minority of states, is that any provision in the will in favor of Ellen will be purged, and she may take nothing under the will. A more common and more lenient view is that Ellen may take under the will but only up to the amount of what her share would have been had the will not been established. Under yet another view, Ellen can take under the will in excess of her intestate share only if she can affirmatively prove that the benefits were not procured through duress, menace, fraud, or undue influence.

 FOCUS: An attested will requires two (and in some states three) witnesses; the fact that a witness stands to benefit under the will has no effect in itself on the validity of the will, although this fact *may* affect the witness's entitlement in benefits under the will.

Witnesses Considered to Be "Interested" Any beneficiary who is also a beneficiary under the will is said to be "interested." In a few states, a beneficiary's spouse would also be considered interested. However, interested witnesses do not include the personal representative, the attorney preparing the will or representing the personal representative of the estate, or a creditor of the testator.

 PRACTICE TIP: The foregoing discussion suggests the exclusive use of disinterested witnesses as standard law-office procedure. If your particular state requires two witnesses to a will, two disinterested staff members—perhaps a paralegal and a secretary—should serve as witnesses. Where the testator is accompanied by a disinterested friend, the friend should nevertheless not serve as a witness; if the testator later amends the will to include the friend, an argument for undue influence might be made respecting the original will.

Declarations of Witnesses. A person may demonstrate that he or she has served as a witness to a will simply by signing the will. However, some form of declaration preceding the witness's signature may provide additional evidence that the will was duly executed. Three such forms are considered here: (1) attestation clauses, (2) self-proved wills, and (3) testimonium clauses.

Attestation Clause An **attestation clause** recites the events of execution and other facts to which it is desired that the witnesses attest. If you examine the attestation clause in Irene Parker's attested will (Appendix A of the Resource Manual, Exhibit 7), notice that the clause purports in essence that the will has been executed in compliance with the requirements for due execution of wills. This particular clause would be appropriate where the state's statute requires all of the following: (1) acknowledgment of the will by the testator; (2) a request by the testator that the persons serve as witnesses; and (3) the simultaneous presence of all witnesses.

If the validity of a will is challenged on the basis that the will was not duly executed, the person applying for probate of the will must attempt to locate the witnesses for testimony in court (see Chapter 5). An attestation clause establishes a presumption that the ceremonial requirements recited therein have been met (as long as the signatures of the witnesses can be identified), thus serving an important evidentiary function if a witness cannot be located, is unavailable to testify in court, or cannot recall the events concerning execution. In fact, the attestation clause may be used to impeach any testimony of a witness that is inconsistent with the facts recited in the clause. Such a clause also serves as a useful procedural guide for execution, facilitating compliance with the required formalities that might otherwise be overlooked. Although not required by statute in any state, an attestation clause should nevertheless be included in all wills prepared by the law firm.

Self-Proved Wills   A minority of states (including New York) authorize the use of the **self-proved will**. If a will is self-proved, compliance with signature requirements for execution is conclusively presumed, and other requirements of execution are presumed subject to rebuttal *without the testimony of any witness*, except under certain circumstances. Declarations by the testator and by the witnesses must be included and signed under oath in the presence of a notary public. The use of a self-proved will obviates the need to locate witnesses and solicit their testimony in the event the will is challenged. A will may be self-proved either at the time it is executed and witnessed or later through the use of written declarations attached as a separate page to the will. The U.P.C. authorizes the use of the self-proved will but requires a specific form for the witnesses' declarations (see U.P.C. § 2-504).

Testimonium Clause   Some states (including California) that do not authorize the self-proved will provide instead for the use of a **testimonium clause**, which enhances the evidentiary strength of an attestation clause by adding a statement that the witness's declaration is made under penalty of perjury (although such a declaration is not made under oath before a notary public). A testimonium clause serves the same function as an attestation clause in establishing a rebuttable presumption of the facts recited therein. In addition, however, if the validity of the will is challenged on the basis that it was not duly executed, the testimonium clause serves as a substitute (just as the self-proved will) for witness testimony, thereby obviating the need to locate witnesses.

REVOCATION OF WILLS

Once a will is executed in compliance with the requirements for a valid will, it may be revoked by any method prescribed by statute or case law. The

U.P.C. (and statutes in most states) permits **revocation** by any one of three methods:

1. By a subsequent instrument executed with the same formalities required for a valid will
2. By a physical act performed upon the will itself
3. By operation of law

Once revoked, a will may be reinstated, or *revived*, but only under certain circumstances.

Revocation by Subsequent Instrument

A will may be revoked in whole or in part by a subsequent instrument. The revoking instrument must be executed with the same formalities required for execution of wills. Where holographic wills are authorized, an attested will may be revoked by a holographic instrument (and vice versa).

*EXAMPLE: On January 23, 1993, T duly executes a typewritten, attested will. Thereafter, T duly executes a holographic instrument that states in its entirety, "I hereby revoke my will of January 23, 1993. [date/signature]." **Result**: If applicable law authorizes holographic wills, T's codicil serves to revoke T's will in its entirety. A valid codicil may serve solely to revoke a prior testamentary instrument; thus, the fact that T's codicil includes no other provisions does not affect its validity.*

*EXAMPLE: T's valid will includes the following provision: "I nominate X to serve as executor of my estate." Thereafter, T executes a valid will that fails to expressly revoke the prior will and that includes the following provision: "I nominate Y to serve as executor of my estate." **Result**: The subsequent will serves to revoke the provision in the prior will nominating X to serve as executor, because the subsequent will is inconsistent with the prior will in this respect.*

PRACTICE TIP: An estate-planning client may wish to make changes in his or her will from time to time, perhaps in order to add a devisee or to nominate a different person as executor. Such changes are generally made by executing a codicil to the will. However, if several changes are desired, it may be preferable to make an entirely new will. A single coherent document is easier to assimilate, and probate of more than one testamentary instrument can be avoided thereby. In either event, the paralegal must ensure that the subsequent instrument, whether it be a codicil or a new will, has the legal effect on the original will that is intended by the client.

PRACTICE TIP: If a codicil is intended to revoke only certain provisions of a prior will, in order to avoid confusion as to the testator's intent, the codicil should (1) *expressly* revoke the relevant provisions of the will, clearly identifying those provisions that the testator wishes to revoke; (2) indicate any provision that the testator desires to add in place of the revoked provision(s); and (3) expressly republish the will in all other respects (see Figure 3-1). Although executing two or more codicils to a will is not uncommon, it becomes increasingly difficult to assimilate the will plan as more codicils are executed. Also, each testamentary instrument must be probated, which compounds the paperwork required during probate proceedings (see Chapter 5). Moreover, through the use of word-processing computer software, preparing an entirely new will may actually be easier and quicker than preparing a codicil. Thus, in responding to a request to prepare a codicil, the paralegal should always consider whether an entirely new will would be more appropriate.

FIGURE 3-1   SAMPLE CODICIL

CODICIL

I, ROBERT T. JONES, declare this instrument to be a codicil to my last will and testament executed by me on October 3, 1993, and hereinafter referred to as "the will." I hereby make the following alterations, deletions, or additions to the will:

FIRST: Referring to Article V, paragraph (1) of the will, I hereby appoint FRANCIS L. LEWIS instead of EUGENE S. LEWIS to serve as executor of the will.

SECOND: Referring to Article III, paragraph (2), I hereby add the following provision:

"To my friend FRANCIS L. LEWIS I give the sum of five thousand dollars ($5,000)."

With the exception of the foregoing alterations, deletions, or additions to the will, I hereby ratify, republish, and reexecute the will.

I, ROBERT T. JONES, executed this codicil on this _____ day of _____ , 19 _____ , at Los Angeles, state of California.

_____
ROBERT T. JONES

[Attestation Clause and Subscribing Witnesses' Signatures]

 PARKER ESTATE: With respect to Irene's letter to Sharon, assuming the letter is valid as a holographic will, although the holograph did not *expressly* revoke any part of the original will, the holograph serves to revoke any provisions in the prior will that are inconsistent with those of the holograph. It is plausible to interpret the holograph as effectively disposing of Irene's entire estate, thereby revoking the entire dispositive scheme under Irene's prior will. Also, whether Irene intended by the letter to nominate Sharon to serve as executor of her estate (thereby revoking the provision in the prior will nominating Fred, Ruth, and John as alternate and successive executors) is unclear—such an interpretation is arguable, because the letter appears to direct or instruct Sharon as though she were acting as executor. This issue will not be significant, however, as you will discover in Chapter 5. (Irene Parker's attested will and holographic codicil are included in Exhibit 7 of Appendix A in the Resource Manual.)

Revocation by Physical Act

Persons acting without the assistance of a lawyer often attempt to revoke a will, either in whole or in part, by a physical act performed upon the will itself. As to whether such acts are effective, U.P.C. § 2-507(2) provides as shown in Figure 3-2.

FIGURE 3-2   U.P.C. § 2-507 (REVOCATION BY WRITING OR ACT)

A will or any part thereof is revoked . . . (2) by being burned, torn, canceled, obliterated, or destroyed, with the intent and for the purpose of revoking it by the testator or by another person in his presence and by his direction.

The act must be accompanied simultaneously by a present intent to revoke the instrument. Thus, a change of mind later on the part of the testator can neither prevent revocation nor reinstate the will. Although most statutes reflect U.P.C. § 2-507(2), some statutes permit total, but not partial, revocation by physical act.

Several issues arise under U.P.C. § 2-507(2), including: (1) whether the testator intended to revoke the entire will or only a portion of the will; (2) the effect on one instrument of an act performed upon another instrument; and (3) whether the particular act is sufficient to effect a revocation.

Total vs. Partial Revocation. Where partial revocation by physical act is authorized, an intent to revoke *only part* of the will may be shown by extrinsic evidence and may be inferred from the nature of the act performed.

EXAMPLE: *After T's death, a duly executed typewritten will is found among T's papers. A particular provision in the will leaving the sum of $1,000 to X is crossed out in pen.* **Result:** *Extrinsic evidence, such as T's relationship to X or statements made by T to others after executing the will, may be admitted to show T's intent to revoke this particular provision only. Also, the very nature of the act of crossing out particular words, also referred to as* interlineation, *suggests an intent to revoke provisions in a selective manner.*

In the foregoing example, extrinsic evidence would also be required to show that the provision was crossed out by the testator rather than by another person. Had the interlineation been accompanied by T's signature or initials, such evidence would help to show T's intent. Where the testator replaces the interlineated words, perhaps above the words or in the margin, the new words would be given testamentary effect only if viewed as a valid holographic or attested codicil (except that in the case of a holographic will, the subsequent addition of handwritten words by the testator constitutes a valid holograph even without a signature because the prior signature on the same paper is adopted).

Effect on One Instrument of Act Performed upon Another. A testator may attempt to revoke a will by performing a physical act upon another instrument, as in the case where a will is executed in duplicate or where one or more codicils exist.

Duplicate Wills Where a will is executed in duplicate—that is, where the testator actually signs two identical instruments—a physical act of revocation performed upon one of the instruments also serves to revoke the duplicate instrument. However, where only one instrument is actually signed by the testator, any physical act performed upon a copy is ineffective to revoke all or any part of the will.

*EXAMPLE: After executing a will, T photocopies the signed will, places the original will in a bank safe-deposit box, and keeps the photocopy at home among T's other important papers. Thereafter, T crosses out on the photocopy several dispositive provisions. **Result**: The attempted revocation by T of the particular dispositive provisions is ineffective, because the only will actually signed by the testator remains undisturbed.*

PRACTICE TIP: The foregoing discussion strongly suggests a number of standard office procedures. First, avoid creating a situation that might allow the client to sign duplicate original wills. Photocopies should be made only of the *signed* will; a photocopy of an unsigned will should never be given to the client. If it is necessary for the client to review rough drafts during the planning process, the word *DRAFT* should be stamped across the face of every page as well as over the signature line to ensure that only a single final draft is signed by the testator and given testamentary effect. Second, all signatures on the original will should be written with a colored pen—perhaps blue—so it is clear that the will is original rather than a photocopy. Third, although the firm may prefer to retain the original will in the firm's vault for safekeeping and to prevent tampering, the paralegal should offer the client the option of keeping the original will at home. In any event, the client should be provided with at least two copies of the will, one for safekeeping in a bank safe-deposit box, and the other either to be kept at home for reference or to give to the person nominated in the will to serve as executor. The client must be cautioned that any attempt to alter the copy will have no effect upon the original will. As an additional safeguard, the word *COPY* should be stamped across the face of each page of all photocopies.

Codicils A physical act of revocation performed upon a codicil does not revoke the will, regardless of the testator's intent. On the other hand, under the law of most states, a similar act performed upon the will revokes a separate codicil, unless it can be shown that the testator intended otherwise.

Where the codicil is written on the same paper as the will, the law varies from state to state and is typically unclear as to the effect on the codicil of a physical act performed upon the will (and vice versa).

EXAMPLE: *After executing a will, T executes a codicil on a separate paper. Thereafter, T tears the codicil into several pieces.* **Result:** *The will is not revoked, regardless of T's intent.*

EXAMPLE: *T executes a will that includes numerous dispositive provisions but fails to nominate an executor. Thereafter, T executes a codicil on a separate paper nominating X to serve as executor of T's estate. Thereafter, T revokes the entire will by tearing it into several pieces.* **Result:** *Under the law of most states, the codicil is revoked as well, unless it can be shown by extrinsic evidence that T intended otherwise (because a valid will may serve solely to nominate an executor, the codicil will be given effect as T's will in this event).*

Sufficiency of the Act. Revocation by physical act requires that a *material part* of the will be affected by the physical act, except in the case of burning, where it is highly unlikely that a person would intend to effect only a *partial* revocation (however, a slight singeing of an envelope containing the will is probably insufficient in itself). The entire will, or more commonly a portion thereof, may be canceled (by drawing an *X* or writing the word *void* across the face of the will, by interlineation, or by another similar act) or obliterated (by interlineation or by erasure). The cancellation or obliteration must actually appear on or touch a material part of the will. Thus, writing the word *void* across the top, in a margin, or on the back of the will is insufficient (unless the writing is valid as a holograph). If only certain portions are to be canceled or obliterated, the act must actually appear on those portions. If it is unclear whether the testator intended to revoke the will in its entirety or only certain portions of the will, extrinsic evidence may be admitted to help determine the testator's intent. Cancellation of the testator's signature serves to revoke the entire will, unless a contrary intent can be shown.

 PRACTICE TIP: A variety of problems may arise where a person attempts to revoke all or part of a will by crossing out words or by other forms of cancellation or obliteration: (1) the attempted revocation may be ineffective if no material part of the will is affected; (2) it may be difficult to tell whether the testator intended to revoke all or only a portion of the will; and (3) the possibility of fraudulent alteration by another person must always be considered. Any of these potential problems may serve to defeat the testator's intent and are likely to add time and expense in probating the will. Accordingly, the paralegal should advise the client to refrain from revoking the will by any physical act (this problem can be avoided if the firm retains the original will in its vault for safekeeping). At the same time, the client should be instructed as to the preferred methods of effecting minor changes in the will plan—for example, through the use of a separate list referred to in the will, by requesting the law firm to prepare a codicil, or by establishing a flexible plan so that minor changes are less likely to be necessary.

Increase by Physical Act. A physical act performed upon the will may serve to revoke a will but cannot serve to *increase* a gift under the will. (Distribution problems relating to increases in gifts are examined in detail in Chapter 8.)

EXAMPLE: A provision in T's will states, "I leave 50% of my shares of stock in ABC Corporation to X." Subsequent to executing the will, T crosses out the words "50% of" in this provision. **Result:** *Although the remaining words might be interpreted as giving to X all of T's shares of ABC stock, the interlineation is ineffective for this purpose, because the result would be to increase the gift to X. In fact, extrinsic evidence may show that T actually intended to eliminate the gift to X by crossing out those words.*

An exception to this rule is made for gifts to residuary beneficiaries, which may be increased by decreasing or eliminating another gift. Also, although a gift cannot generally be increased by physical act, a gift can be *decreased* by physical act. In the foregoing example, for instance, T may decrease X's gift to 5% by crossing out the number "0."

Lost or Destroyed Wills. It is possible for a valid will that has not been revoked nevertheless to be denied probate—a lost or destroyed will is presumed to be revoked, and it must be shown that the will was lost or destroyed by accident in order to overcome the presumption and allow probate of the will. By so proving, the lost or destroyed will may be admitted to probate (even though it is not available physically) upon adequate proof of contents, in the absence of a statute to contrary. Some states have enacted statutes that limit or prohibit the probate of lost or destroyed wills.

FOCUS: A variety of potential revocation problems, including (1) inadvertent alterations of a will, (2) attempted but ineffective alterations of photocopies by a client, and (3) loss or destruction of the will, may be avoided by employing certain basic office procedures for handling original wills and photocopies.

Revocation by Operation of Law

In most states, a will or part of a will may be revoked by operation of law under certain circumstances—for example, in the event of subsequent marriage, divorce, or birth of children. The rationale is that the testator probably would not have wanted the will (or relevant provision in the will) to remain effective under such a change in circumstances. Statutes vary widely in this area.

Effect of Marriage. Statutes in about half the states provide that a will is revoked automatically and in its entirety upon subsequent marriage. In the remaining states, instead of providing for revocation, statutes allow the surviving spouse (at the time of the testator's death) to take a portion of the estate regardless of the provisions of the will (see *Restrictions on Dispositive Powers*).

Effect of Birth of Children. Only a few states provide for revocation of the will upon the subsequent birth of a child. In most states, an afterborn child is protected by allowing the child to take a portion of the estate against the provisions of the will (see *Restrictions on Dispositive Powers, Omitted Heirs*).

Effect of Divorce. Statutes in nearly all states reflect U.P.C. § 2-508, which provides that any disposition of property to a spouse is revoked by divorce and that the former spouse is deemed to have predeceased the testator. Accordingly, any gift to that spouse will pass instead to the residuary devisee under the will (or, in the absence of a residuary devisee, to the decedent's intestate heirs).

PRACTICE TIP: Wills prepared by lawyers often name the testator's spouse specifically (for example, see the Will of Irene Parker, Appendix A of the Resource Manual, Exhibit 7). This practice helps to clarify that gifts to the testator's spouse are to that particular spouse only but is unnecessary because revocation is automatic upon divorce in any event. Also, upon divorce or marriage, in most cases clients would want to revise their will plan if asked about it. However, clients typically procrastinate in reviewing their will upon occurrence of these events. Although it is not feasible for the law firm to develop a system for monitoring the marital status of its clients, as part of standard office procedure, all estate-planning clients should be informed at the time a will is executed to contact the law firm in order to review the will plan upon the occurrence of certain events, such as divorce, marriage, or the birth of children.

FOCUS: Whether or not the will of a married person identifies a spouse by name, upon divorce any provision benefiting the former spouse is automatically revoked; if the will is thereafter admitted to probate, the former spouse is deemed to have predeceased the testator for the purpose of distributing the estate in accordance with the will.

WILL CONTESTS

A **will contest** is a proceeding in probate challenging the validity of a will or a part thereof. A will contest may be based upon any of the following grounds:

1. Lack of due execution
2. Revocation of the will
3. Lack of testamentary capacity
4. Undue influence (including duress and menace)
5. Fraud
6. Mistake

Procedural Aspects of Will Contests

A will contest is in the nature of a civil action—it is subject to the rules of civil procedure and is often appropriately handled by the litigation department of the law firm. Will contests are often heard before a court of general civil jurisdiction rather than before the probate court. Nevertheless, the probate paralegal should expect some involvement in the area of discovery—for example, in locating witnesses as required under statutes akin to U.P.C. § 3-406 (relating to necessity of testimony of witnesses to the will). At a minimum, the probate paralegal must be aware of the basic procedural rules relating specifically to will contests as they affect probate proceedings.

Any party who stands to benefit from a successful will contest is considered an "interested person" in this context and has standing to initiate a contest. The party contesting the will is the plaintiff and has the burden of proving that the will is invalid. The administrator of the estate is the defendant. The specific procedural steps relating to will contests are provided by statute. Although the U.P.C. does not provide specific procedural guidelines for will contests, U.P.C. § 3-407 does establish certain evidentiary burdens in contested probate matters.

Once the will is offered for probate, the plaintiff (contestant) may initiate a contest by filing a petition in the court stating the ground for opposing the probate of the will, but the plaintiff must do so either before the will is admitted to probate or within a certain time period thereafter (typically 120 days). Within the same period of time, the contestant must also notify the defendant/administrator, generally in the same manner as required for the service of summons in civil actions. The contestant may also be required to notify the beneficiaries under the will and heirs of the decedent (including minors, incompetent persons, and representatives of deceased heirs and beneficiaries). Statutes also generally require responsive pleadings to be filed within 30 days after service of the citation.

PARKER ESTATE: Under the attested will of Irene Parker, her estate passes to her issue by representation. The will also requires a four-month survivorship period, by which definition John has failed to survive Irene and his share would pass equally to his children. Accordingly, the "interested" parties who may contest the validity of the holograph include Dennis as well as John's unborn child and possibly John's stepson Todd. Because these children are obviously unable legally to assert their rights, their mother Susan would initiate the will contest on their behalf as guardian *ad litem* (see Chapter 11).

Grounds for Contesting a Will

The validity of a will may be challenged on the grounds that it was not duly executed or that it was revoked. In addition, a will may be challenged on the grounds that the testator was not competent to execute the will or that the testator executed the will under physical or mental coercion. Also, all or part of a will may be denied probate in certain cases where the will resulted from a fraudulent statement or a mistake (see Figure 3-3).

Lack of Testamentary Capacity. A person's competency to execute a will is referred to as **testamentary capacity**. U.P.C. § 2-501 provides that "any person 18 years of age who is of sound mind may make a will." Generally speaking, a "sound mind" requires that the testator know and understand the nature and extent of the testator's property, the persons who are the natural objects of the testator's bounty, and the nature of the disposition the testator is making. A person who has been adjudged by a court as incompetent does not necessarily lack testamentary capacity, although such an adjudication creates a presumption to this effect.

FIGURE 3-3   QUESTIONS AFFECTING THE ENFORCEABILITY OF A WILL

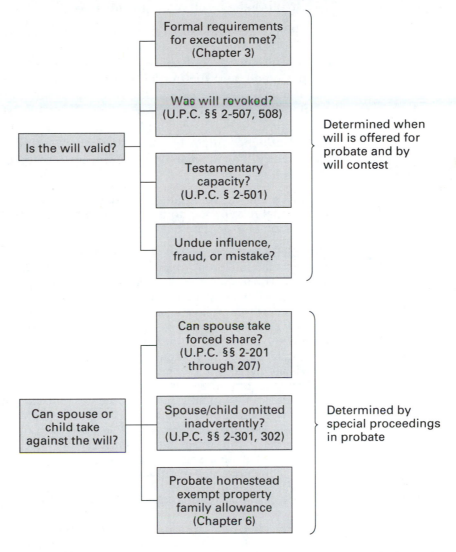

Undue Influence. Undue influence (including menace and duress) requires some sort of mental or physical coercion that impinges upon the testator's freedom and substitutes the wishes of another person for those of the testator. Four elements are ordinarily required in order to establish undue influence:

1.   The testator must be susceptible to undue influence.
2.   The other person must have had the opportunity to exert undue influence.
3.   The other person must have had the disposition to influence the testator for the purpose of personal benefit.

4. The provisions of the will must appear to be unnatural and therefore the result of undue influence.

Where a confidential relationship exists between the testator and a devisee—that is, where the testator relied heavily upon and placed more than a normal amount of confidence in the other person—undue influence is often presumed, and the burden shifts to the proponent of the will to show that the will was *not* made as the result of undue influence. A confidential relationship exists between attorney and client, between doctor and patient, and in some states between husband and wife. In addition, a presumption of undue influence might be established where a devisee participated in preparing the will or in some other significant activity related to the execution of the will.

 PRACTICE TIP: The foregoing discussion strongly suggests that no person in a confidential relationship to the testator should be involved in any way in the preparation or execution of the will.

 PARKER ESTATE: In the Parker matter, Dennis may have a colorable claim that Irene's letter to Sharon resulted from Sharon's undue influence. Irene was somewhat unsophisticated in financial and legal affairs and therefore may have been susceptible to undue influence. Also, Sharon served as Irene's primary if not sole caretaker following the death of Irene's husband, and thus probably had sufficient opportunity to exert undue influence. Moreover, Sharon benefits greatly under the holographic instrument—the distribution scheme appears to leave to Sharon Irene's entire estate, an unnatural result considering Irene is survived by two children (Sharon and Dennis) as well as by issue of a third child (John). However, whether Sharon was disposed to exert such influence is not known at this point. Also, the fact that Sharon came to the aid of her mother in her last years would tend to show that Irene's holographic instrument was executed of her own volition and will, motivated by gratitude, as Irene herself expressed in the will. Furthermore, since no confidential relationship existed between Sharon and Irene, Dennis (or any other person contesting the will) has the burden of proving undue influence. Consider Dennis' position as a potential will contestant in light of the no-contest clause included in Irene's attested will and discussed later (see *No-Contest Clauses*).

Fraud. Fraud occurs where a person procures some benefit under a will by intentionally misrepresenting certain facts to the testator. **Fraud in the execution**, or fraud *in the factum*, refers to an intentional misrepresentation to the testator by another person as to the nature or contents of the will, relied upon by the testator in executing the will. **Fraud in the inducement** refers to a misrepresentation as to other facts that motivate the testator to make the will or to make a particular gift in the will. With either type of fraud, it must be shown that the devisee intentionally deceived the testator and that the testator acted in reliance upon the misrepresentation. The will may be denied probate if the fraud taints the entire will; on the other hand, if the fraud affects only certain portions of the will, then only those provisions will be denied probate.

*EXAMPLE: T, a widow, mentions to B, her brother, that she is considering leaving a large portion of her estate to a particular charitable organization in her will. B states to T that the organization no longer exists. In fact, the organization still exists, and B is aware of this fact. Shortly thereafter, T makes a will giving her entire estate in equal shares to B, T's husband H, and T's only child C. **Result:** B's misrepresentation appears to have been intentional. If it can be shown that T was in fact deceived by and relied upon this misrepresentation, then B's statement might constitute fraud in the inducement. If so, it is likely that the will would be admitted to probate but that the gift to B would be struck.*

Mistake. A **mistake in the execution** refers to a mistake on the part of the testator as to the nature or contents of the executed instrument. Generally speaking, a mistake in the execution renders the will invalid on the basis that the contents do not reflect the true intent of the testator (except in the case of reciprocal wills; see Chapter 2). However, proper execution of a will establishes a strong presumption that the testator understood its contents. Although inadvertent execution of the wrong document occurs occasionally, a far more common mistake involves the inadvertent inclusion of a particular provision in the will. Some courts would admit the will to probate minus the particular provision, as long as this reflects the testator's true intent. Other courts would deny probate of the entire will.

A mistake by the testator as to certain facts, other than the nature or contents of the will, which motivates the testator to make the will or to include or exclude a particular provision is referred to as **mistake in the inducement**. Generally speaking, there is no relief for this type of mistake (unless the mistake resulted from fraud), except in the highly unlikely event that both the fact of the mistake and what the testator would have done but for the mistake are evident on the face of the will.

PRACTICE TIP: The problem of mistake in the execution is of particular importance to the probate paralegal. The production of two or more drafts of the will prior to the final will is quite common. The lawyer's instruction to delete a particular provision can easily be overlooked. Also, undesired provisions may be inadvertently added at the word-processing stage. It is highly recommended that all but the first draft be "red-lined" to facilitate comparison between drafts, and that all drafts be saved and compared prior to execution. Standard office procedure should also require a final and careful reading by the client prior to execution.

No-Contest Clauses

The term **no-contest clause** refers to a special provision included in a will for the purpose of discouraging will contests. Any contesting devisee forfeits his or her inheritance if a no-contest clause is included in the will, but if the contestant defeats the will, the no-contest clause is also defeated. A no-contest clause is effective only against beneficiaries under the will because only contestants who are beneficiaries stand to lose if the clause is effective. Although no-contest clauses are made expressly enforceable by statute in most states, some states refuse to recognize their validity.

PRACTICE TIP: Disinheritance of a natural heir, such as a spouse or child, or leaving a nominal amount, such as one dollar, is generally not recommended because it creates animosity and conflict among surviving family members and may invite a will contest, since the contestant has nothing to lose (except costs and attorneys' fees) if the contest fails. Although wills prepared by lawyers almost invariably include a general provision expressly disinheriting omitted heirs (see *Will of Irene Parker*, Appendix A of the Resource Manual, Exhibit 7), if a client insists on disinheriting a natural heir, such as a spouse or child, it is recommended that the will expressly state that the person is excluded as well as the reason for the exclusion. Such a statement makes the testator's intent and motivation clear and renders the will less susceptible to challenge.

PARKER ESTATE: In the Parker matter, although Irene's attested will contains both a no-contest clause and a general provision disinheriting omitted heirs, do these provisions also apply in a contest respecting the second will (i.e., the letter to Sharon)? Probably so, because the original will is revoked by the holograph only to the extent the two instruments are inconsistent. Consider, however, whether these provisions would deter Dennis from contesting the validity of the holograph, since he appears to have nothing to lose by doing so. Also consider the discussion later in this chapter concerning the rights of children omitted from the will (see *Restrictions on Dispositive Powers, Omitted Heirs*).

RESTRICTIONS ON DISPOSITIVE POWERS

Assuming that the will has survived any and all challenges, the court will not necessarily follow the precise dispositive scheme under the will. Under certain circumstances, the decedent's surviving spouse or children may be entitled to a portion of the decedent's estate *against* the will—that is, regardless of the terms of the decedent's will (see Figure 3-3). Statutes vary considerably in their protective measures. Of primary concern here are statutes entitling the surviving spouse to a certain percentage of the estate in lieu of any provision under the will, as well as statutes entitling an inadvertently omitted spouse or child to an intestate share of the estate. Other measures designed to protect surviving family members, including allowances, homestead rights, and exemptions, will be discussed in Chapter 6.

Minimum Rights of the Surviving Spouse

Statutes vary widely in the rights afforded the surviving spouse to take against the will, as discussed below.

Choice of Law. Because statutes vary considerably regarding the rights of the surviving spouse to share in the estate against the will, choice of law is of vital importance. In some states, the court must apply the law of the place where the decedent was domiciled at the time of death. In other states, the surviving spouse's rights with respect to *personal property* are determined in a similar manner, although the spouse's rights with respect to *real property* are governed by the law of the place where the property is located. The U.P.C. adopts the former approach (see *Right to an Elective Share*).

Dower and Curtesy. A diminishing number of states perpetuate the common-law concepts of *dower* and *curtesy*. Under the right of **dower** (in the case of a widow) or **curtesy** (in the case of a widower), the surviving spouse is entitled to a life estate in one-third of all real property of the decedent acquired during the marriage, regardless of the decedent's will, and free of all creditors' claims or conveyances made by the decedent without the spouse's consent. In nearly all states, the rights of dower and curtesy have been replaced by rights arising from community property laws or from forced-heirship statutes.

Right to an Elective Share. In nearly all separate-property states, the surviving spouse is entitled to a specified share of the estate (including personal as well as real property), referred to as an "elective share," regardless of the terms of the deceased spouse's will. Most community-property states do not so provide, because the surviving spouse is afforded some measure of protection by way of shared ownership in community property. Under most "elective share" statutes, the surviving spouse's elective share is simply one-third of the decedent's *net* estate. Computing the surviving spouse's elective share is a bit more complicated, however, under the U.P.C. The spouse's elective share is based upon the decedent's "augmented estate," which includes not only the decedent's property but also gifts made to the surviving spouse as well as gifts made during the marriage to others where the decedent still retained some benefit, measure of control, or other incident of ownership in the property (which would include transfers to most types of trusts as well as transfers in which the decedent retains a joint-tenancy interest).

The surviving spouse must affirmatively elect to take his or her elective share of the estate by filing a petition for an elective share in a timely manner; otherwise, the right is waived. The U.P.C. requires the procedural steps shown in Figure 3-4.

Statutory procedures may differ somewhat from those of U.P.C. § 2-205. For example, some states require the surviving spouse to file the election while requiring the personal representative to file a separate petition at a later time for determination of the elective share. In any event, where the law firm represents the surviving spouse, the paralegal should compute the amount of the elective share to determine whether an election would be advantageous for the client (see Practice Tip, below).

PRACTICE TIP: The law firm might represent the surviving spouse rather than the administrator of the decedent's estate. Where the surviving spouse receives only a portion of the estate, it is generally the duty of the probate paralegal to determine whether and to what extent an election to take an elective share would be beneficial to the surviving spouse. Great care must be exercised in computing the surviving spouse's elective share under applicable statute. The foregoing procedural requirements suggest the use of a tickler system to ensure that in cases where the firm represents the surviving spouse, any election is filed (and mailed or delivered to the personal representative, if any) prior to expiration of the time period specified by statute. Also, in the

FIGURE 3-4   U.P.C. § 2-205 (PROCEEDING FOR ELECTIVE SHARE; TIME LIMIT)

(a) The surviving spouse may elect to take his elective share in the augmented estate by filing in the Court and mailing or delivering to the personal representative, if any, a petition for the elective share within 9 months after the date of death, or within 6 months after the probate of the decedent's will, whichever limitation last expires. However, non-probate transfers, described in Section 2-202(1), shall not be included within the augmented estate for the purpose of computing the elective share, if the petition is filed later than 9 months after death. The Court may extend the time for election as it sees fit for use shown by the surviving spouse before the time for election has expired.

(b) The surviving spouse shall give notice of the time and place set for hearing to persons interested in the estate and to the distributees and recipients of portions of the augmented estate whose interests will be adversely affected by the taking of the elective share.

(c) The surviving spouse may withdraw his demand for an elective share at any time before entry of a final determination by the Court.

(d) After notice and hearing, the Court shall determine the amount of the elective share and shall order its payment from the assets of the augmented net estate or by contribution as appears appropriate under Section 2-207.

common situation where the surviving spouse is serving as representative of the estate, the spouse must nevertheless comply with the procedural requirements in order to preserve the right to an elective share in lieu of the gift under the will. (As to whether the law firm's representation of an administrator/beneficiary constitutes a conflict of interest, see Chapter 12.)

FOCUS: The surviving spouse must affirmatively elect to take an elective share of the deceased spouse's estate (typically one-third of the net estate), and the election must be filed with the court and served on the personal representative in a timely manner; otherwise, the right is waived. If acting as personal representative, the surviving spouse must nevertheless comply with all procedural requirements in order to preserve the right to take an elective share.

Rights of Omitted Heirs

If a spouse or a child is neither mentioned specifically in the will nor provided for under the terms of the will, that spouse or child may under certain circumstances take a portion of the estate against the will, under the theory that the testator's failure to leave a portion of the estate to the spouse or child was *inadvertent*—that is, that the testator simply forgot to so provide. An inadvertently omitted heir is also referred to as a **pretermitted heir** (literally meaning ''forgotten heir'').

Omitted Spouse. All states have enacted legislation for the benefit of inadvertently omitted spouses where the will was executed *prior* to the marriage.

Under these statutes, the omitted spouse is entitled to his or her intestate share of the deceased spouse's estate. Where the will omitting the spouse is executed *during* the marriage, the omitted spouse is not similarly protected because it is presumed that the testator had the spouse in mind and thus intentionally excluded the spouse (however, the omitted spouse in this situation may be entitled to a portion of the decedent's estate under forced-heirship or dower/curtesy statutes). Also, where the spouse is expressly mentioned in the will but excluded from sharing in the estate, omitted-spouse statutes afford no protection to the spouse, because it is clear that the spouse's exclusion was intentional.

EXAMPLE: *While unmarried, T executes a will under which T's entire estate passes to T's children. Thereafter, T marries S but takes no action prior to death to revoke or modify the will executed prior to the marriage. However, during the marriage, T purchases a life insurance policy in the amount of $10,000 payable at T's death to S.* **Result:** *S is entitled to an amount equal to what S would have taken had T died intestate, unless it can be shown that the life insurance policy was intended by T to serve as a substitute for a gift to S under T's will. The amount of the proceeds ($10,000) in proportion to the size of T's estate, as well as any statements T might have made to others regarding T's intentions, would be helpful to demonstrate T's probable intent.*

Omitted Children. In addition to protecting omitted spouses, all states have enacted legislation for the benefit of *inadvertently* omitted children born or adopted after execution of the will, whereby the omitted child is entitled to his or her intestate share of the deceased parent's estate, except under certain circumstances. Omitted children born or adopted *before* the will is executed are not similarly protected because it is presumed that the testator had them in mind and thus intentionally excluded them. Also, where the child is expressly mentioned in the will but excluded from sharing in the estate, omitted-child statutes afford no protection to the child, because it is clear that the child's exclusion was intentional.

EXAMPLE: *T executes a will leaving her entire estate to her sister. At the time the will is executed, T has two children—X and Y. Thereafter, T has a third child—Z. Both during and after T's pregnancy, T made statements to several people to the effect that the pregnancy was an accident and that Z is an unwanted child. T dies without revoking or modifying the will.* **Result:** *Z might be entitled to Z's intestate share of the estate, because Z was born after the will was executed. However, T's statements, together with the fact that T also excluded her other two children from the will, may be sufficient to prove that T intentionally omitted to provide for Z by altering T's will plan. T's other two children—X and Y—are not entitled in any event to share in T's estate as omitted children, because they were born prior to the execution of the will.*

 PRACTICE TIP: Where a spouse or child is omitted from the will, a special proceeding may be required during probate to determine the omitted heir's rights. To avoid the delay and expense of such a proceeding, lawyers often include a general provision in their clients' wills providing for forfeiture of inheritance rights of any heir who claims his or her intestate share against the will (see Figure 3-5). As an additional measure to prevent such a proceeding, it is universally recommended that the will be reviewed and modified as necessary in the event of marriage or the birth of a child. As noted earlier, every estate-planning client should be instructed to contact the law firm promptly upon any such event to review the will plan. With respect specifically to the birth of a child, an additional safeguard is provided by drafting the will so that gifts to the testator's children are treated as gifts to a group, or *class*, the members of the class determined as of the testator's death. This type of provision would serve to include automatically children born or adopted after the will is executed. (The subject of class gifts is discussed in Chapter 8.)

FIGURE 3-5   SAMPLE WILL PROVISION—CLAIMANT HEIR TAKES ONE DOLLAR

> If any person who, if I had died intestate, would be entitled to any part of my estate, shall either directly or indirectly, alone or in conjunction with any other person, claim in spite of my Will an intestate share of my estate, including any stepchild or foster child, I give that person One Dollar ($1.00), and no more, in lieu of any other share or interest in my estate.

 PARKER ESTATE: In the Parker matter, Irene's holographic instrument excludes both Dennis and John, omitting to mention either one of these two children. However, because both Dennis and John were born prior to the execution of the holograph, they cannot be considered pretermitted heirs for the purpose of determining their entitlement in Irene's estate.

Other Testamentary Restrictions

In addition to protective measures for the surviving spouse and children, other testamentary restrictions are also provided for in all states, either under common law or by statute. The more common such restrictions are discussed below.

Contracts Relating to Wills.   If a testator enters into a contractual agreement to make a will or a particular testamentary gift (or to refrain from so doing), is such an agreement enforceable? If so, and if the testator violates the agreement, can the will nevertheless be admitted to probate? If the will is admitted to probate, what are the promisee's remedies? Under the law in nearly all states, such contracts are indeed valid and enforceable, but only if in writing or referred to in the will. An enforceable contract regarding the making of a will or particular testamentary gift provides a basis for a cause of action against the estate of the promisor, but it will not prevent probate of the will. The promisee's usual remedy in such a case is to impose a constructive trust upon the appropriate beneficiaries under the will (see Chapter 9).

Restrictions on Gifts to Charity.   Statutes in a few states protect the testator's surviving family members by restricting the percentage of the testator's estate that may be given to charity. Statutes in a few other states prohibit testamentary gifts to charity where the will was executed shortly before the testator's death. However, the U.P.C. and a substantial majority of states place no restrictions on charitable testamentary gifts.

Prohibited Beneficiaries. Restrictions on the rights of certain persons, such as aliens and persons responsible for the testator's death, to the *intestate estate of a decedent* were discussed in Chapter 2. By statute, these restrictions generally apply equally to cases of testamentary gifts to such persons. A far more common problem involves gifts to family pets, such as dogs or cats. The law treats animals as property, and because property cannot own other property, any testamentary gift to an animal will fail. Where the testator wishes to ensure that a pet is provided for, it is generally recommended that the testator identify in the will a specific trusted family member or friend whom the testator would prefer to care for the pet, perhaps leaving that person a specific monetary gift as compensation if the devisee accepts responsibility for the pet.

Paralegal Assignment 3

Recall that your third assignment for Ms. Cargis is to develop a form letter to be sent to will clients shortly after they have established a will plan. Because the letter deals with questions that the paralegal often answers for clients, it is appropriate to send the letter out under your name. Based upon the materials presented in this chapter, particularly the practice tips, a draft for Ms. Cargis' review may be prepared as indicated below. This form letter should be revised as necessary in the event that the law firm retains the original will. Italicized portions were added by Ms. Cargis after reviewing the draft.

> The purpose of this letter is to address some of the most common questions that might occur to you now that you have established your will plan. Some of these questions may have been discussed at our offices, while you may be considering others here for the first time:
>
> *Where should I keep the original will?* The original will is the only will that you actually signed. Keep this will at home with your other important papers, preferably in a fireproof box. Your will should be readily accessible immediately upon your death. Thus, inform a trusted family member or friend (preferably the person you nominated in your will to serve as executor) as to the location of the will and how to gain access to it. You should not keep the will in a bank safe-deposit box, because immediate access upon your death to the contents of a bank box may be a problem.
>
> *What about photocopies of the will?* We are retaining a photocopy of your will in our files. Also, you have been provided with two photocopies of the original signed will. You may wish to provide your executor

with one photocopy while retaining the other photocopy for ready reference. However, do not under any circumstances attempt to change your will plan by altering a photocopy—any changes made to a photocopy are ineffective. If you wish to make changes to your will plan, see below.

How should I make changes in my will? Attached to your original will as "Schedule A" is a list of certain items of tangible personal property together with the name of the person you wish to receive each item. If you wish to add to this list or make changes in the list from time to time, you may do so without our assistance. However, please be sure to make any and all changes in your handwriting, and sign your initials next to each change or addition when made. Identify the item of property and the devisee as specifically as possible so that no confusion results concerning their identity. Remember also that this list may be used for items of personal tangible property only, such as furniture, clothing, jewelry, automobiles, tools, or artwork—you may not use this list to dispose of real estate, cash, or monetary investments, such as stocks, bonds, or bank accounts. Any other changes in your will plan should be made only by executing a formal amendment to the will with our assistance. Do not attempt to alter the will in any way—for example, by writing on the face of the will.

Under what circumstances should I change my will? Contact our offices if you know that you wish to revise your will plan. In addition, we recommend that you contact our office to review your plan upon the occurrence of any of the following events: (1) your marriage; (2) your divorce; (3) the birth of a child; *(4) a sizeable inheritance or other dramatic increase in your net worth; or (5) if you sell or otherwise dispose of a sizeable asset you left to a particular devisee under your will.* Also, you may be tempted in the future to take particular actions that might affect your will plan, such as entering into a contract to leave a particular person a gift in your will *or making a gift during your lifetime as an advancement of the donee's inheritance.* These acts create many potential legal problems and are likely to result in undue delay and expense prior to the distribution of your estate. Therefore, please discuss these ideas with us first.

4 INTRODUCTION TO ESTATE ADMINISTRATION AND DISTRIBUTION WITHOUT FORMAL ADMINISTRATION

Formal estate administration is not always necessary to transfer a decedent's assets to the heirs or devisees. A less formal procedure may be available under certain circumstances. Also, certain estates may be distributed under a summary proceeding in which the court plays an even smaller role; summary proceedings may also be available for property passing to the surviving spouse. Finally, certain "nonprobate" transfers may be made immediately and entirely without resort to the court system, regardless of whether a probate estate is established to distribute other assets of the estate.

The Parker matter presents two possibilities for distribution of assets without formal administration. First, the proceeds from Irene's life insurance policy may be distributed to the beneficiary as a "nonprobate" transfer. Second, recall that in the Parker matter, title to Irene's residence is held in joint-tenancy form with her husband Fred. Because no action was taken prior to Irene's death to establish for the record that she was entitled to the property after Fred's death, it is now the responsibility of the personal representative—in all likelihood, Sharon Madson—to do so before this asset can be distributed to Irene's devisees. As you will discover in this chapter, a simple affidavit procedure in which the court plays no role is available for this purpose. Ms. Cargis has asked you to follow up on this matter, obtaining all necessary information from Susan and preparing all documents necessary to complete the transaction.

SETTLING DECEDENTS' ESTATES: AN OVERVIEW

As noted in Chapter 1, one of the probate paralegal's primary functions is to assist in the settlement of decedents' estates. The procedural steps required to settle an estate depend upon the extent of the court's involvement in this process, as discussed in the following materials and as summarized in Figure 4-1.

Alternative Methods of Settling Decedents' Estates

In some cases, no court involvement is necessary to settle a decedent's estate. For example, in all states, certain "nonprobate" transfers may be made entirely without resort to the court system. Also, some states provide for transfer of certain *entire* estates upon affidavit of the distributees and without resort to the courts, but usually only when the estate is sufficiently low in value. Where court involvement is required, a variety of systems have emerged, requiring varying degrees of court supervision. The type of system most widely adopted requires continual court supervision of the entire process, except under certain circumstances. Under this type of system, a formal court hearing, or *adjudication*, requiring prior notice to persons whose interests may be affected by the outcome, is required for probate of a will, for appointment of a personal representative, and for distributions of estate property. Other matters, such as sales of estate property, payment of a family allowance, and payment of the decedent's debts, may also require adjudication.

Although administration under continual court supervision is the best method of ensuring that the decedent's wishes are carried out and that the interests of the decedent's creditors, heirs, and devisees are protected, this method may be unduly burdensome in settling estates where few, if any, matters are disputed, because all essential steps of the process are closely monitored by the court. As a response, in all states where court-supervised administration is the rule, one or more forms of summary administration may be available, depending upon the circumstances. Some form of summary proceeding might be available (1) where certain members of the decedent's family are the sole heirs or devisees; (2) where all property passes to the surviving spouse; or (3) where all of the heirs or devisees join in the application or petition filed with the court. Some states go even further in limiting court involvement, making no provision for continual court supervision, instead providing for formal court proceedings only as requested for particular matters. The statutory trend is toward limiting court involvement to cases in which court supervision or adjudication is requested, and the U.P.C. provides a model for this progressive approach, as discussed below.

FIGURE 4-1   METHODS OF TRANSFERRING A DECEDENT'S ESTATE

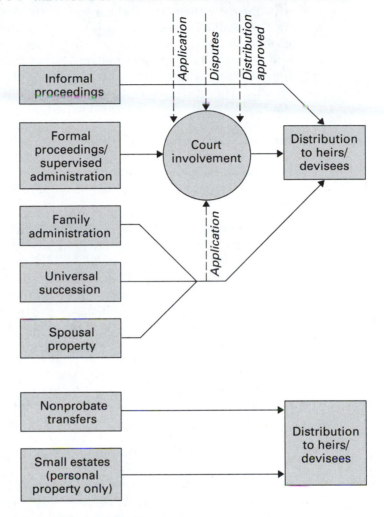

The U.P.C.'s Flexible System of Administration

Under the U.P.C.'s flexible system of administration, court supervision is required only to the extent that it is requested. The U.P.C. provides for three levels of court involvement (in ascending order):

1. Informal proceedings
2. Formal proceedings
3. Supervised administration

An **informal proceeding** involves a verified "application" to a nonjudicial officer of the court, referred to in the U.P.C. as the **Registrar**, who may either "accept" or "deny" the application. The Registrar's decision has the same authoritative weight as that of a judge, although the Registrar has no discretionary powers. Informal proceedings may be used in combination with **formal proceedings**, which involve a "petition" to the court, a court hearing (adjudication), and prior notice of the hearing. Each proceeding, whether formal or informal, is independent from all others involving the same estate; thus, any question relating to the estate may be resolved by a formal proceeding without necessarily subjecting the estate to the necessity of judicial orders for other questions. This flexible "in and out" system facilitates settlement of the estate while still allowing for adjudication of contested matters. The U.P.C. also provides an alternative system, referred to as **supervised administration**, in which the administration of the estate is treated as a single, continuous formal proceeding to secure complete administration and settlement under the continuing authority of the court.

The essential characteristics of this flexible system may be summarized as follows:

- Neither probate of a will nor appointment of a personal representative is compelled, but is left to be obtained by persons having an interest in the consequence of probate or appointment.

- A will may be probated either through formal probate proceedings or informal probate proceedings. Proceedings to determine the testacy status of the decedent may occur without any attending proceeding for appointment of a personal representative. Unless a request for probate of a will is made within three years after the decedent's death, a statute of limitations bars probate of the will, and the will is ineffective. This statute of limitations also applies to any proceeding to determine whether the decedent died intestate.

- A personal representative may be appointed either through formal or informal appointment proceedings, but appointment proceedings must commence within three years after the decedent's death; otherwise, a statute of limitations bars appointment of a personal representative.

- Supervised administration is provided for testators and persons interested in the decedent's estate, whether testate or intestate, who desire to use it. Supervised administration encompasses formal testacy and appointment proceedings as well as complete settlement of the estate under continuing supervision of the court. Supervised administration is not required unless the decedent's will stipulates it, an interested person requests it, or the court otherwise determines in its discretion that it is necessary under the circumstances.

- A personal representative, whether appointed formally (after notice) or informally, and whether supervised or not, is given statutory powers enabling him or her to collect, protect, sell, distribute, and otherwise handle all steps in administration without further court order, except that a supervised personal representative may be subjected to special restrictions on his or her power as determined by the court at the time of appointment.

PARKER ESTATE: In the Parker matter, applicable law does *not* provide for informal proceedings. Except for the proceeds from Irene's life insurance policy, which may be transferred outside of probate, distribution of Irene's entire estate will be subject to court-supervised administration.

Concerns Common to All Proceedings and Forms of Administration

Whether the law firm proceeds formally, informally, or by summary proceeding, all available information must be gathered to determine the beneficiaries of the decedent's estate, the decedent's debts must be settled, and title in the decedent's assets must be transferred to the recipients. Also common to any court proceeding involving a decedent's estate are certain procedural concerns, including (1) determining the proper court, (2) satisfying notice requirements, and (3) satisfying requirements for filing papers with the court. Each of these three procedural concerns is discussed below.

Determining the Proper Court. Just as in civil and criminal legal proceedings, the appropriate court in which to initiate estate proceedings must be determined beforehand. In determining the proper court in which to initiate estate proceedings, it is important to distinguish between the concepts of *jurisdiction* and *venue*, as well as between *domiciliary* and *ancillary* administration.

Jurisdiction The term **jurisdiction** refers generally to the power and authority of a court to hear and decide certain types of cases; with respect to decedents' estates and protective proceedings (guardianships and conservatorships), as well as matters involving trusts, jurisdiction lies with a court that is referred to in most states as the *probate court*. The probate court's jurisdiction is defined and established by statute in each state (see, e.g., U.P.C. § 3-105).

Venue While the court's powers are defined in terms of jurisdiction, the *location*—that is, the appropriate state and county (or city)—for estate proceedings is referred to as **venue**. The proper venue for initiating estate proceedings depends upon where the decedent was domiciled as well as where the decedent's property was located at the time of death (see Figure 4-2). The issue of venue is particularly significant for the purpose of determining which state is entitled to payment of death taxes on the decedent's property (see Chapter 7). U.P.C. § 3-201, shown in Figure 4-3, reflects a typical statute concerning the proper venue for estate proceedings.

Domiciliary Administration Administration at the decedent's domicile is referred to as **domiciliary administration**. The decedent's domicile is the proper venue for all testacy proceedings and for the administration of all assets located in that state. The decedent's domicile is the place that he or she considered to be a permanent home and is not necessarily the decedent's place of residence at the time of death. This distinction may come into play, for example, in the common situation where the decedent died while living with relatives or at a convalescent home, which may have been the decedent's residence at the time of death but would probably be considered

FIGURE 4-2   PROPER VENUE FOR ESTATE PROCEEDINGS

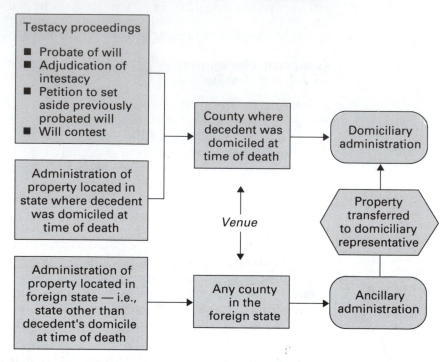

FIGURE 4-3   U.P.C. § 3-201 (VENUE FOR FIRST AND SUBSEQUENT ESTATE PROCEEDINGS; LOCATION OF PROPERTY)

(a) Venue for the first informal or formal testacy or appointment proceedings after a decedent's death is: (1) in the [county] where the decedent had his domicile at the time of his death; or (2) if the decedent was not domiciled in this state, in any [county] where property of the decedent was located at the time of his death. . . . (d) For the purpose of aiding determinations concerning location of assets which may be relevant in cases involving non-domiciliaries, a debt, other than one evidenced by investment or commercial paper or other instrument in favor of a non-domiciliary is located where the debtor resides or, if the debtor is a person other than an individual, at the place where it has its principal office. Commercial paper, investment paper and other instruments are located where the instrument is. An interest in property held in trust is located where the trustee may be sued.

the decedent's domicile only if the decedent had no intention of returning to his or her prior home. All of the following factors should be considered in determining the decedent's domicile:

1.   The length of time that the decedent resided at various places
2.   The location of the decedent's assets and accounts

3. The address used for filing tax returns
4. Where the decedent was registered to vote

Ancillary Administration All property owned by the decedent at his or her death and located in a state other than the decedent's domicile is subject to **ancillary administration** in the foreign state (unless the property can be transferred outside of probate altogether). U.P.C. § 3-201(d) establishes guidelines for determining the location of a particular item of personal property (see Figure 4-3).

EXAMPLE: *Edward dies leaving a valid will while domiciled in Cuyahoga County, Ohio. Edward left among other assets the following: (1) Edward's home and tangible personal property located in Cuyahoga County, Ohio; (2) Edward's vacation home, also located in Ohio but in Hamilton County; (3) a parcel of real property in Campbell County, Kentucky; and (4) various stock certificates and bonds kept in a bank safe-deposit box in Kenton County, Kentucky.* **Result:** *Edward's will must be probated in Cuyahoga County, Ohio. Edward's home, tangible personal property, and vacation home are subject to domiciliary administration in Cuyahoga County, Ohio. However, ancillary administration, either in Campbell County or Kenton County, Kentucky, is required with respect to the real property, stock certificates, and bonds located in that state.*

In the foregoing example, as to whether Campbell County or Kenton County is the proper venue for ancillary administration, consider U.P.C. § 1-303(a), shown in Figure 4-4.

FIGURE 4-4   U.P.C. § 1-303 (VENUE; MULTIPLE PROCEEDINGS; TRANSFER)

> (a) Where a proceeding under this Code could be maintained in more than one place in this state, the Court in which the proceeding is first commenced has the exclusive right to proceed. . . . In the event ancillary administration is necessary, a personal representative must be appointed in the foreign state.

Some states permit the domiciliary personal representative to also serve as ancillary representative, while other states do not. The domiciliary representative is not entirely relieved of his or her duties until ancillary administration is complete and the domiciliary representative has collected the assets administered in the foreign state and distributed them to the appropriate heirs or devisees.

Notices Required in Estate Administration. The right to due process of law under the U.S. Constitution requires that all parties who are affected by the settlement of a decedent's estate be notified of formal court proceedings that may affect their interests. In the case of supervised administration, notice requirements can become quite burdensome, because court approval (adjudication) may be required for a variety of different matters throughout the process. The use of informal probate or appointment proceedings, such as those under the U.P.C., alleviates the necessity of notice (except to certain parties), since the proceeding is conducted by a nonjudicial officer of the court without court adjudication.

One of the probate paralegal's primary tasks in estate administration is to provide notices as required by applicable statute. Therefore, it is crucial that the paralegal become thoroughly familiar with all notice requirements, including the circumstances under which notice is required, the method and time of providing notice, as well as the parties entitled to it. The U.P.C. requirements typify those of most states. Thus, throughout this chapter as well as in subsequent chapters, the U.P.C. provisions regarding general notice requirements, as discussed below, will be assumed.

Forms of Notice   In all states, two forms of notice are provided: (1) notice by advertisement (or ''publication''), and (2) written notice to persons whose interests are affected by the proceeding. The persons entitled to notice must be afforded sufficient opportunity to respond. Consider the U.P.C. provision relating to the method and time for providing notice to interested persons (Figure 4-5).

FIGURE 4-5   U.P.C. § 1-401 (NOTICE; METHOD AND TIME OF GIVING)

(a) If notice of a hearing on any petition is required and except for specific notice requirements as otherwise provided, the petitioner shall cause notice of the time and place of hearing of any petition to be given to any interested person or his attorney if he has appeared by attorney or requested that notice be sent to his attorney. Notice shall be given: (1) by mailing a copy thereof at least 14 days before the time set for the hearing by certified, registered or ordinary first class mail addressed to the person being notified at the post office address given in his demand for notice, if any, or at his office or place of residence, if known; (2) by delivering a copy thereof to the person being notified personally at least 14 days before the time set for the hearing; or (3) if the address, or identity of any person is not known and cannot be ascertained with reasonable diligence, by publishing at least once a week for 3 consecutive weeks, a copy thereof in a newspaper having general circulation in the county where the hearing is to be held, the last publication of which is to be at least 10 days before the time set for the hearing.

(b) The Court for good cause shown may provide for a different method or time of giving notice for any hearing.

(c) Proof of the giving of notice shall be made on or before the hearing and filed in the proceeding.

Parties Entitled to Written Notice   Prior to a court hearing (adjudication), written notice must be provided to all interested persons as well as to all persons who have properly requested it. The U.P.C. refers to a person requesting notice as a ''demandant.'' The U.P.C. defines an ''interested person'' as illustrated in Figure 4-6.

FIGURE 4-6   U.P.C. § 1-201 (GENERAL DEFINITIONS)

> . . . (20) "Interested person" includes heirs, devisees, children, spouses, creditors, beneficiaries and any others having a property right in or claim against a trust estate or the estate of a decedent, ward or protected person which may be affected by the proceeding. It also includes persons having priority for appointment as personal representative, and other fiduciaries representing interested persons. The meaning as it relates to particular persons may vary from time to time and must be determined according to the particular purposes of, and matter involved in, any proceeding.

An interested person may wish to be informed of certain matters relating to the estate in addition to court hearings. If so, the person can make a request or *demand for notice* of such matters. At any time after the death of the decedent, demand for notice may be made by any person who has a financial or property interest in the estate. Typically, the demand must comply with statutory requirements as to form and content, it must be filed with the court, and a copy must be presented to the personal representative. Under the U.P.C., to be effective, demand must be made in accordance with U.P.C. § 3-204, which requires the demandant to file the demand for notice with the court stating the name of the decedent, the nature of the demandant's interest in the estate, and the demandant's address or that of his or her attorney. The court clerk then mails a copy of the demand to the personal representative if one has been appointed. The personal representative, whether formally or informally appointed, must notify the demandant as to any matters regarding which the demandant requested notice. Typically, the demandant will demand notice of all hearings and copies of all papers filed with the court. No order or filing to which the demand relates should be made or accepted by the court without notice to the demandant. However, the validity of an order that is issued or filing that is accepted by the court without compliance with the notice requirement is not affected by this error. The personal representative may be liable, however, for any damage caused by failing to give notice to the demandant.

Court Records, Certified Copies, and Verification of Documents. Whether a proceeding to settle a decedent's estate is formal or informal, the clerk of the court keeps a separate record for each decedent. The title used as the caption for all applications, petitions and other pleadings—for example, "Estate of Irene Parker"—may vary somewhat according to local court rules. Upon payment of a small fee, any person may obtain a *certified copy* of any probated will, of any letters issued to the personal representative signifying his or her authority, or of any other record or paper filed with the court. As you will learn throughout the next four chapters, it is likely that the paralegal will be required to obtain several certified copies both of the decedent's will (if any) and of the letters issued to the personal representative.

As a general rule, each document filed with the court, including applications, petitions, and demands for notice, must be *verified*; that is, it must include an oath, affirmation, or other statement to the effect that its representations are true as far as the person executing it knows or is informed. Penalties for perjury may result from deliberate falsification. Under the U.P.C., every document filed with the court is deemed to include such an oath. Sworn affidavits made before a notary public are generally not required.

INFORMAL ESTATE PROCEEDINGS UNDER THE UNIFORM PROBATE CODE

The U.P.C. provisions for informal proceedings streamline the process of estate administration by permitting the accomplishment of routine procedures without court supervision, thereby alleviating congestion in the court system as well as making the job of the personal representative and of the probate paralegal easier. A key feature of informal estate proceedings is that notice requirements are minimal, thereby alleviating a significant amount of paperwork. A second important feature is that papers filed with the court are reviewed by a nonjudicial officer of the court (the Registrar) rather than by a judge; thus, in many cases the entire process of estate administration may be conducted without any court hearings. The court is still available, however, to settle formally a dispute or to instruct the personal representative (if requested to do so), after which informal estate proceedings resume.

Limitations on Availability

Informal estate proceedings are not permitted under the U.P.C. in the following situations:

1. Where the application indicates the existence of a possible unrevoked testamentary instrument that has not been filed with the court and that may relate to property subject to the laws of the state where appointment is sought (U.P.C. § 3-311)
2. Where the will is comprised of one or more of a known series of testamentary instruments (other than a will and one or more codicils thereto), the latest of which does not expressly revoke the earlier (U.P.C. § 3-304)
3. Where a personal representative has been appointed in another county of the state or if it appears that this or another will of the decedent has been the subject of a previous probate, unless an authenticated copy of the will and of the statement probating it from the office or court where it was first probated is deposited with the court (U.P.C. § 3-303[b],[d])

 PRACTICE TIP: The restriction indicated by § 3-311 strongly suggests that, in cases where a will is to be offered for probate (either formally or informally), the will should be filed with the court either prior to or at the time that application is made for informal appointment of the personal representative. Where informal appointment of the personal representative and informal probate of the will are both desired, it is generally recommended that applications for informal appointment and for informal probate be filed *concurrently* (see *Initial Procedural Steps*).

When to Use Informal Estate Proceedings

If informal proceedings are available, it is generally recommended that the applicant proceed informally. Application for informal appointment does not prevent the personal representative from proceeding under the rules of supervised administration instead. The Registrar's acceptance (approval) of an application for informal appointment permits the personal representative to proceed informally at his or her election; the personal representative may choose at any time to proceed formally instead, even though the court is not requiring supervised administration. Application to proceed informally should be made even where disputes or other problems are anticipated, because the personal representative may always switch to formal administration without delay.

However, in some situations, informal estate proceedings may be inappropriate. Informal proceedings are designed for use in relatively simple estates where they will be less cumbersome than supervised administration. In more complex estates—particularly, those involving significant creditor or tax problems as well as those in which disputes are likely to occur—settlement of the estate may be delayed in any event, and informal estate proceedings will be of little or no advantage. Also, an even less cumbersome alternative may be available—for example, a summary proceeding where all heirs or devisees join in the application to the court (see *Summary Distribution, Universal Succession under the U.P.C.*).

 PRACTICE TIP: Applications are generally processed and evaluated promptly (within one to two weeks), so that only a short delay has resulted if the application is denied and you are required to proceed formally instead. Nevertheless, the lawyer and the paralegal should carefully assess whether informal estate proceedings are available prior to application to the court so as to avoid even this short delay.

Initial Procedural Steps

The initial procedural steps for informal estate proceedings are summarized in Figure 4-7. A person applying for informal *probate of a will* must give notice of the application to any person properly demanding notice as well as to any personal representative whose appointment has not been terminated (U.P.C. § 3-306). An applicant must give notice of his or her intention to seek an *appointment* informally to any person properly demanding notice as well as to any person having a prior or equal right to appointment not waived in writing and filed with the court (U.P.C. § 3-310).

FIGURE 4-7   INFORMAL PROBATE AND APPOINTMENT: PROCEDURAL STEPS

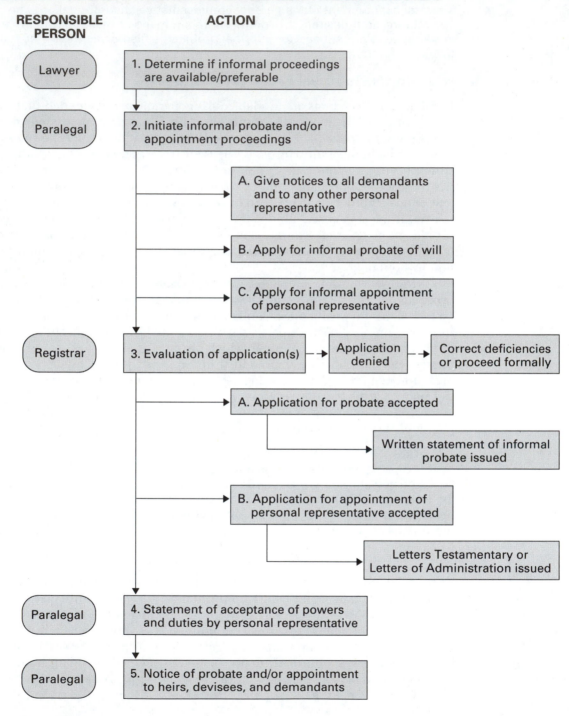

Applications for informal probate of a will or appointment of a personal representative must generally contain the same information required in petitions in formal probate or appointment proceedings (see Chapter 5). Once an application for informal appointment of the personal representative and/or for informal probate of a will is made to the court, the court's Registrar reviews the application to ensure that all of the statutory requirements are satisfied. If the application fails to conform to all requirements, the Registrar will deny the application. Unintentional mistakes or omissions may be corrected at this point. However, if the Registrar denies the application because informal probate or appointment is not permitted under the circumstances, the applicant must initiate formal appointment and/or probate proceedings instead (U.P.C. § 3-305, § 3-309). In any event, the Registrar may not accept (approve) an application for informal appointment or probate of a will until at least 120 hours have elapsed since the decedent's death.

Upon accepting an application for informal probate of a will, the Registrar issues a written statement of informal probate. If the application turns out to be defective, the probate is still effective until superseded by an order in a formal testacy proceeding (U.P.C. § 3-302). Upon accepting an application for informal appointment of a personal representative, the Registrar appoints the applicant subject to qualification and acceptance (see below).

Procedures after Appointment of Personal Representative

Appointment of the personal representative is subject to *qualification* by his or her filing with the appointing court a *statement of acceptance* of the duties of the office and any *bond* that might be required (although bond is generally not required where the personal representative is appointed informally) (U.P.C. § 3-601). Under U.P.C. § 3-306, the personal representative must, within 30 days after his or her appointment, give written notice of informal *probate* of a will (if any) to all heirs, devisees, and demandants (unless the applicant is required to give notice of his or her appointment as personal representative under U.P.C. § 3-705). Under § 3-705, the personal representative must, within 30 days after appointment, give notice of his or her *appointment* to all heirs, devisees, and demandants. In the case of informal appointment of an *intestate* estate, notice must also be given to devisees in any will mentioned in the application for appointment of the personal representative. If the personal representative fails to give notice as required, the probate or appointment is nevertheless effective, although such failure does constitute a breach of duty to the heirs and devisees, and the personal representative may be held personally liable for any damages resulting from his or her failure to provide notice.

No further notices are required by the personal representative (except to demandants) in carrying out his or her duties when proceeding informally. Otherwise, personal representatives proceeding informally are generally charged with the same duties as those who proceed under supervised administration (as discussed in Chapters 6 through 8). However, in closing the estate, the personal representative proceeding informally may be discharged by simply filing an affidavit with the court (pursuant to U.P.C. § 3-1003), while a more formal method of discharge is required where the personal representative has proceeded under supervised administration.

SUMMARY DISTRIBUTION

In most states as well as under the U.P.C., certain estates that otherwise would be subject to estate administration (or to "probate") may be distributed summarily without the necessity of appointing a personal representative (see Table 4-1). In addition, many property interests may be transferred outside of probate in any event (see *Nonprobate Transfers*). Nearly all states have enacted statutes providing for one or more forms of summary distribution for relatively simple estates, for estates passing entirely to certain family members, or for property passing to the surviving spouse. The discussion that follows highlights the more common types of statutory provisions as well as outlines summary proceedings available under the U.P.C. It is important to keep in mind that this discussion is intended only as an overview; because statutes vary from state to state in their specific requirements, the probate paralegal must become familiar with the statutory scheme in his or her own state as well as the materials in this text.

If the law firm assists in a summary distribution, these services are rendered not to an estate or to a personal representative but rather directly to the recipient(s) of the property. It is the lawyer's responsibility to determine whether summary distribution is available under applicable law. The paralegal assists the lawyer in collecting the information required to make this determination and performs the paperwork necessary to complete the transfers.

Collection of Personal Property by Affidavit

Under a common statutory scheme, where the estate is sufficiently small, the heirs or devisees may obtain title to and possession of *personal* property of the decedent *entirely* outside of the court system by presenting an affidavit complying in form and content to statutory requirements to the holder of the property—for example, to an officer of the financial institution where the decedent kept a savings account. Where the affidavit procedure is used, a waiting period is generally required to afford creditors and other claimants to the decedent's property an opportunity to assert these claims before title and possession are transferred to the heirs/devisees. After the transfer, the heirs/devisees assume personal liability for the decedent's debts just as in universal succession.

Under U.P.C. § 3-120, if the value of the decedent's estate, less liens and encumbrances, does not exceed $5,000, then the heirs or devisees may collect the decedent's *personal* property (including debts owed to the decedent) by an affidavit which states that:
1. The value of the entire estate, wherever located, less liens and encumbrances, does not exceed $5,000.

TABLE 4-1 FORMAL ESTATE ADMINISTRATION VS. ALTERNATIVE PROCEDURES

Method of Transfer	Extent of Court Involvement	Minimum Delay before Distribution to Heirs/Devisees
Formal proceedings/ supervised administration	Noticed court hearing and approval required for certain transactions and distributions	6 months*
Informal proceedings under U.P.C.	Application to Registrar for probate of will and appointment of personal representative No court hearings required	6 months*
Universal succession under U.P.C.	Application to Registrar No further court involvement	120 hours**
Collection of small estates	Affidavit (no court involvement)	None** (30 days if decedent was nonresident, unless exception applies)
Family administration Summary transfer to surviving spouse	Noticed court hearing	Approximately one month

*See Chapters 6, 7, and 8.
**Obtaining a death certificate may take several days (or longer).

2. Thirty days have elapsed since the death of the decedent.
3. No application or petition for the appointment of a personal representative is pending or has been granted in any jurisdiction.
4. The claiming successor is entitled to payment or delivery of the property.

The person to whom the affidavit is presented may pay or transfer the property to the claimant without inquiring as to the truthfulness of the statements made in the affidavit and without requiring any additional evidence of the claimant's entitlement in the property (U.P.C. § 3-1202).

EXAMPLE: *Hazel dies intestate, leaving a small estate that includes the following: (1) a bank certificate of deposit and a checking account at the same bank; (2) tangible personal belongings, such as furniture and clothing, which remain in Hazel's rented apartment; and (3) a security deposit held by Hazel's landlord under the terms of the rental agreement. The total value of Hazel's estate, including her security deposit for the apartment, is approximately $4,000. Hazel's heirs are her two children, Gerald and Alan, who wish to collect their mother's assets as soon as possible. **Result:** Either Gerald or Alan may present to the bank and to the landlord an Affidavit for Collection of Personal Property, signed by Gerald and Alan. Gerald and Alan may simply take possession of Hazel's personal belongings, if they have ready access to her apartment.*

In the foregoing example, if Gerald had collected Hazel's property using the affidavit procedure but without Alan's participation or knowledge, Gerald would remain personally liable to Alan for his share of the property; however, neither the bank nor Hazel's landlord would incur liability to Alan, because they are under no obligation to inquire further as to Gerald's right to the property.

Transfer of title in *real* property requires application or petition to the court, unless the real-property interest is sufficiently low in value, in which case other documents—such as a certified copy of a death certificate and document of title—are also generally required.

Family Administration

Another common statutory provision for summary distribution involves estates that pass entirely (except for gifts of minor value) to certain members of the decedent's family, such as the decedent's spouse, issue, and ascendants (parents, grandparents, and so forth). All beneficiaries may be required to join in the application for distribution. Consider, for example, the Florida Probate Code provision shown in Figures 4-8 and 4-9.

FIGURE 4-8   FLORIDA PROBATE CODE § 735.101 (FAMILY ADMINISTRATION; NATURE OF PROCEEDINGS)

Family administration may be had in the administration of a decedent's estate when it appears:

(1) In an intestate estate, that the heirs at law of the decedent consist solely of a surviving spouse, lineal descendants, and lineal ascendants, or any of them.

(2) In a testate estate, that the beneficiaries under the will consist solely of a surviving spouse, lineal descendants, and lineal ascendants, or any of them, and that any specific or general devise to others constitutes a minor part of the decedent's estate.

(3) In a testate estate, that the decedent's will does not direct administration as required by chapter 733 [*providing for a form of supervised administration*].

(4) That the value of the gross estate, as of the date of death, for federal estate tax purposes is less than $60,000.

(5) That the entire estate consists of personal property or, if real property forms part of the estate, that administration under chapter 733 has proceeded to the point that all claims of creditors have been processed or barred. [Emphasis added.]

FIGURE 4-9   FLORIDA PROBATE CODE § 735.101 (PETITION FOR FAMILY ADMINISTRATION)

. . . The petition shall be signed and verified by all beneficiaries and the surviving spouse, if any. The petition may be signed on behalf of a minor or incompetent by his legal guardian or, if none, by his natural guardian.

The U.P.C. includes a similar but more liberal proceeding in which there are no restrictions as to the identity of the decedent's heirs or devisees and no limit as to the total value of the estate (see *Universal Succession under the U.P.C.*).

Property Passing to the Surviving Spouse

Apart from the other methods of transfer discussed in this chapter, in many states property of a decedent to which a surviving spouse is entitled may be set aside for distribution to the surviving spouse without passing through probate. The surviving spouse may elect instead, however, to allow probate of the assets. The appropriate procedure depends upon the nature of the property involved as well as logistical concerns.

Spousal Property Petition. Generally, the spouse must petition the court to approve a distribution outside of probate. This procedure may be used even where formal estate proceedings are established to distribute the remainder of the estate to the other heirs or devisees. If the decedent died leaving a valid will, the will must accompany the petition, although a petition for formal probate of the will is not necessarily required (depending upon the particular statutory requirements). Notice of the hearing to approve the petition must be given to all heirs and devisees, as well as to the personal representative (if other than the surviving spouse) and to all persons demanding notice.

Wages Owed to Decedent. The surviving spouse may also be authorized by statute to collect unpaid wages of the decedent to which the surviving spouse is entitled by using an affidavit procedure and entirely without resort to the court system.

Community Real Property. In community-property states, the surviving spouse may have the right, without court approval, to dispose or otherwise deal with the deceased spouse's community real property passing to the surviving spouse. However, the deed must clearly state that the property is owned by the spouses "as husband and wife" or "as community property." The title company handling the transaction involving the property will require an affidavit by the surviving spouse (or by the personal representative of the surviving spouse's estate) that the spouse is entitled to the decedent's community-property interest prior to completing the transaction.

Community Property Held in Joint-Tenancy Form. Property held by a husband and wife in joint-tenancy form might actually be community property instead. The form of title is not necessarily conclusive. The law in this area is complex and varies among community-property states. The lawyer must examine all property held in joint-tenancy form by a husband and wife to determine its true nature and the appropriate procedure to transfer the decedent's interest to the spouse. The community-property form of ownership presents a distinct income-tax advantage over the joint-tenancy form upon subsequent sale by the surviving spouse (see Chapter 9).

PARKER ESTATE: With respect to Irene Parker's residence, although in joint-tenancy form, it might actually be community property in nature. If so, the affidavit procedure referred to above (see *Community Real Property*), even if provided for under statute in this state, is unavailable to clear title in Irene's name because the property was held in joint-tenancy form. However, this state might authorize the use of a spousal-property petition, which may be submitted by the personal representative of the surviving spouse's estate (if the surviving spouse died before clearing title in the property). This procedure would circumvent a formal probate estate simply for the purpose of transferring title in the property to Irene's name and may avoid the necessity of probating Fred's will. If Ms. Cargis were to decide to employ this method, Sharon Madson must wait until her appointment as personal representative before submitting the spousal-property petition. Ms. Cargis has determined, however, that the true nature of the ownership interests was joint tenancy and that the affidavit procedure should be used to establish title in Irene's name alone (see *Paralegal Assignment 4*).

Universal Succession under the U.P.C.

Under the U.P.C., if certain requirements are met, a decedent's estate that otherwise would require the appointment of a personal representative may be distributed outright—that is, without administration. This type of distribution is referred to in the U.P.C. as **universal succession** and is governed by U.P.C. § 3-312 through § 3-222; the distributees under these provisions are referred to as *universal successors*. There are no limitations as to the value of an estate that may be distributed to universal successors under the U.P.C. Many states have adopted the U.P.C. provisions for universal succession, either in their entirety or with minor modifications.

The availability of universal succession is subject to limitations similar to those associated with informal appointment and probate, and the application is similar in content (see U.P.C. § 3-313). In addition, however, all universal successors (except for minors and incapacitated, protected, and unascertainable persons) must join in the application for universal succession. In the case of total or partial intestacy, all heirs must apply jointly, while application for universal succession under a will must be made jointly by all *residuary* devisees and must be combined with informal probate of the will, unless the will has already been admitted to probate in the same state (U.P.C. § 3-313[a] [1],[2]). Application for universal succession will not be accepted until at least 120 hours have elapsed since the decedent's death (U.P.C. § 3-315). Upon granting the application, the Registrar issues a written statement of universal succession as evidence of the universal successors' title in the assets of the estate. Within 30 days thereafter, the universal successors must give notice to all heirs and devisees who did not join in the application (U.P.C. § 3-319).

Generally speaking, universal successors acquire title as a group to the decedent's assets, and thereafter may apportion and distribute the assets without further court involvement. Universal successors assume personal liability for:

1. Taxes owed by the decedent and by the decedent's estate
2. Debts of the decedent
3. Claims against the decedent or against the estate
4. Distributions to other heirs and devisees (U.P.C. § 3-312, 317)

However, the personal liability of any single universal successor for a debt or claim is limited to the proportion of the debt or claim that the universal successor share bears to the share of all heirs and residuary devisees (U.P.C. § 3-321).

FOCUS: In all states where court-supervised administration is the rule, one or more forms of summary administration or distribution may be available in which the appointment of a personal representative is not necessary. Some form of summary proceeding might be available (1) where the value of the decedent's estate is sufficiently low; (2) where certain members of the decedent's family are the sole heirs or devisees; (3) for all property passing to the surviving spouse; or (4) where all of the heirs or devisees join in the application or petition filed with the court.

NONPROBATE TRANSFERS

Many property interests may be transferred outside of probate, even where a probate estate is established. These property interests include (1) property interests in which the transferee is determined by the *form of title*, such as property held in joint-tenancy form, and (2) property interests such as life insurance proceeds and various retirement and death benefits that pass at death under the terms of a *contract* (see Table 4-2). Consider U.P.C. § 6-101 (Figure 4-10), which provides for nonprobate transfer of such interests.

The law firm representing the probate estate typically assists with "nonprobate" transfers as well, although these services are rendered not to the personal representative but rather directly to the recipients of the nonprobate property. The dual representation by the law firm of nonprobate transferees and of the probate estate presents a potential conflict of interest for the firm. This fact must be disclosed to the personal representative and to the transferees, and the firm should withdraw its representation of the transferees in the event of an actual conflict.

PRACTICE TIP: It is ultimately the lawyer's responsibility to determine the extent to which the decedent's property may be transferred outside of probate. The paralegal assists the lawyer in collecting the information required to make this determination and performs the paperwork necessary to complete the transfers. Also, assets that are not subject to probate may nevertheless be subject to death taxes as well as to the rights of the decedent's creditors (see Chapters 6 and 7). As a result, where a probate estate is established, the lawyer and the paralegal must collect information about *all* of the decedent's assets, not just those assets that are subject to probate.

Joint-Tenancy Interests and Multiple-Party Accounts

As discussed in Chapter 1, if property is held in joint tenancy form, upon the death of any joint tenant, the decedent's interest terminates and automati-

TABLE 4-2 NONPROBATE TRANSFERS

Asset	Procedure	Minimum Delay
Joint-tenancy property and multiple-party accounts*	Real property:record affidavit Personal property: submit documents as required by holder of property	None**
Life insurance proceeds and death benefits passing to named beneficiary*	Submit claim form to policy or plan administrator	None**
U.S. Savings Bonds owned in beneficiary or co-ownership form*	Redeem or reissue through commercial bank	None**
Social Security death and survivor's benefits*	Submit claim form to local Social Security District office	None**
Community real property passing to surviving spouse	Affidavit	Waiting period (e.g., 40 days) may be required
Decedent's unpaid wages to which surviving spouse is entitled	Affidavit	None

*All states.
**Except to obtain and prepare forms and to obtain death certificate.

cally passes to the remaining owners in equal shares. This rule applies irrespective of any other provision made by the decedent for the disposition of his or her interest—for example, under the terms of a will. Accordingly, joint-tenancy property is not subject to probate. The procedural steps required to terminate a joint-tenancy interest upon the death of a co-owner— that is, to "clear title"—depends upon the type of property involved, as discussed below.

Real Property. A joint-tenancy interest in real property may be terminated upon the death of a co-owner in several different ways. The simplest and most commonly used method is an affidavit procedure. A similar procedure may also be used to terminate a life estate upon the death of the life tenant.

Affidavit—Death of Joint Tenant This affidavit states that the decedent's name on the death certificate (which must be attached to the affidavit) is the same person named on the original joint-tenancy deed. The affidavit may be signed by the surviving joint tenant(s) either in the presence of a notary public or, in some states, by declaration under penalty of perjury. If there is no surviving joint tenant, the affidavit may be executed by another person, usually the personal representative of the estate of the last joint tenant to die, so that the record shows that title is held solely in the name of the last surviving joint tenant.

FIGURE 4-10 U.P.C. § 6-101 (NON-PROBATE TRANSFERS ON DEATH)

(a) A provision for a nonprobate transfer on death in an insurance policy, contract of employment, bond, mortgage, promissory note, certificated or uncertificated security, account agreement, custodial agreement, deposit agreement, compensation plan, pension plan, individual retirement plan, employee benefit plan, trust, conveyance, deed of gift, marital property agreement, or other written instrument of a similar nature is nontestamentary. . . . If the law firm assists in collecting and transferring a decedent's property outside of probate, these services are rendered not to an estate or to a personal representative but rather directly to the recipient(s) of the property. Where a probate estate has also been established, the law firm often assists with non-probate transfers as well; fee arrangements must of course be made with the recipients of the non-probate property, and not with the personal representative of the estate, although if the amount of additional effort or time involved is minimal, these services are often rendered free of charge.

EXAMPLE: *During Kelly's lifetime, she transfers title in real property to Keith and David as joint tenants. Thereafter, Keith dies, although no action is taken to clear title prior to David's subsequent death.* **Result:** *The personal representative of David's estate must sign an Affidavit—Death of Joint Tenant with respect to the death of Keith before title to the property can be passed to David's heirs or devisees.*

A certified copy of the death certificate must be attached to the affidavit. (More detailed information regarding obtaining copies of death certificates is included in Chapter 5.) As soon as possible after the decedent's death, the affidavit should be recorded at the recorder's office in the county where the real property is located. The death certificate will be recorded as the second page of the document. The paralegal should contact that office to determine the necessary recording fees. The affidavit may be hand delivered if it is practical to do so; otherwise, the affidavit, along with death certificate and fee payment, should be mailed to the recorder's office with a cover letter requesting that the affidavit be returned to the address indicated near the upper left corner of the affidavit.

 PRACTICE TIP: Most of the information needed to complete the affidavit can be obtained from the original joint-tenancy deed. If the decedent's name on the death certificate differs from the name on the deed, additional proof may be required to show that the decedent and the joint tenant were the same person, except for minor discrepancies in the names. The paralegal should use a form affidavit provided by a local title company; otherwise, if the property is subsequently sold, the title company may want to examine the affidavit more carefully, which could result in delays in closing the transaction.

PRACTICE TIP: In order to verify that the document was received and promptly recorded by the recorder's office, it is highly recommended that the document be returned to the law firm rather than to the surviving owner/client. After receiving the recorded affidavit, the paralegal should make a copy to retain and return the original affidavit (and attached death certificate) to the owner, instructing the owner to keep it in a safe place.

Alternative Procedures If a certified copy of the death certificate cannot be obtained, the joint tenancy may be terminated by a proceeding to establish the fact of death (this proceeding can also be used to terminate a life estate upon the death of a life tenant). In cases where the decedent's joint-tenancy interest passes to the surviving spouse, it may be desirable to treat the interest as community property instead of using the foregoing affidavit procedure.

 PARKER ESTATE: In the Parker matter, Fred's joint-tenancy interest in the residence must be terminated in order for the record to show that Irene was the sole owner at her death. Sharon may sign the affidavit even though not yet appointed as personal representative of Irene's estate (see, however, Paralegal Assignment 4).

Securities. Securities include financial assets such as stocks, bonds, and mutual-fund accounts. Upon the death of a joint tenant, securities should be re-registered in the name of the surviving owner(s). The actual transfer is made by a *transfer agent*, except in the case of mutual funds in which transfers are made by the company that manages the fund or by its *custodian*. In order to transfer title in securities (other than mutual funds) to the surviving joint tenants, the paralegal must assemble and provide to the transfer agent the following documents:

1. A certified copy of the death certificate
2. The original stock certificate or bond
3. A *stock or bond power* signed by all surviving joint tenants (forms are available from a stockbroker); all signatures must be guaranteed by a bank or broker
4. An affidavit, signed by all surviving joint tenants, whose signatures must be notarized, as to their respective domiciles
5. A transmittal letter to the agent signed by all surviving joint tenants

In the case of mutual funds, the certificate evidencing ownership is retained by the company's custodian. Also, the fund management company may have different requirements or specific forms for transfers; the paralegal should contact the company (or its custodian) directly to determine its particular requirements. Appropriate addresses and telephone numbers are generally listed on account statements.

 PRACTICE TIP: The name and address of the transfer agent usually appears on the face of the stock certificate or bond. However, the current transfer agent may be different from that indicated; the paralegal should contact either the transfer agent or a stock brokerage firm in advance to confirm the name and address of the current agent. The law firm may wish to use the services of a stock broker to handle the entire transfer; brokers can generally accomplish this task more quickly than can the paralegal and for only a modest fee.

Multiple-Party Accounts. Lending institutions, such as banks, savings-and-loan companies, and credit unions, may provide one or more types of multiple-party accounts. A "joint-tenancy" account may be *for convenience only*, with no right of survivorship, or it may be a true joint-tenancy account with a *survivorship* feature. **Totten trust accounts** and **P.O.D. (payable-on-death) accounts** are types of accounts in which any balance remaining in the account at the death of the account holder(s) is immediately payable to a beneficiary specified by the account holder(s). When the type of account is not specified, the identity of the person entitled to the balance of the account upon the owner's death is a question of fact and is a frequent subject of litigation. The Uniform Multiple-Person Accounts Act, which is included in the U.P.C. (U.P.C. § 6-201, *et seq.*), establishes certain rules intended to provide certainty with respect to the nature of multiple-party accounts. (This Act has been adopted by Colorado and North Dakota, and several other states have enacted similar legislation.)

In order to terminate any of these multiple-party accounts, the paralegal should instruct the surviving owner or beneficiary to present to the lending institution a certified copy of the death certificate and (for a savings account) the passbook or (for a checking account) a check drawn for the amount of the balance of the account.

 PARKER ESTATE: In the Parker matter, Irene and Sharon owned a joint checking account for paying Irene's monthly bills and as a depository for Irene's Social Security benefits. According to Sharon, the purpose of including Sharon on the account was to allow her to handle these matters in the event her mother was unable to do so. The account failed to indicate whether Sharon is entitled to the balance in the account by right of survivorship. However, the circumstances under which the joint account was created suggest that the joint feature was for convenience only. The balance remaining in the account at Irene's death is approximately $1,000. These funds may properly be applied by Sharon toward payment of Irene's unpaid bills and toward meeting Irene's other financial obligations, such as the mortgage. In the event Sharon is required to advance her own funds to meet the obligations, or if it is later determined that Sharon was entitled to the account balance as surviving co-owner, then Sharon may seek reimbursement from the estate. (For a complete discussion of these and other immediate postmortem concerns, see Chapter 5.)

Motor Vehicles. Whether a motor vehicle is owned in joint-tenancy form depends upon the particular requirements of the state's vehicle code. In order to terminate a joint-tenancy interest in an automobile or other motor vehicle, the paralegal should instruct the surviving joint tenant to sign the ownership certificate in the appropriate places and to present it, along with the registration card for the vehicle and a certified copy of the death certificate, to the state department of motor vehicles. A certificate of compliance with smog pollution control laws may also be required.

Contractual Benefits Payable at Death

Certain contractual benefits payable at death may pass to designated beneficiaries outside of probate. Such benefits include

1. Life insurance proceeds
2. Death benefits under retirement plans
3. U.S. Savings Bonds
4. Social Securities benefits

Life Insurance Proceeds. The proceeds of a life insurance policy owned by the person whose life is insured are not included in the decedent's probate estate if payable to a named beneficiary rather than to the decedent's estate or to a personal representative of the estate. However, a life insurance policy purchased by a person on the life of another will be included in the policy owner's (purchaser's) probate estate in the event that he or she predeceases the person whose life is insured.

EXAMPLE: Merle purchases a life insurance policy on his own life, the proceeds payable upon Merle's death to his wife Benita; Merle predeceases Benita. Result: Upon Merle's death, the proceeds are payable directly to Benita, and the distribution is not subject to probate.

EXAMPLE: Juanita purchases a life insurance policy on the life of Stephen, the proceeds payable upon Stephen's death to Rose, or if Rose predeceases Stephen, to Stephen's estate; Rose predeceases Stephen, who in turn predeceases Juanita. Result: The proceeds will be included in Stephen's probate estate and will pass to Stephen's heirs or devisees.

EXAMPLE: Klaus purchases a life insurance policy on his father George's life, the proceeds payable upon George's death to Klaus's mother (George's wife) Helen. Klaus predeceases George. Result: Because Klaus owned the policy, the policy is an asset of Klaus's probate estate; the heirs or devisees of Klaus's estate will become the new owner(s) of the policy, subject to probate administration.

To collect proceeds for a named beneficiary, the paralegal should contact the death claims office of the insurance company to request a claim form (each insurance company uses its own form). If an estate-tax return will be filed, the paralegal should also request from the insurance company IRS Form 712 for estate-tax purposes. Upon receipt, the claim form should be prepared by the paralegal, signed by the beneficiary, and returned to the insurance company along with the original policy and a certified copy of the death certificate.

In cases where insurance proceeds (or other death benefits) are payable to a named beneficiary, the law firm representing the decedent's probate estate is not obligated to assist the beneficiary in collecting these proceeds/benefits. However, it is highly recommended that the law firm assist in collecting these proceeds and benefits when the firm anticipates filing an estate-tax return for the decedent's estate; the paralegal must maintain accurate records for this purpose, and life insurance proceeds and most types of death benefits must be reported on the estate-tax return regardless of whether the proceeds or benefits are subject to probate.

Death Benefits under Retirement Plans and Other Contracts.

Death benefits include those payable under employee retirement programs, I.R.A.s (Individual Retirement Accounts), or Keogh plans, as well as deferred compensation benefits, annuities, and veteran's benefits. As in the case of life insurance proceeds, benefits payable to a named death beneficiary (rather than to the decedent's estate or to a personal representative of the estate) are not included in the decedent's probate estate. The paralegal should contact the administrator of the appropriate plan under which the benefits are payable to inquire as to the proper procedure for claiming benefits.

 PRACTICE TIP: In the initial letter of request to the insurance company or plan administrator, the paralegal should refer to the policy number or other identifying number (often the decedent's Social Security number), indicate the law firm's representation, and ask for verification of the amount of the proceeds or benefits and the person entitled to receive them. A self-addressed stamped envelope should also be enclosed.

 PARKER ESTATE: In the Parker matter, recall that Sharon had found a blank change-of-beneficiary form from a life insurance company among Irene's papers. Sharon has since contacted the insurance company. It appears that Fred and Irene each purchased modest life insurance policies on their respective lives, naming the other as primary beneficiary and their son John as secondary beneficiary. After Fred's death, Irene collected the proceeds from Fred's policy and changed the beneficiary under her own policy to her granddaughter (Sharon's daughter Cindy). Accordingly, the proceeds from Irene's policy, which total $50,000, will pass to Cindy and will not be included in Irene's probate estate. However, because Cindy is a minor, she is not legally permitted to receive the proceeds outright. The subject of property ownership by minors and other legally incompetent persons is discussed in Chapters 9 and 11.

U.S. Savings Bonds.

U.S. Savings Bonds are included in the owner's probate estate unless the bonds are registered in *beneficiary* form—for example, "P.O.D. to Joseph Smith"—or in *co-ownership* form—for example, "Joseph Smith or Mary Smith." Ownership in the bonds passes automatically to the surviving beneficiary or co-owner, who may either redeem the bonds or have them reissued. To redeem the bonds, the surviving beneficiary or co-owner must simply endorse the bond (by signing it on the back as with a personal check) and present it to a commercial bank; if the bond was owned in beneficiary form, a certified copy of the death certificate must also be presented. To reissue the bonds, either in the name of the surviving beneficiary, co-owner, or fiduciary (such as a conservator of the surviving beneficiary or co-owner), the endorsed bonds and certified copy of the death certificate must be presented to the bank together with certain federal tax forms that are provided by the bank. All signatures must be certified by an officer of the bank.

 PRACTICE TIP: Most commercial banks provide the necessary forms as well as assistance and advice in redeeming or reissuing U.S. Savings Bonds. In most cases, the paralegal may simply inform the surviving beneficiary or co-owner as to the proper procedure and allow him or her to follow through without further assistance by the law firm.

Social Security Benefits. If the decedent was covered under Social Security, the surviving spouse or dependent children may be entitled to a small lump-sum death benefit as well as to survivor's benefits. The lump-sum death benefit is currently $255 and must be claimed within two years after the decedent's death. The paralegal should contact the local district office of the Social Security Administration to obtain claim forms. After completing the forms and obtaining the claimant's signature as required, the paralegal should return the forms, along with a certified copy of the death certificate, to the local district office. In claiming survivor's benefits, it may also be necessary to include certified copies of documents showing the claimant's relationship to the decedent (for example, a birth certificate or marriage license).

 PRACTICE TIP: If the claimant wishes to receive these benefits as soon as possible, the paralegal should instruct the claimant to visit the Social Security Administration office in person with the necessary documents.

 PARKER ESTATE: In the Parker matter, Irene's primary source of income prior to her death was her Social Security benefits. Although Irene was covered under Social Security, no lump-sum or survivor's benefit is payable to any surviving family member, because Irene was not survived by a spouse or by a dependent child. Also, any payments received after Irene's death must be returned, and Irene's death should be reported promptly to the Social Security Administration.

Paralegal Assignment 4

Your fourth assignment involves the residence of Fred and Irene Parker which they owned as joint tenants prior to Fred's death. Ms. Cargis has asked you to assist Sharon in terminating the joint tenancy—specifically, to obtain all necessary information from Sharon and to prepare and process all documents necessary to complete the transaction. To complete this task, you must prepare an Affidavit—Death of Joint Tenant for Sharon's signature and ensure that the affidavit, together with a certified copy of John Parker's death certificate, is properly recorded. Perform the following tasks to complete this assignment:

- Obtain the following items:
  1. The joint-tenancy deed (a high-quality photocopy will suffice for this purpose)
  2. A certified copy of Fred Parker's death certificate
  3. The appropriate blank affidavit form (from a local title insurance company)

- Obtain the following information to prepare the affidavit:
  1. Tax Assessor's Parcel Number (if applicable)
  2. Decedent's name as it appears on the joint-tenancy deed
  3. Decedent's name as it appears on the death certificate
  4. Name(s) of the person(s) signing the joint-tenancy deed
  5. Names(s) of the person(s) who own the property as joint tenants as shown on the deed
  6. Recording information shown on the joint-tenancy deed
  7. County where the real property is located
  8. Legal description of the property

  With the exception of item 3, all of this information may be obtained from the joint-tenancy deed.

- Mail the completed affidavit to Sharon Madson, instructing her to sign it in the presence of a notary public and return it promptly to the law firm.
- Call the recorder's office in the county where the property is located to verify their mailing address and to determine their recording fee for a two-page document.
- Mail the completed, signed, and notarized affidavit (with death certificate attached) to the office of the county recorder, along with payment for the recording fee. The cover letter (as well as the affidavit) should request return of the recorded affidavit to the law firm.

The joint-tenancy deed and completed affidavit are included in the Parker file (Appendix A of the Resource Manual) as Exhibits 5 and 6, respectively.

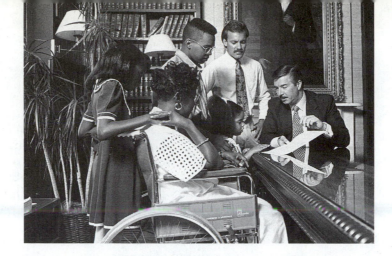

5 PREPARING FOR ESTATE ADMINISTRATION

Prior to initiating estate proceedings, some of the decedent's legal and financial matters may require immediate attention, and the paralegal must gather from the decedent's family all of the information and documents necessary to address these concerns as well as to proceed appropriately with the collection and transfer of the decedent's assets. If estate proceedings are required, the attorney must determine who the petitioner and prospective personal representative will be and the proper court in which to initiate the proceedings. The paralegal plays a vital role in gathering and organizing information and in assisting the prospective personal representative with urgent postmortem tasks.

In the Parker matter, all of the information and documents have been collected and all urgent postmortem tasks have been accomplished by the department's other probate paralegal (as noted throughout this chapter). Ms. Cargis has instructed you to prepare and file with the court a petition for probate of Irene's will and for Sharon's appointment as personal representative, together with all necessary supporting documents. After securing a hearing date, you must also provide notice of the hearing as required by law.

TASKS PRIOR TO INITIATING ESTATE PROCEEDINGS

The paralegal often provides the first significant contact between the law firm and the decedent's family. Typically, a member of the decedent's family

111

calls the law firm within a few days after the decedent's death. In many cases, however, several months may pass before the decedent's family seeks legal advice and assistance. During the initial contact, the paralegal must ask pointed questions to determine whether certain matters must be addressed immediately. If so, an initial meeting with appropriate members of the decedent's family should take place as soon as possible. Based upon the information gathered at the interview, the attorney will determine whether probate is required and what other procedures are necessary to transfer the decedent's assets. The paralegal must then establish a file and organize all of the information and documents provided by the decedent's family. The paralegal may be required to conduct additional interviews and discovery to collect the documents and information required to initiate estate proceedings and nonprobate transfers. In addition, particular actions may be required prior to appointment of a personal representative in order to protect or preserve the estate.

Immediate Postmortem Concerns

Immediately after the decedent's death but prior to a formal probate interview between the lawyer and the surviving family members, certain legal questions and procedures respecting the proper disposition of the decedent's bodily remains may call for the law firm's assistance. Concurrently, the lawyer must determine whether to accept employment as well as determine what person (or entity) should serve as personal representative of the decedent's estate. These various immediate postmortem concerns are discussed in the following materials.

Anatomical Gifts. The Uniform Anatomical Gift Act, adopted by all 50 states, permits any person who is competent to make a will to donate all or part of his or her body for medical research, organ transplantation, or other specified purposes. Of immediate concern after the decedent's death, then, is whether the decedent made such a donation. Funeral and burial arrangements should not be finalized until after thorough investigation into this matter. The paralegal should check the following sources, any of which might indicate an anatomical donation:

1. The decedent's will
2. The records of the state department of motor vehicles where the decedent was licensed
3. The decedent's wallet or purse, which may contain a wallet-sized card with organ-donation information
4. Any power of attorney for health care executed by the decedent (see Chapter 11)

Institutions that accept anatomical donations often provide their own forms for this purpose. The paralegal should also ask the decedent's physician, immediate family, close friends, attorney, and clergy whether the decedent mentioned any such gifts.

Funeral Arrangements. Funeral and burial arrangements are often made prior to the decedent's death. The paralegal should determine whether prior arrangements were made, obtain a copy of the contract, and inform appropriate family members of these arrangements. However, the decedent may instead have provided funeral and burial instructions in his or her will. If so, the instructions in the will must be carried out, even if the validity of the will is in doubt and the will has not yet been probated. If the decedent's purported will nominated an executor, that person is typically authorized by statute to carry out any written instructions by the decedent respecting disposition of the body prior to appointment of a personal representative (see, e.g., U.P.C. § 3-701). In the absence of any prior arrangements or testamentary instructions, the paralegal should encourage family members to agree among themselves about funeral and burial arrangements. In the event that family members cannot agree, the order of priority as to who may dispose of the decedent's remains may be specified by statute.

If funeral and burial expenses have not been paid, a family member often makes the required payments. If the decedent's will authorizes the personal representative to pay for funeral and burial expenses (or for expenses of the decedent's last illness) out of the estate's assets, the contributing family member may file a creditor's claim with the estate. If the decedent died as a result of work-related injuries, the decedent's employer may be liable under the state's worker's compensation laws for payment of reasonable funeral and burial expenses.

Obtaining Copies of the Decedent's Death Certificate. When a person dies, an official death certificate is filed in the health department or vital statistics office of the county where the decedent died. Certified copies of the death certificate are needed for recording an Affidavit—Death of Joint Tenant and for filing insurance claims, as well as for several other purposes. The paralegal should estimate the total number of certificates that will be required and obtain them as soon as possible from the local bureau of vital records. A small fee is required for each certificate.

 PRACTICE TIP: It is generally recommended that the paralegal obtain at least five certified copies of the decedent's death certificate in any event. A quick and easy method of obtaining death certificates is to request the mortuary that is handling the decedent's funeral and burial to obtain them and add the fee for this service to the bill. In the event an autopsy is required, a delay in obtaining the death certificate will result; however, a preliminary death certificate may be obtained in the meantime to provide adequate proof of death for the purpose of collecting and transferring the decedent's assets (the cause of death is not indicated in the preliminary death certificate).

Locating the Will. The paralegal should ensure that a thorough search for all wills and codicils is conducted as soon as possible, since the will may indicate anatomical gifts or funeral and burial instructions. Most people keep their will in an obvious place—for example, among their important personal papers at home or in a bank safe-deposit box. However, it is always possible that the decedent executed one or more codicils without informing anyone. Thus, an immediate and thorough search of the decedent's personal papers should be conducted in any event. If a will is not found, the paralegal should ask the decedent's family, friends, and employer whether the decedent mentioned to them the existence and location of a will. In many cases, a family member or professional advisor may have possession of the will. Any person in custody of a document appearing to be a will or other testamentary instrument of a decedent is generally required by statute to deliver the document to a person able to secure its probate or, if none is known, to an appropriate court (see, e.g., U.P.C. § 2-902).

All safe-deposit boxes to which the decedent had access should be opened for the purpose of finding the most recent will and codicils as well as any funeral or burial instructions. Bank practices vary regarding requirements for gaining access to a safe-deposit box; most banks require at a minimum a certified copy of the decedent's death certificate. Until a personal representative is appointed (or until an affidavit is presented to the bank indicating right of succession to the box contents), only wills, codicils, and funeral/burial instructions may be removed from the box. Many states require a state-conducted inventory of the contents of bank safe-deposit boxes. (As to removal of remaining contents after appointment, see Chapter 6.)

 PRACTICE TIP: The paralegal should contact the bank beforehand to determine its requirements for gaining access to the decedent's safe-deposit box. If the decedent's key to the box cannot be located, the paralegal should make arrangements to have the box drilled. In any event, the paralegal should be present when the box is first opened.

Accepting Employment. Because of the obvious urgency of the immediate postmortem concerns discussed above, the law firm often assists in these matters prior to establishing a formal employment agreement with a prospective personal representative. This is understandable, because the extent of the services and the identity of the client (i.e., the personal representative) may not be ascertainable at this early stage. In the event that the law firm provides no further services, the firm is entitled, of course, to reasonable compensation for its services to this point. If the parties agree to the law firm's continued representation of the estate, the agreement should be reduced to writing.

The law firm must decline employment if a conflict of interest would result. Perhaps the most obvious conflict occurs where the firm has agreed to represent a beneficiary or creditor in opposition to the estate. The paralegal should conduct a thorough conflict-of-interest search before a formal employment agreement is reached. (Employment agreements and conflicts of interest are discussed in detail in Chapter 12.)

Determining the Personal Representative. Once the law firm has determined the need to establish an estate and appoint a personal representative, the attorney must determine the appropriate person to serve as personal representative (see Table 5-1). An individual personal representative must be a U.S. citizen. A corporation or trust may act as personal representative if nominated as executor in the decedent's will or otherwise entitled to so serve under applicable priority statute (see below).

Priority among persons seeking appointment is established by statute, as reflected in U.P.C. § 3-203 (Figure 5-1). Where the decedent left a valid will naming an executor, that person must be appointed by the court if willing to serve and not under the age of 21 or found unsuitable by the court (U.P.C. § 3-203[e]). Wills typically nominate two or three persons as alternate executors having priority for appointment in the order specified in the will. If the decedent's valid will fails to nominate an executor, or if no executor (including alternate executors) nominated in the decedent's will is able and willing to serve, the court must appoint an **administrator C.T.A.** (*cum testamento annexo*), also referred to as an *administrator with the will annexed*, in accordance with applicable priority statute, except in the case of a special administrator (see *Appointment of a Special Administrator*). A person having priority for appointment may renounce his or her right to appointment or may nominate another qualified person to act as personal representative by appropriate writing filed with the court (U.P.C. § 3-203[c]). In this event, however, the nominee may not necessarily have priority for appointment vis-à-vis other members of the decedent's family, depending upon applicable law.

PARKER ESTATE: With respect to the Parker matter, recall that Irene's attested will nominated her husband Fred, her sister Ruth, and her son John to serve alternately and successively in that order as executor. Since Fred is deceased, Ruth has priority to serve. Since John is Qalso deceased, Irene's other competent devisees—i.e., Sharon and Dennis—are each next in line of priority to serve as administrator with the will annexed. Thus, if Ruth is unwilling or unable to serve, the court may be required to determine in formal appointment proceedings whether Sharon or Dennis has priority for appointment.

The Probate Interview

Assuming that the law firm has decided to accept employment and that the immediate postmortem concerns discussed above have been addressed, the next step is a formal and thorough interview with the prospective personal representative and certain members of the decedent's family. A formal probate interview serves two important functions. First, it allows the law firm to gather information and documents needed to proceed further. Second, it provides an opportunity to educate the decedent's family regarding probate procedures and to instruct them regarding the respective roles of the personal representative, the attorney, and the paralegal in the process.

Arranging the Interview. The attorney must determine who should be present at the interview. In addition to the prospective personal representative, those persons most familiar with the decedent's financial and legal affairs

TABLE 5-1   DETERMINING THE PERSONAL REPRESENTATIVE

Scenario	Personal Representative	Letters Issued by Court
Valid will nominates executor who is willing and able to serve	Nominee appointed as "executor"	Letters Testamentary
Valid will fails to nominate executor	Appointee determined by priority statute and appointed as "administrator C.T.A. (with the will annexed)"	Letters of Administration with the Will Annexed
Valid will nominates one or more executors, but none are willing and able to serve		
No will	Appointee determined by priority statute and appointed as "administrator"	Letters of Administration
Immediate action required to protect or preserve estate	"Special administrator" appointed; person nominated in will as executor has priority (otherwise, court may appoint any proper person)	Letters of Special Administration
Property located in state other than decedent's domicile	Ancillary administrator appointed in foreign state	Letters of Administration
Disability, death, resignation, or removal of personal representative	Successor personal representative determined by priority statute and appointed as "administrator," "administrator C.T.A.," or "administrator D.B.N."*	Letters of Administration

*See Chapter 6.

FIGURE 5-1   U.P.C. § 3-203 (PRIORITY AMONG PERSONS SEEKING APPOINTMENT AS PERSONAL REPRESENTATIVE)

(a) Whether the proceedings are formal or informal, persons who are not disqualified have priority for appointment in the following order:

(1) the person with priority as determined by a probated will including a person nominated by a power conferred in a will;

(2) the surviving spouse of the decedent who is a devisee of the decedent;

(3) other devisees of the decedent;

(4) the surviving spouse of the decedent;

(5) other heirs of the decedent;

(6) 45 days after the death of the decedent, any creditor.

should be present. The attorney will then instruct the paralegal to contact the appropriate persons to arrange for a formal probate interview.

Prior to the interview, the paralegal should provide to the prospective personal representative (or to the person most familiar with the decedent's financial and legal affairs) three important forms to complete as fully as possible for the interview (see Exhibits 1, 2, and 3 in the Parker file):

1. A Probate Questionnaire
2. A Document Checklist
3. A Preliminary Inventory

The Probate Questionnaire The purpose of this form is to assemble basic factual information about the decedent and his or her family that will be required for estate proceedings as well as for nonprobate transfers. Among other information, the Probate Questionnaire should provide personal information about the decedent (e.g., residence history, marriages, pending and prior civil law suits, and divorce proceedings) and the decedent's family (e.g., names, ages, relationship, addresses, and telephone numbers).

The Preliminary Inventory This form is essentially a worksheet for assembling financial information about the decedent. The Preliminary Inventory should give the attorney and paralegal a complete picture of the decedent's estate, including the decedent's assets and their value and location, as well as the decedent's debts and obligations. This form will serve as a useful reference in:

1. Determining the necessity of and proper venue for estate proceedings
2. Identifying all nonprobate transfers required
3. Preparing an inventory and appraisement for the court
4. Determining the estate's tax liability and preparing tax returns
5. Addressing problems that may arise during the course of administration relating to the management of estate assets

The Document Checklist A complete list of all types of documents that might be relevant to the administration of a decedent's estate can serve as a useful checklist for the personal representative, as well as for the paralegal, to ensure that no important documents are overlooked. The paralegal can also use the Document Checklist later as an index for locating documents in the probate file and for recording routing information with respect to original documents.

 PRACTICE TIP: These forms must be comprehensive and must be properly and consistently used by the law firm to ensure that the decedent's estate is administered as expeditiously and competently as possible. The probate paralegal should assist in developing these forms if they are not already used by the law firm. The paralegal should provide to the prospective personal representative, along with these forms, a letter requesting that the forms be completed as fully and accurately as possible prior to the probate interview. The letter should also stress the importance of obtaining all available information for prompt administration of the estate. The paralegal may wish to meet with the prospective personal representative prior to the formal probate interview to assist in completing the Probate Questionnaire and Preliminary Inventory, especially if he or she is relatively unsophisticated in financial matters or if the decedent's important papers and records were left in a state of disorganization.

PRACTICE TIP: In arranging the interview, the paralegal must be sensitive to the effects of grief on the decedent's closest family members; although the interview should be conducted as soon as practicable, the decedent's family, particularly the surviving spouse, may require additional time to regain sufficient emotional stability to contribute to a productive interview. Also, key family members may not all be available at the same time, in which event separate interviews may be required to gather all of the necessary information and documents.

FOCUS: The paralegal must at the outset gather and assemble, in an organized manner, all information and documents that will be relevant for estate administration, for collecting and transferring nonprobate property, and for payment of taxes. The importance of maintaining and updating a comprehensive Probate Questionnaire, Preliminary Inventory, and Document Checklist for this purpose cannot be overemphasized.

Conducting the Interview. The attorney and paralegal should both be present at the probate interview. The paralegal must be present at the interview to establish contact with the decedent's family, to assure them of the paralegal's competence in handling probate matters, and to gain familiarity with the details of the decedent's estate. The family should be informed as to the respective roles of the personal representative, the attorney, and the paralegal. The family must understand that the paralegal plays much more than a merely clerical role in the process; otherwise, the family will invariably insist on communicating directly with the attorney rather than with the paralegal to discuss even the most trivial matters.

During the interview, the attorney will review the information presented in the Probate Questionnaire and Document Checklist and will outline the necessary procedures for distributing the estate (at least to the extent ascertainable at this point). The attorney may wish to disclose the contents of the decedent's will at this time, depending on the likelihood that the will is valid and on who is present at the interview. Once the will is offered for probate, it becomes a matter of public record in any event.

It is the paralegal's job to collect and organize all documents provided by the prospective personal representative and by the family members, to review the Probate Questionnaire and Preliminary Inventory to determine whether any necessary information is not yet provided, and to follow up in obtaining this information, if possible, during the interview. The paralegal should indicate on the Document Checklist which documents have been received, the location of all documents not yet received, and the person who intends to provide a particular document or piece of information to the paralegal.

PRACTICE TIP: Because the probate paralegal serves as the family's primary contact with the law firm, the paralegal may initially be barraged with telephone calls from various family members who have various demands and requests. It is important, therefore, that the paralegal, the attorney, and the personal representative all make clear to the family that the law firm's client is the personal representative only, and that other family members should contact the personal representative for basic information.

PRACTICE TIP: When the decedent's family arrives at the office for the interview, a staff member should obtain the completed Probate Questionnaire and Preliminary Inventory for the attorney and paralegal to review briefly immediately prior to the interview. By reviewing the Probate Questionnaire beforehand, the attorney will have a clearer idea as to whether probate will be required, whether additional information or documents should be requested, and whether certain matters should be discussed further during the interview. The probate interview will be more productive as a result.

Follow-Up Procedures. After the probate interview, additional documents and information may still be required prior to initiating estate proceedings. It may be prudent for the paralegal to arrange for a second interview with the prospective personal representative in order to follow up on these matters. Also, in the event that the prospective personal representative and family members cannot ascertain important information, the paralegal might be required to perform some investigative work, perhaps with the assistance of a private investigative firm.

Other Tasks Prior to Initiating Estate Proceedings

As discussed in Chapter 4, prior to initiating estate proceedings, the attorney must determine the proper court in which to initiate the proceedings. Other tasks prior to initiating proceedings are discussed below.

Opening the Probate File and Handling Documents. Immediately after the probate interview, the paralegal should establish or "open" a probate file according to established law-office procedure. The Probate Questionnaire and Preliminary Inventory should be kept near the top of the file for ready reference (see Figure 5-2). After reviewing all original documents provided by the client, the attorney may wish to retain certain original documents, while retaining copies of some other documents. It is the paralegal's responsibility to route all documents according to the attorney's instructions and to maintain careful records concerning their current location. Routing may be indicated directly on the Document Checklist; the paralegal should indicate on the checklist when the document was obtained, whether the law firm is retaining the original document or a copy, and when the document was returned to the client.

FIGURE 5-2   OPENING THE PROBATE FILE AND HANDLING DOCUMENTS

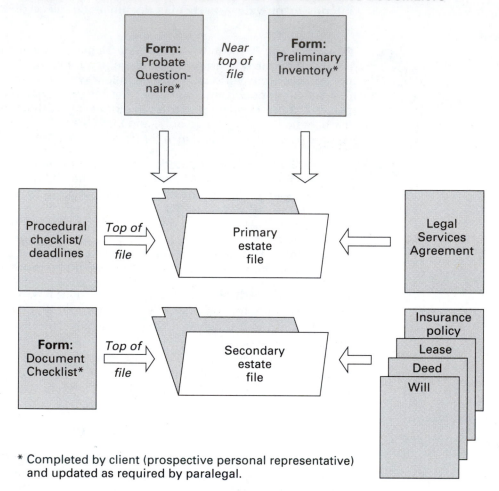

* Completed by client (prospective personal representative)
  and updated as required by paralegal.

Copies of documents should be kept in a separate file; the Document Checklist should be kept at the top of this file both as an index to the file's contents and as a reference for current location of original documents. Original documents retained by the law firm should be kept in a fireproof filing cabinet or safe. Also, the client may wish the law firm to keep certain valuable personal items, such as jewelry or collectibles, belonging to the decedent; if so, these items must be kept in a fireproof safe and their location and estimated value recorded on the Preliminary Inventory.

 PRACTICE TIP: The paralegal should obtain a signed receipt from the client for all original documents returned to the client personally. If an original document is returned by mail, the paralegal should use certified or registered mail. All routing information should be recorded promptly on the Document Checklist. With respect to valuable personal items left with the law firm, the paralegal should also provide a receipt with a detailed description of the item and should record the item and its location on the Preliminary Inventory.

Characterizing Assets and Determining the Need for Probate. Based on the information and documents provided to the law firm, the attorney must identify the character (joint tenancy, community property, etc.) of each of the decedent's assets as well as the value of the estate to determine whether probate is needed and what other or additional methods of transfer are appropriate. As discussed in Chapter 4, even where a probate estate will be established, certain assets may be collected and transferred outside of probate. Because nonprobate transfers are not part of estate administration, the paralegal should initiate procedures for the collection of benefits and transfer of nonprobate assets only after the attorney reaches a clear agreement with the beneficiaries regarding whether and by whom the law firm will be compensated for these services.

Meeting Immediate Financial Needs and Protecting the Estate. Some of the decedent's financial and legal matters pending at the decedent's death may require immediate attention prior to initiating probate and appointment procedures, as discussed below.

Payment of the Decedent's Debts The paralegal should determine the nature and extent of the decedent's debts from the Preliminary Inventory. The decedent's unopened mail should be examined for bills that may be due, and arrangements should be made to have the decedent's mail forwarded to the prospective personal representative. Also, the decedent's credit cards should be destroyed, and card issuers should be informed of the decedent's death. In protection of the estate's interest, payment of most debts should be postponed until after a personal representative is appointed and the attorney determines whether the debt is legally enforceable. Known creditors must be notified of the appointment of the personal representative in any event, and their claims will be barred unless filed with the estate in a timely manner. (Creditor's claims are discussed in Chapter 6.)

The attorney and the prospective personal representative must determine, however, whether any particular debts require attention prior to appointment. Funeral and burial expenses are often paid for right away by a family member (who may seek reimbursement later from the estate by filing a creditor's claim if the decedent's will authorizes payment of these expenses out of the estate's assets). Significant installment payments such as mortgage and automobile loan payments are generally postponed until they can be made by the personal representative from the estate assets. However, where the loan is made to another person as well, such as the surviving spouse, or where the loan is co-signed, or where the debt is a community debt of the decedent and the surviving spouse, it may be prudent to arrange for immediate payment in order that the surviving debtor's credit is not adversely affected. In any event, it is important to maintain communication with the lender; the paralegal should inform the lender by telephone and by letter as soon as possible of the decedent's death, the law firm's representation, and the anticipated time at which payments will be brought current. If the lender has agreed to postpone payments, the paralegal should request written confirmation of this agreement from the lender.

 PARKER ESTATE: Irene's attested will authorizes the personal representative to pay for funeral and burial arrangements with estate funds. In the meantime, Sharon has paid for these arrangements partly by depleting the funds remaining in Irene's checking account (owned jointly with Sharon) and partly with her own funds. Assuming that Sharon's name was included on the account for convenience only (which is probably the case), Sharon may file a creditor's claim for reimbursement only to the extent her own funds were used for this purpose.

Sharon has been instructed to collect her mother's unopened mail and to arrange with the post office to have all of Irene's mail forwarded to Sharon's address. She has also been instructed to pay various utilities bills—for water, gas, electricity, and telephone service—as they come due, keeping a record of all bills paid with her own funds. Sharon may wish to continue utilities service to the house until access to it is no longer necessary.

Income Received after Death The decedent might continue to receive income from various sources (e.g., stock dividends, investment interest, rent) prior to appointment of the personal representative. The prospective personal representative may open an estate bank account prior to his or her appointment for the purpose of depositing income, although no withdrawals may be made at this time. The personal representative should monitor and record income during this interim period. With respect to payments such as Social Security benefits, unemployment compensation, and other disability and retirement benefits, if the attorney determines that the benefits should properly be terminated at death, the paralegal should instruct the personal representative to return the payments to the payor and inform the payor of the decedent's death.

 PARKER ESTATE: Sharon has been instructed to check Irene's mail carefully for any further payment of Social Security benefits and to return any such payments. The other paralegal has written to the local S.S.A. office to inform them of Irene's death.

Pending Court Proceedings The paralegal should determine at the probate interview whether the decedent was a party to a civil law suit at the time of his or her death. Causes of action generally survive a person's death, and the estate substitutes for the decedent as a party to the litigation. If the decedent's family members are uncertain whether any court proceedings were pending, the paralegal should check the local court index. Pending litigation may require the appointment of a special administrator.

Insurance Coverage The paralegal should determine at the probate interview whether any of the decedent's assets were insured. If so, the paralegal should ascertain the name of the insurer and obtain a copy of the policy. The lawyer will want to examine all insurance policies to determine whether existing coverage is adequate, as well as whether insurance should be obtained for any uninsured assets. Additional or new coverage should be obtained if necessary to protect the estate.

Continuation of the Decedent's Business Affairs The decedent may have owned and operated all or a portion of a business (as a sole proprietor, general partner of a partnership, or shareholder of a closely held corporation). If so, arrangements should be made for the continued operation of the business in order to preserve its value as an asset of the estate. After appointment of the personal representative, final decisions can be made concerning the continuation and ownership of the business. The paralegal should obtain copies of partnership agreements, corporate bylaws, lease agreements, and insurance policies for review by the attorney. The attorney or the paralegal should contact key employees or partners of the business to determine whether the immediate cash and management needs of the business are being met. If not, it may be necessary to appoint a special administrator to protect and preserve the business during this interim period.

Investment Property If the decedent owned and rented investment property at the time of death, the paralegal should obtain all lease agreements for the attorney to review. Decisions regarding termination or renewal of current leases should be postponed until appointment of the personal representative. However, immediate arrangements should be made for the continued maintenance of the property and for the collection of rent; the paralegal should inform tenants to send rent to the prospective personal representative during this interim period (payable to the decedent and deposited in the estate's checking account). If appointment of the personal representative is likely to be delayed, and if the decedent's investment holdings are substantial, a special administrator should be appointed.

INITIATING ESTATE PROCEEDINGS

The remainder of this chapter will examine the specific procedures involved in initiating *formal* proceedings to determine the testacy status of the decedent and for the appointment of a personal representative (see Figure 5-3). Informal testacy and appointment proceedings were discussed in Chapter 4.

Formal Testacy and Appointment Proceedings

If the lawyer determines, based upon all of the information supplied by the decedent's family, that formal testacy and/or appointment proceedings are appropriate, the paralegal will then prepare the appropriate petition(s) and accompanying documents for filing with the court. Attention to detail is crucial in this process; to avoid delays, the paralegal must be sure that all documents are submitted in their proper form and that any errors or omissions are corrected prior to the scheduled court hearing. The following materials examine the specific paralegal tasks during this process.

In General. In the event that informal probate and appointment proceedings, such as those under the U.P.C. (see Chapter 4), are not authorized by applicable law or are otherwise unavailable, formal proceedings requiring

FIGURE 5-3   INITIATING ESTATE PROCEEDINGS

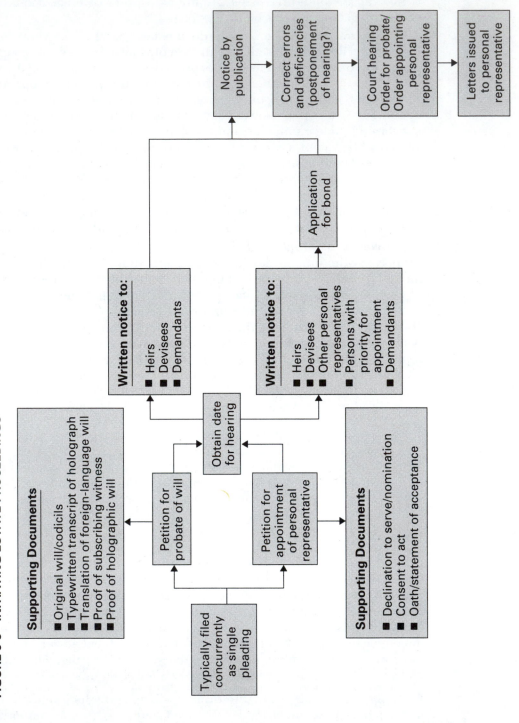

notice to interested persons and a court hearing are necessary. The probate paralegal plays an important role in this process—it is his or her job to prepare the petition and supporting documents, to ensure that all notice requirements are satisfied, to file with the court all necessary documents, and to correct mistakes and deficiencies prior to the hearing.

Any interested person may initiate formal testacy proceedings by filing an appropriate petition with the court. A petition for probate of the decedent's will (or for adjudication of intestacy, if there is no will) is usually combined and filed simultaneously with the initial petition for appointment of a personal representative. This is not always the case, however. Under certain circumstances, formal testacy proceedings may be initiated *after* a personal representative is appointed—for example, where a will or codicil is discovered thereafter, or if an interested person seeks to set aside a will that has been probated. Also, formal appointment proceedings might under certain circumstances be initiated where a personal representative has already been appointed. For example:

1. Appointment of the personal representative might terminate due to the personal representative's death, disability, or resignation.
2. An interested person might seek the removal of the personal representative and the appointment of another person.
3. An ancillary administrator might be appointed after appointment of the domiciliary personal representative.
4. The personal representative already appointed might be a special administrator, whose appointment is only temporary until a general personal representative can be appointed.

Preparing the Petition for Probate of the Will. If the decedent died leaving a valid will, the will must be probated before a personal representative is appointed to administer the decedent's estate. It is the paralegal's job to prepare and file the petition, together with any attachments and other documents that may be required. Attention to detail is important, since the court will require correction of all mistakes and deficiencies, no matter how minor, prior to hearing the matter. A comprehensive Probate Questionnaire and Preliminary Inventory will provide all information necessary for the paralegal to prepare the petition for probate of the will (as well as to prepare any other petition to initiate testacy or appointment proceedings).

The required contents of the petition are determined by statute. In addition, many courts either require or permit the use of a standard form (see Exhibit 7 of the Parker file). Under the U.P.C. (see U.P.C. § 3-402[a] [2]), a petition for probate of a will in formal (as well as informal) testacy proceedings must contain the following:

■ An oath or affirmation by the applicant that all statements contained in the application are accurate and complete to the best of his or her knowledge and belief

■ A statement of the interest of the applicant

- The name and date of death of the decedent, the decedent's age, the county and state of the decedent's domicile at the time of death, and the names and addresses of the spouse, children, heirs, and devisees and the ages of any who are minors so far as known or ascertainable with reasonable diligence by the applicant
- If the decedent was not domiciled in the state at the time of his or her death, a statement showing venue (the proper court in which to initiate proceedings)
- A statement identifying and indicating the address of any personal representative of the decedent appointed in this state or elsewhere whose appointment has not been terminated
- A statement indicating whether the applicant has received a demand for notice or is aware of any demand for notice of any probate or appointment proceeding concerning the decedent that may have been filed in this state or elsewhere

Petitions for adjudication of intestacy (and appointment of an administrator in intestacy) under the U.P.C. are governed by slightly different requirements as to content (see U.P.C. § 3-402[b]). Common sources of error in preparing the petition for probate of a will are discussed below.

Listing the Decedent's Heirs and Devisees The petition must include the names and addresses of the decedent's spouse, children, and heirs, as well as all devisees under the will. *Contingent* devisees—that is, devisees whose interests are conditioned upon the occurrence or nonoccurrence of a certain event—must also be listed. If the person is deceased, the petition should indicate so and should identify any current estate proceeding with regard to that person. The court may require the ages of all minors who are included to be indicated.

 PARKER ESTATE: As determined in Chapter 2, Irene's heirs include Sharon and Dennis, as well as John's unborn child. No estate proceedings will be required to transfer John's modest estate to his surviving heirs, and so there are no pending proceedings to indicate in the list of heirs. Since John is deceased, his surviving issue must be listed—his unborn child—and the child's legal guardian (Susan Burns) must be listed. The petition must list devisees under the holograph as well as under Irene's attested will—Irene's two granddaughters should be listed as possible devisees under the holographic instrument, even though the validity and interpretation of the provisions of the holograph are uncertain at this point. (See Exhibit 7, Attachment 8, of the Parker file.)

Name of the Decedent and Petitioner All known names of the decedent should be included in order to avoid problems later dealing with title companies, insurance companies, transfer agents, and other third parties. The name used most commonly by the decedent should be indicated first and will be used as the court's title of the estate. The name of the petitioner should be the one that he or she uses most often. If the petitioner is nominated in the will as executor but under a different name, the petition should indicate both names—for example, "John Doe, named in the will as J.T. Doe."

Petitioner's Signature and Verification The petitioner must sign the petition as well as an oath or affirmation that the contents of the petition are complete and accurate to the best of his or her knowledge and belief. The verification is generally included in the same form used for the petition. The person petitioning for probate of the will and the person seeking appointment as personal representative need not be the same person.

Proving the Will. Unless the will is self-proved, the court will require proof that it was duly executed. If the will is uncontested, a declaration (Proof of Subscribing Witness) by one subscribing witness that the will was properly signed and witnessed may serve this purpose. Most states require a notarized affidavit. The paralegal should locate one subscribing witness and should mail the form, together with a copy of the signature page of the will, to the witness for him or her to sign and return to the paralegal. If no subscribing witness can be located, the will may be proved by someone who can identify the handwriting of the testator and of one of the subscribing witnesses.

If a will or codicil is offered for probate as a holographic instrument, the decedent's handwriting must be proved. The paralegal should identify a person who may have seen the testator write the will or who is familiar with the testator's handwriting to obtain an appropriate declaration (Proof of Holographic Instrument), which must be filed with the court prior to the hearing (see Exhibit 8 of the Parker file). The paralegal must file the holograph together with a typewritten transcription; it is recommended that each line of the transcription correspond to each line of the holograph to assist the court in deciphering the testator's handwriting (see Exhibit 7, Attachment 3[E], of the Parker file).

If the will is written in a foreign language, the paralegal must file with the court both the original will and a written translation of the will. The paralegal must also obtain a signed declaration (Certificate of Translation of Foreign Language Will) from the translator that (1) he or she reads and writes both languages, (2) he or she personally translated the will, and (3) the translation is true and accurate.

PARKER ESTATE: Irene's attested will is self-proved, while the holograph is unattested. Accordingly, the use of a declaration (Proof of Subscribing Witness) to prove either will is inappropriate. Irene's letter to Sharon must be proved as a holograph by obtaining the Proof of Holographic Instrument discussed above. Sharon is familiar with her mother's handwriting and has agreed to sign this declaration.

Preparing the Petition for Appointment of a Personal Representative. As noted earlier, a petition for appointment of a personal representative is usually combined and filed simultaneously with a petition for probate of a will (or for an adjudication of intestacy). A petition in formal appointment proceedings must either contain or adopt many of the statements required in a petition in formal testacy proceedings. In addition, a petition in appointment proceedings must state who has priority for appointment and must describe any question relating to priority or qualification of the personal representative that is to be resolved (see, e.g., U.P.C. § 3-414).

The petitioner and the person whose appointment is sought need not be the same person. If not, or if one or more prospective co-representatives does not join in the petition, a Consent to Act form must be signed by each nonpetitioning representative and must be filed with the court prior to the hearing. In this event, the remaining personal representative may serve alone unless the will specifies otherwise. If the person nominated in the decedent's will as executor declines to serve, a written renunciation and/or nomination of another person to serve instead must be signed by that person and filed with the court prior to the hearing.

Under the U.P.C., a request by the petitioner for "supervised administration" may be included in petition for administration of the estate (U.P.C. § 3-502). Such a request may also be made by any interested person or by the personal representative at any other time. (Supervised administration is discussed further in Chapter 6.)

PARKER ESTATE: Fred's sister, Ruth Adams, has priority for appointment under the terms of Irene's attested will. Ruth has agreed not to serve because she does not reside nearby and is not as familiar with Irene's affairs as Sharon is. Ruth has agreed to sign an appropriate form nominating Sharon to serve in her place (see Exhibit 7 in the Parker file, Attachment 3[F][1]). With this nomination, Sharon clearly has priority for appointment, and any objection by Dennis (or by any other interested person) to Sharon's appointment is likely to fail. Able, Berman & Cargis has advanced costs for filing and probate fees and for initial probate bond premiums. This is common practice, and the attorney is reimbursed upon application to the court at final distribution.

Filing the Documents and Correcting Errors. After preparing the petition for probate of the will and for appointment of the personal representative, the paralegal must file the petition with the court, along with a filing fee. An additional fee may be required for filing the will. When the petition is filed, the court will set a time and place for hearing on the petition (although a hearing is not always required; see *The Court Hearing, Unopposed Hearings*). Prior to the scheduled date for the hearing, the court's personnel (e.g., the Registrar) will examine the petition and supporting documents and provide a written report to the law firm indicating any mistakes or deficiencies. Some deficiencies may require postponement of the hearing—for example, where notice was not given to a particular person entitled to it. After correcting errors and deficiencies as required, the paralegal should confirm with the court prior to the hearing that all necessary corrections have been made and should ascertain whether an appearance by the attorney will be required at the hearing.

PRACTICE TIP: Before an original will is filed, several copies should be made. Staples should not be removed from the will for this purpose; removing staples could result in an accusation that pages were removed or lost. If the court hears probate matters on more than one day of the week, for the convenience of both the attorney and paralegal, the paralegal should try to arrange with the court for all of the firm's probate matters to be heard consistently on one particular day of the week. The paralegal should check local rules to ascertain whether there is a deadline before the hearing date to file all documents with the court. Local court rules vary as to the proper procedure for correcting particular errors or deficiencies. The paralegal may be able to simply file a supplement to the petition with the court or may have to file an amendment requiring notification to all persons originally entitled to notice, which may result in postponement of the hearing.

Notice Requirements. After the petition is filed and a time and place for the hearing are set, notice of the hearing must be given as required by statute.

    Persons Entitled to Notice U.P.C. § 3-403 reflects a typical notice statute, requiring notice of formal testacy proceedings to the following persons:

- The surviving spouse, children, and other heirs of the decedent
- The devisees and executor named in any will that is being, or has been, probated, or offered for informal or formal probate in the county, or that is known by the petitioner to have been probated, or offered for informal or formal probate elsewhere
- Any personal representative of the decedent whose appointment has not been terminated
- Any persons properly demanding notice

    If a petition for appointment of a personal representative is filed at a later time—for example, where an interested person seeks to remove the original personal representative—notice must be given to interested persons, including all alternate executors nominated in the decedent's will, any previously appointed personal representative, and any person having or claiming priority for appointment as personal representative (U.P.C. § 3-414[b]).

    The petitioner must comply with a request by any person entitled to notice that notice be given to his or her attorney. Notice to a minor must be addressed to the minor as well as to the minor's legal guardian or, if none, to the adult in custody of the minor. Notice to foreign citizens residing in another country may be addressed to that country's consular in the United States. Notice of charitable gifts under the decedent's will to unspecified recipients may be given to the state attorney general.

    If the death of the decedent is in doubt, or upon written demand of any interested person, notice must be sent by registered mail to the alleged decedent at his or her last known address. The court may also require the petitioner to conduct a reasonably diligent search for the alleged decedent (see U.P.C. § 3-403[b]).

 PARKER ESTATE: In the Parker matter, all persons listed as heirs and devisees are entitled to notice. Dennis has not as yet filed a demand for notice but is entitled to notice of the hearing in any event as an heir and as a devisee under Irene's attested will. Fred's sister Ruth is entitled to notice as an executor nominated in Irene's attested will. Since Sharon is serving as personal representative, she need not mail notice to herself. However, her name should appear on the list of persons receiving notice.

Form, Time, and Manner of Notice A standard form is generally used for providing notice of the hearing (see Exhibit 10 of the Parker file). Under a typical notice statute, notice must be given to each person entitled to it (unless the address or identity of a person entitled to notice is not known or cannot be ascertained with reasonable diligence) at least 14 days before the time set for the hearing and may be given either by personal delivery or by mail (certified, registered, or ordinary first class). Notice statutes also generally require publication of notice in a newspaper of general circulation in the county where the hearing is to be held. Notice under this method must be published at least once a week for three consecutive weeks, and the last publication must be at least ten days before the time set for the hearing. Some newspapers will begin publication without further notification from the law firm if requested in the petition. Proof that notice has been given as required must be provided on or before the hearing and filed with the court. A standard proof-of-service form may be used for this purpose and is typically included on the back of the notice form.

PRACTICE TIP: A cover letter is typically included in order to explain the purpose of the notice and to inform the decedent's heirs and devisees of their right to disclaim their inheritance within the time specified by law (see Exhibit 9 of the Parker file). The attorney may or may not wish to inform the decedent's surviving spouse of his or her right to an elective share of the estate, depending upon whether this would conflict with the attorney's duty to the estate.

FOCUS: Proper notice of testacy or appointment proceedings requires notice to all interested persons whose names and addresses are reasonably ascertainable as well as notice by publication in a newspaper of general circulation. Notice must be given well in advance of the hearing; as a result, at least three to four weeks must pass between the time the petition is filed and the time of the hearing.

The Court Hearing. Whether a hearing in open court will be required and, if so, the extent of the judge's inquiry at the hearing usually depend upon whether there is any opposition to the petition, as discussed below.

Unopposed Hearings If a petition in a testacy or appointment proceeding is unopposed, a hearing in open court may not be necessary if the court is satisfied by examining the documents submitted to the court that all conditions for granting the petitioner's requests have been met. Local court rules vary as to whether an appearance by the attorney is required in this situation. If not, within a matter of a few weeks the attorney's office receives the court order(s) through the mail. In other situations, the court will conduct a hearing in open court to receive additional evidence or proof of the matters necessary to support the order sought. If evidence concerning the execution of a will is necessary, the affidavit or testimony of one subscribing witness is sufficient. If the affidavit or testimony of a subscribing witness cannot be obtained, execution of the will may be proved by other evidence or affidavit (U.P.C. § 3-405).

Contested Hearings Probate of a will may be opposed on a variety of grounds, as discussed in Chapter 3. If the validity of an attested will is challenged on the basis that it was not duly executed, the testimony of at least one of the subscribing witnesses, if within the state and competent and able to testify, is required, unless the will is self-proved. If no attesting witness is available, or if the will is unattested, due execution of the will may be proved by other evidence (U.P.C. § 3-406[a]). If the validity of a self-proved will is challenged on the basis that it was not duly executed, compliance with signature requirements for execution is conclusively presumed, and no additional evidence will be required by the court. Other requirements for execution (for example, the requirement of testamentary capacity, testamentary intent, and freedom from fraud, duress, or undue influence) are presumed subject to rebuttal but without the necessity of testimony of any attesting witness, at least under certain circumstances (U.P.C. § 3-406[b]). In a contested appointment proceeding, the judge may require testimony or other evidence to help in determining what person should be appointed as personal representative.

The Court's Findings and Order. In formal testacy proceedings, at the hearing the court will determine the decedent's domicile, the decedent's heirs, and the decedent's state of testacy. If a personal representative was previously appointed, the court will also determine whether his or her appointment should be terminated or confirmed. If more than one testamentary instrument was filed, the court will also determine which provisions control regarding the nomination of an executor, if any. The court may, but need not, also indicate how any provisions of a particular instrument are affected by the other instrument (U.P.C. § 3-410). All of these findings are included as appropriate in the court order. In appointment proceedings, the court will determine the person qualified and entitled to serve as personal representative and will issue a formal instrument—either **Letters Testamentary** (where the person appointed was nominated in the decedent's probated will) or **Letters of Administration** (in other cases)—signifying the personal representative's power and authority (see Exhibit 14 of the Parker file). In some states, Letters of Administration are issued in all cases.

The paralegal usually prepares and submits an order conforming to the petitioner's requests for the judge's signature (see Exhibit 13 of the Parker file), although a court-generated order may be appropriate in certain cases. Unless and until the court's order is modified or vacated, the order is final and binding in all jurisdictions (U.P.C. §§ 3-408, 412, 413).

 PARKER ESTATE: In the Parker matter, if Sharon is appointed as personal representative, the court will issue Letters of Administration with Will Annexed to her as Administrator with Will Annexed. Also, rather than requesting a ruling at this time about the effect of the holograph on the attested will, Ms. Cargis has decided to file a separate petition after Sharon's appointment for the purpose of determining heirship (see Chapter 6).

Qualification of the Personal Representative. Prior to receiving Letters Testamentary or Letters of Administration, the personal representative must qualify by filing with the court any required bond (see *Probate Bonds*) and a signed oath of office (U.P.C. § 3-601; see Exhibit 11 of the Parker file). The bond and oath are typically included on the same form. The bonding agent submits the completed form to the court immediately after the hearing. If the personal representative is a corporation, a separate Statement of Acceptance must be completed and filed with the court, although no bond will be required. By signing the oath or statement of acceptance, the personal representative submits personally to the jurisdiction of the court in any proceeding relating to the estate that may be instituted by any interested person (U.P.C. § 3-602).

Appointment of a Special Administrator

If a delay in appointment of the personal representative (referred to here as "general personal representative") is anticipated (for example, if a will contest has been filed or if a prior appointment has been terminated suddenly due to death or disability), an application may be filed with the court for the appointment of a **special administrator** who may act immediately to protect the estate of the decedent pending the appointment of a general personal representative. Appointment of a special administrator may be necessary in order to continue the decedent's business, to attend to litigation in which the decedent was a party at the time of death, to meet urgent cash needs, to preserve assets, or to complete contractual obligations. In many states, the order of priority for appointment of a special administrator is determined by statute and is typically the same as for the appointment of a general personal representative.

Procedure for Appointment. Because time is of the essence, a special administrator may generally be appointed without notice (although some courts may require 24-hour notice to certain parties such as the surviving spouse and executor named in the will). The court may in its discretion require bond of the special administrator (see *Probate Bonds*). Most courts require that an application for probate of a will or for appointment of a general personal representative be filed with the court before an application for appointment of a special administrator will be granted. Typically, application for appointment of a special administrator and for appointment of a general personal representative are filed simultaneously. Application for appointment of a special administrator is similar in form and content to an application for appointment of a general personal representative, except that an attachment is usually required to explain the reasons for seeking special administration and to specify the powers requested (see below). Once the attorney determines that special administration is desired and decides on the identity of the applicant, the paralegal should prepare the application, attachment (stating grounds for appointment and requested powers), and the order conforming to the requested powers. If the court agrees that a special administrator would be in the best interests of the estate, the court will issue Letters of Special Administration to the administrator.

Powers and Duties of the Special Administrator. The court may require the applicant to specify in the application those powers being sought; the requested powers should be limited to those necessary to protect the estate pending the appointment of the general personal representative. However, if it is anticipated that special administration will continue for a lengthy time period, the applicant should request full powers—that is, the same powers as those of a general personal representative.

Termination of Appointment. The appointment of the special administrator terminates on the appointment of a general personal representative. However, other events, including the administrator's death or disability, resignation, or removal for cause, may also serve to terminate the special administrator's appointment (U.P.C. §§ 3-608 through 611, 618). Also, the court may specify in its order a certain time period after which appointment terminates regardless of whether a general personal representative has been appointed. In this event, if an extension is desired, the paralegal must prepare and file a request for extension along with an order conforming to the request. The request must be filed in a timely manner to avoid a lapse in the administrator's authority.

Probate Bonds

A **probate bond** is a promise to pay in the event of a breach of trust by the personal representative—for example, if the personal representative fraudulently uses estate assets for his or her personal benefit. The promisor, usually a corporation, is referred to as a *surety*; personal sureties are rarely used. A probate bond is similar in some respects to an insurance policy—it is typically obtained through a local agent representing the corporation, and payment is made in the form of a premium based upon the amount of protection desired. If bond is required, the personal representative must file bond with the court before he or she can receive Letters Testamentary or Letters of Administration. The cost of the bond is allowed as an expense of administration and thus may be paid for out of the estate's assets. The specific bond requirements and procedures discussed below reflect U.P.C. §§ 3-603 through 606 and are typical of statutory requirements.

Determining the Necessity and Amount of the Bond. Probate bonds are not required of a personal representative appointed in informal proceedings under the U.P.C., except upon the appointment of a special administrator or if the decedent's will expressly requires bond. If the personal representative is appointed in formal proceedings, the court may in its discretion require bond, except where the decedent's will expressly relieves the personal representative of bond. Bond may also be requested by an interested party, and the court may require it if satisfied that bond is desirable. Bond required by the decedent's will may be dispensed with in formal proceedings if the court determines that it is not necessary. Probate bonds are not required of a corporate representative such as a bank or trust company.

If bond is required, the appropriate amount of the bond must be determined. Bond must be filed in an amount no less than the total value of the personal estate of the decedent and of the income expected from all the estate's property during the next year. In certain unusual situations—for example, where the personal representative fails to qualify for the required bond—it may be necessary to deposit estate assets in lieu of bond in a special *blocked* bank account to which the personal representative cannot gain access without a court order.

 PRACTICE TIP: The paralegal may use the Preliminary Inventory for the purpose of determining the amount of bond. If the value of an asset is in doubt, undervaluation should be avoided.

Bonding Procedures. To obtain the probate bond, the paralegal must prepare an application for probate bond as well as the bond form itself (appropriate forms are provided by the bonding company's agent), obtain the prospective personal representative's signature on both documents, and submit the application and bond form to the agent. If the applicant qualifies for bond, the agent will obtain the required premium from the prospective personal representative and file the original bond with the court.

Under certain circumstances—for example, if real property is sold, thereby increasing the value of the personal estate, or after a preliminary distribution or payment of taxes that would decrease the value of the personal estate—the court may increase or reduce the amount of the bond. The cost to the estate of the bond (that is, premium payment) will also increase or decrease. The attorney is responsible for bringing to the court's attention the need to increase the bond amount. If the bond amount is increased, surety companies generally prefer to file an additional bond rather than cancel an existing bond and file a new one in a larger amount.

 PARKER ESTATE: Irene's attested will states that no executor nominated in the will shall be required to file bond. Although Sharon is not a named executor, the court might waive bond in this situation, since the value of Irene's personal property is low and since it appears that she might inherit most of the estate (depending on the legal effect of the holograph). However, by filing an appropriate request with the court, an interested person such as Dennis might influence the court in this matter. Thus, Ms. Cargis has decided that Sharon should file bond to avoid the possibility of delay or objection.

Paralegal Assignment 5

Recall that Ms. Cargis has instructed you to prepare and file with the court a petition for probate of Irene's will and for Sharon's appointment as personal representative, together with all necessary supporting documents, as well as to provide notice of the hearing as required by law. Fred's sister Ruth has agreed to nominate Sharon to serve in her place as personal representative. Upon his attorney's advice, Dennis has decided not to object to probate of Irene's letter or to Sharon's appointment as personal representative.

Based upon the information provided by Sharon and upon the textual materials in this chapter, you can now prepare/assemble and file with the court the following documents:

1. Petition for Probate of Will and for Letters of Administration with Will Annexed
2. Irene's attested will (original document)
3. Irene's holographic instrument (i.e., the letter to Sharon)
4. Typewritten transcript of the holographic instrument
5. Proof of Holographic Instrument (signed by Sharon Madson)
6. Declination to Serve as Executor and Nomination (signed by Ruth Adams)
7. Duties and Liabilities of Personal Representative and Acknowledgment of Receipt (signed by Sharon Madson) and Letter of Instructions to Personal Representative
8. Order for Probate/Order Appointing Administrator with Will Annexed (for the judge's signature)
9. Letters of Administration with Will Annexed (for judge's signature)

In addition, you can now prepare and provide to the bonding company's agent the following documents:

1. Application for bond
2. Bond upon qualification

After filing the petition and obtaining a case number and hearing date, you can now initiate publication of notice and provide notice (Notice of Petition to Administer Estate) to the following persons:

1. Dennis Parker (heir and devisee)
2. Sharon Madson (heir and devisee)
3. Cindy Madson (devisee) (addressed both to Cindy and to her mother Sharon Madson)
4. Deborah Madson (devisee) (addressed both to Deborah and to her mother Sharon Madson)
5. John Parker's unborn child (heir) (addressed to Susan Burns)
6. Ruth Adams (priority for appointment as personal representative and nominated as executor under attested will)

These documents are included in the Parker file as Exhibits 7 through 14 (only one notice form is included, since all notices are identical except as to the addressee).

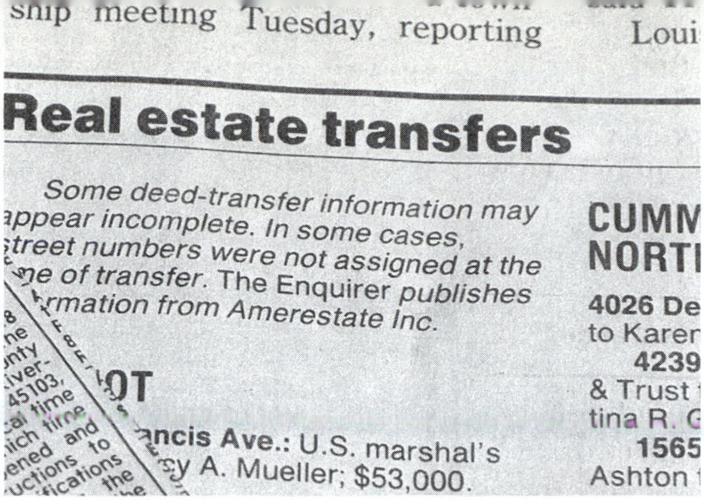

6 FORMAL ESTATE ADMINISTRATION

Paralegal Assignment 6

In the Parker matter, now that the court has probated Irene's will and issued Letters of Administration to Sharon Madson, Sharon may collect Irene's assets under her authority as personal representative. Before the estate can be distributed to Irene's devisees, however, a complete inventory and appraisement of Irene's estate must be filed with the court, and all of Irene's potential creditors must be notified of the estate proceedings and provided an opportunity to assert their claims. Ms. Cargis has asked you to assist Sharon in these matters. In addition, Sharon has decided to sell Irene's house during estate administration, and court approval of the sale is required. You will be assisting Sharon in this matter as well.

INTRODUCTION

Before allowing distribution of a decedent's probate estate, the court must be satisfied that all of the decedent's assets have been collected, that the decedent's debts have been paid, and that the proposed distribution is in accord with the terms of the decedent's will or, in the case of intestacy, with the laws of intestate succession. Also, the decedent's surviving spouse and minor children are entitled during this interim period to certain measures of protection against impoverishment and against the decedent's creditors. Because this process is administrative, it may be handled largely by the personal representative and by the paralegal, while the estate's attorney typically plays only a limited role as advisor to the personal representative and as supervisor to the paralegal. The attorney also provides legal representation for the personal representative in the event of disputes with creditors, beneficiaries, or other interested persons. Despite the attorney's limited role, it is important to keep in mind that the attorney is ultimately responsible to the personal representative and that the paralegal must maintain continual communication with the attorney throughout the process, consulting the attorney with respect to all matters outside of the paralegal's expertise or authority.

COMMENCING ESTATE ADMINISTRATION

Immediately upon appointment of the estate's personal representative, the paralegal may expect to assist in instructing the personal representative, establishing a bank checking account for the estate, obtaining a federal tax identification number for the estate, and notifying certain parties (including the Internal Revenue Service) of the personal representative's appointment. These specific tasks are examined in detail in the following materials.

Instructing the Personal Representative

The attorney and paralegal should meet with the personal representative immediately after his or her appointment to discuss the personal representative's duties and to outline the procedural steps involved in administration and the respective roles that the personal representative, attorney, and paralegal will perform in the process. In addition, the personal representative should be provided, either at the meeting or as soon as possible thereafter, with a detailed letter alerting the personal representative to his or her duties. Some lawyers prefer to provide such a letter to the client at the time the petition for his or her appointment is filed. This letter serves as a useful guide for the personal representative, thereby minimizing telephone calls by the personal representative to the law firm, as well as protecting the law firm in the event of a subsequent claim that the firm failed to adequately advise the personal representative. The paralegal should obtain proof of receipt by the personal representative of this letter, either by written acknowledgment of receipt at the meeting or by sending the letter by certified mail. (For a list of duties of a personal representative and a sample letter of instructions, see Exhibits 11 and 12 in the Parker file.)

Establishing Accounts and Determining a Bookkeeping System

Of immediate concern to the personal representative is the handling of income and expenses of the estate. The personal representative must understand at the outset that the estate is a separate legal entity and should be managed like a business. Accordingly, all estate income and expenses must be kept separate from those of the personal representative and beneficiaries through the use of separate bank accounts. A checking account for the estate should immediately be established at a commercial bank. An interest-bearing account should also be established as a depository for all excess cash. The following items will also be required:

1. A certified copy of the Letters of Administration
2. A signature card signed by the personal representative
3. A certified copy of the decedent's death certificate
4. A federal tax identification number (see *Obtaining a Tax Identification Number*)

If the personal representative wishes to establish a bank account for the estate prior to his or her appointment, a copy of the application or petition for appointment, stamped or signed by the court clerk as proof that the original document has been filed with the court, may be presented to the bank in lieu of Letters of Administration. Estate accounts should be opened in the name of the personal representative. Bank practice varies as to the specific form used—for example, "Estate of Irene Parker by Sharon Madson, Administrator" or "Sharon Madson as Administrator of the Estate of Irene Parker." The personal representative's signature on checks should indicate his or her office—for example, "/s/ Sharon Madson, Administrator."

 PRACTICE TIP: For the purpose of accounting to the court (as well as for reporting income as a distinct tax-paying entity to the federal and state tax authorities), the personal representative must establish a bank checking account for the estate and must keep complete and accurate records of all expenses of the estate. If the personal representative is unsophisticated in financial matters or unwilling to maintain the records, the paralegal may function as the estate's bookkeeper, writing checks for the personal representative as needed. In any event, the estate's records of income and expenses should be monitored regularly by the law firm to identify and correct errors and improprieties.

Notice of the Appointment

Notice of the personal representative's appointment should be provided to the decedent's creditors as soon as possible. This subject is discussed in detail later in this chapter (see *Payment of the Decedent's Debts, Notice to Creditors*).

Obtaining a Tax Identification Number

Every taxpayer must have a federal taxpayer identification number for the purpose of filing income tax returns with the Internal Revenue Service. Individuals use their Social Security number. However, other tax-paying entities, including decedents' estates, must obtain a federal Employer Identification Number (EIN) by submitting an appropriate application (IRS Form SS-4) to the IRS. Form SS-4 is the appropriate form for a decedent's estate even though an estate is not usually an employer. The same EIN is used by state taxing authorities. The personal representative must provide the EIN to all banks, corporations, and other institutions paying interest or dividends to the estate. (See Exhibit 15 in the Parker file.)

PRACTICE TIP: It generally takes two to three weeks for the IRS to process Form SS-4. The paralegal should consider preparing and submitting Form SS-4 at the same time that the petition to administer the estate is prepared for filing with the court. The EIN may then be obtained by the time the personal representative is appointed. If an EIN is needed immediately, the paralegal may obtain an EIN over the phone by calling the IRS district office; Form SS-4 should be filed as soon as possible thereafter with the EIN indicated on the form.

Notification of Fiduciary Relationship

Because the personal representative is responsible for the decedent's income taxes, the personal representative should inform the IRS of this fiduciary relationship. For this purpose, the paralegal should obtain and prepare IRS Form 56 (Notice Concerning Fiduciary Relationship) for the personal representative's signature. The estate's EIN must be indicated on the form and therefore must be obtained beforehand. Form 56 should be sent to the IRS service center where the decedent filed his or her income-tax returns. A copy should also be sent to the appropriate state taxing authority in the state where the decedent filed state income-tax returns. A certified copy of the Letters Testamentary or Letters of Administration should be attached to Form 56 and to each copy.

When the duties of the personal representative terminate, either after the estate is closed or after the appointment of a successor representative, the paralegal should prepare and send a second Form 56 to the IRS (and to appropriate state taxing authorities), indicating on the form that the fiduciary relationship has terminated. A certified copy of the court's order discharging the personal representative must be attached to Form 56. (See Exhibit 16 in the Parker file.)

COLLECTION AND INVENTORY OF THE DECEDENT'S ASSETS

One of the most primary purposes of court-supervised administration of decedent's estates is to ensure that all of the decedent's assets are collected and are accounted for to the estate's beneficiaries. The specific paralegal tasks associated with the collection and inventory of the decedent's assets are discussed in the following materials.

Discovery and Collection of the Decedent's Assets

Complete knowledge of the decedent's assets is necessary for administration of the estate. The paralegal plays a vital role in the discovery and collection of the decedent's assets. Some of the more common tasks the paralegal may be required to perform in this area are examined below.

Determining the Decedent's Assets—In General. Complete knowledge of the decedent's assets is necessary for administration of the estate. Much of the necessary information can usually be obtained by examining the documents, papers, and files kept by the decedent at his or her residence. Key items generally kept at home include bank books, insurance policies, tax returns, and deeds. The decedent's will should be examined for specific gifts. The decedent's bank safe-deposit box may contain valuable tangible personal property as well as documents such as deeds and stock certificates that provide information about the decedent's assets. Mail addressed to the decedent and delivered both before and after the decedent's death may also provide useful information. The paralegal should also contact the decedent's family, friends, and business associates, as well as the decedent's professional advisors, including the decedent's accountant, attorney, stockbroker, insurance agent, and other financial advisors. If it is believed that the decedent owned particular assets unaccounted for from the foregoing sources, the paralegal may be required to investigate still further.

To assume control of estate assets that are accompanied by a document of title, such as deeds, stock certificates, bills of sale, or other ownership certificates, it is not necessary to change the title from the decedent's name to the name of the personal representative. However, in the case of financial accounts with respect to which the personal representative intends to make withdrawals and deposits, the account should be transferred to the estate's name.

Accounts in Financial Institutions. If it is believed that the decedent owned bank accounts that have not been discovered, the paralegal should conduct appropriate inquiries among local banks by circulating copies of a standard letter of inquiry, countersigned by the personal representative and requesting information concerning account numbers, balance at death, accrued interest, and account names; a certified copy of the Letters of Administration should be enclosed. Once an account is located, the personal representative may deal with the asset by presenting a copy of the Letters of Administration to the bank.

Contents of Safe-Deposit Boxes. The paralegal should determine all bank safe-deposit boxes leased by the decedent, either solely or jointly. The paralegal and the personal representative should both be present to open the box in order to examine and inventory its contents. Many states also require a representative from the state taxing authorities to be present when the box is opened and its contents inventoried. Generally, the contents are then kept in the box which is transferred to the estate's name. If the box is leased jointly, the surviving joint tenant should also be present when the box is opened. If a dispute arises over whether the estate or the surviving joint tenant is entitled to possession of any particular contents, the bank may hold the contents in its vault and require a court order or written instructions signed by both parties before releasing the items.

Stocks and Bonds. The personal representative should take possession of all stock and bond certificates and should deposit them in the estate's safe-deposit box or the law firm's vault for safekeeping. The number of shares owned by the decedent should be verified by comparing the certificate(s) against any dividend checks or statements. In the event of a discrepancy, the paralegal may write to the stock transfer agent to verify the decedent's holdings as well as to determine whether any stock splits or stock dividends have been declared that may affect the decedent's holdings. Stock valuation services also provide information concerning mergers, stock splits, and stock dividends. If no information about the corporation can be obtained from these sources, the corporation may no longer exist; the paralegal may write to the appropriate secretary of state to determine the corporation's status.

Life Insurance Proceeds and Policies. After the attorney examines all life insurance policies to determine the beneficiary, the paralegal should file a claim on behalf of the estate (if the estate is beneficiary), obtaining the appropriate claim form directly from the insurance company. (For collection of proceeds on behalf of beneficiaries other than the estate, see Chapter 4.) If the decedent owned life insurance on the life of another person, the policy is part of the probate estate. The paralegal should request the insurance company to provide the appropriate forms to change ownership of the policies.

Real Property. If it is believed that the decedent owned real property as yet unaccounted for, the paralegal should employ a title company to conduct a search among the records in the county where the property might be located. For each parcel of real property owned by the decedent, the paralegal should obtain the following items as applicable for the attorney to examine:

1. Deeds
2. Title insurance policies
3. Fire insurance policies
4. Current title reports
5. Leases
6. Notes and deeds of trust
7. Tax bills
8. Contracts to sell
9. Agency agreements

Original documents should be kept in the estate's safe-deposit box or in the law firm's vault.

The personal representative must monitor real-property assets closely, because various important deadlines may be involved in managing these assets, including deadlines for mortgage payments, property-tax payments, and insurance payments. For rental property, additional dates may be important, including deadlines for payment of rent and lease termination or renewal dates. The paralegal or personal representative should notify the decedent's tenants to make payments to the personal representative and should arrange for the maintenance of the property. Costs for maintenance and repair are properly chargeable to the estate.

FOCUS: Where an asset of the estate is accompanied by a document of title, such as a deed, stock certificate, bill of sale, or other ownership certificate, it is not necessary to change the title from the decedent's name to the name of the personal representative. However, in the case of financial accounts with respect to which the personal representative intends to make withdrawals and deposits, the account should be transferred to the estate's name.

Tangible Personal Property. The paralegal should instruct the personal representative to collect and store the decedent's personal belongings, such as motor vehicles, furniture, clothing, and other household and personal items, until they can be sold or distributed. If the identity of the devisee is not in doubt, distribution can be made prior to closing the estate, as long as the property has not been set apart for the decedent's family and as long as it is clear that remaining assets are sufficient to satisfy all creditors and to make any required payments of the family allowance. A receipt should be obtained from the distributee and filed with the court either prior to or at the time a petition for an order of final distribution is filed.

PARKER ESTATE: Regarding Irene's personal tangible property, you will learn later in this chapter that in a special proceeding the court has determined that Irene's granddaughters (Sharon's daughters), Cindy and Deborah, are entitled to contents of the safe located in the basement of Irene's house. The safe contains items of jewelry—specifically, a pearl necklace and a pair of diamond earrings. Although the court will appoint an appraiser to determine the value of the jewelry, Ms. Cargis has advised Sharon to obtain an independent appraisal of the jewelry as well (see *Preparing and Filing the Inventory and Appraisement, Appraising the Estate's Assets*). In the event the jewelry's value is significant, distribution should be delayed until the extent of Irene's debts and taxes can be determined.

Sharon has estimated the total value of Irene's other tangible personal property (aside from her automobile) at $1,000. Because the value of this property is not significant, Ms. Cargis has advised Sharon to distribute the property in kind as she wishes under the general power of appointment conferred to her under Irene's holographic codicil, although distribution must wait until after appraisal by the court-appointed appraiser. Sharon has decided to divide the property between herself, Dennis, Susan, and Irene's sister Ruth, equally between herself, Dennis, and Susan, consistent with the terms of Irene's attested will, even though Sharon is not legally obligated to do so. Sharon will obtain receipts from these distributees to file with the court. Sharon estimates the total value of all remaining property (furniture, housewares, clothing, jewelry, and so forth), aside from Irene's automobile, at approximately $1,000. Ms. Cargis has advised Sharon either to liquidate the belongings at public auction or to arrange with Dennis and Susan for the division of this property between the three of them. Sharon has decided to arrange to meet Dennis and Susan at the house in order to divide the property among them; she will then sell the remainder at auction only if its value is substantial (which is unlikely). Sharon has also invited Irene's sister Ruth to meet with them at the house; even though Ruth is not entitled to share in the estate, Sharon has decided that Ruth should have the opportunity to select certain items that may hold sentimental value for her.

Although Dennis has expressed a particular interest in Irene's automobile, Ms. Cargis has advised Sharon to refrain from distributing this asset to Dennis as part of his share of the estate. Depending upon the extent of Irene's debts and of the expenses and costs of estate administration, the value of the automobile might exceed Dennis' rightful share of Irene's estate; moreover, Sharon may discover that sale of the automobile is necessary to pay all of Irene's debts and the costs of administration. Although Sharon would have the authority to take back possession from Dennis if necessary, there would be no assurance that the asset would be available later. Sharon has decided to sell the automobile to avoid continuing insurance payments and because the automobile is a depreciating asset. Written notice to interested persons of the intended sale is required under applicable law (see Exhibit 23 in the Parker file).

Other Assets. Collection of debts owed to the decedent is generally not a matter in which the probate paralegal assists, except to the extent of determining such debts. The attorney must determine whether the debt can and should be enforced and whether compromise or litigation may be appropriate. Business interests of the decedent must be evaluated by the attorney and the personal representative to determine whether the estate should sell or continue the business; valuation typically requires independent appraisal. Any interest of the decedent as a beneficiary of another decedent's estate or of an *inter vivos* or testamentary trust must be included in the probate estate. Contingent and other future interests may pose valuation problems that should be resolved by the attorney.

The attorney should also determine as promptly as possible whether an interest in a decedent's estate or trust should be disclaimed. A *disclaimer* by a beneficiary of an interest in the estate or trust of another is generally motivated by income-tax or inheritance-tax considerations. An effective disclaimer must be in writing and must either be submitted to the estate (or trustee of a trust) or filed with the court in which the estate proceedings are conducted, within the time period permitted under applicable law (typically nine months after the decedent's death).

Preparing and Filing the Inventory and Appraisement

An inventory of the decedent's assets must generally be filed with the court. To ensure that the inventory represents a complete and accurate picture of the decedent's estate at the time of death, the paralegal may be required to work with both independent and court-appointed appraisers to determine the value of certain assets. Preparing and processing the inventory, discussed in detail below, is one of the probate paralegal's primary functions.

In General. Assisting the attorney and the personal representative in preparing the inventory and appraisement is one of the probate paralegal's primary tasks. An inventory and appraisement (hereafter referred to simply as "inventory") must be filed with the court within a certain time period, as determined by statute, after appointment of the personal representative (three months under U.P.C. § 3-706). The inventory includes all *probate* assets but should include nonprobate assets only in states that levy an inheritance tax. Otherwise, including nonprobate assets in the inventory may be misleading to the beneficiaries and to the decedent's creditors and will result in accounting problems when a final account for the estate is prepared, as well as undermine the decedent's privacy respecting these assets, since the inventory is a matter of public record once it is filed with the court.

An inventory serves several useful purposes:

1. It assists the court in ensuring the proper administration of the estate.
2. It enables the court to determine attorney's and executor's fees, which are determined by the value of the estate assets.
3. It serves as a guide for the personal representative and the paralegal in preparing federal and state death tax returns.
4. It assists the paralegal in preparing the final accounting, since all assets included in the inventory must also appear in the final account.
5. It provides a source of information for the decedent's creditors and beneficiaries.

The paralegal should prepare the inventory and provide it to the personal representative as soon as possible to review and resolve any valuation problems. If the personal representative agrees that the inventory is complete and accurate, the paralegal should file it with the court and should mail copies to all interested persons who request it, as well as to the state inheritance-tax authorities as required. Under the U.P.C., the personal representative may choose either to file the inventory with the court or to send a copy to all interested persons. (See Exhibit 17 in the Parker file.)

Appraising the Estate's Assets. The inventory must indicate the fair market value of each asset as of the date of the decedent's death. The personal representative may employ qualified and disinterested appraisers to assist in ascertaining the value of any asset whose fair market value is in doubt. Assets that may require independent appraisal include real property, business assets, furniture, collectibles (antiques, art objects, stamp and coin collections), and jewelry. The cost of employing appraisers is an expense of administration.

Most states where supervised administration is the rule require the appraisal of nonliquid assets (assets other than cash, bank accounts, and publicly traded securities) by an appraiser appointed by the court. The appraiser's fees are determined by statute, either as a percentage of the value of the appraised assets or, more typically, as any reasonable fee within certain parameters. If the court has appointed an appraiser, the paralegal should first provide the inventory to the appraiser (completed except for values of those assets to be appraised by the referee), who will appraise the listed assets as required and submit the appraisal to the law firm. This appraisal should not be accepted blindly by the personal representative and the paralegal. The personal representative should determine independently the value of these assets, and significant discrepancies should be resolved prior to filing the inventory with the court.

 PRACTICE TIP: Fraudulent undervaluation of assets is all too common an occurrence, because undervaluation decreases death-tax and inheritance-tax liability. However, undervaluation also decreases attorney's fees and executor's fees, while increasing income-tax liability upon subsequent sale of an appreciating asset. Thus, undervaluation is often to little or no advantage, while it is ethically improper and illegal from a tax standpoint. The paralegal should record the deadline for filing the inventory and determine a realistic time schedule for obtaining, evaluating, and revising appraisals and for preparing and filing the inventory in a timely manner. The attorney should determine whether any delays in securing appraisals are likely and anticipate filing a request for an extension of time to file the inventory as the deadline approaches.

 PARKER ESTATE: In the Parker matter, the court's order for issuance of Letters of Administration (see Exhibit 13 in the Parker file) included an order appointing an appraiser for the purpose of determining the value of Irene's residence and tangible personal property. Sharon has obtained an independent appraisal at $500 for Irene's jewelry, which coincides with the probate referee's appraisal. Because the value of the jewelry is insignificant, Sharon will take possession of the jewelry on behalf of her daughters (Cindy and Deborah), since these devisees are minors. Sharon will sign a receipt for the jewelry, which will be filed with the court prior to or at the time the petition for an order of final distribution is filed.

Preparing the Inventory. It is typically the paralegal's job to prepare the inventory. The Preliminary Inventory may be used as a guide for this purpose. Many jurisdictions require no specific form for the inventory and appraisement. If permissible, however, the paralegal should adopt a form for the inventory and appraisement (as well as for the law firm's Preliminary Inventory) that resembles the schedules for the federal estate-tax return (see Chapter 7). This will facilitate the preparation of the estate-tax return if it is required. Assets should be described in reasonable detail—for example, bank-account locations and account numbers should be specified, and street addresses of real property should be indicated, although complete legal descriptions are unnecessary. Information regarding encumbrances, such as a mortgage, should be indicated with the description of the asset subject to the encumbrance. The paralegal must ensure that all assets properly included appear on the inventory. (The inventory for the estate of Irene Parker is included in the Parker file as Exhibit 17.)

Partial and Supplementary Inventories. The inventory must reflect a picture of the decedent's assets (except for nonprobate assets) *at the date of death.* Immediately upon appointment, however, the personal representative may begin to alter this picture by selling assets, by closing, transferring or merging accounts, and so forth. Thus, it may be advisable to prepare a *partial* *inventory* of certain assets before they are transformed in order to preserve this picture.

After the inventory is filed, the personal representative or the paralegal may discover assets that were not included in the inventory or may learn that the value or description indicated in the inventory for a particular asset is erroneous or misleading. In this event, the paralegal should assist the personal representative in preparing a *supplemental inventory* showing the new item or revised value as well as the appraiser or data relied on for any revised value. The supplementary inventory must be processed in the same manner as the original inventory.

ESTATE TRANSACTIONS

The personal representative acquires legal title to the decedent's assets and may deal with them as legal owner, subject to his or her fiduciary duty as well as to certain other limitations, as discussed in the following materials.

Sales of Estate Property

Estate property may be sold for a variety of different reasons:

1. The will may direct that particular property be sold.
2. Cash may be needed for a family allowance, to pay the decedent's debts, or to pay taxes.
3. Sale of a depreciating asset may be prudent to help preserve the estate.
4. The sale of certain property may be required to effect the proper distribution among the heirs or devisees in accordance with their proportionate interests, either under the decedent's will or under the laws of intestate succession.

The attorney and personal representative should determine jointly whether particular property should be sold and whether it would be more advantageous to sell the property by private sale or at a public auction. Either method is generally permitted, unless the decedent's will directs otherwise. As a general rule, however, only tangible personal property belonging to the decedent is sold at a public auction, while other property is sold privately. Additional bond may be required upon the sale of real property, because the value of the estate's personal property will increase as a result.

Under certain circumstances, sales of estate property require notice to interested persons and must be approved by the court before title in the property may be transferred to the purchaser. Circumstances dictating whether notice and court approval are required include:

1. Whether estate administration is subject to the court's continuing supervision
2. Whether the will requires it
3. The type of property sold (the sale of real property requires court approval unless the will indicates otherwise, while the sale of securities and perishable property does not)

4. The particular statutory requirements in the jurisdiction where the estate is administered

If required, notice must be given by publication and by writing to all persons properly requesting it. In addition, the property sold must first be appraised and included in the estate's inventory, so that the court can determine whether the amount paid is reasonable. The specific statutory requirements for sales of personal property may differ from those for sales of real property.

If court approval of a sale is required, the paralegal may expect to perform the following tasks:

1. Publish notice of the sale
2. Prepare and send written notices of the hearing to all interested persons requesting it
3. Prepare the petition for court approval
4. Prepare the order confirming the sale

If the sale involves real property, the paralegal may also be required to perform additional tasks:

1. Consult a title company to determine the status of title in the property
2. Assist the personal representative in determining and employing a broker
3. Prepare and file a petition (and court order) for execution of a listing agreement with a broker

Also, if the personal representative *sells* real property during the course of administration (rather than distributing the property in kind to a distributee), an *executor's deed* or *administrator's deed* will be required to complete the transfer of title. (Real-property interests may be transferred in kind to a distributee by delivering the deed to the distributee and recording a certified copy of the court order for final distribution in the county where the real property is located.)

PARKER ESTATE: In the Parker matter, Sharon has the authority as personal representative to sell the house, and she has decided to do so. Although Irene's attested will expressly permits any executor nominated in the will to sell estate property without court approval, Sharon is not authorized to sell the house without court approval because she is not a named executor. Ms. Cargis anticipates no problem in obtaining court approval, as long as the sale price is not significantly below the appraised value of the property. If Irene had left this asset to someone other than Sharon, however, the court would carefully examine whether the sale was necessary. (The problem of disposing of estate property that is included as a specific gift under the decedent's will is addressed later in this chapter and in Chapter 8.)

Borrowing Money

As an alternative to selling estate property to satisfy debts, the personal representative may wish to borrow money. As with estate sales, the personal representative might be authorized, either under the decedent's will or by statute, to do so without court approval. However, if approval is required, a petition must be filed showing the purpose of the loan and the advantage to the estate of securing the loan over some other course of action. If the loan is secured by estate property, a detailed description of the property must be included (if the property is included in the inventory, referring to the inventory may be sufficient). As in the case of a sale of real property, additional bond may be required when borrowing money, since the value of the estate's personal property will increase as a result.

 PRACTICE TIP: If real property of the estate is used to secure a loan, a document evidencing the security interest of the lender (such as a deed of trust) must be executed and recorded by the personal representative. It is generally the paralegal's function to prepare the necessary document, which should state that it is executed by authority of a court order as well as indicate the date of the order.

Self-Dealing

In a variety of situations, the personal representative may wish to enter into a transaction with the estate—for example, to purchase an asset from or loan money to the estate. Since the personal representative may benefit personally from such a transaction, a conflict arises between the interests of the estate and those of the personal representative. To protect the estate's heirs, devisees, and creditors, the personal representative may be required to obtain court approval for the transaction, although most states follow the U.P.C. approach illustrated in Figure 6-1.

FIGURE 6-1   U.P.C. § 3-713 (SALE, ENCUMBRANCE OR TRANSACTION INVOLVING CONFLICT OF INTEREST; VOIDABLE; EXCEPTION)

> Any sale or encumbrance to the personal representative, his spouse, agent or attorney, or any corporation or trust in which he has a substantial beneficial interest, or any transaction which is affected by a substantial conflict of interest on the part of the personal representative, is voidable by any person interested in the estate except one who has consented after fair disclosure, unless (1) the will or a contract entered into by the decedent expressly authorized the transaction; or (2) the transaction is approved by the Court after notice to interested persons.

Even if a provision such as U.P.C. § 3-713 applies, the attorney is likely to advise the personal representative to disclose any proposed transaction of this nature to interested persons in order to guard against a claim that the transaction was improper.

Co-representatives

The decedent's will may require the appointment of two or more co-representatives. Under the U.P.C., co-representatives must concur with respect to transactions and all other acts connected with the administration of the estate and distribution of the estate, except:

1. As otherwise provided in the will
2. If concurrence of all co-representatives cannot be obtained in the time reasonably available for emergency action necessary to preserve the estate
3. When a co-representative has been delegated to act for the others (U.P.C. § 3-717)

In many states, however, acts performed in the regular course of administration by one are deemed to be acts of all co-representatives. Whether a particular act is in the "regular course of administration" is determined in each state adopting this view by judicial decision rather than by statute. In general, each co-representative is responsible only for his or her own acts, and so liability for breach of fiduciary duty is separate and not joint.

FAMILY ALLOWANCES, PROBATE HOMESTEADS, AND EXEMPT PROPERTY

Statutes in every state make some provision to protect the decedent's family against impoverishment and against the decedent's creditors. One or more of the following provisions exist in each state (see, e.g., U.P.C. § 2-401, *et seq.*):

1. A family allowance
2. Probate homestead rights
3. Rights to set apart certain personal property

The Family Allowance

The purpose of a family allowance is to meet the continuing financial needs of the decedent's surviving spouse and minor children during estate administration, as an extension of the decedent's support obligation. In some states, the decedent's dependent adult children and parents may also receive an allowance. Remarriage of the surviving spouse terminates a right to an allowance but does not terminate the rights of the decedent's minor children to an allowance. Payment of a family allowance is given priority over all other claims to the estate, except for those relating to funeral expenses, expenses of administration, probate homestead rights, and rights to exempt personal property. However, once the family allowance is paid, the property is subject to existing liens and contractual rights of the decedent's creditors. If the estate is insolvent, payments for a family allowance may nevertheless be made, although under a typical statute the payments must discontinue in this case after one year has passed since the decedent's death. Otherwise, a family allowance may be paid until the estate is closed. Family-allowance payments are not chargeable against the recipient's eventual share of the decedent's testate or intestate estate.

In some states, the surviving spouse is entitled to an allowance as a matter of right, regardless of his or her needs, while in other states an allowance may be granted or denied at the court's discretion. If court approval is not required, notice is generally not required. If court approval is required, the person seeking an allowance (rather than the personal representative) must file a petition with the court within a reasonable time after the decedent's death. There is usually no difficulty obtaining court approval for a reasonable allowance to the surviving spouse and/or minor children. However, if the estate is insolvent and the devisees under the decedent's will are persons other than those seeking an allowance, the court will carefully scrutinize the petition to determine the need for the allowance.

If the decedent left a valid will, the will may designate which assets should be used to pay the allowance; if not, allowance payments are chargeable first against the residue of the estate. Specific gifts under the decedent's will should not be resorted to unless all other estate assets (other than homestead property and exempt personal property) have been exhausted. Income should be used before resorting to principal, in order to preserve the estate to the extent possible.

PRACTICE TIP: The attorney should determine the need for an allowance, those family members entitled to the allowance, and whether court approval is required. If approval is required, the paralegal should consult the attorney to determine what supporting statements and documents should be included in the petition to ensure that the court approves the allowance for the amount requested. If the surviving spouse is the petitioner but is not a devisee, the law firm may be unable to assist him or her in obtaining a family allowance, because of conflict of interest.

Probate Homesteads

In nearly all states, constitutional or statutory **probate homestead** rights provide additional security to the surviving spouse and minor children. A probate homestead is distinct and separate from a family allowance and from the family's rights respecting exempt personal property. A probate homestead must also be distinguished from the more common type of "homestead," which protects *any* person from losing ownership and possession in his or her residence to creditors.

Under a typical probate-homestead statute, the family residence, if part of the decedent's probate estate or acquired with estate assets, may be set apart and protected from all claims against the estate, although the spouse must first file a petition with the court. Notice of a petition to set apart a probate homestead is generally not required, since a homestead claim is a matter of right and is not subject to the court's discretion. Probate-homestead rights typically extend for the life of the surviving spouse. However, homestead protection for minor children terminates when they reach the age of majority.

In some states, homestead protection may also extend to other property. Under U.P.C. § 2-401, the decedent's surviving spouse and minor children are entitled to a total of $5,000 as a *homestead allowance.* This allowance is exempt from and has priority over all claims against the estate and is not chargeable against the recipients' shares in the estate (including the surviving spouse's elective share).

Exempt Personal Property

After the inventory is filed, upon petition by the spouse, the court may set apart certain tangible personal property, such as furniture, clothing, automobiles, and other household necessities, for the spouse and minor children exempt from all claims against the estate. As with a family allowance and probate homestead, this measure of protection is available whether or not the decedent's spouse and children are devisees under the decedent's will. Under the U.P.C., the right to set apart personal property is in addition to the right to a homestead allowance, and exempt personal property is limited to $3,500 in net value (U.P.C. § 2-402).

PAYMENT OF THE DECEDENT'S DEBTS

One of the purposes of supervised estate administration is to protect the decedent's creditors by affording them an opportunity to collect their debts from the estate prior to distribution of the remaining estate to the decedent's heirs and devisees. To facilitate the settlement and distribution of the estate, nearly all states impose, under what are generally referred to as "nonclaim" statutes, certain time limits for the decedent's creditors to assert their claims after proper notice or be barred forever (although other remedies might be available to creditors under certain circumstances). The paralegal assists the personal representative in notifying the decedent's creditors, in monitoring the status of each of the decedent's debts, and in processing a creditor's claim after it has been filed. Deadlines and procedures are important in the area of creditors' claims, and statutes and local rules vary somewhat in these respects.

Notice to Creditors

The decedent's creditors have a certain period of time after being given proper notice of the administration of the estate to present their claims to the personal representative (and/or file a claim with the court). The estate cannot be closed until the time period allowed for creditors to present claims has passed. Accordingly, in order to move the estate toward final distribution and closing as quickly as possible, the paralegal should ensure that all appropriate notices are provided expediently.

Notice by Publication. The purpose of notice to creditors by publication is to establish a "claim period"—typically four months in duration—upon which several key deadlines relating to creditors' claims are based. In some states, notice to creditors by publication is satisfied by publication of the notice of the hearing on the petition to administer the estate, and the claim period begins to run upon appointment of the personal representative. In other states (and under the U.P.C.), notice to creditors by publication is a separate matter required after the personal representative is appointed. In the latter situation, publication requirements are similar to those regarding the petition to administer the estate.

Written Notice. Known and "reasonably ascertainable" potential creditors who are unlikely to receive *actual* notice as a result of publication—for example, where the creditor resides (in the case of a potential individual creditor) or is engaged in business (in the case of a potential business creditor) in another state—may be entitled to written notice of the administration of the estate. In many states now, written notice must be given to these potential creditors either within the claim period or within a certain time period—typically 30 days—after the personal representative discovers the potential creditor, whichever occurs later, and the personal representative may be held personally liable for failure to take reasonable steps to ascertain and notify creditors in a timely fashion. The requirements of the form and content of written notice are the same as those for notice by publication.

 PRACTICE TIP: Either the paralegal or the personal representative should conduct a thorough search of the decedent's papers as well as inquire among the decedent's family, friends, and business associates for this purpose. The paralegal should also check the court index of the county where the decedent resided and any county where the decedent owned real property to determine whether the decedent was named as a defendant in any pending law suit there. The paralegal should establish a separate file for creditors' claims and keep on the inside of the file cover an updated list of all potential creditors, noting the current status of their claims. As further protection from liability, the personal representative and the paralegal should record in this file all steps taken to ascertain creditors, and when the right of a "potential creditor" to receive written notice is in doubt, the personal representative should send the notice.

 PARKER ESTATE: In the Parker matter, under applicable law, publication of the notice of hearing to administer the estate also served as notice to creditors, and the four-month claim period began when Letters of Administration were issued to Sharon. Applicable law also requires written notice to *all* potential creditors who are known or reasonably ascertainable to Sharon. After a reasonably diligent search, only one potential creditor has been identified—specifically, First National Bank and Trust (the lender who provided refinancing for Irene's house). Sharon must provide written notice to this creditor (see Exhibit 18 in the Parker file).

Filing of Claims by Creditors

Creditors must present their claims within a certain time period after notice by publication or after written notice is provided (whichever occurs later); a statute of limitations also limits the time period within which claims may be asserted. However, late claims may be allowed under some circumstances. Specific procedures, limitations, and exemptions for filing creditors' claims are examined below.

Filing Procedures. To assert a claim against the decedent's estate, a creditor of the decedent must either present a creditor's claim to the personal representative or file a claim with the court, or possibly both, depending upon applicable law. The personal representative's attorney has the authority to receive claims on behalf of the personal representative. Although the claim need not be in any particular form, it must state the nature and amount of the claim as well as provide enough additional information to enable the personal representative to act advisably on it. If the claim is based upon a written contract or note, a copy of the contract or note must generally be attached to the claim. Claims must be signed and verified by the claimant. (See Exhibit 19 in the Parker file.)

The decedent's creditors must meet certain deadlines in filing their claims (see Figure 6-2). Generally speaking, a creditor must file a claim either within the claim period or within a certain time period—typically 30 or 60 days—after written notice is provided by the personal representative. Also, a statute of limitations bars any creditor of a decedent from asserting a claim against either the estate, the personal representative, or the heirs and devisees after a certain period of time (typically one year) has passed since the decedent's death. However, this statute of limitations is tolled from the time a creditor files a claim until such time that the claim is rejected, if at all. Nonclaim statutes in some states allow a creditor to present a late claim under special circumstances—for example, where the creditor was out of the state during the entire claim period and did not have knowledge of the administration of the estate.

An Illustrative Example. How these various deadlines come into play can best be understood by example. Assume that just prior to Richard's death, he purchased a product from DirectShop, Inc., a mail-order merchandise company located in another state. Richard died on 2/20, without having paid for the product. Letters Testamentary for the administration of his estate were issued to Stephanie on 4/15. The first notice to creditors by publication occurred on 5/1. Applicable law provides for a four-month claim period as well as a one-year statute of limitations, and the personal representative has 30 days after learning of a potential creditor to provide written notice, while a potential creditor has 30 days after written notice is provided to file a claim. Examine Figure 6-2 in light of the following alternative scenarios involving Richard's estate:

*SCENARIO 1: Stephanie was aware even prior to Richard's death that Richard had purchased the product from DirectShop and was aware that Richard had not paid for the product. **Result**: Stephanie must provide written notice to DirectShop by 9/1 (four months after notice by publication). Assuming notice is provided by 8/1 (see Figure 6-2), DirectShop has until 9/1 to file a claim. However, if Stephanie delays until after 8/1 in providing written notice, Direct-Shop has until 30 days after written notice to file its claim, even though the claim will be filed after 9/1—i.e., after the four-month period for filing claims has expired.*

FIGURE 6-2   TIME PERIOD FOR PRESENTING A CREDITOR'S CLAIM

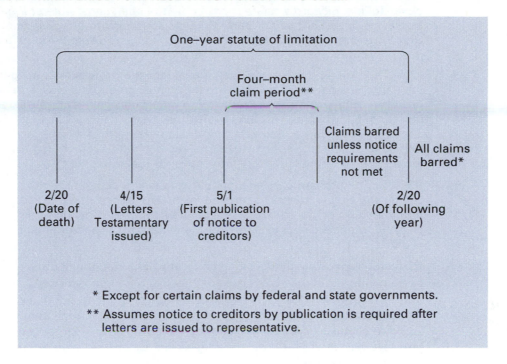

SCENARIO 2: On 9/20, Stephanie receives a "Notice of Payment Due" addressed to Richard from DirectShop for the product that Richard apparently had purchased but not paid for. Stephanie had conducted a reasonably diligent search for potential creditors and had no previous knowledge of DirectShop's claim. **Result:** Stephanie must provide written notice to DirectShop, Inc., by 9/20 (i.e., within 30 days after discovering the potential claim). DirectShop then has 30 days—i.e., until 10/20—in which to file a claim, even though the four-month period for filing claims has expired.

SCENARIO 3: Stephanie has conducted a reasonably diligent search for potential creditors and has no knowledge of this potential creditor. DirectShop makes no attempt to notify Richard of its potential claim. **Result:** Stephanie is not required to provide written notice to DirectShop, Inc., since she did not discover the potential claim, despite taking reasonably diligent steps to do so. Notice by publication serves to bar any claim by DirectShop presented after 9/1, unless (depending upon applicable law) it can show to the court that it had no actual knowledge within the claim period of the administration of the estate.

SCENARIO 4: Assume the same facts as in Scenario 2, except that Stephanie takes no action to provide written notice to DirectShop, in the hope that the company will make no further attempt to collect the debt allegedly owed by the decedent. As of 2/20 of the year following Richard's death, DirectShop has made no further attempt to collect the debt. **Result:** Regardless of whether

Stephanie has failed to provide adequate notice to DirectShop, DirectShop's claim against Richard's estate is barred by the one-year statute of limitations. However, DirectShop is not barred by this statute from bringing suit against Stephanie personally for failing to provide notice to DirectShop as a known potential creditor doing business outside of the state.

PRACTICE TIP: The foregoing scenarios suggest a professional obligation on the part of the paralegal to ensure that potential creditors are ascertained and provided with written notice as soon as possible; delays might extend the period for filing claims, resulting in an unnecessary delay in closing the estate. Scenario 4 suggests a potential ethical dilemma—if the law firm is aware of a potential creditor to whom the personal representative refuses to provide written notice, how should the law firm respond? (See Chapter 12.)

FOCUS: The probate paralegal should establish a separate file for creditors' claims and should maintain complete records of efforts made to ascertain and notify the decedent's creditors. The paralegal must closely monitor the status of each potential claim, since the estate cannot be closed until all claims are settled.

Claims Arising after the Decedent's Death. The deadlines discussed above pertain only to claims arising *before* the death of the decedent, including debts that are not yet due (unmatured debts), contingent debts, and unliquidated (disputed) debts (see, e.g., U.P.C. § 3-803[a]). The deadlines do not apply to claims against the decedent's estate or against the personal representative arising *at or after* the decedent's death (with the exception of claims for funeral expenses, in many states). Claims arising after the decedent's death include such claims as:

1. Claims for services rendered to the estate by the estate's attorney, accountant, or personal representative
2. Claims arising from a contract entered into by the personal representative in the regular course of estate administration
3. Tort claims against the personal representative for mismanagement of the estate or breach of other fiduciary duties

Such claims may either be subject to different deadlines or to other statutes of limitation, depending upon the type of claim involved (see, e.g., U.P.C. § 3-803[c],[d]).

Debts for Which No Creditor's Claim Is Required. Certain claims may be preserved without presenting a creditor's claim. Although statutes vary widely in this area and may differ from the U.P.C., the most common examples include:

1. Claims for which a civil law suit has been commenced
2. Claims by the state and federal governments
3. Secured claims
4. Claims covered by insurance
5. Claims based upon community debts—that is, debts incurred by both spouses

Handling Creditors' Claims

For each claim filed, the attorney must determine whether to allow the claim, reject it, or take some other appropriate action. As a general rule, the personal representative's allowance, rejection, or compromise of a claim is subject to the court's approval, although in some states (and under the U.P.C.) the personal representative may handle creditors' claims without court approval, except that all claims by the personal representative or by the personal representative's attorney must be approved by the court before they will be allowed.

Claims are usually rejected either because they are filed late or because the attorney determines that the debt is not legally enforceable, but not merely because the claim is defective in some way. A claim may be defective in any number of different ways; for example, a form may have been used that is unacceptable to the court, the creditor's signature may be missing, or additional documents or statements may be needed to substantiate the claim. If the defect is minor, the personal representative may choose to waive the defect; otherwise, the paralegal should send a letter to the claimant identifying the defect and requesting that the defect be corrected. It may also be appropriate to return the claim form to the claimant (for example, where the claimant's signature is missing). If the claimant has made a written demand for payment of a debt on the estate, the personal representative may elect to treat the demand as a claim.

Whether the attorney has decided to allow or reject the claim, the paralegal should prepare an appropriate form (Notice of Allowance or Rejection of Creditor's Claim) for the personal representative's signature and mail or deliver to the claimant a copy of the notice with a copy of the claim attached. A proof-of-service form should be completed at this time. If court approval is required or if the claim is disputed, the original notice and proof-of-service should be filed with the court. Otherwise, local court rules vary as to whether notices of approval or rejection must be filed with the court. By allowing a claim, the personal representative need not (and in many cases should not) pay the creditor at the same time (see *Payment of Allowed Claims*). If a controversy arises over a rejected claim and the parties cannot resolve their differences through negotiation and compromise, a summary proceeding in the probate court may be available to resolve the dispute quickly and informally; otherwise, the creditor may initiate a civil law suit.

 PARKER ESTATE: Sharon has advanced a portion of her own funds to pay for Irene's funeral expenses and is entitled to reimbursement. Even though the claim arose after Irene's death, applicable law requires that the personal representative file a claim for all funds advanced to the estate for this purpose. Accordingly, Sharon must present a claim. She cannot pay the claim until she obtains the court's approval, since she is acting as personal representative.

Payment of Allowed Claims

Certain debts must be given priority in the event that the estate is insolvent—that is, if the estate assets are insufficient to pay all of the decedent's debts. The order of priority for payment is determined by statute. Typically, funeral expenses and costs and expenses of administration are given first priority, followed by debts and taxes with preference under federal law. Also, judgment creditors and secured creditors are usually given priority over other creditors. In some states, as a separate matter, some debts must be paid as soon as the personal representative has sufficient funds, as long as the remaining assets are sufficient to pay all higher-priority debts.

Although the personal representative may pay allowed claims before expiration of the four-month claim period, this is generally not recommended, since the personal representative may be held liable to a high-priority creditor if payment to a lower-priority creditor resulted in insufficient assets to pay the higher-priority creditor (see, e.g., U.P.C. §§ 3-807, 808). If the personal representative is ready to close the estate and certain debts are still owing but are not yet due, the court may conduct a special proceeding on petition of either the personal representative or the creditor to determine arrangements for payment (see U.P.C. § 3-810).

 PRACTICE TIP: When an allowed claim is paid in full, the paralegal should request the creditor to withdraw any demand for special notice that may have been previously made. Also, some claimants may not know the precise amount of their claim at the time of filing—for example, providers of medical services may not know what portion of their fees will be paid by insurers. Such claimants typically do not amend their claims as they are paid from other sources. Thus, prior to instructing the personal representative to pay any such claim, the paralegal should contact the claimant to confirm the amount of the claim. Finally, the paralegal should check whether interest is payable on a claim, either by written contract or by statute. For example, interest may be payable by statute once payment of the claim is approved by the court. Also, funeral expenses typically bear interest after a certain number of days following the decedent's death.

The Decedent's Debts and Nonprobate Assets

As demonstrated in the foregoing materials, estate administration protects the decedent's creditors by affording them a clear opportunity to secure payment prior to distribution of the estate. Estate administration also serves the interests of the decedent's heirs and devisees by establishing a clear and relatively short time period during which the decedent's creditors must assert their claims. However, as discussed in Chapter 4, all or part of the decedent's property might be transferred outside of probate. The personal representative (if any) has no authority to resort to nonprobate property to pay the decedent's debts. Accordingly, the decedent's creditors cannot ''reach'' nonprobate assets by filing a claim with the estate. Although other remedies may be available to the decedent's creditors where the estate is insolvent or where there is no probate estate, discussion of such remedies is beyond the scope of this text and is more properly covered in a debtor-creditor text.

SPECIAL PROCEEDINGS IN PROBATE

Particular circumstances during estate administration may require one or more special proceedings. Appointment of a successor representative may be required if the original representative fails to complete the duties of the office. Ancillary administration may be required for the administration of assets located in another state. Other special proceedings in probate might include

1. Appointment of a trustee or guardian
2. Proceedings to resolve title disputes
3. A petition to determine heirship
4. A petition for instructions

Appointment of Successor Representatives

In the event that appointment of the original personal representative is terminated (due to death, disability, removal, or resignation), a successor personal representative must be appointed to perform the remaining duties of the office. Wills typically nominate two or three alternate executors to serve successively in the order listed. A successor representative is referred to specifically in many states as an **administrator D.B.N.** or *de bonis non* (*de bonis non* means "of goods not administered").

The procedure for appointment of a successor is generally the same as for the initial personal representative. However, most of the statements included in the petition for appointment of the initial personal representative are not required; the petition for appointment of a successor typically need only state the right of the petitioner to appointment as successor and the reason why appointment of a successor is necessary.

Ancillary Administration

Recall from Chapter 5 that while the place of the decedent's domicile at the time of death is the proper *venue* for testacy proceedings, the proper venue for administration of the decedent's assets is the place where the assets are located. Accordingly, property located in a nondomiciliary state is subject to ancillary administration. The decedent's creditors may assert their claims in either the domiciliary or ancillary estate, and a family allowance may be paid out of either estate as well.

Priority for appointment of an ancillary administrator may differ from priority for appointment of a domiciliary personal representative. Many states permit the domiciliary representative to serve also as ancillary administrator, and some states give the domiciliary personal representative priority for appointment (see, e.g., U.P.C. § 4-204). Otherwise, certain heirs or devisees of the decedent are typically given priority.

In most respects, ancillary administration is no different from domiciliary administration. However, while the law of the decedent's domicile governs the distribution of the ancillary estate, the law of the ancillary state governs the payment of the decedent's debts out of the ancillary property as well as governs matters regarding administration of the estate (unless the decedent's will specifies otherwise). In some states, an ancillary administrator may not be appointed unless and until a domiciliary estate is established; other states, however, do not follow this rule. If a domiciliary representative has been appointed, a certified copy of the Letters Testamentary or Letters of Administration, along with a certified copy of the decedent's will, if any, must be filed with the court in the ancillary state before an ancillary administrator can be appointed.

The ancillary administrator must collect and take inventory of all of the decedent's assets located in that state, making payment of allowed claims out of the estate. As for distribution of the remaining estate, the court generally has discretion as to whether the property should be distributed directly to the decedent's heirs and devisees or should be delivered to the domiciliary representative (if any) for distribution. In any event, the domiciliary personal representative's final account to the court must include all assets administered in ancillary proceedings. The domiciliary estate cannot be closed until the ancillary administrator is relieved of his or her duties, since estate tax liability cannot be determined until all of the decedent's property, wherever located, is accounted for by the personal representative.

 PRACTICE TIP: The paralegal should determine as soon as possible whether ancillary administration is required and begin making arrangements for ancillary administration even before the domiciliary representative is appointed to ensure that delays in closing the estate are minimized.

Heirship Proceedings

In many cases, the proper distribution of an estate, either under the laws of intestate succession or under the terms of the will, is in doubt or is disputed. Such issues may be resolved by way of one of three different proceedings:

1. Some courts permit a petitioner in *testacy proceedings*—for example, a proceeding for probate of the decedent's will or for determination of intestacy—to request that dispositive issues be settled during the testacy proceedings. Local court rules vary as to whether the court will hear these matters at the same time.

2. When the estate is in a position to be closed, the personal representative in supervised administration must prepare and file with the court a *petition for order of final distribution.* The personal representative may include in the petition a request that the court rule on

certain dispositive issues and include the rulings in the order of distribution.

3. As a third alternative, special *heirship proceedings* may be initiated, either by the personal representative or by any interested person, at any time prior to the court's order of final distribution. Notice must be provided to all interested persons, who must be afforded an adequate opportunity to appear in the proceedings. Where a party other than the petitioner appears, the proceeding becomes adversarial in nature, as in the case of a will contest. The court will typically determine issues of both law and fact, particularly with respect to the construction and interpretation of provisions in the decedent's will. (Problems of construction and interpretation of wills are discussed in detail in Chapter 8.)

 PARKER ESTATE: In the Parker matter, Irene's will and holographic codicil present several issues concerning the proper distribution of her estate. Local court rules do not permit dispositive issues to be determined during testacy proceedings. Ms. Cargis has decided to initiate heirship proceedings as soon as practicable after Sharon's appointment, so that Sharon can deal properly with Irene's personal belongings in order to prepare the house for sale. (The petition, notice of hearing, and court order are included in the Parker file as Exhibits 20, 21, and 22.)

Other Special Proceedings

A variety of other matters arising during the course of administration may require special proceedings. Some of the more commonly occurring such matters include the following:

- If the decedent's will establishes a testamentary trust, a court proceeding is required to establish the trust and appoint a trustee.
- If a portion of the decedent's estate passes outright to a person who is legally incompetent (a minor or incapacitated adult), a court proceeding is required to give another person the legal authority as guardian (or conservator) to manage and deal with the inheritance on behalf of the heir or devisee (see Chapter 11).
- The decedent may have held title to or possession of property claimed by another or, conversely, may have a claim of an interest in the property of another. Either the personal representative or the other interested party may petition the court to determine who is entitled to the property. If the personal representative agrees that the claim of another is valid, a petition is nevertheless required.
- The personal representative may petition the court at any time, whether or not the estate is administered under the court's continued supervision, to instruct the personal representative in any matter or to approve any action considered or taken by the personal representative. As a general rule, transactions involving large sums

or actions that raise complex legal issues call for prior petition to the court for instructions.

Paralegal Assignment 6

Recall that Ms. Cargis has directed you to assist in the following matters relating to the administration of Irene Parker's estate: (1) providing notice as required to Irene's potential creditors; (2) preparing and filing the inventory and appraisement; and (3) preparing and filing the documents necessary to obtain court approval of the sale of Irene's house. The other paralegal has assisted in the heirship proceedings.

Under applicable law, publication of notice of the hearing on the petition to administer the estate also served as notice by publication to creditors. Applicable law requires written notice (see Exhibit 18 of the Parker file) to all potential creditors who are known or reasonably ascertainable by Sharon; Irene's only known creditor is First National Bank and Trust, the lender that provided refinancing for Irene's house. Since administration of Irene's estate is supervised by the court, Dennis Parker will receive notice of all transactions, petitions, and so forth that may affect his interest as an heir and devisee. Thus, his attorney has decided that it is unnecessary to submit a demand for special notice of estate proceedings in order to protect Dennis' interests.

Applicable law requires Sharon to file the inventory and appraisement with the court (Exhibit 17 of the Parker file). The court-appointed appraiser has appraised Irene's residence but is authorized to accept Sharon's independent appraisal of Irene's tangible personal property. Sharon has accepted the appraisal of the residence and has submitted it to the court.

With respect to the heirship proceedings, no other party appeared, and the court has ruled as follows: (1) Irene's granddaughters Cindy and Deborah are entitled to share equally in the contents of Irene's safe; (2) Irene's holographic codicil confers upon Sharon a general power of appointment with respect to Irene's *tangible* personal property (except for the contents of the safe), but not with respect to Irene's other assets; and (3) the last two sentences of the holographic codicil are insufficient to establish an intent on Irene's part to create a testamentary trust for the benefit of Irene's grandchildren. (See Exhibits 20, 21, and 22 in the Parker file.)

Sharon has entered into a written agreement for the sale of Irene's home for an amount above the appraised value of the property, and a deposit has been placed into escrow. Under the terms of the agreement, the sale must be approved by the court before escrow can close and title can be transferred to the buyer. The small gain resulting from the sale will be reflected in the final account (see Chapter 8). An administrator's deed (Exhibit 27 of the Parker file) will be executed by Sharon and will be recorded, along with the court order approving the sale, with the recorder's office in the county where the residence is located. Sharon will file additional bond to reflect the increase in personal assets of the estate resulting from the sale of the residence. (The petition, notice of hearing, and court order confirming the sale of Irene Parker's residence are included in the Parker file as Exhibits 24, 25, and 26, respectively.)

Irene's jewelry has been appraised and its value is only $500; accordingly, Sharon has distributed the jewelry to Cindy and Deborah; a receipt signed by Sharon on behalf of her minor children has been filed with the court. After a notice of proposed action to all interested persons (Exhibit 23 of the Parker file), Sharon has sold Irene's automobile at a price of $2,050, which is $50 below wholesale "blue-book" value; the loss from the sale will be reflected in the final account (see Chapter 8). Sharon has distributed the remaining tangible personal property among Dennis, Susan, Ruth, and herself, pursuant to the general power of appointment conferred upon her under the terms of Irene's holographic codicil; receipts have been obtained from all distributees and have been filed with the court. Table 6-1 shows a summary of the administration transactions.

TABLE 6-1   PARKER ESTATE—SUMMARY OF TRANSACTIONS DURING ADMINISTRATION

Asset	Inventory Value	Activity during Administration
Real property (residence) ■ 6704 Renault Street, Carson, California	$220,000.00 Encumbrance: $64,730	■ Sold at private sale ■ Sale confirmed by court order ■ Sale price: $227,500.00 ■ Gain on sale after commission and expenses: $1,122.00
Checking Account ■ Joint tenancy for convenience only ■ First National Bank & Trust	$1,122.00	■ Depleted to pay for funeral/burial expenses ■ Account closed
Passbook savings account ■ First National Bank & Trust	$6,023.00	■ Account maintained and transferred to estate's name ■ Proceeds from sale of residence and automobile deposited in account
Certificate of Deposit ■ Southern California Savings & Loan Association ■ 5-year term; matures on 5/5/95	$21,325.00	■ No activity ■ Distributed in kind at final distribution to avoid penalty for early withdrawal
1985 Buick LeSabre automobile	$2,100.00	■ Sold at private sale for $2,050 after notice of proposed action to interested persons ■ Proceeds deposited in estate accounts
Contents of safe (jewelry) in basement of house	$500.00	■ Distributed to Sharon on behalf of minor devisees (Cindy and Deborah) ■ Receipt filed with court
Furniture, household goods, personal effects	$500.00	■ Distributed to Sharon, Dennis, Susan, and Ruth, under Sharon's general power of appointment conferred by holograph ■ Receipts obtained and filed with court
Life insurance policy ■ Metropolitan Life Insurance Co. ■ Beneficiary: Cindy Madson	$50,000.00 (Not included in inventory)	■ Nonprobate asset

7 TAXATION OF DECEDENTS' ESTATES

Paralegal Assignment 7

In the Parker matter, because the value of Irene's estate is modest, no death taxes will be owing. However, certain other taxes are of concern, including: (1) federal and state income taxes for income to Irene Parker during the final year of her life and (2) federal income taxes for income to Irene's probate estate. Sharon plans to seek the assistance of a certified public accountant to prepare these tax returns. However, according to Ms. Cargis, the law firm should in all cases make a preliminary determination as to (1) what tax returns might be required, (2) what types of taxes might be owing, and (3) when these returns and taxes are due. She has asked you to develop a checklist of federal tax forms and deadlines for this purpose.

INTRODUCTION

During the initial probate interview, one of the first concerns often expressed by the decedent's family involves the payment of taxes. Most people are unfamiliar with the subject of death taxes, and misconceptions are quite common in this area. One of the probate paralegal's important functions is to assist in the preparation and filing of various tax forms. Almost invariably, final federal and state income-tax returns must be filed on behalf of the decedent. In many cases, the probate estate is also liable for income taxes as a separate tax-paying entity. Federal estate taxes may be owed by certain large estates, and many states impose their own estate tax or inheritance tax (a tax on the beneficiaries of the estate). Claims by the federal and state government for taxes have priority over all other claims to the estate, except for claims resulting from:

1. Probate homestead rights
2. Rights to exempt personal property
3. Funeral expenses
4. Expenses of administration

With the exception of state inheritance taxes, these taxes are levied against the decedent's estate rather than against the distributees of the decedent's estate. The decedent's will (or trust), if any, may specify which assets should be applied first toward payment of taxes (as well as other claims)—for example, out of the residue of the estate. Otherwise, this matter is governed by statute.

ALLOCATION OF RESPONSIBILITIES

The personal representative (if any) assumes ultimate responsibility for filing all tax returns as required by law and for payment of death taxes as well as income taxes on behalf of the decedent and the estate. The personal representative of an insolvent estate is personally responsible for any tax liability of the decedent or of the estate if, before distribution of the estate's assets and before being discharged from duties, he or she had notice of such tax obligations or had failed to exercise due care in determining whether such obligations existed. In most cases, the law firm assists the personal representative in determining tax liability and filing the necessary returns. In fact, in many cases the law firm may be professionally obligated to do so (see Chapter 12). Tax issues relating to decedents are often quite complex, and competent handling of them frequently requires specialized knowledge. Accordingly, many lawyers prefer to employ an accountant to handle all tax matters relating to decedents' estates. Other lawyers, however, particularly those who specialize in estate planning and probate law, are sufficiently competent in this area to handle most of these matters themselves, employing accountants only when significant problems or complex tax issues arise. In any event, the personal representative may employ an accountant as a reasonable expense of administration.

The discussion in this chapter assumes that the law firm assists the personal representative in preparing all required tax returns, in which event the paralegal may expect to perform a variety of functions:

1. Respond to all routine questions by the personal representative in this area
2. Monitor the progress in preparation of tax returns in order to ensure that filing deadlines are met
3. Assemble the information needed to prepare the necessary tax forms
4. Assist in the preparation and filing of all required tax forms

When assisting in preparing tax forms, the paralegal must be extremely cautious to perform only those tasks that he or she has been thoroughly trained to perform and that do not involve specialized knowledge or judgment calls. Although this advice holds true for any task performed by the paralegal, it is perhaps most important in the area of taxes, where potential liability may be quite considerable. Particularly, the paralegal should refrain from making independent determinations about the following matters:

1. Whether the estate is liable for any particular tax
2. In the case of death-tax returns, valuation of noncash assets or the appropriate valuation date
3. Whether a particular deduction, exemption, or credit is available to reduce or eliminate tax liability
4. The appropriate state(s) with which to file state death-tax returns

An in-depth treatment of the subject of taxes as they relate to decedents' estates is far beyond the scope of this text; the following discussion provides the paralegal with an overview. For more detailed information about preparing and filing tax returns, the paralegal should refer to the instructions that accompany the tax forms. Other resources that the paralegal will find helpful include IRS Publication 559 (*Tax Information for Survivors, Executors, and Administrators*) and the looseleaf tax services published by Prentice Hall and Commerce Clearing House (CCH).

FEDERAL INCOME TAXES

In nearly all decedents' estates, the personal representative must report to the federal tax authorities any income earned by the decedent prior to death but for which the decedent failed to report as well as all postmortem earned income. The specific procedures and appropriate tax forms for reporting this income are examined in the following materials.

The Decedent's Final Income-Tax Return (IRS Form 1040)

In all likelihood, a final federal income-tax return (IRS Form 1040) must be filed on behalf of the decedent. It is generally the responsibility of the personal representative to file (and sign) the decedent's final income-tax return. If a joint return for the decedent and the surviving spouse is filed, both the personal representative and the surviving spouse must sign the return. If no probate estate is established (and thus no personal representative is appointed), the surviving spouse generally files the return. If there is no surviving spouse or personal representative, a member of the decedent's family or a friend may file the return. The due date for the final 1040 is the same as if the decedent were still living. If the decedent died early in the year, the personal representative may have to file two returns, one for the year in which the decedent died and one for the previous year.

 PRACTICE TIP: At the time the probate file is opened, the paralegal should determine whether the decedent filed an income-tax return for the previous year and if not, should indicate on the estate calendar the time schedule for preparing and filing the return. If there is insufficient time to meet the filing deadline, the personal representative should apply for an automatic four-month extension with IRS Form 4868 (Application for Automatic Extension of Time to File U.S. Individual Income Tax Return). Extending the deadline for filing does not extend the time to *pay*. If there is insufficient time to estimate the amount of tax owing, a penalty for underpayment may be avoided in most cases by paying the same amount owed for the previous year, assuming that funds are available for this purpose. If the amount of income and the increase in income from the prior year are both substantial, however, an estimated tax payment may be required in order to avoid a penalty.

 PARKER ESTATE: Irene died on March 20, 1993. Irene had not yet prepared or filed an income-tax return for 1992. IRS Form 1040 must be filed on her behalf for 1992, and a final 1040 must be filed on her behalf for 1993. The deadlines for filing these returns are April 15, 1993 and April 15th, 1994, respectively. It is unlikely that Irene's 1992 income-tax return can be prepared and filed by April 15th without risking error or oversight. Accordingly, Ms. Cargis has directed you to file Form 4868 to extend the filing deadline to August 15, 1993. Ms. Cargis has determined that any amount owing in addition to taxes already withheld from Irene's Social Security payments will be insubstantial. Accordingly, the amount of taxes Irene paid in 1992 will be used as the estimated tax liability for 1993, and no payment will be made when filing Form 4868.

Income and Deductions in Respect of the Decedent

All gross income that the decedent would have received had death not occurred and that was not properly included on the decedent's final income-tax return (IRS Form 1040) is referred to as *income in respect of the decedent*. This income must be included in the gross income of (1) the decedent's estate, if the estate receives it; or (2) the beneficiary, if the right to the income is passed directly to the beneficiary and beneficiary receives it; or (3) any person to whom the estate properly distributes the right to receive it.

*EXAMPLE: Kirk, an insurance agent, used the cash method (as opposed to the accrual method) of accounting to report income to the IRS. His compensation as an insurance agent was comprised in part of renewal commissions on policies that he originally sold. Kirk's son Robert inherited the right to receive the renewal commissions that Kirk did not receive during his lifetime. During the administration of Kirk's estate, some but not all of the remaining commissions are paid by the insurance company. The rest of the commissions are not paid until after the estate is closed. **Result:** While all commissions paid during Kirk's lifetime are included as income on Kirk's final income-tax return, the commissions received by the estate in respect of Kirk are included in the gross income of the estate. The commissions received by Robert after the estate is closed must be included in Robert's gross income during the year(s) he received them.*

Items such as business expenses, income-producing expenses, interest, and taxes, for which the decedent was liable but which are not properly allowable as deductions on the decedent's final income-tax return, will be allowed when paid as a deduction to the estate or, if the estate was not liable for them, as a deduction to the person who acquired an interest in the decedent's property (subject to such obligations) because of death.

Fiduciary Income Taxes (IRS Form 1041)

A decedent's probate estate (as well as certain types of trusts) is a separate legal entity for federal tax purposes. As a general rule, if the estate's assets have produced sufficient income during the course of administration (greater than $600 in a given tax year), the personal representative must file IRS Form 1041 (Fiduciary Income-Tax Return) and pay income taxes for the estate based upon the fiduciary income-tax rates (see Table 7-1). If one or more of the beneficiaries of the estate are nonresident alien individuals, the personal representative must file Form 1041 even if the gross income of the estate is less than $600. If an ancillary estate is established, the domiciliary and ancillary representative must each file a separate Form 1041.

TABLE 7-1   FEDERAL INCOME-TAX RATES FOR ESTATES AND TRUSTS

If taxable income is over:	But not over:	The tax is:
$0	$3,450	15% of the amount over $0
$3,450	$10,350	$517.50 + 28% of the amount over $3,450
$10,350	—	$2,449.50 + 31% of the amount over $10,350

If an Employer Identification Number (EIN) has not already been obtained (see Chapter 6), the personal representative must obtain an EIN to identify the estate on Form 1041. The tax is due on April 15, unless a tax year other than the calendar year is used. The first filing is likely to cover a period shorter than one full year. If the estate is closed before the first return is due, or if no probate estate is established, the income may instead be passed through to the decedent's heirs or devisees and reported on their respective individual income-tax returns. The last fiduciary income-tax return is not filed until the estate is distributed, since income up to that time is reported by the estate rather than by the heirs or devisees. Accordingly, filing Form 1041 is typically one of the personal representative's final tasks and may occur after a court order discharging the personal representative of his or her duties.

An estate computes its gross income in much the same manner as an individual; generally, the deductions and credits allowed to individuals are also allowed to estates. However, an estate is also allowed an *income distribution deduction* for distributions of income to beneficiaries. The income distribution deduction is computed on Schedule B of Form 1041 and determines the amount of the distribution that is to be taxed to the beneficiary as income for the year of the distribution. If Form 1041 is required, the personal representative must also file a separate schedule (Schedule K-1 of Form 1041) for each beneficiary of the estate to report the beneficiary's share of current income required to be distributed by the estate.

*EXAMPLE: Margarite's estate includes two parcels of real property that produce monthly rental income. Other income and the general assets of Margarite's estate are more than adequate to satisfy Margarite's debts and tax obligations, and so the personal representative of Margarite's estate has obtained the court's approval to distribute current rental income to Spencer, the eventual recipient of the property under the terms of Margarite's will, even though the estate is not yet in a position to be closed. **Result:** All rental income distributed to Spencer is included in Spencer's gross income, and Margarite's personal representative must file a Schedule K-1 reporting the income.*

Schedule K-1 must include the beneficiary's tax identification number, and the personal representative must provide a copy of the schedule to the beneficiary at the time Form 1041 is filed with the IRS.

PRACTICE TIP: An extension of time to file Form 1041 may be granted if the personal representative clearly describes the reasons that will cause a delay in filing the return. Form 2758 (Application for Extension of Time To File Certain Excise, Income, Information, and Other Returns) should be used for this purpose. The extension is not automatic, so Form 2758 should be filed in sufficient time to allow the IRS to act on it before the regular due date of Form 1041. An extension of time to file Form 1041 does not extend the time for payment of tax due.

PARKER ESTATE: The gain over appraised value from the sale of Irene's residence is sufficient in itself to require the filing of a federal fiduciary income-tax return. The return will not be filed (and taxes will not be paid) until *after* the estate is closed. The petition for final distribution will include a request to withhold from final distribution a reserve of cash in order to pay taxes (as well as to accommodate other possible unforeseen expenses).

FOCUS: For most estates, a final income-tax return for the decedent as well as an income-tax return for the estate must be filed by the personal representative. The paralegal should record the deadlines for filing the returns and ensure that they are filed in a timely manner or that appropriate extensions are requested.

Request for Prompt Assessment of Tax (IRS Form 4810)

The IRS ordinarily has three years from the date an income-tax return is filed or its due date, whichever is later, to charge any additional tax that is due. However, a prompt assessment of the tax may be requested at or after the time an income-tax return is filed by submitting separately IRS Form 4810 (Request for Prompt Assessment Under Internal Revenue Code Section 6501(d)). A request for prompt assessment reduces the time for making the assessment to 18 months from the date the IRS received the request and may be made for the income-tax return of the decedent as well as for the fiduciary income-tax return (but not for the decedent's estate-tax return). The request permits quicker settlement of the tax liability of the estate and may permit an earlier final distribution of the estate assets.

PRACTICE TIP: Form 4810 should be sent to the IRS by certified mail. Although filing this form is likely to trigger an audit by the IRS, an audit is actually a desirable consequence from the standpoint of the law firm, since it serves to protect the law firm from liability in the event the personal representative (or any other person) failed to disclose, either intentionally or otherwise, certain assets of the decedent or other important information.

THE FEDERAL UNIFIED TRANSFER TAX SYSTEM

The Internal Revenue Code (I.R.C.) provides a single "unified" system for taxing *inter vivos* gifts as well as transfers upon death. Thus, although gift taxes and estate taxes are distinct, it is helpful to think about these two types of taxes as parts of one unified tax system. Under the unified system, liability for gift taxes and for estate taxes is determined under a single Unified Rate Schedule (Table 7-2). A *unified transfer tax credit* of $192,800 may be used to offset gift-tax liability as *inter vivos* gifts are made. Any portion of the unified credit not used to offset gift-tax liability may then be used to offset estate-tax liability.

TABLE 7-2   FEDERAL UNIFIED TRANSFER TAX RATE SCHEDULE

Column A	Column B	Column C	Column D
			Rate of tax or excess over
Taxable amount over	Taxable amount not over	Tax on amount in column A	amount in column A
			(Percent)
0	$10,000	0	18
$10,000	20,000	$1,800	20
20,000	40,000	3,800	22
40,000	60,000	8,200	24
60,000	80,000	13,000	26
80,000	100,000	18,200	28
100,000	150,000	23,800	30
150,000	250,000	38,800	32
250,000	500,000	70,800	34
500,000	750,000	155,800	37
750,000	1,000,000	248,300	39
1,000,000	1,250,000	345,800	41
1,250,000	1,500,000	448,300	43
1,500,000	2,000,000	555,800	45
2,000,000	2,500,000	780,800	49
2,500,000	3,000,000	1,025,800	50

Note: The benefits of the graduated estate and gift tax rates and $192,000 tax credit are phased out for estates/gifts over $10 million.

Estate taxes are computed by applying the Uniform Rate Schedule to the *cumulative* value of all taxable lifetime gifts and transfers upon death; in other words, taxable lifetime gifts are brought back into the estate for the purpose of determining estate-tax liability under the rate schedule. All gift taxes previously paid are then credited against the estate tax. Only post-1976 gifts are cumulated to determine estate-tax liability, since the unified system did not take effect until January 1, 1977.

In examining the Unified Rate Schedule, notice that the tax rate is progressive, beginning at an initial marginal rate of 18% up to a maximum marginal rate of 50%. Also notice that the unified credit ($192,800) will serve to offset the tax on a total of $600,000 in transfers (the tax on a $600,000 transfer is $155,800 + 37% of $100,000). Accordingly, as a general rule, no tax liability is incurred until the aggregate value of all taxable transfers exceeds $600,000. However, the benefits of the progressive tax rates and $600,000 exemption equivalent are gradually phased out when total transfers exceed $10,000,000 in value. Thus, except for estates exceeding this amount, every person may transfer up to a total of $600,000 in property, either as lifetime gifts or as transfers upon death, without incurring federal gift-tax or estate-tax liability. All taxable transfers in excess of $600,000 are effectively taxed at the initial marginal rate of 37%. Although the federal gift- and estate-tax system is unified in the sense that transfers are treated cumulatively and are taxed under a single rate schedule, it is important to bear in mind that gift taxes and estate taxes are distinct and are subject to different rules.

All of the features of the transfer-tax system are continually subject to change through federal legislation. At the current time, only about 2% of all estates incur some federal estate-tax liability; estate taxes are not a significant source of revenue for the federal government. The primary function of gift taxes and estate taxes is not to generate revenue but rather to prevent the sort of concentration of wealth, through accumulation within a single family over a period of several generations, that existed in feudal England. However, in light of the growing federal deficit, particularly in the 1980s, the federal government has begun to look at the unified transfer-tax system as a potential source of revenue. A variety of revenue-enhancing proposals relating to the transfer-tax system have been introduced. Some proposals have called for the reduction of the unified credit (a reduction of the exemption equivalent from $600,000 to $200,000 would increase the percentage of estates that are subject to transfer taxes from 2% to about 15%), while others would place additional limitations on the use of the annual gift-tax exemption (see *Federal Gift Taxes [IRS Form 709]*). Another proposal would eliminate or reduce the stepped-up tax basis for postmortem transfers (as discussed in Chapter 9). What proposals, if any, are passed into law by Congress will depend on the country's economic and political climate during the remainder of the 1990s and beyond.

FEDERAL GIFT TAXES (IRS FORM 709)

Federal gift taxes are levied upon *inter vivos* transfers of property made without adequate or full consideration. IRS Form 709 (United States Gift Tax Return) or Form 709-A (United States Short Form Gift Tax Return) is used on an annual basis to report all taxable gifts made during the year. The deadline for filing is April 15 following the end of the calendar year in which the gift is made. The person making an *inter vivos* gift is referred to as the *donor*, while the recipient of the gift is the *donee*. The donor is responsible for reporting the gift and paying the tax; however, if the donor fails to do so, the donee is liable for the gift tax. The income-tax laws do not generally treat gifts as income, and so the donee need not report the gift to the IRS on his or her income-tax return. However, the donee may be required to report a subsequent transfer of the property to another person either as a gift or as a sale, depending upon the nature of the transfer. If the donor dies before the gift tax is paid, the personal representative is responsible for paying the tax out of the estate. If there is no personal representative, the decedent's heirs or devisees are liable for the tax in proportion to their respective shares in the estate.

Certain deductions and exemptions, the most notable of which are listed below, are allowed under the gift-tax provisions of the I.R.C.

1. The donor may exclude the first $10,000 in gifts to each and every donee each year. If the donor's spouse joins in the gift, the exclusion of both spouses may be used, resulting in a $20,000 exemption per donee each year; this is referred to as *gift splitting*. Any gift not exceeding the exemption amount need not be reported.

   EXAMPLE: *During 1993, Quincy, a married man, makes a gift to each of his three sons as follows: a $5,000 gift to Adam; a $15,000 gift to Stuart; and a $25,000 gift to Thomas.* **Result:** *The entire gift to Adam qualifies for the annual exclusion and need not be reported. The gift to Stuart may be treated as made by both Quincy and his spouse, and the entire gift is exempt and need not be reported since it does not exceed $20,000. Similarly, a $20,000 exemption is available for the gift to Thomas, resulting in a taxable gift of $5,000. Thus, the total value of taxable gifts reportable by Quincy on his 1994 gift-tax return is $5,000.*

2. Any amounts paid on behalf of an individual for certain educational expenses and for medical care may be excluded.

3. An unlimited *marital deduction* is allowed for all gifts to the donor's spouse.

4. A deduction is allowed for gifts to qualifying charitable organizations, although the amount of the deduction may be limited according to the type of gift and type of organization.

The federal gift tax is cumulative in nature. Each year that gifts are made, the tax on the total value of all post-1976 gifts is recomputed by applying the Uniform Rate Schedule, and any gift tax previously paid is subtracted from (or credited against) the tax. The unified credit is applied against the cumulative tax, so that no gift tax will be owing until the total tax exceeds $192,800—that is, until the cumulative taxable gifts exceed $600,000 in value.

EXAMPLE: *Carlita makes taxable lifetime gifts during only three years—in 1991, Carlita's taxable gifts total $400,000; in 1992, Carlita's taxable gifts total $300,000; and in 1993, Carlita's taxable gifts total $200,000.* **Result:** *No gift tax is owed for the 1991 gift, since the aggregate value of all gifts does not yet exceed $600,000. However, the 1992 gift increases the aggregate value of all gifts above $600,000 to $700,000, and so Carlita incurs gift-tax liability at this time. Referring to the tax-rate schedule (Table 7-2), the tax at the time the 1992 gifts are reported is $229,800 [$155,800 + (37% × $200,000)]. Applying the unified credit against the tax, the net tax due by April 15, 1993, is $37,000. After the 1993 gift, additional gift-tax liability is determined by recomputing the tax based upon cumulative taxable gifts of $900,000. The tax is $306,800 ($248,300 + 39% of $150,000). After subtracting the unified credit and a credit for gift tax previously paid, the net tax due on April 15, 1994, is $77,000.*

PRACTICE TIP: The paralegal should obtain sufficient information (either at or soon after the initial probate interview) to determine whether the decedent made any gifts prior to death for which a gift-tax return has not been filed and if so, the value of the gift. The attorney or accountant should then determine whether filing is required. If a return must be filed, the decedent's tax records from previous years should be examined carefully to determine whether prior gift-tax returns were filed; the most recently filed return may be used to compute additional gift-tax liability resulting from the unreported gift. The paralegal should note the filing deadline on the estate calendar and, if necessary, file a request for an automatic extension (IRS Form 4868 is used to extend the filing deadline for gift-tax returns as well as income-tax returns).

FEDERAL ESTATE TAXES (IRS FORM 706)

One of the most important functions of the probate paralegal is to assist in the preparation of the federal estate-tax return (IRS Form 706), which is examined in detail below. The rules of federal estate taxation are very complex; accordingly, a comprehensive treatment of this topic is not practicable in this text. The paralegal is admonished to consult the IRS instructions for Form 706 and in all circumstances to consult the estate's attorney and/or accountant in preparing Form 706.

In General

The federal estate tax is levied upon all property owned by the decedent at the time of death. IRS Form 706—United States Estate (and Generation-Skipping Transfer) Tax Return—is used for this purpose. An estate-tax return must be filed if the property owned by the decedent at death plus all taxable post-1976 gifts exceeds $600,000 in total value, before subtracting debts, liens, encumbrances, and other liabilities. If the value is under

$600,000, no estate-tax return is required, because the unified credit will reduce tax liability to zero. It is important to keep in mind that filing Form 706 does not necessarily mean that tax will be owing, since various deductions and other credits may be allowed.

For the purpose of estate taxation, property owned by the decedent at death is generally valued as of that date. As an alternative, however, the value of the estate's assets six months after the decedent's death may be used. Use of this *alternate valuation date* may be advantageous if the estate declines in value during these six months, since tax liability might decrease accordingly. If the alternate valuation date is used in determining estate-tax liability, the federal tax laws require that any property distributed, sold, exchanged, or otherwise disposed of within six months after the decedent's death be valued on the date title passes as a result of the disposition. The paralegal should consult the attorney early to determine whether the alternate valuation date will be used and if so, should schedule appraisals as necessary on the estate calendar.

IRS Form 706 must be filed within nine months after the decedent's death. Certified copies of the decedent's will (if any) and death certificate must be attached to the return. Although an extension of the time to file may be obtained, the personal representative should pay an estimated amount of the tax when applying for an extension. The estate will be charged interest on any unpaid tax from the due date. If the return is not filed in a timely manner, in addition to interest, the IRS charges a penalty of 5% per month (up to a maximum of 25%) from the date the return was due up to the time the tax is paid. An extension of time to *pay* the tax may be available (thereby avoiding a penalty) for good cause—for example, where payment would result in undue financial hardship to the estate. However, such an extension is available only if the IRS has approved the request prior to the filing deadline. IRS Form 4768 may be used to request an extension of the time to file Form 706 and/or pay estate taxes.

Figure 7-1 shows how the tax is computed. All property owned by the decedent at death is included in line 1 as the *gross estate* (see *Determining the Gross Estate*). Subtracting allowable deductions (line 2) from the gross estate results in the *taxable estate* (line 3) (see *Determining the Taxable Estate*). Post-1976 taxable gifts are then added to the taxable estate (line 4 of Form 706), and a *tentative tax* (line 6 of Form 706) is computed based upon the resulting tax base (line 5 of Form 706) by referring to the Unified Rate Schedule. Next, all gift taxes previously paid are subtracted, resulting in the *gross estate tax*. Finally, the unified credit and other credits are subtracted from the gross tax (lines 11 through 20 of Form 706), resulting in the *net estate tax* (line 21 of Form 706) (see *Estate Tax Credits*).

IRS Form 706 is long and detailed. It includes a variety of schedules (see Table 7-3) that are essentially worksheets for computing figures entered on the appropriate lines on the first three pages of the return. The paralegal should consult the IRS instructions and loose-leaf tax services for completing

FIGURE 7-1   COMPUTING THE FEDERAL ESTATE TAX

Gross Estate
– <u>Deductions</u>
Taxable Estate

+ <u>Post-1976 Taxable Gifts</u>
Tax Base

⇩ (Compute from Unified Rate Schedule)

Tentative Tax on Total Transfers
– <u>Gift Taxes Payable for Post-1976 Gifts</u>
Gross Estate Tax

– Allowable Unified Credit
– <u>Other Tax Credits</u>
Net Estate Tax

the various schedules. As discussed in Chapter 6, many law firms prepare the inventory and appraisement in a manner that resembles the schedules for Form 706 so that it can be used for both purposes. Computer programs are readily available to assist in completing Form 706 and computing the tax.

PRACTICE TIP: If the value of the estate approaches but does not exceed the minimum value required for filing a return, to protect the law firm against liability, the paralegal should request the personal representative by letter to verify the property included and the values used to determine the gross estate. Also, the paralegal should consult the attorney early about whether an extension will be requested. If so, the paralegal should prepare and submit the application as soon as possible and should monitor the status of the request, following up by contacting the IRS if the filing deadline is near and the IRS has not yet responded to the request.

FOCUS: A federal estate-tax return must be filed only if the property owned by the decedent at death (gross estate) plus all taxable post-1976 gifts exceeds $600,000, before deductions. The personal representative may be required to file a federal estate-tax return even though no estate tax is owing. If the estate approaches but does not exceed $600,000 in total value, the paralegal should request written verification by the personal representative of the property included and the values used to determine the gross estate in order to protect the law firm against liability.

Determining the Gross Estate

All property owned by the decedent at the time of death is referred to as the decedent's **gross estate** (or more specifically, the *gross tax estate*). Property interests that terminate automatically at death, such as life estates and interests in trust for life, are *not* included in the gross estate. The rationale for

TABLE 7-3   COMPONENTS OF THE FEDERAL ESTATE TAX RETURN

Form 706 (pages 1-3)	PART 1—Decedent and Executor
	PART 2—Tax Computation
	PART 3—Elections by the Executor
	PART 4—General Information
Gross Estate	Schedule A—Real Estate
	Schedule A-1—Section 2032A Valuation
	Schedule B—Stocks and Bonds
	Schedule C—Mortgages, Notes, and Cash
	Schedule D—Insurance on the Decedent's Life
	Schedule E—Jointly Owned Property
	Schedule F—Other Miscellaneous Property Not Reportable Under Any Other Schedule
	Schedule G—Transfers During the Decedent's Life
	Schedule H—Powers of Appointment
	Schedule I—Annuities
Deductions	Schedule J—Funeral Expenses and Expenses Incurred in Administering Property Subject to Claims
	Schedule K—Debts of the Decedent, and Mortgages and Liens
	Schedule L—Net Losses During Administration and Expenses Incurred in Administering Property Not Subject to Claims
	Schedule M—Bequests, etc., to Surviving Spouse
	Schedule O—Charitable, Public, and Similar Gifts and Bequests
Credits	Schedule P—Credit for Foreign Death Taxes
	Schedule Q—Credit for Tax on Prior Transfers
Additional Taxes	Schedule R—Generation-Skipping Transfer Tax
	Schedule S—Increased Estate Tax on Excess Retirement Accumulations

excluding such interests is that the decedent has no power over the transfer of the property interest upon his or her death (the interest automatically either reverts to the fee owner or passes to a remainderman), and so the decedent is not considered to own any interest in the property at death. However, other interests shorter in potential duration than a life estate might be included in the gross estate; for example, the remaining value of a ten-year tenancy interest would be included in the gross estate if it extends beyond the decedent's death.

It is important to distinguish between the gross tax estate and the decedent's probate estate. The gross tax estate includes *all* property owned by the decedent at the time of death, regardless of whether the property is subject to probate. The gross estate must also be distinguished from the *taxable estate*, which is computed by subtracting allowable deductions from the gross estate. On Form 706, the total gross estate (line 1) is determined by totaling in Part 5 (Recapitulation) all items from Schedule A through Schedule I. The following materials discuss briefly which assets should be included on each of these schedules (and in the total gross estate). For more detailed information on completing these schedules, refer to the IRS instructions for each schedule.

Real Estate (Schedule A). Schedule A should include real estate owned by the decedent as well as real estate for which the decedent had contracted to purchase. If an item of real estate is subject to a mortgage for which the estate is liable—that is, if the debt can be charged against other property of the estate that is not subject to the mortgage—or if the decedent was personally liable for the debt, the *full* value of the property must be listed on Schedule A; the amount of the mortgage may then be deducted on Schedule K. On the other hand, if the creditor can resort only to the property subject to the mortgage to satisfy the debt, then only the value of the equity (but not less than zero) should be reported on Schedule A (the amount of the mortgage is not deducted on another schedule). Any appraisals upon which the reported value is based should be attached to Schedule A. Certain real-property interests should be included on other schedules instead:

- Joint-tenancy interests in real property (but not tenancies in common) are reported on Schedule E.
- Promissory notes owned by the decedent and secured by a mortgage, deed of trust, or other interest in real property are reported on Schedule C.
- Real property that is part of a sole proprietorship is reported on Schedule F.
- Real estate transferred by the decedent within three years before the decedent's death is reported on Schedule G.
- A general power of appointment regarding real estate is reported on Schedule H.

Section 2032A Valuation (Schedule A-1). Section 2032A of the Internal Revenue Code permits a personal representative to value certain classes of real estate used in farming or in a closely held business at its current use rather than its highest, best, or most suitable use. The special use valuation election is available only if:

1. At least 50% of the adjusted value of the gross estate consists of real or personal property devoted to a qualifying use at the time of the owner's death.

2. The real property devoted to a qualifying use comprises at least 25% of the adjusted value of the gross estate.
3. The qualifying property passes to a qualifying heir of the decedent (a qualifying heir includes certain family members).
4. The real property has been owned by the decedent or the decedent's family for five of the eight years ending on the date of the decedent's death and was devoted to qualifying use during that period of time.
5. The decedent or a member of the decedent's family has participated materially in the operation of the farm or closely held business during the period of time specified under condition 4.

The attorney or the estate's accountant determines whether the election is available and whether it is desirable, based not only on estate-tax considerations but also on the fact that the election will affect the qualifying heirs' income-tax basis in the property (see Chapter 9).

For real property, legal descriptions and copies of appraisals must be attached to Schedule A-1, and all real property listed on Schedule A-1 must also be listed on Schedules A, E, F, G, or H as applicable. For personal property, a description of the method used to determine the special value based on qualified use must be attached.

Stocks and Bonds (Schedule B). All stocks and bonds owned by the decedent are reported on this schedule, except that jointly owned stocks and bonds are reported on Schedule E. Mutual funds are reported on Schedule F. Bonds that are exempt from federal income taxes are generally not exempt from estate taxes and must be reported. In completing Schedule B, the paralegal must be careful to (1) describe each item in the required detail, (2) value each item properly, and (3) list the items in the proper order, all as required in the instructions for Schedule B.

Mortgages, Notes, and Cash (Schedule C). The following items are reported on Schedule C:
1. Mortgages and notes *payable to* the decedent at the time of death
2. Contracts by the decedent to sell land
3. Cash in possession
4. Cash in banks, savings and loan associations, and other types of financial organizations

Mortgages, notes, and contracts involving jointly owned property are reported on Schedule E.

Insurance on the Decedent's Life (Schedule D). Because life insurance proceeds often account for a large portion of the wealth transferred among family members, life insurance is often the key factor in determining estate-tax liability. Any insurance *on the decedent's life* must be reported on Schedule D, whether included in the gross estate or not. Insurance on the decedent's life is includable in the decedent's gross estate either if (1) the decedent's estate is the beneficiary under the policy or if (2) the decedent possessed at death certain *incidents of ownership*, exercisable either alone or in conjunction with any person. Incidents of ownership in a life insurance policy include:

- The right of the insured or estate to its economic benefits (for example, if the proceeds are used to satisfy claims against the estate for debts, taxes, and so forth)
- The power to change the beneficiary
- The power to surrender or cancel the policy
- The power to assign the policy or to revoke an assignment
- The power to pledge the policy for a loan
- The power to obtain from the insurer a loan against the surrender value of the policy
- A reversionary interest if the value of the reversionary interest was more than 5% of the value of the policy

EXAMPLE: *Akira was employed by ABC Corporation for many years. As one of the benefits provided to Akira, ABC purchased a life insurance policy on Akira's life and paid all of the required premiums. Akira was permitted not only to designate the beneficiary but also to change the beneficiary at any time. Akira designated his wife as beneficiary at the time the policy was purchased on his behalf and died without ever changing the beneficiary.* **Result:** *Even though the policy is owned and paid for by ABC, the proceeds are includable in Akira's gross tax estate. By retaining the power to change the beneficiary, he is treated under the tax laws as the owner of the policy.*

The redemption or "cash" value (if any) of a life insurance policy owned by the decedent on the life of another (who is still alive) is reported on Schedule F.

For each life insurance policy reported on Schedule D, the paralegal must request IRS Form 712 (Life Insurance Statement) from the company that issued the policy. Form 712 is completed by the insurance company; it identifies the policy and indicates the amount of insurance and to whom and in what manner the insurance is payable. The insurance company provides the completed Form 712 to the person requesting it (e.g., the paralegal), and the information from the form is included on Schedule D. Also, Form 712 must be attached to Schedule D.

Jointly Owned Property (Schedule E). Any jointly owned property owned in part by the decedent at the time of death must be reported on Schedule E, whether or not the decedent's interest is includable in the gross estate. Jointly owned property includes all property, whether real estate or personal property (including bank accounts), in which the decedent held at the time of death an interest either as a joint tenant with right of survivorship or as a tenant by the entirety. Generally, the *full value* (not just the value of the decedent's undivided share) of the jointly owned property must be included in the decedent's gross estate. However, less than the full value may be included if the taxpayer can show that either: (1) a part of the property originally belonged to the other joint owner(s) and was never received or acquired by the other owner(s) from the decedent by less than adequate and full consideration, or (2) the property was acquired partly with consideration furnished by a surviving joint owner. In either case, only the portion attributable to the decedent would be included in the gross estate. However, the taxpayer must attach to Schedule E adequate proof of the extent, origin, and nature of the decedent's interest and the interest(s) of the joint owner(s).

EXAMPLE: *X and Y acquire property as joint tenants, although X contributes the entire amount required for the purchase while Y contributes nothing.* **Result**: *Although X and Y each own an equal one-half interest in the property, the total value of the property will be included in X's gross tax estate, while no portion of the property will be included in Y's gross tax estate (assuming Y dies before X).*

An important exception to the foregoing rule involves interests held by the decedent and his or her surviving spouse (unless the spouse is not a U.S. citizen) as the only joint owners (either as tenants by the entirety or as joint tenants with right of survivorship). Such interests are referred to on Schedule E as "qualified joint interests" and are computed equally for estate-tax purposes, regardless of the respective contributions of each spouse toward purchasing (and improving) the property.

Other Miscellaneous Property Not Reportable Under Any Other Schedule (Schedule F). Assets reported on Schedule F include such items of intangible personal property as debts due the decedent (other than notes and mortgages included on Schedule G), insurance on the life of another, leaseholds, royalties, reversionary or remainder interests, and shares in trust funds. Also reported on Schedule F are interests in a partnership (unless the partnership interest is jointly owned), sole proprietorship, or other unincorporated business. For each business, a statement of assets and liabilities at the valuation date as well as for each of the five years before the valuation date must be attached to Schedule F. Also reported on Schedule F are items of tangible personal property, such as household goods, collectibles, personal effects, wearing apparel, and automobiles, as well as farm products, growing crops, livestock, and farm machinery. For articles of artistic or intrinsic value (e.g., jewelry, artwork, and coin and stamp collections), if any one article is valued at more than $3,000, or any collection of similar articles is valued at more than $10,000, a written appraisal by an expert under oath and a statement regarding the appraiser's qualifications must be attached to Schedule F.

Transfers during the Decedent's Life (Schedule G). Five types of transfers should be reported on Schedule G:
1. The total value of the gift taxes that were paid by the decedent or the estate on gifts made by the decedent or the decedent's spouse within three years before death

2. Certain other transfers made by the decedent within three years before death—specifically, any transfer with respect to a life insurance policy—and transfers of retained life estates, reversionary interests, and certain powers
3. Transfers in which the decedent retained the income from the transferred property or the right to designate the person(s) who will possess or enjoy the transferred property or the income from the transferred property
4. Transfers taking effect at the decedent's death—that is, where possession or enjoyment can be obtained only by surviving the decedent, but only if the decedent retained a reversionary interest in the property that immediately before the decedent's death had a value of more than 5% of the value of the transferred property
5. Transfers in which the enjoyment of the transferred property was subject at the decedent's death to any change through the exercise of a power to alter, amend, revoke, or terminate

The most frequently occurring instance where property must be reported on Schedule G and included in the gross tax estate involves property held by the decedent in a revocable *inter vivos* trust. Property transferred during the decedent's lifetime to an irrevocable trust may in some cases be includable in the decedent's gross estate as well. Such property will be included in the gross estate if the trustor either (1) retained the right to receive the economic benefits of the trust property for the duration of his or her life, or (2) retained a significant right to determine who will receive the benefits (either present or future) or in what manner benefits may be received. Alternatively, a transfer of property to an irrevocable trust might be subject to gift tax at the time of the transfer. Irrevocable *inter vivos* trusts are generally used in planning large estates to reduce income-tax liability and possibly estate-tax liability as well. The rules in this area are among the most complex in the federal tax law. Where a decedent's estate involves such a trust, the personal representative should employ an accountant to prepare and file all of the decedent's tax returns.

Powers of Appointment (Schedule H). A **power of appointment** refers to a power conferred by one person, either by deed or by will, on another person to select the person(s) entitled to receive and enjoy particular property and/or income from the property. A *general* power of appointment authorizes the holder to select any person, including himself or herself, as the recipient, whereas a *limited* power does not (a limited power may place additional restrictions on the holder's authority as well). Powers of appointment are not usually considered to be "property interests." However, property that is subject to a *general* power of appointment is included in the holder's gross tax estate if the holder failed to exercise the power either during his or her lifetime or by will in favor of another person.

Annuities (Schedule I). Lump-sum death benefits under pension plans, annuities, and retirement plans are generally included in the gross estate. However, if death benefits are payable to the survivor(s) in installments, some portion of the benefits might be excluded from the gross estate, depending upon the terms of the plan. The rules in this area are very complex and are best left to the attorney or to the estate's accountant.

Determining the Taxable Estate

If the decedent's gross estate exceeds $600,000, although an estate-tax return must be filed, this does not necessarily mean that tax will be due. Not unlike the income tax laws, the rules for estate taxation allow various deductions that serve to reduce or eliminate tax liability. These deductions are subtracted from the gross estate, and the resulting figure is the *taxable* estate. Deductions are permitted for the following five items, each of which must be described on the appropriate schedule.

Funeral Expenses and Expenses Incurred in Administering Property Subject to Claims (Schedule J). Funeral expenses may be deducted from the gross estate, less any amounts paid as reimbursement for funeral expenses—for example, as death benefits payable by the Social Security Administration or the Veteran's Administration. "Property subject to claims" refers to property administered as part of the decedent's probate estate. Deductions are allowed for

1. Commissions and fees earned by the personal representative
2. Attorney fees
3. Accountant fees
4. Miscellaneous expenses

Deductions for fees are generally allowed even if the amount of the fees has not been fixed by decree of the proper court and the fees have not yet been paid. If the personal representative has not yet been paid the commissions and fees claimed at the time of the final examination of the return by the IRS, the personal representative must support the amount deducted with an affidavit or statement signed under penalty of perjury that the amount has been agreed upon and will be paid. Expenses claimed on Schedule J and allowed as a deduction for estate-tax purposes are not allowable as a deduction in computing the taxable income of the estate for federal income-tax purposes. They are allowable as an income-tax deduction on Form 1041 only if a waiver is filed to waive the deduction on Form 706.

Debts of the Decedent, and Mortgages and Liens (Schedule K). Only valid debts that the decedent owed at the time of death are listed on Schedule K and included in the gross estate. If the amount of the debt is disputed, only the amount that the estate concedes to be a valid claim may be deducted. Property taxes and income taxes accrued before the date of the decedent's death may be deducted. Federal taxes on income received during the decedent's lifetime are also deductible, but taxes on income received after death are not deductible. If an item of real estate is subject to a mortgage for which the estate is liable—that is, if the debt can be charged against other property of the estate that is not subject to the mortgage—or if the decedent was personally liable for the debt, the *full* value of the property must be listed on Schedule A, and the amount of the mortgage may then be deducted on Schedule K. If the creditor can resort only to the property subject to the mortgage to satisfy the debt, then only the equity is included in the gross estate, and the amount of the mortgage is not deductible.

Net Losses during Administration and Expenses Incurred in Administering Property Not Subject to Claims (Schedule L). The taxpayer may deduct only the amount not reimbursed by insurance or other sources for losses from thefts, fires, storms, shipwrecks, or other casualties that occurred during the settlement of the estate. Losses claimed as deductions on a federal income-tax return (either Form 1040 or 1041) may not be claimed as a deduction for federal estate-tax purposes. Also, no deduction is allowed for depreciation in the value of securities or other property. Property ''not subject to claims'' refers to property that is not part of the probate estate. Thus, certain expenses incurred in the administration of an *inter vivos* trust (see Chapter 10) or in the collection of other nonprobate assets (see Chapter 4) may be claimed on Schedule L.

Bequests, Etc., to Surviving Spouse (Schedule M). The most significant deduction in most estates is an unlimited deduction, referred to as the **marital deduction**, for all property passing to the decedent's surviving spouse. Because of this deduction, in most situations where there is a surviving spouse to whom a large portion of the estate passes, no estate tax will be due upon the death of the first spouse. The marital deduction is generally not allowed if the surviving spouse is not a citizen of the United States, unless the property passes to such a surviving spouse in a **qualified domestic trust (QDT)** or if such property is transferred or irrevocably assigned to such a trust before the estate-tax return is filed. A qualified domestic trust is any trust:

1. That requires at least one trustee to be either an individual who is a citizen of the United States or a domestic corporation
2. That requires that no distribution of corpus from the trust can be made unless such a trustee has the right to withhold from the distribution the tax imposed on the QDT
3. That meets the requirements of any applicable regulations
4. For which the executor has made an election on the estate-tax return of the decedent

As a general rule, the marital deduction is available only for property passing outright to the surviving spouse; if the spouse is not given complete control over the use, enjoyment, and disposition of the property, the marital deduction cannot be used. The QDT is one important exception to this rule. There are other exceptions as well, the most widely used involving what is referred to under the tax laws as *qualified terminable interest property (QTIP)*, which is placed in trust for the use and benefit of the surviving spouse until his or her death (see Chapter 9). The tax rules in this area are complex, requiring careful examination by an attorney with specialized knowledge or by the estate's accountant. The availability of the marital deduction, both for outright transfers and for transfers in trust to the surviving spouse, suggests a variety of estate-planning strategies for spouses with large combined estates. (An introduction to this subject is provided in Chapter 9.)

Charitable, Public, and Similar Gifts and Bequests (Schedule O). A deduction is permitted for any disposition to or for the use of any of the following:

- The United States or any political subdivision thereof
- Any corporation or association organized and operated exclusively for religious, charitable, scientific, literary, or educational purposes, as long as no benefit inures to any private individual and no substantial activity is undertaken to carry on propaganda or otherwise attempt to influence legislation or participate in any political campaign on behalf of any candidate for public office
- A trustee or trustees of a fraternal society, order, or association operating under the lodge system if the transferred property is to be used exclusively for religious, charitable, scientific, literary, or educational purposes and no substantial activity is undertaken to carry on propaganda or otherwise attempt to influence legislation or participate in any political campaign on behalf of any candidate for public office
- Any veteran's organization incorporated by an Act of Congress (or any of its subdivisions) as long as no benefit inures to any private individual

The deduction is limited to the amount actually available for charitable uses. Thus, any death taxes (federal or otherwise) paid out of the charitable gift pursuant to the terms of the decedent's will or for any other reason will serve to reduce the amount of the deduction (computing the deduction in this case is problematic and may require the use of special tax-accounting tables or a computer program). If the charitable transfer was made by a written instrument (will, trust, etc.), a copy of the instrument must be attached to Schedule O. In the case of a charitable transfer under a will, a copy of the court order admitting the will to probate must also be attached. In addition, in the case of a residuary gift to charity (under the decedent's will or trust), a detailed statement showing how the amount of the deduction was determined must be attached.

Computing the Gross Estate Tax

Once the taxable estate (line 3) is determined by subtracting allowable deductions (line 2) from the gross estate, the taxable estate is adjusted by adding all post-1976 *inter vivos* taxable gifts (line 4), and the *tentative tax* (line 6) is computed based upon the resulting figure (line 5) by referring to the Unified Rate Schedule. Taxable post-1976 gifts are valued at the time the gift was made, not at the time of the decedent's death.

EXAMPLE: *In 1991, Judy made taxable gifts totaling $50,000. In 1992, Judy made taxable gifts totaling $75,000. Judy made no other taxable* inter vivos *gifts. The total value of all property owned by Judy at the time of her death is $500,000. No estate-tax deductions are available.* **Result:** *The taxable* inter vivos *gifts will be included in Judy's estate for the purpose of computing the tax. Taxable* inter vivos *gifts ($125,000) are added to Judy's gross (and taxable) estate ($500,000), and the tentative tax is computed based upon a figure of $625,000.*

In the foregoing example, Judy incurred no gift-tax liability at the time of the *inter vivos* gifts because the total value of all post-1976 taxable *inter vivos* gifts never exceeded $600,000. If the total had exceeded $600,000 (and gift tax had been paid accordingly), the gifts would nevertheless be brought back into the estate to recompute tax liability.

EXAMPLE: *The total value of all post-1976 taxable gifts made by Fred was $750,000. Gift-tax returns were filed as required, and a total of $55,500 ($248,300 – $192,800) was paid in gift taxes during Fred's lifetime. The total value of all property owned by Fred at the time of his death was $450,000. No estate-tax deductions are available.* **Result:** *The total value of Fred's gross estate is $450,000. The* inter vivos *gifts ($750,000) are added to the gross estate for the purpose of computing the tentative tax, which is $427,800 ($345,800 + 41% of $200,000). After subtracting gift taxes previously paid by Fred ($55,500) and the unified credit ($192,800), the net estate tax is $179,500.*

Estate Tax Credits

Once the gross estate tax is computed, five credits are available to offset the amount of the tax. If the gross estate tax does not exceed the total credits, then no estate tax will be owed.

The Unified Credit. The most significant credit in most cases is of course the unified credit of $192,800 (line 11). Because all post-1976 gifts are added back into the estate, the entire unified credit, not just the unused portion, is subtracted. If the decedent made gifts (including gifts made by the decedent's spouse and treated as made by the decedent by reason of gift splitting) after September 8, 1976, and before January 1, 1977, for which the decedent claimed a specific exemption, the unified credit must be reduced by 20% of the amount of the exemption claimed for these gifts.

Credit for State Death Taxes. A credit is allowed for state death taxes, including estate, inheritance, legacy, or succession taxes (line 15). The amount of the credit is computed by subtracting $60,000 from the tax base (line 5) and applying a separate tax-credit table (Figure 7-2) to the resulting figure. If a credit is claimed, evidence of payment of state death taxes must be attached to Form 706.

Credit for Federal Gift Taxes on Pre-1977 Gifts. A credit is allowed for federal gift taxes on pre-1977 gifts (line 17). However, the amount of the credit may not be more than the amount figured by the formula indicated in Figure 7-2. This computation may be made by using IRS Form 4808 (Computation of Credit for Gift Tax). A copy of Form 4808 and all available copies of Forms 709 filed by the decedent should be attached to Form 706 to verify the amount of this credit.

Credit for Foreign Death Taxes (Schedule P). A credit is allowed for foreign death taxes (line 18), but only if the decedent was a citizen or resident of the United States. If a credit is also available under a treaty between the United States and the foreign country where the death taxes are paid, whichever credit is most advantageous to the estate is allowed. If death taxes are paid in more than one foreign country, a separate computation of the credit must be made for each foreign country. The amount of the credit is computed and reported on Schedule P. If a credit is claimed, IRS Form 706CE (Certificate of Payment of Foreign Death Tax) must be completed and attached to Schedule P.

Credit for Tax on Prior Transfers (Schedule Q). A credit is allowed for all or part of the tax on prior transfers to the decedent from a transferor who died within ten years before or two years after the decedent (line 19). This credit is determined by using a separate table (see Figure 7-2) and is computed and reported on Schedule Q.

An Illustrative Example

The following example, involving the estate of Marie Bohlinger, illustrates the use of deductions and credits to reduce federal estate tax liability. Figure 7-3 shows the first page of IRS Form 706 for Marie Bohlinger's estate.

EXAMPLE: Marie Bohlinger, an unmarried widow, died in 1992 and is survived by two children—Trevor and Lindsey. In 1990, Marie made a taxable gift (properly reported on IRS Form 709) of $66,000 to Trevor to assist him during a financial emergency. Marie made no other taxable gifts. Marie's gross estate at the time of her death was $1,480,520. At her death, all of Marie's assets were held in a revocable trust. Under the terms of the trust, the trustee is directed to distribute the trust estate at Marie's death as follows: 25% to Marie's church, free of death taxes, and the residue equally to Trevor and Lindsey. Marie's debts, along with funeral expenses and expenses and fees involved in terminating the trust and distributing the estate, total $261,940. Liability for state death taxes exceeds the maximum credit allowed against the federal estate tax. Result: Debts and expenses ($261,940) are reported on Schedule L and may be deducted from the gross estate. After payment of debts and expenses (but before payment of death taxes), the amount available totals $1,218,580 ($1,480,520 less $261,940). Of this amount, 25% ($304,645) passes to Marie's church. This amount may be reported as a charitable transfer on Schedule O and may be deducted from the gross estate. Allowable deductions (line 2) total $566,585, and the taxable estate is $848,450 (line 3). Marie's $66,000 taxable

FIGURE 7-2   COMPUTING ESTATE TAX CREDITS

Computation of Maximum Credit for State Death Taxes
Adjusted Taxable Estate = Taxable Estate – $60,000

(1) Adjusted taxable estate equal to or more than—	(2) Adjusted taxable estate less than—	(3) Credit or amount in column (1)	(4) Rate of credit on excess over amount in column (1) (Percent)
0	$40,000	0	None
$40,000	90,000	0	0.8
90,000	140,000	$400	1.6
140,000	240,000	1,200	2.4
240,000	440,000	3,600	3.2
440,000	640,000	10,000	4.0
640,000	840,000	18,000	4.8
840,000	1,040,000	27,600	5.6
1,040,000	1,540,000	38,800	6.4
1,540,000	2,040,000	70,800	7.2
2,040,000	2,540,000	106,800	8.0
2,540,000	3,040,000	146,800	8.8
3,040,000	3,540,000	190,800	9.6
3,540,000	4,040,000	238,800	10.4
4,040,000	5,040,000	290,800	11.2
5,040,000	6,040,000	402,800	12.0
6,040,000	7,040,000	522,800	12.8
7,040,000	8,040,000	650,800	13.6
8,040,000	9,040,000	786,800	14.4
9,040,000	10,040,000	930,800	15.2
10,040,000		1,082,800	16.0

Computation of credit for tax on prior transfers

Period of Time Exceeding	Not Exceeding	Percent Allowable
—	2 years	100
2 years	4 years	80
4 years	6 years	60
6 years	8 years	40
8 years	10 years	20
10 years	—	none

Computation of maximum credit for federal gift taxes on pre-1977 gifts

$$\frac{\text{Gross estate tax minus (the sum of the state death taxes and unified credit)}}{\text{Value of gross estate minus (the sum of the deductions for charitable, public, and similar gifts and bequests and marital deduction)}} \times \text{Value of included gift}$$

gift to Trevor is added to this figure (line 4) to determine the tax base (line 5). Based upon the adjusted taxable estate, a tentative tax of $312,435.50 (lines 6 and 8) is computed by referring to the unified tax rate schedule ($248,300 + 39% of $164,450). The unified credit is applied against the tentative tax (line 13), resulting in a gross tax of $119,635.50. The maximum credit for state death taxes, computed by referring to Table B, is $25,125.60. Since liability for state death taxes exceeds this amount, the maximum credit is allowed (line 15). The net estate tax, after subtracting the amount of the credit for state death taxes, is $94,509.90 (lines 21, 24, and 28).

Generation-Skipping Transfer Taxes (Schedule R)

The underlying purpose of the federal estate-tax system is to tax significant family wealth as it is passed down from one generation to another. Where a decedent's wealth is transferred down one generation to his or her children, the wealth will be subject to estate tax again at the death of the children. However, if the decedent's estate plan calls for the estate to "skip" the first generation, then the second estate tax is likely to be delayed (since the decedent's children are likely to die before the grandchildren). To offset this delay, a **generation-skipping transfer tax** (GSTT) is levied on significant wealth that is transferred to the decedent's grandchildren (or to subsequent generations). This tax is levied in addition to the federal estate tax and is reported on the same form (see IRS Form 706, line 23). The GSTT applies not only to direct skips but also to *indirect* skips—for example, where the property is left in trust for the benefit of a child's lifetime and, upon the child's death, is transferred to the grandchildren.

The GSTT is a flat (not progressive) tax. The tax is computed by applying a complex formula and is reported on Schedule R of Form 706. A $1,000,000 exemption from the GSTT is allowed per transferor; accordingly, only large estates will be subject to the tax. Generation-skipping transfers may raise complex issues that should be addressed by the attorney or by the estate's accountant.

Increased Estate Tax on Excess Retirement Accumulations (Schedule S)

The federal income-tax laws provide a number of tax incentives for saving money in the form of retirement plans. One such advantage is that income from funds invested in certain plans accumulates tax-free until it is distributed. However, if a sufficient amount accumulates in certain "qualified plans" until the decedent's death, the federal tax laws provide for an increase in the estate tax to offset the delay. A "qualified plan" includes certain pension, profit-sharing, stock bonus, and annuity plans, as well as certain annuity contracts, custodial accounts, retirement income accounts, and bond purchase plans. Whether the decedent's estate has any "excess retirement accumulations" in qualified plans is determined by comparing the accumulation with a hypothetical life annuity (computed in Part III of Schedule S). A flat tax of 15% of any excess accumulation is then added to

FIGURE 7-3   UNITED STATES ESTATE (AND GENERATION-SKIPPING TRANSFER) TAX RETURN

Form **706** (Rev. October 1991) Department of the Treasury Internal Revenue Service	**United States Estate (and Generation-Skipping Transfer) Tax Return** Estate of a citizen or resident of the United States (see separate instructions). To be filed for decedents dying after October 8, 1990, and before January 1, 1993. For Paperwork Reduction Act Notice, see page 1 of the instructions.	OMB No. 1545-0015 Expires 6-30-93

Part 1.—Decedent and Executor

1a Decedent's first name and middle initial (and maiden name, if any) MARIE M.	1b Decedent's last name BOHLINGER	2 Decedent's social security no. 123 : 45 : 6789
3a Domicile at time of death (county and state, or foreign country) Los Angeles , California	3b Year domicile established 1962	4 Date of birth 2/3/37	5 Date of death 10/12/92

6a Name of executor (see instructions) Trevor Bohlinger	6b Executor's address (number and street including apartment or suite no. or rural route; city, town, or post office; state; and ZIP code) 7044 Hillsdale Avenue N. Hollywood, California, 91601
6c Executor's social security number (see instructions) 234 : 56 : 7890	

7a Name and location of court where will was probated or estate administered Los Angeles County Superior Ct., 111 N. Hill St. Los Angeles CA 90012	7b Case number 76543

8 If decedent died testate, check here ▶ [X] and attach a certified copy of the will. 9 If Form 4768 is attached, check here ▶ ☐

10 If Schedule R-1 is attached, check here ▶ ☐

Part 2.—Tax Computation

1	Total gross estate (from Part 5, Recapitulation, page 3, item 10)	1	1,480,520 00
2	Total allowable deductions (from Part 5, Recapitulation, page 3, item 20)	2	566,585 00
3	Taxable estate (subtract line 2 from line 1)	3	848,450 00
4	Adjusted taxable gifts (total taxable gifts (within the meaning of section 2503) made by the decedent after December 31, 1976, other than gifts that are includible in decedent's gross estate (section 2001(b))	4	66,000 00
5	Add lines 3 and 4	5	914,450 00
6	Tentative tax on the amount on line 5 from Table A in the instructions	6	312,435 50
7a	If line 5 exceeds $10,000,000, enter the lesser of line 5 or $21,040,000. If line 5 is $10,000,000 or less, skip lines 7a and 7b and enter -0- on line 7c . 7a		
b	Subtract $10,000,000 from line 7a . 7b		
c	Enter 5% (.05) of line 7b	7c	
8	Total tentative tax (add lines 6 and 7c)	8	312,435 50
9	Total gift tax payable with respect to gifts made by the decedent after December 31, 1976. Include gift taxes by the decedent's spouse for such spouse's share of split gifts (section 2513) only if the decedent was the donor of these gifts and they are includible in the decedent's gross estate (see instructions)	9	
10	Gross estate tax (subtract line 9 from line 8)	10	312,435 50
11	Maximum unified credit against estate tax 11 192,800 00		
12	Adjustment to unified credit. (This adjustment may not exceed $6,000. See instructions.) 12		
13	Allowable unified credit (subtract line 12 from line 11)	13	192,800 00
14	Subtract line 13 from line 10 (but do not enter less than zero)	14	119,635 50
15	Credit for state death taxes. Do not enter more than line 14. Compute the credit by using the amount on line 3 less $60,000. See Table B in the instructions and **attach credit evidence** (see instructions)	15	25,125 60
16	Subtract line 15 from line 14	16	94,509 90
17	Credit for Federal gift taxes on pre-1977 gifts (section 2012) (attach computation) 17		
18	Credit for foreign death taxes (from Schedule(s) P). (Attach Form(s) 706CE) 18		
19	Credit for tax on prior transfers (from Schedule Q) 19		
20	Total (add lines 17, 18, and 19)	20	
21	Net estate tax (subtract line 20 from line 16)	21	94,509 90
22	Generation-skipping transfer taxes (from Schedule R, Part 2, line 10)	22	
23	Section 4980A increased estate tax (from Schedule S, Part I, line 17) (see instructions) . .	23	
24	Total transfer taxes (add lines 21, 22, and 23)	24	94,509 90
25	Prior payments. Explain in an attached statement 25		
26	United States Treasury bonds redeemed in payment of estate tax . . 26		
27	Total (add lines 25 and 26)	27	
28	Balance due (or overpayment) (subtract line 27 from line 24)	28	94,509 90

Under penalties of perjury, I declare that I have examined this return, including accompanying schedules and statements, and to the best of my knowledge and belief, it is true, correct, and complete. Declaration of preparer other than the executor is based on all information of which preparer has any knowledge.

/s/ TREVOR BOHLINGER   3/20/93

Signature(s) of executor(s)   Date

Signature of preparer other than executor   Address (and ZIP code)   Date
Cat. No. 20548R

the estate tax. The tax on excess retirement accumulations will not apply to most decedents because the present value of the hypothetical annuity is usually so large that very few decedents will have a total interest in qualified plans and individual retirement plans. If the tax applies, Schedule S must be filed regardless of whether the estate is otherwise required to file Form 706. However, Schedule S may be filed only as an attachment to Form 706.

STATE DEATH TAXES AND OTHER TAXES

Nearly all states impose their own income tax on individuals, and the attorney must determine the state in which the decedent resided at the time of death for the purpose of filing a final state income-tax return. Some states impose an inheritance tax on the beneficiaries of a decedent's estate who reside in that state. Many states impose an estate tax (either in lieu of or in addition to an inheritance tax) on all property owned by the decedent at the time of death and located in that state. If the property is located in a state other than the state of the decedent's domicile at the time of death, the property will be subject to ancillary administration in that state, although the tax may usually be paid from the assets of the domiciliary estate.

A detailed discussion of estate-tax schemes at the state level is beyond the scope of this text, since the laws vary widely among the states. However, the generally statutory schemes can be described briefly here. While some states impose a tax that is entirely independent of the federal estate tax, estate taxes imposed in other states are dependent to one extent or another on federal estate taxes. For example, in some states, the entire state death-tax liability is simply the maximum amount allowed for federal estate-tax purposes as a credit. In other states, a "sponge tax" is added to an inheritance tax if the amount of the inheritance tax is less than the maximum amount allowed for federal estate-tax purposes as a credit. The amount of the sponge tax is the difference between these two figures. Other states impose a "piggyback tax" in which the state simply receives a small percentage of any federal taxes paid by the estates of decedents who resided in that state at the time of death.

Other taxes might be of concern to the decedent and the estate as well. Most notably, if the decedent was engaged in a business, the estate might be liable for business, employment, or sales taxes. The personal representative may also be responsible for payment of additional such taxes if the personal representative continues the business. Although the paralegal should of course become familiar with his or her own state's requirements in these areas, handling such matters is not normally one of the paralegal's functions.

Paralegal Assignment 7

Recall that Ms. Cargis has asked you to develop a checklist of federal taxes and forms, including all appropriate deadlines, that may be required in matters involving decedents. A checklist such as the one shown in Table 7-4 can help you avoid penalties and interest for late filing and/or payment of taxes.

TABLE 7-4   FEDERAL TAX FORMS COMMONLY FILED BY THE PERSONAL REPRESENTATIVE

Form #	Title	Due Date
SS-4	Application for Employer Identification Number	As soon as possible. The EIN must be included in returns, statements, and other documents
56	Notice Concerning Fiduciary Relationship	As soon as all the necessary information is available*
706	United States Estate (and Generation-Skipping Transfer) Tax Return	9 months after date of decedent's death
712	Life Insurance Statement	Part 1 to be filed with estate-tax return
1040	U.S. Individual Income-Tax Return	Generally, April 15 of the year after death
1041	U.S. Fiduciary Income-Tax Return	15th day of 4th month after end of tax year
4868	Application for Automatic Extension of Time to File U.S. Individual Income Tax Return	Due date of Form 1040
2758	Application for Extension of Time to File Certain Excise, Income, Information, and Other Returns	Sufficiently early to permit IRS to consider the application and reply before the due date for Form 1041
4768	Application for Extension of Time to File U.S. Estate (and Generation-Skipping Transfer) Tax Return and/or Pay Estate (and Generation-Skipping Transfer) Taxes	Sufficiently early to permit IRS to consider the application and reply before the estate tax is due

*A second Form 56 should be filed to report termination of the estate.

8 SETTLING, DISTRIBUTING, AND CLOSING A DECEDENT'S ESTATE

Paralegal Assignment 8

In the Parker matter, once all necessary tax returns have been filed and all taxes have been paid, a final account may be filed with the court that recapitulates the administration of the estate and reconciles the beginning inventory with the property currently on hand. The final account will also include a request for a court order for final distribution according to a proposed plan. After the court approves the final account and distribution plan, Sharon may then transfer all of the estate assets to the estate's devisees. Ms. Cargis has asked you to prepare the final account and to assist Sharon in completing all of the necessary transfers, as well as to take the necessary steps to close the estate and obtain a discharge of Sharon's duties from the court.

PRELIMINARY DISTRIBUTIONS

Although final distribution of the estate cannot be made until after all of the decedent's debts have been settled, most states allow preliminary distribution of at least part of the estate after notice and a hearing where it appears the distribution can be made without jeopardizing the interests of the decedent's creditors. The fact that a will may still be open to contest does not necessarily preclude preliminary distribution. Some statutes require the distributee to file a bond to protect creditors, unless the creditor's claim period has passed and it is clear from the circumstances that the creditors' interests would not be endangered by allowing the distribution. Under a typical statute, a petition for preliminary distribution must indicate in detail:

1. The property on hand
2. The property proposed to be distributed
3. The property remaining in the estate after the proposed distribution
4. An estimate of the total amount of unpaid taxes and other liabilities, including unpaid claims against the estate
5. All other facts necessary to apprise the court of the estimated expenses in closing the estate

The desirability and timing of a preliminary distribution may depend upon income-tax and estate-tax considerations. Distributions of any portion of the residuary estate will shift taxable income from the estate to the distributees, which may either be advantageous or disadvantageous, depending upon the relative income-tax brackets of all taxpayers involved. If the alternate valuation date is used in determining estate-tax liability, the federal tax laws require that any property distributed, sold, exchanged, or otherwise disposed of within six months after the decedent's death be valued on the date title passes as a result of the disposition; this rule may either work to the advantage or disadvantage of the estate, depending upon how the value of the property changes immediately after disposition.

Under the U.P.C., interim orders approving or directing "partial" (preliminary) distributions may be issued by the court at any time during the pendency of a supervised administration on the application of the personal representative or any interested person (U.P.C. § 3-505). The U.P.C. also provides for summary distribution of the *entire* estate under certain circumstances. Under U.P.C. § 3-1203, once the inventory and appraisal is filed, the personal representative may immediately distribute the estate to the persons entitled thereto if it appears the value of the entire estate, less liens and encumbrances, does not exceed the total of the following:

1. Homestead allowance
2. Exempt property
3. Family allowance
4. Costs and expenses of administration
5. Reasonable funeral expenses
6. Reasonable and necessary medical and hospital expenses of the last illness of the decedent

The personal representative may close an estate administered under this summary procedure by filing a verified statement that the foregoing requirements have been met. Where the estate is distributed pursuant to § 3-1203, the personal representative must send a copy of the closing statement to all distributees of the estate and to all creditors or other claimants of whom he or she is aware whose claims are neither paid nor barred. The personal representative must also provide a full account in writing of the administration to the distributees whose interests are affected.

 PRACTICE TIP: The information included in a petition for preliminary distribution must generally be provided without reference to any inventory already on file. In preparing a petition for preliminary distribution, the paralegal must be familiar with the local court rules because they vary considerably. Although some states allow preliminary distributions before the inventory is filed, since the information required in the petition amounts to an inventory, as a practical matter preliminary distributions are not commonly made until after the inventory is filed.

COMPENSATION OF THE PERSONAL REPRESENTATIVE AND THE ESTATE'S ATTORNEY

The rules and procedures for payment of attorney's fees and the personal representative's fees are generally the same and therefore are discussed together here. Generally speaking, the personal representative and the attorney are each entitled to reasonable compensation commensurate with the value of their services. The amount of compensation allowed for ordinary services—that is, for those services performed in the regular course of administration—is typically determined by statute and is based upon the value of the estate. Absent such a statute, fees for ordinary services are based upon the time expended, the size and complexity of the estate, and the difficulty of the duties performed. Fees for extraordinary services are based upon the time expended. Compensation is in addition to any inheritance from the decedent.

Statutory Commission

In nearly all states, the personal representative is entitled to a commission computed as a percentage of the value of the estate. This commission is referred to as the **statutory commission** or *statutory fee*. The statutory commission is intended to compensate for time expended and for incidental expenses, such as secretarial services, telephone calls, and postage. Under a typical commission schedule, statutory fees as a percentage of the estate's value decrease as the value of the estate increases. In many states, statutory fees for the estate's attorney are computed using the same schedule, while in other states the attorney's fees are largely a matter of negotiation between the attorney and personal representative. Consider the Oregon statutes shown in Figure 8-1, which adopt the latter approach.

The base value used to determine the statutory commission varies among the states. One commonly used base is simply the gross value of the estate at the time of the decedent's death, as reflected in the inventory. However, this method fails to account for increases or decreases in the value of the estate after the decedent's death owing, for example, to effective management or to mismanagement of the estate. Another commonly used base includes gains over the appraised value on sales, plus receipts, less losses

FIGURE 8-1   OREGON STAT. ANN.

Section 116.173 (Compensation of Personal Representative)

(1) . . . The compensation is a commission upon the whole estate, as follows:
(a) Upon the property subject to the jurisdiction of the court, including income and unrealized gains:
   (A) Seven percent of any sum not exceeding $1,000.
   (B) Four percent of all above $1,000 and not exceeding $10,000.
   (C) Three percent of all above $10,000 and not exceeding $50,000.
   (D) Two percent of all above $50,000.
(b) One percent of the property, exclusive of life insurance proceeds, not subject to the jurisdiction of the court but reportable for Oregon inheritance tax or federal estate tax purposes.

Section 116.183 (Expenses of Personal Representative; Determination of Attorney's Fees)

(1) A personal representative shall be allowed in the settlement of his final account all necessary expenses incurred in the care, management and settlement of the estate, including reasonable fees for appraisers, attorneys and other qualified persons employed by him. An award of reasonable attorney fees under this section shall be made after consideration of the customary fees in the community for similar services, the time spent by counsel, counsel's experience in such matters, the skill displayed by counsel, the excellence of the result obtained, any agreement as to fees which may exist between the personal representative and his counsel, the amount of responsibility assumed by counsel considering the total value of the estate, and such other factors as may be relevant. No single factor shall be controlling.

under the appraised value on sales. By including gains and losses on sales while excluding "paper" gains and losses (i.e., unrealized gains and losses resulting from appreciation or depreciation), changes in the value of estate assets are not reflected unless the asset is sold rather than distributed in kind to the devisee or heir. In some states that adopt this method, gains (but not losses) upon sale that are due solely to inflation rather than to effective management are excluded. In some states, assets that are distributed in kind are entirely excluded from the base value.

Where the decedent's will stipulates the amount of fees, or states that the personal representative is not entitled to fees, the personal representative can renounce the provision in the will and take his or her statutory commission instead, although a written renunciation must be filed with the court within the time specified by statute. Although a provision in the decedent's will need not bind the personal representative, a contract entered into by the personal representative and a distributee governing fees is generally binding. Co-representatives share the statutory commission in proportion to their respective services rendered. Similarly, where the initial appointment terminates as a result of the death, removal, disability, or resignation of the original personal representative, the initial personal representative and the successor personal representative(s) share the statutory commission in proportion to their respective services rendered, although fees for prior personal representatives are generally not payable until the estate is closed.

The personal representative may waive his or her fees. One common situation where a waiver may be advantageous is where the personal representative is also a beneficiary. Fees for services as personal representative are includable as income for income-tax purposes, whereas inheritances are not. Thus, depending upon the personal representative's income-tax bracket and the portion of the estate to which he or she is entitled, it may be advantageous to waive the fees and receive all or a portion of those fees as an inheritance instead. Also, personal representatives often waive their fees out of a sense of devotion to the decedent.

The statutory commission should properly reflect the value and quality of the services rendered. Accordingly, although in most situations the court will approve fees in the full amount allowed by statute, the court may in its discretion reduce the statutory commission in cases of negligence, bad faith, or dishonesty.

 PARKER ESTATE: In the Parker matter, applicable law provides for a statutory commission for the personal representative based upon the value of the estate, plus gains on sales, plus receipts, minus losses on sales. Attorney fees (for ordinary services) are determined in the same manner. Since Sharon is the primary devisee of her mother's estate, Ms. Cargis has determined that it would be advantageous from an income-tax standpoint for Sharon to waive her statutory commission. The statutory fee for Able, Berman & Cargis is computed and requested in the First and Final Account.

Fees for Extraordinary Services

In addition to any commission computed as a percentage of the estate's value, the personal representative and the estate's attorney (if the attorney is entitled to a statutory fee as well) are each entitled to fees for extraordinary services rendered on behalf of the estate—that is, for services that are not ordinarily required and that are not routine. Whether the personal representative and the attorney are entitled to such fees and the amount of the fees are at the discretion of the court. Services typically categorized as extraordinary include those related to the following activities:

- Transactions involving real property, including sales, leases, exchanges, mortgages, or foreclosures
- Negotiation or litigation of claims against the estate or the decedent as well as claims by the decedent or the estate
- Payment of taxes, including preparation of returns, adjustments, and litigation
- Carrying on the decedent's business under court order

- Will contests
- Proceedings for construction and interpretation of the decedent's will
- Petition for instructions with a showing of actual need for instructions
- Heirship proceedings brought by the personal representative
- Termination of joint tenancy of a predeceased joint tenant

 PARKER ESTATE: In the Parker matter, Able, Berman & Cargis assisted Sharon Madson not only with the regular matters of estate administration but also with the following matters: (1) termination of Fred Parker's joint-tenancy interest in the residence; (2) sale of the residence and confirmation of the sale; and (3) proceedings for construction and interpretation of the will. Services in connection with these matters constitute extraordinary services, and fees for these services are requested in the First and Final Account. Although Sharon expended some time as well in connection with these matters, she will not request a fee for such extraordinary services, since she is the primary devisee of the estate and since she has expressed that her services are motivated in part by a sense of devotion to her mother.

Compensation for Services in Another Capacity

If the personal representative is also an accountant and provides services to the estate in this capacity, additional compensation for these services is allowed, although the court must approve the payment. Whether a personal representative acting also as the estate's attorney is entitled to statutory commissions for both services depends upon the circumstances and applicable law. The decedent's will may expressly allow both fees. Otherwise, in states where fees are based upon the value of the estate, the personal representative–attorney must typically obtain the written consent of all distributees in order to receive both fees, while in states where fees are based upon time expended, it is more likely that both fees will be allowed, even without the consent of the distributees.

Procedures and Payment of Fees

Court approval is generally required for payment of fees. Most states allow partial payment of fees after a certain time period has elapsed since the appointment of the personal representative, although partial fees are typically limited to a specified portion of the statutory commission, based upon the value of the estate as reflected in the inventory. If partial fees are requested, an interim account may be required. It is the paralegal's job to prepare the appropriate petition, all supporting documents for extraordinary fees, and the court order, as well as to provide notice of the hearing to all nonpetitioning personal representatives and to all interested persons properly requesting notice.

A petition for fees must state the amount of the statutory commission and how the amount was computed. Extraordinary services must be described in detail—each task involved should be described, and the time expended for each task should be indicated. The court will determine whether the time expended with respect to a particular extraordinary service was reasonable. Accordingly, if more than one type of extraordinary service was provided, the time expended for each service should be indicated separately. The law firm is entitled to fees for extraordinary services performed by the paralegal as well as by the attorney; thus, the paralegal should keep careful record of tasks performed and time expended related to any extraordinary service. The court is likely to require a separate affidavit or declaration in support of all allegations of extraordinary services performed by the personal representative, the attorney, and the paralegal. The paralegal's affidavit should include a statement as to his or her training and expertise so that the court can determine that the services are those of a paralegal rather than of a secretary.

 FOCUS: The law firm is entitled to fees for extraordinary services performed by the paralegal as well as by the attorney; thus the paralegal should keep careful record of tasks performed and time expended related to any extraordinary service. The court is likely to require a separate affidavit or declaration in support of all allegations of extraordinary services performed by the personal representative, the attorney, and the paralegal.

Uniform Probate Code

Under the U.P.C., the personal representative may fix his or her own fees and those of the estate's attorney; this approach marks a significant departure from the prevailing rule that both fees are determined by the court. To protect the beneficiaries of the decedent's estate, any interested person may request judicial review of the fees (as well as the propriety of employing any attorney, auditor, investment advisor, or other specialized agent or assistant) by petition (or by motion in the case of supervised administration) (see U.P.C. § 3-721 and official Comment to this section). Under U.P.C. § 3-719, if a will provides for compensation of the personal representative and there is no contract with the decedent regarding compensation, the personal representative may renounce the provision and be entitled to reasonable compensation, but must do so before qualifying to serve as personal representative. A personal representative may also renounce his or her right to all or any part of compensation; a written renunciation may be filed with the court.

ACCOUNT AND PETITION FOR ORDER OF FINAL DISTRIBUTION

Under court-supervised administration, the personal representative must account to the court for his or her administration of the estate and must obtain the court's approval before making final distribution of the estate (preliminary distributions may be made without an accounting). This procedural step actually involves three distinct elements. First, the personal representative must submit to the court a complete financial *account* that lists all transactions and itemizes all receipts and disbursements, as well as lists all property currently on hand. Second, the personal representative must submit a *report* in narrative form regarding matters not self-explanatory from the account, including a description of remaining liabilities, detailed information about creditors' claims, and the purpose and advantage to the estate of transactions for which court approval has not already been obtained, including a showing that any sales were made at or above fair market value. Third, the personal representative must request or *petition* the court for various court orders, including an order for settlement of the account, for distribution of the estate in accordance with a proposed plan, for allowance of fees for the personal representative and for the estate's attorney, and for ratification of certain transactions for which court approval had not previously been obtained. The account, report, and petition are generally combined (and are collectively referred to hereafter simply as the "final account") (see Exhibit 28 in the Parker file), although some lawyers prefer to file the account separately from the report and petition. In any event, one order is entered rather than an order settling the account and a separate order for final distribution. A noticed court hearing is required, and the personal representative must provide a copy of this document to all interested persons properly requesting it.

Time for Filing an Account

The time within which the *final* account must be filed is determined by statute, subject to a court order extending the time. A final account cannot be filed until all claims have either been allowed or rejected and until the time for initiating a suit on all rejected claims has elapsed or litigation has concluded. Otherwise, the estate is not in a position to be closed. Before preparing the final account, the paralegal should review the entire file to determine if there are any pending matters that may have been overlooked and should bring any such matters to the attorney's attention. After determining that the estate is in a position to be closed, a final account should be filed as soon as possible. Where a final account is otherwise required, the personal representative may be relieved from this duty by obtaining and filing with the court written waivers from *all* beneficiaries of the estate. Even if the final account is waived, the personal representative may be required to submit a less-detailed report to the court, although a noticed hearing will not be required in this event.

If the estate is not completely settled within the statutory time period, the personal representative may be required by statute to file one or more *interim* or *periodic* accounts. An interim account is typically combined with a request for partial compensation for the personal representative and/or the estate's attorney. A personal representative who resigns or is removed from office must submit a complete accounting to the court (as well as deliver the estate assets to the successor) before he or she can be relieved of the liabilities of office. If the personal representative dies in office, it is the duty of his or her personal representative to file the account.

Content and Form of the Final Account

Although most states pose no statutory requirements as to the form of a final account, local court rules typically impose their own requirements for the purpose of processing the paperwork in an efficient manner. It is the paralegal's job to recapitulate the administration of the estate and to transform the records provided by the personal representative into a form that is acceptable to the court. As noted earlier, the final account actually includes three elements—an account, a report, and a petition (see Figure 8-2). Items typically required by statute in the account, report, and petition are discussed in more detail below (these elements are separated here for the purpose of discussion but are actually incorporated into a single document).

FIGURE 8-2   FORM AND CONTENT OF FINAL ACCOUNT

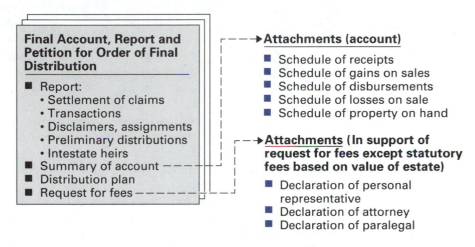

The Account. The account must generally include a summary of the account as well as detailed lists of receipts, disbursements, gains and losses, and property on hand, including full legal descriptions for all real property. Just as the initial inventory filed with the court provides a "snapshot" of the decedent's estate at the time of death, the account should provide a complete picture of the property on hand after the estate has been fully administered. The personal representative must account for the differences between these two pictures by listing receipts, disbursements, and transactions, including the dates thereof, during the course of administration. In other words, the inventory must be reconciled with the property on hand after administration. Total charges against the estate must equal total credits, as shown in Figure 8-3.

FIGURE 8-3   RECONCILING THE ESTATE'S ACCOUNT

CHARGES	=	CREDITS
⇩		⇩

•Inventory amount
•Receipts
•Gains on sales

•Disbursements
•Losses on sales
•Property on hand

SALE OF IRENE PARKER'S RESIDENCE

	Charges	Credits	
Inventory amount	$220,000	$63,820	Disbursement (mortgage pay-off)
Gain on sale	1,122	7,388	Disbursement (expenses of sale)
		149,914	Property on hand (net proceeds from sale)
Total charges	$221,122	$221,122	Total credits

The amount of detail required in listing and describing receipts, disbursements, and transactions may either be determined by local court rules or may lie within the court's discretion. Complete descriptions of assets acquired or disposed of are typically required—reference to the description included in the inventory is usually not sufficient. In any event, the account should be readily understood by the lay person and should contain sufficient information to enable one to determine what has happened to the estate assets during administration and to determine what is left for distribution.

Typically, a summary of the account is included in the petition, while detailed lists of such items as receipts, gains on sales, disbursements, losses on sales, and property on hand are each attached to the petition as separate schedules. Generally speaking, these lists may be organized in one of two ways: by category or chronologically. Categorized accounts separate receipts and disbursements into categories, such as principal, dividends, interest, and rent, while chronological accounts list them in order of time, separating receipts and disbursements. The paralegal should consult local court rules to determine what approach is acceptable. If organization by category is required, the paralegal might be permitted simply to list receipt totals for each particular account or asset rather than list each and every receipt. Local rules may require that income and principal be listed separately, particularly where income is payable to a trust beneficiary. In community-property states, local rules typically require that all property on hand be identified as either community property, separate property, or quasi-community property.

The Report. The purpose of the report is to recapitulate the activities of the estate and must generally include the following items:

- A statement showing compliance with the prerequisites for closing the estate
- A list of the decedent's intestate heirs and their relationship to the decedent, where appropriate
- A list and full description of creditors' claims submitted to the estate, indicating whether the claim was allowed, rejected, or other action taken in response (if the estate is insolvent, the description should indicate the proper proration of remaining assets among creditors)
- A detailed description of every transaction (e.g., sales, purchases, loans) not already approved by the court, including an explanation of the purpose and advantage to the estate of the transaction
- A description of all disclaimers, assignments, and preliminary distributions

The Petition. The petition should include the following:

- A plan for the distribution of the remaining estate (indicating all distributees, their relationship to the decedent, and the specific property or fractional share to which they are entitled)
- A recapitulation of the dispositive terms of the decedent's will (if any), tracking the terms of the will as to disposition of assets, including an explanation of abatements, ademption, or other unusual circumstances
- Calculation of the statutory compensation of the personal representative and attorney, including partial payments already made (if fees are to be shared among two or more personal representatives or attorneys, computation of their respective shares should be included)
- If compensation for extraordinary services is requested, a complete description of the services provided, including the specific tasks performed and the time expended for each task
- All appropriate requests for relief, including orders for allowance of fees, settlement of the account, distribution of the estate, approval or ratification of prior transactions, and any other desired relief

 PRACTICE TIP: If the proposed distribution plan is simple, the details can be set forth in the petition. However, if the distributees or assets are numerous, the proposed distribution should be attached as an exhibit. A separate exhibit should also be used if the will is unclear or the distributions complex; in this event, the report should paraphrase the will or state the issues to be resolved by the court respecting the identity of an heir or the distribution of property. The proposed distribution plan should be attached as an exhibit and referred to in the report; this avoids the need to retype the report if corrections or revisions are required and makes the petition easier to read and assimilate.

PARKER ESTATE: The Final Account for the Irene Parker Estate is included in the Parker file as Exhibit 28. The proposed distribution plan (which has been approved by the court) is summarized in Table 8-1. Since administration of the estate began, John Parker's widow Susan Burns gave birth to a daughter, Tracy Parker. Pursuant to Article 3 of Irene's attested will, the petition for final distribution requests an order for Tracy's share of Irene's estate to be held in a "custodian" account until she reaches the age of 18, with her mother Susan acting as custodian (see Chapter 11).

TABLE 8-1 DISTRIBUTION OF IRENE PARKER ESTATE

Property	Distributee	Controlling Instrument
Net proceeds from sale of residence (and income from proceeds)	Sharon Madson	Holograph
Contents of safe (jewelry) in basement of residence	Equally to Cindy Madson and Deborah Madson	Holograph
Tangible personal property	Equally to Sharon and Dennis (Susan Burns and Ruth Adams included in distribution by informal consent and agreement)	Attested will
Remaining assets	Equally to Sharon Madson, Dennis Parker, and Susan Burns (as custodian for Tracy Parker)	Attested will

DISTRIBUTION OF TESTATE ESTATES—RULES OF CONSTRUCTION

In preparing the petition for final distribution of a testate estate or otherwise instructing the personal representative regarding making distributions of estate assets, the paralegal must be careful not to overlook potential issues regarding the interpretation and construction of the will. Words used in the will to identify a devisee or a devise may be susceptible to more than one meaning. The will itself may clarify the meaning of important terms; indeed, a properly drafted will should leave no ambiguities. If not defined in the will, the proper interpretation of many important terms, such as *heir, devisee, children,* and *issue,* may be specified by statute. The meaning and legal effect of a disposition in a will is determined by the law of the particular state selected by testator in the will; otherwise, the law of the state where the will was executed governs these matters.

Aside from problems relating to the definition of terms used in the will, a variety of issues respecting the proper construction of the will for the purpose of determining distribution may arise. These problems are introduced below. In reviewing these materials, keep in mind two important considerations. First, the intention of a testator as expressed in his or her will controls the legal effect of his or her dispositions; the rules of construction discussed below apply only in the absence of a contrary intention by the decedent as expressed in the will. Second, this discussion is intended only as an introduction for the purpose of alerting the paralegal to some of the more common problems relating to construction of the dispositive provisions of a will. The paralegal should not determine the distribution plan under a will without first alerting the lawyer to potential problems and awaiting the lawyer's instructions.

Classification of Gifts

Every gift made under a will may be classified as either

1. A specific gift
2. A general gift
3. A demonstrative gift
4. A residuary gift

The classification of gifts made under a will is important for a variety of purposes, as discussed shortly (see *Distribution Problems*).

Specific Gifts. A **specific gift** is a gift of a particular item of property distinct from all other property in the testator's estate. The testator must intend the donee to receive a particular thing, and only that thing. The following will provisions create specific gifts:

- "I give to X my diamond wedding ring."
- "I give whatever automobile I own at my death to X."
- "I leave my 20 acres of farmland in Jackson County to X."

General Gifts. A **general gift** is a gift of a general economic benefit, payable out of the general assets of the estate. In contrast to a specific gift, a general gift does not entitle the donee to any particular thing. The most prevalent example of a general gift is a gift of a particular sum of money:

- "I give $20,000 to X."

A gift of property other than a sum of money may also be categorized as a general gift, as long as the gift is not of a particular thing. Consider, for example, the following will provisions:

- "I leave all of my real property to X."
- "I leave 20 acres of farmland located in Jackson County to X."
- "I leave 50 shares of common stock in I.B.M. Corporation to X."

A gift of "all" of the decedent's real property (as in the first example above) or personal property is usually held to be a general rather than a specific gift.

In the last two examples, assuming the testator did acquire, either before or after execution of the will, the type of property indicated in the provision (whether or not the amount acquired is the same), the provision is likely to be viewed as creating a general gift. Some courts, however, would hold that a specific gift is created if the testator, at the time the will was executed, owned the type and precise amount of property described in the provision. In the less likely event that the testator *never* owned the type of property described in the provision—for example, where the testator intended to acquire certain property but never did—then the provision creates a general gift that authorizes the personal representative to purchase from the general assets of the estate the type and amount of property described in the provision. In the foregoing examples, if the testator had instead left "*my* 20 acres" or "*my* 50 shares" to X, then the provisions would clearly create specific gifts since they refer to particular things.

Demonstrative Gifts. A **demonstrative gift** is one that is payable first from particular property of the estate and then out of the general assets of the estate if the particular property is insufficient to satisfy the gift. A demonstrative gift is, in a sense, a hybrid between a specific and a general gift. If the gift is payable only from particular property, the gift is specific rather than demonstrative. Consider the following will provision, which creates a demonstrative gift:

- "I give $50,000 to X; my shares of IBM stock should be sold to pay for this gift."

In this example, if the value of the IBM stock is less than $50,000, the general assets of the estate must be used to satisfy the gift. A demonstrative gift is actually a particular type of general gift. The distinction between a general and a demonstrative gift comes into play when shares of the estate must be reduced to satisfy obligations of the decedent or of the estate. As long as the particular fund or property identified in the will is available to satisfy a demonstrative gift, the gift will not be used along with other general gifts to satisfy the obligations (see *Distribution Problems, Abatement*).

Residuary Gifts. A **residuary gift** is a gift of what remains of the testator's property after payment of debts, expenses, and taxes as well as after satisfying all specific, general, and demonstrative gifts. A *residuary clause* is invariably included in all wills prepared by lawyers in order to avoid partial intestacy.

Distribution Problems

Classification of gifts made under a will is important for a variety of purposes, including the following: *ademption, satisfaction, increase, exoneration,* and *abatement*. In addition, the problem of *lapse* may arise independent of how a gift is classified. Each of these subjects is discussed below.

Ademption by Extinction. The concept of **ademption by extinction** applies only to specific gifts. A specific gift is *adeemed* (revoked) if the property is not part of the testator's estate at the time of death, and the donee is not entitled to any property in lieu of that particular property.

EXAMPLE: *T's probated will includes the following provision: "I give to X my diamond wedding ring." After execution of the will, T divorced and sold the ring and did not acquire another diamond wedding ring.* **Result:** *Since T did not own the particular property at her death, the gift is adeemed. X is not entitled to the proceeds from the sale of the ring or to any other property of T's estate in lieu of the specific gift (the ring).*

In many states (and under U.P.C. §§ 2-607, 608), ademption may be avoided if it can be inferred by the circumstances that, at the time the property was disposed of, the testator did not intend the gift to adeem, for example:

- Where the property was disposed of by the testator's conservator
- In the case of shares of stock, where the stock is exchanged for new stock in another corporation as the result of a merger or consolidation
- Where the property is accidentally destroyed at the time of or shortly before the testator's death

A variety of other means are provided in many states to avoid ademption, including the following:

- Allowing the devisee the balance of the purchase price still owed by the purchaser to the decedent at the time of the decedent's death
- Allowing the devisee any proceeds unpaid at the decedent's death on fire or casualty insurance on the property
- Allowing the devisee the net proceeds from the sale of the property if the proceeds are traceable to a particular fund (e.g., a savings account)
- Classifying the gift as a demonstrative gift rather than a general gift
- Classifying the disposition of the property during the testator's lifetime as a change in form rather than substance
- Construing the will at the time of death rather than at the time of execution

Ademption by Satisfaction. The doctrine of **ademption by satisfaction** is similar to the doctrine of advancements discussed in Chapter 2, except that the former applies to gifts made under a will while the latter applies to intestate inheritances. A gift under a will may be satisfied either in whole or in part by an *inter vivos* transfer from the testator to the devisee subsequent to (but not prior to) execution of the will. The testator must intend that the transfer serve as satisfaction of the gift, and many states require written evidence of such intent, either by a contemporaneous writing signed by the testator or by written acknowledgment by the devisee (see, e.g., U.P.C. § 2-612). For the purpose of partial satisfaction, the property is valued as of the time the devisee comes into possession or enjoyment of the property or as of the time of the testator's death, whichever occurs first. However, if the value of the gift is stated in the writing, in many states the writing is conclusive as to the value. As with advancements, the principle of "hotchpot" is used to compute the share of a devisee who shares a portion of the estate with one or more other devisees (e.g., a residuary devisee) receiving the gift as partial satisfaction of his or her share of the estate.

EXAMPLE: *Tony executes a valid will in which he leaves his entire estate equally to his three children—Judith, Mary Beth, and Lawrence. Shortly thereafter, Tony gives a computer system to Judith and in a contemporaneous writing declares that this gift is in partial satisfaction of Judith's inheritance. The value of the computer system at the time of the gift is $7,000. After administration of Tony's estate, a total of $80,000 is available for distribution to Tony's three children.* **Result:** *Since the gift was made after the will was executed and since Tony's intention was that the gift serve in partial satisfaction of Judith's inheritance, the value of the gift at the time it was made must be deducted from Judith's share. To accomplish this, the gift is brought into hotchpot and deducted from Judith's $29,000 share. Consequently, Judith will receive $22,000, while Mary Beth and Lawrence will each receive $29,000.*

Increase during the Testator's Lifetime. After execution of the will, the amount or quantity (as opposed to the value) of property specifically devised may increase before the decedent's death. Problems of increase during the decedent's lifetime usually involve stock splits or stock dividends. A *stock split* occurs where the corporation issues additional shares to existing stockholders based upon their current holdings. For example, if a shareholder owns 100 shares of stock that splits "2 for 1," the shareholder would own 200 shares after the split. A *stock dividend* occurs when a corporation pays a dividend in the form of shares of stock rather than cash. The effect of a "100% stock dividend" would be the same as that of the stock split mentioned above—although the number of shares owned by the shareholder doubles, the total value of his or her ownership interest in the corporation remains unchanged after the split or dividend. Suppose the shareholder had executed a will prior to the split or dividend that gives "100 shares" of the stock to a particular devisee. There are two alternative views: In some states, the devisee would be entitled to 100 shares if the gift is classified as a general gift, or 200 shares if the gift is classified as a specific gift. Other states would focus on the economic benefit that the testator intended to give to the devisee, entitling the devisee to all 200 shares regardless of whether the gift is specific or general.

Income after the Decedent's Death. After the decedent's death but prior to distribution of the estate, certain assets are likely to continue producing income in the form of rent, interest, dividends, and so forth. A specific gift carries with it the right to earnings or profits produced by the particular property subsequent to the date of the testator's death. The devisee of a specific gift is entitled to all rent or interest earned, or *accrued*, as of the date of the testator's death, even if the rent or interest is paid later. Whether the devisee of a specific gift is entitled to dividends from the particular property depends upon the "record date" indicated by the corporation at the time it declares the dividend.

EXAMPLE: *XYZ Corporation declares a dividend payable to all persons who are shareholders of record on April 1, although the dividend will not be received until April 15. Under the terms of Douglas's will, Douglas leaves all of his XYZ stock to Russell. Douglas dies on March 29.* **Result:** *Since Douglas died before the record date (April 1), Russell is entitled to the dividend. However, if Douglas had died after April 1, the dividend would pass instead to Douglas's residuary devisee(s).*

The issue of income after the decedent's death is not applicable to general gifts, because particular property is not involved. However, nearly all states provide for interest to be paid on general pecuniary devises after a certain period of time has elapsed (e.g., one year) since the appointment of the original personal representative (see, e.g., U.P.C. § 3-904).

Exoneration. Property specifically devised by the testator may be subject to an obligation such as a lien or encumbrance (for example, a mortgage against real property or a lien by a bank for an automobile loan). **Exoneration** occurs when the devisee entitled to the particular property is freed from the obligation, which must instead be paid from other assets of the estate (at least to the extent possible). The testator may indicate in the will whether the devisee should or should not be exonerated from the obligation, although a general directive for the payment of the testator's debts is insufficient for this purpose. Absent a directive in the testator's will, exoneration is provided for by common law, but only if the testator was personally liable for the obligation. Because the common-law rule results in a harsh result for the residuary devisee and more often than not runs contrary to the testator's intent, in many states the devisee takes the property subject to the lien or encumbrance, whether or not the testator was personally liable for the obligation (see U.P.C. § 2-609).

PARKER ESTATE: Neither Irene's attested will nor her holographic codicil provided for exoneration of any devisee. Accordingly, with respect to the testamentary gift of the house to Sharon, Sharon is entitled only to those proceeds from the sale of the house that remain after the proceeds are applied to pay off the mortgage debt.

Abatement. The reduction of a distributee's share for payment of the decedent's debts and taxes, as well as for payment of a family allowance and other valid claims against the estate, is referred to as **abatement** (the distributee's share is said to be *abated* for this purpose). Wills prepared by lawyers invariably include a provision specifying the order of abatement—that is, which assets of the estate should be abated prior to others to satisfy claims against the decedent or the estate. A typical provision provides for abatement of all residuary devises first. Absent such a provision or absent a will, the order in which the estate property is applied toward the payment of allowed claims is determined by statute. Consider U.P.C. § 3-902, shown in Figure 8-4, which exemplifies a typical statute.

FIGURE 8-4   U.P.C. § 3-902 (DISTRIBUTION; ORDER IN WHICH ASSETS APPROPRIATED; ABATEMENT)

> (a) . . . [S]hares of distributees abate, without any preference or priority as between real and personal property, in the following order: (1) property not disposed of by the will; (2) residuary devises; (3) general devises; (4) specific devises. . . . Abatement within each classification is in proportion to the amounts of property each of the beneficiaries would have received if full distribution of the property had been made in accordance with the terms of the will.

*EXAMPLE: Under the terms of Edward's will, Edward's estate is to be distributed as follows: (1) a specific gift of $10,000 to Eugene; (2) a gift to Julia of certain real property with a value of $200,000; (3) two-thirds of the residue to Sally and one-third of the residue to Shannon. The total value of the probate estate at death, as indicated on the estate's inventory, is $330,000. Debts, taxes, expenses of administration, and all other obligations of Edward and of the estate total $190,000; a mortgage debt for the real property devised to Julia accounts for $160,000 of the total amount. Edward's will does not provide for exoneration. **Result:** Under U.P.C. § 3-902, the shares of Sally and Shannon are abated first. Since the mortgage debt is paid from Julia's share, Sally's two-thirds share of the residue is abated by $20,000 (two-thirds of the remaining debts and expenses), while Shannon's one-third share is abated by $10,000 (one-third of the remaining debts and expenses). Thus, Sally will receive $60,000, and Shannon will receive $30,000. Neither Eugene's share or Julia's share will be abated.*

Under some statutes, gifts of personal property are abated prior to gifts of real property in the same class.

*EXAMPLE: Assume the same facts as in the preceding example, except that: (1) total expenses, debts, etc., are $290,000 instead of $190,000; and (2) applicable law provides for abatement of personal property before real property within each classification. **Result:** The shares of Sally and Shannon are abated first and are entirely depleted to satisfy $120,000 of the total debts, expenses, etc. (aside from the $160,000 mortgage debt abating Julia's share alone). Eugene's $10,000 gift is abated in its entirety to satisfy the remaining $10,000 in obligations. Thus, only Julia actually receives any portion of Edward's estate.*

Lapse, Class Gifts, and Antilapse Statutes. As discussed in Chapter 2, when an intestate heir predeceases (by a sufficient period of time) the decedent, his or her intestate share passes instead to the decedent's other intestate heirs. When a devisee under the decedent's will predeceases the decedent (by a sufficient period of time as determined under the will or by applicable law), the gift to the devisee is said to **lapse**. A set of rules distinct from the intestate-succession laws govern the disposition of lapsed gifts. An alternative disposition may be made by the will, which is typically the case in wills prepared by lawyers. Otherwise, under the common law, the gift passes to the residuary devisee (or to the intestate heirs if the will fails to indicate a residuary beneficiary or if the lapsed gift is a residuary gift). However, if the gift is to a *class* of devisees, such as to "my brothers and sisters" or to "the children of X," the share that would have gone to a class member who predeceased the testator is divided among the surviving members of the class.

Nearly all states have enacted **antilapse statutes** that depart from the common-law rules discussed above. A typical antilapse statute provides for a gift that otherwise would lapse to pass to the devisee's issue. Antilapse statutes in some states apply only where the decedent was related by blood (either by blood or marriage in some states) to the predeceased devisee, as reflected in the U.P.C. (Figure 8-5).

FIGURE 8-5   U.P.C. § 2-605 (ANTILAPSE; DECEASED DEVISEE; CLASS GIFTS)

If a devisee who is a grandparent or a lineal descendant of a grandparent of the testator is dead at the time of execution of the will, fails to survive the testator, or is treated as if he predeceased the testator, the issue of the deceased devisee who survive the testator by 120 hours take in place of the deceased devisee and if they are all of the same degree of kinship to the devisee they take equally, but if of unequal degree then those of more remote degree take by representation. One who would have been a devisee under a class gift if he had survived the testator is treated as a devisee for purposes of this section whether his death occurred before or after the execution of the will.

Where a gift fails, even where an antilapse statute applies, a device other than a residuary device becomes part of the residue. Under the U.P.C., if the residue is devised to two or more persons and the share of one of the residuary devisees fails, his or her share passes to the other residuary devisee, or to other residuary devisees in proportion to their interests in the residue (U.P.C. § 2-606).

FINAL DISTRIBUTION OF THE ESTATE ASSETS

In supervised administration, the court's order for final distribution (see Exhibit 29 in the Parker file) authorizes the personal representative to distribute the remaining property on hand. Except for transfers of real property interests, the paralegal should prepare a written receipt for each distributee in which the distributee acknowledges that the property received constitutes his or her entire entitlement in the estate (see Exhibit 30 in the Parker file). The receipts should then be filed with the court, so that the court can determine whether all of the property has been properly distributed. Receipts are typically filed at the time application for discharge of the duties of the office is made to the court.

Transferring Cash and Tangible Personal Property

Assets such as cash and tangible personal property may be distributed by delivering or simply relinquishing dominion or control to the distributee. For tangible personal property, a certified copy of the order for distribution should be provided to the distributee as proof of ownership. Cash is typically distributed either by a check drawn on the estate's checking account or by cashier's check. The amount of cash distributed to a residuary beneficiary is likely to differ from the amount indicated in the order for distribution; thus, a reconciliation form indicating receipts and disbursements since the time the final account was filed should be attached to the receipt provided to the distributee.

In order to transfer ownership of motor vehicles, the personal representative must present a certified copy of the letters of administration to the bureau of motor vehicles in the state where the vehicle is registered, although a copy of the court order for distribution is not required. The personal representative must also sign the ownership certificate in the appropriate place and present it along with the current registration card to the bureau. Once ownership and registration have been transferred to the distributee, either the paralegal or the personal representative should contact the insurance company to discontinue the policy. It is the responsibility of the distributee to obtain insurance coverage at this point.

Transferring Real-Property Interests

If the personal representative *sells* real property (rather than distributes the property in kind to a distributee) during the course of administration, an *executor's deed* or *administrator's deed* will be required to complete the transfer of title (see Exhibit 27 in the Parker file). However, if the real property is distributed in kind, then the interest may be transferred by delivering the deed to the distributee and recording a certified copy of the court order for final distribution in the county where the real property is located. As an alternative to delivering the deed to the distributee, an executor's deed or administrator's deed may be prepared and recorded concurrently with the court order for distribution. If the latter method is used, the executor's deed should explicitly refer to the order for distribution. An executor's deed is recommended (although not required) where the order for distribution is unclear. Otherwise, recordation of the court order adequately alerts a subsequent transferee or a title company that ownership has been transferred from the decedent to the distributee by the estate's personal representative. If the real property that is transferred is subject to a mortgage or deed of trust, the paralegal should provide a copy of the court order to the lender, although it is the distributee's responsibility to inform the lender where to send future statements and payment requests.

Transferring Securities

In order to transfer securities of a closely held corporation (rather than shares of publicly traded stocks or bonds), a new stock certificate or bond should be prepared, and the order for distribution should be provided to the corporate secretary for its records. The procedures for transferring registered (i.e., publicly traded) securities are governed by Article 8 of the Uniform Commercial Code (U.C.C.), which has been adopted in all states except Louisiana. The U.C.C. requirements have been modified somewhat in many states, so that transfer procedures may vary somewhat depending upon the particular state of incorporation. Registered securities must be transferred through the corporation's *transfer agent*. Although the agent may be indicated on the bond or stock certificate, this information may be obsolete. A better source for current information about names and addresses of transfer agents is the Commerce Clearing House Stock Transfer Guide. This important resource also lists each state's requirements for transferring securities. In all states, the original stock certificate or bond as well as a *stock or bond power* (see below) must be provided to the transfer agent. In addition, one or more (and typically all) of the following must be provided to the transfer agent:

1. A copy of the personal representative's Letters, certified within 60 days prior to the requested transfer
2. An *Affidavit of Domicile*, signed by the personal representative, with the signature notarized
3. A *tax waiver* or *consent*
4. A *transmittal letter*

It is not necessary to submit a copy of the court order for distribution or of the decedent's death certificate (except where the transfer is to a surviving joint tenant) to the transfer agent. If the original stock or bond certificate has been lost, the paralegal should write to the transfer agent to obtain a new one.

A **stock or bond power** is actually a special power of attorney (see Chapter 11) and authorizes the actual transfer of the securities. It must be executed by a person having the authority to sign on behalf of the decedent (e.g., the personal representative). Although a stock or bond power is typically printed on the back of the stock or bond certificate, a separate form, called "Stock or Bond Assignment Separate from Certificate" or "Irrevocable Stock or Bond Power" is normally used instead. These forms may be obtained from a bank, stockbroker, or stationery store; a suitable form may also be drafted by the law firm. Because the transfer agent has no means of identifying the signature of the person who signs the stock or bond power, the agent will require that the signature be *guaranteed* either by an officer of a national bank or by a stockbroker at a firm that is a member of a nationally recognized securities exchange. Usually, the personal representative's bank or the broker handling the transfer will provide the signature guarantee.

States that impose their own inheritance or death taxes will require evidence that these taxes have been paid before securities of a corporation incorporated in the state may be transferred if the decedent was a resident of the same state where the corporation is organized. If the decedent was not a resident of the state, evidence of this fact must be provided. An **Affidavit of Domicile**, also referred to as an *affidavit of residence*, should be provided to the transfer agent for either purpose. A suitable form may be obtained from a bank or stockbroker, and the personal representative's signature on the form must be notarized. In some states, a *tax waiver* or *tax consent* must first be obtained from the state by the personal representative; this document must in turn be provided to the transfer agent.

A *transmittal letter*, signed by the personal representative, is used to request the transfer and should provide the name, Social Security number, and address of the new owner so that the agent knows to whom to send dividends and proxies and so the agent can report certain information to the IRS. If the securities are to be apportioned between two or more owners, the number of shares going to each owner should be indicated. One transmittal letter may be used for all securities transferred through the same transfer agent.

The procedure for transferring shares of mutual funds and money-market funds is simpler than for transferring securities. The fund's management company or a *custodian* for the fund generally retains the original certificates, and each company provides its own forms to complete the transfers.

 PRACTICE TIP: It is generally recommended that original stock or bond certificates be mailed separately from the stock or bond power (unless the power on the back of the certificate is used) and that these documents be mailed separately from all other documents. The purpose of mailing documents under separate covers is to prevent fraudulent transfers in the event the documents are misdelivered. Original certificates should be sent by registered mail with return receipt requested and should be insured. If the transfer agent is located in New York or Florida, a stock transfer tax (2.5 cents per share) must be paid to the transfer agent (regardless of the state of the decedent's residence). The paralegal should select a transfer agent in another state if possible; otherwise, the paralegal should contact the transfer agent ahead of time to confirm the amount of the tax and should include payment with the other documents. Because transferring securities involves a substantial amount of paperwork, the law firm may wish to have a bank or stock brokerage firm handle the transfers; the fee for this service is nominal, and a bank or stock brokerage firm can generally handle the transfers more efficiently than the law firm.

CLOSING THE ESTATE AND OBTAINING AN ORDER DISCHARGING THE DUTIES OF OFFICE

Under supervised administration, after the personal representative has distributed all of the assets to the distributees pursuant to the court's order for final distribution, application to the court should be made for an order discharging the personal representative from his or her duties (see Exhibit 31 in the Parker file). All receipts obtained from the distributees should be filed at this time if the paralegal has not already done so. If the personal representative filed a bond, after discharge there is no reason to continue payment of bond premiums. However, the bonding company will not automatically be notified of the discharge. Thus, the paralegal should provide the bonding company with a certified copy of the court's order discharging the personal representative. The bonding company will then cancel the bond and, if the estate has been open for more than one year, will give a *pro rata* refund of the unearned bond premium to the estate.

PRACTICE TIP: In most cases, the estate checking account should be kept open for some period of time after final discharge. After the final account is filed, the estate may still continue to receive income in the form of interest, dividends, rent, insurance and bond premium refunds, and so forth. Also, additional fees, taxes, and unexpected expenses may arise. In the final account, the personal representative may petition the court to maintain a reserve of cash in the estate checking account to meet such expenses.

REOPENING THE ESTATE

After final settlement of the estate, it may be necessary or proper to issue Letters of Administration and "reopen" the estate. The most common scenario requiring that the estate be reopened is where additional property owned by the decedent is discovered after final distribution. Reopening the estate for this purpose can be avoided by the inclusion of a request, referred to as an **omnibus clause**, in the petition for final distribution that after-discovered property be distributed to specified persons, such as the residuary beneficiary or a trustee of a testamentary trust. If the estate must be reopened, the original personal representative generally has priority for appointment. If the estate is reopened because of newly discovered property, interested persons must be provided notice, and it will be necessary to file a new inventory and possibly an amended estate-tax return as well.

UNIFORM PROBATE CODE

The U.P.C. provides several methods for closing the estate, as set forth in U.P.C. § 3-1001, *et seq.* The choice as to which method is used depends upon the degree of court supervision desired by the personal representative and by interested persons. Although the U.P.C. does not expressly provide for it, the personal representative may distribute the estate without any court proceeding and without filing anything with the court. If the personal representative chooses to proceed in this manner, however, the personal representative is afforded no protection against further claims from interested persons that the personal representative breached his or her fiduciary duty. Thus, one of the three following methods of closing the estate is preferred.

Complete Settlement Proceedings

Any estate may be closed by a complete settlement proceeding. A complete settlement proceeding is required for estates in supervised administration proceedings. Either the personal representative or any interested person may file a petition for complete settlement of the estate, although an interested person may not initiate settlement proceedings until one year has passed since appointment of the original personal representative. In any event, the petition cannot be filed until the creditors' claim period has elapsed (for claims arising prior to the decedent's death). The petition may request the court to determine testacy (if not previously determined), to consider the final account or compel or approve an accounting and distribution, to construe any will or determine heirs, and to adjudicate the final settlement and distribution of the estate. After notice and a hearing, the court may issue orders determining the persons entitled to distribution of the estate, approving settlement and directing or approving distribution, and discharging the personal representative from any further claims.

Settlement Order in a Testate Estate

Where an estate is being administered under an *informally* probated will, the personal representative or any devisee may file a petition for an order of settlement that will not adjudicate the testacy status of the decedent. This proceeding is not available in the case of partial or total intestacy. The proceeding is similar to a complete settlement proceeding. After notice to all devisees and a hearing, the court may make a final determination of the rights of all devisees vis-à-vis one another and vis-à-vis the personal representative, even though there has been no formal testacy proceeding. This proceeding affords the personal representative protection against further claims by the devisees but not by the decedent's heirs, creditors, or other third parties.

Verified Closing Statement

Except in supervised administration and unless prohibited by court order, the personal representative may close the estate by filing a verified *closing statement.* The statement may not be filed until at least 6 months have elapsed since the original appointment of a personal representative. The closing statement must declare that the personal representative has:

- Published notice to creditors and that the first publication occurred more than six months prior to the date of the statement
- Fully administered the estate by making payment, settlement, or other disposition of all claims that were presented, by making payment of all expenses of administration and death taxes (except as specified in the statement), and by ensuring that the assets of the estate have been distributed to the persons entitled thereto
- Distributed the estate, if any claims remain undischarged, with the agreement of the distributees or made other arrangements (described in detail) to accommodate outstanding liabilities
- Sent a copy of the statement to all distributees and to all creditors or other claimants of whom the personal representative is aware whose claims are neither paid nor barred

■ Furnished a full account in writing of his or her administration to the distributees whose interests are affected thereby

The filing of a closing statement affirms that the personal representative believes the business of the estate to be completed and begins a six-month statute of limitations for interested persons to assert claims against the personal representative for breach of fiduciary duty. At this point a creditor whose claim has not been paid or whose claim is not barred may assert the claim against the distributees. The personal representative's authority is not terminated until one year after filing a closing claim. The personal representative remains liable to suit even after termination of his or her authority unless protected by a statute of limitations.

Paralegal Assignment 8

Recall that Ms. Cargis has asked you to prepare the Final Account and to assist Sharon in completing all of the necessary transfers of the remaining estate assets to the distributees, as well as to take the necessary steps to close the estate and obtain a discharge of Sharon's duties from the court. You have prepared and processed the following documents according to this final assignment for the Irene Parker Estate:

1. First and Final Account and Report of Executor and Petition for Settlement of Estate, for Allowance of Attorney's Fees for Ordinary and Extraordinary Services, and for Final Distribution (Exhibit 28)
2. Order for Settlement of Estate, for Allowance of Attorney's Fees, and for Final Distribution (Exhibit 29)
3. Receipt of Distributee (Exhibit 30)
4. Declaration for Final Discharge and Order (Exhibit 31)

The property on hand (except for a $2,500 cash reserve) has been distributed among Sharon, Dennis, and Susan (acting as custodian for her newborn daughter, Tracy Burns). Receipts have been obtained from all distributees and have been filed with the court. An order for discharge has been issued, and you have also contacted the bonding company to arrange for their release of bond (although no *pro rata* refund will be due because the period of coverage did not exceed one year). Sharon has indicated that she will prepare and file IRS Form 1041 without the firm's assistance.

9 ESTATE PLANNING AND THE USE OF TRUSTS

We are now returning to your first week as a probate paralegal with Able, Berman & Cargis. Recall from Chapter 1 that you sat in on Ms. Cargis' estate-planning interview with Walter and Betty Taylor. At this point, you may wish to review the basic facts about the Taylors from Chapter 1 (see *Two Case Studies for the Paralegal*). You will learn in this chapter that the Taylors' estate-planning objectives can best be achieved through the use of a complex but commonly used form of trust. Ms. Cargis has explained to you that, before you will be able to assist her effectively in the Taylor matter or in other estate-planning matters, you must learn how lawyers plan estates and must develop an appreciation for the complexity of the estate-planning process and for the knowledge and judgment that an experienced estate-planning attorney brings to this process. Accordingly, Ms. Cargis has provided you with the materials in this chapter, not for the purpose of performing any particular task, but rather to prepare you for your next task relating to the Taylor matter (see Chapter 10).

While this chapter provides an overview of the estate-planning process, its primary focus will be the law of trusts and the uses of trusts in the estate-planning process. The federal tax laws as they relate to the estate-planning process will also be examined in detail. Other aspects of estate planning are treated in detail elsewhere in this text. The law of wills was examined in Chapters 2 and 3. Planning for incapacity, which is just as important as and arguably more important than planning for postmortem transfers of wealth, will be discussed in Chapter 11.

THE NATURE OF TRUSTS

Perhaps no legal concept is as difficult to explain as the trust, because trusts appear in so many different forms and serve so many different purposes. The following materials are intended only as an introduction to this complex area of law.

The Trust Concept

As you examine these materials (as well as the materials in Chapter 10), bear in mind that the law of trusts, like the law of wills, is determined by state law and that questions of construction, interpretation, and choice of law are generally resolved in the same manner as in the area of wills by the probate court, which has subject-matter jurisdiction over matters involving trusts.

The Restatement (Second) of Trusts defines the term as illustrated in Figure 9-1.

FIGURE 9-1   RESTATEMENT (SECOND) OF TRUSTS § 2

> . . . A trust . . . is a fiduciary relationship with respect to property, subjecting the person by whom the title to the property is held to equitable duties to deal with the property for the benefit of another person, which arises as a result of a manifestation of an intention to create it.

The trust concept is best understood by example. Consider the following two scenarios. Both scenarios involve a trust relationship, although the first is far more typical.

SCENARIO 1: *Salvador's will provides as follows: "I leave my estate to my brother Miguel to hold, manage, and invest until my youngest child attains the age of 21, at which time Miguel shall distribute my estate equally to my then living children."*

SCENARIO 2: *Stephen declares the following to his three children: "I am setting aside $10,000 in a special account for the first one of you three children to marry."*

As suggested by the Restatement's definition of a trust, a trust requires two parties: a trustee and a beneficiary. Most trusts also involve a third party, referred to as the settlor (see Figure 9-2). Each of these three parties to a trust is discussed further below.

The Trustee

The person who holds title to the property is referred to as the *trustee*. The trustee is said to hold *legal title* in the property interests held in trust and is

FIGURE 9-2   PARTIES TO A TRUST

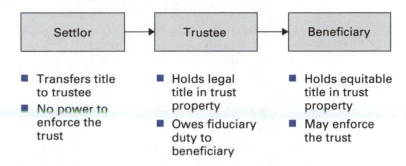

considered the owner of the trust property as to third parties. In Scenario 1, Miguel is the trustee while in Scenario 2 Stephen is the trustee. A trustee is essential for the creation of a trust. However, a trust will not necessarily fail for want of a trustee; if the settlor fails to name a trustee or if the named trustee cannot perform, a trustee may be appointed by the court upon application of an interested person. Although the settlor may also be the trustee, if the trustee is also the *sole* beneficiary, legal and equitable title are said to merge, and the trust fails. Some active duty must be placed upon a trustee, although duties may be implied where the other essential elements of the trust are present. Thus, a provision in a will stating simply "to T in trust for B," although failing to indicate any duties of T, implies that T is under an affirmative duty to deal with the property for B's benefit.

The Beneficiary

A person for whose benefit the property is held by the trustee is referred to as a **beneficiary**. The beneficiary has an equitable interest in the property in that the property must be used for his or her benefit. Accordingly, the beneficiary is said to hold *equitable title* in the trust property. The trustee stands in a fiduciary relationship to the beneficiary and must exercise a very high standard of care in managing the trust property. The beneficiary, as holder of equitable title, may enforce the trust against the trustee, if necessary, by resort to the court system. In Scenario 1 above, the beneficiaries of the trust include Salvador's children living at the time Salvador's youngest child reaches the age of 21, while in Scenario 2 the beneficiaries include Stephen's three children (and only those three children).

A beneficiary, like a trustee, is essential for the creation of a trust, since only the beneficiary, as holder of equitable title, can enforce the trust. Except in the case of certain trusts established for charitable purposes, the beneficiary must be ascertainable based upon the settlor's description, unless the settlor has granted to the trustee or to another person the power to choose the beneficiary. Class descriptions such as "my family" or "my spouse's relatives" are generally deemed sufficient to permit identification of the beneficiaries, although descriptions such as "my friends" are usually deemed too vague.

The Settlor

Most trusts are created by the express and intended direction of the owner of property, who is referred to either as the *settlor, trustor,* or *grantor* (the term *settlor* will be used hereafter). The settlor relinquishes title in the property to the trustee and has no power to enforce the trust. Some types of trusts may be created without a settlor (see *Trusts Arising by Operation of Law*).

The Requirement of a Trust *Res*

Creation of an express trust requires that an existing property interest be placed in trust. Trust property is also referred to as the trust *res* (from the Latin term meaning ''thing'' or ''object''), *corpus,* or *principal.* Without a *res,* there can be no trust. The trust *res* may be either a tangible or intangible property interest, either a present or future interest, and either a vested or contingent interest. However, the trust *res* must be an existing interest in existing property.

EXAMPLE: *Kathryn declares: ''All profits I make henceforth from ABC Corporation I hereby place in trust for the benefit of Dorothy.''* **Result:** *The trust will fail because the intended trust* res *is merely an expectation rather than an existing property interest.*

One notable exception to the requirement of a trust *res* involves life insurance trusts, which are valid even though the trust remains unfunded until the death of the settlor.

The Requirement of Present Intent

As a general rule, the settlor must have a *present intent* to create a trust; that is, the settlor must intend for the trust to take effect immediately rather than at some future time. A testamentary trust meets this requirement as long as the settlor intends for the trust to take effect at his or her death.

EXAMPLE: *Geri declares: ''Chris owes me $10,000. When I collect this debt from Chris, I will be setting aside the money in trust until my death, at which time the executor of my estate shall distribute the money to Bobbi.''* **Result:** *The trust is invalid because Geri does not intend to create a trust* now. *If Geri had intended that the trust take effect immediately, assuming Chris's debt to Geri was legally enforceable, the debt would be considered a property interest, and the trust would be valid.*

However, if a promise to create a trust in the future is supported by consideration, a valid trust is created at the time the trustee acquires the trust property.

An intent to create a trust may be manifested either by words or conduct, although a trust involving a real-property interest must be evidenced by a writing. Oral trusts present obvious evidentiary problems, so nearly all enforceable trusts are reduced to some sort of writing. The settlor need not express his or her intent to create a trust to the beneficiary, nor is it necessary that the settlor know that what he or she is creating is called a trust. If the words used in attempting to create the trust merely express a preference, hope, wish, or suggestion as to how the transferee should deal with the property, rather than expressing a clear and unequivocal command or directive, the trust is likely to fail for lack of sufficient intent.

Allowable Trust Purposes

A trust may be created for any lawful purpose that is not contrary to public policy. Accordingly, a trust will not be enforced if its purpose is to operate an illegal business or to operate a business in an illegal manner. Also, trust provisions requiring the trustee to act in a tortious manner are unenforceable. Examples of trusts that may violate public policy include trusts in restraint of marriage and trusts created for the primary purpose of avoiding creditors.

TYPES OF TRUSTS

Because trusts may be used to serve any lawful purpose (as noted above), they appear in many different forms. Although the probate paralegal deals primarily only with a few different types of trusts, he or she should at least be familiar with all of the common types, as discussed in the following materials and classified in Figure 9-3.

Express Trusts—General Types

An **express trust** is created by the express and intended direction of the property owner (settlor). An express trust is usually created by a transfer of property from the settlor to another person as trustee, either during the settlor's lifetime or by testamentary disposition in the settlor's will. After the transfer, the settlor relinquishes all title to the property and has no power to enforce the trust. Alternatively, an owner of property may create an express trust during his or her lifetime without transfer of the property to another by a **declaration of trust** in which the owner declares that he or she holds the property (as trustee) henceforth for the benefit of another. A trust in which the settlor and trustee are the same person is referred to under the federal tax laws (and throughout this chapter) as a **grantor trust**. An express trust created by the settlor during his or her lifetime is called an *inter vivos* trust (also referred to as a *living trust*), while an express trust created after the settlor's death under the terms of the settlor's will is referred to as a *testamentary trust*. *Inter vivos* trusts can be further classified either as revocable or irrevocable (testamentary trusts are inherently irrevocable). In creating a **revocable trust**, the settlor retains the power to revoke the trust and take back legal and equitable ownership of the trust property (the revocable trust is commonly referred to as a *revocable living trust*). Most revocable trusts are also grantor trusts. By contrast, an **irrevocable trust**, once established, forever terminates the settlor's rights with respect to the trust property. The holder of a power of appointment may also create an express trust by exercising the power in favor of another as trustee. Express trusts can also be classi-

FIGURE 9-3   TYPES OF TRUSTS

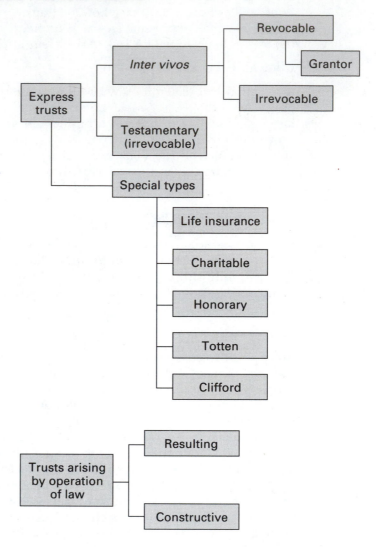

fied as either *private* or *charitable*. Charitable trusts, as well as other special types of express trusts, are discussed in the materials that follow.

FOCUS: Although trusts may take many different forms and serve varied purposes, the types of trusts of primary concern to the probate paralegal are the testamentary trust and the revocable *inter vivos* (living) trust; irrevocable *inter vivos* trusts are generally used only in larger estates for income-tax and estate-tax purposes.

Express Trusts—Specific Types

In dealing with testamentary trusts and revocable *inter vivos* trusts (see above), the probate paralegal should be familiar with certain particular types of express trusts that serve very specific purposes. Some of the more common specific types include

1. Life insurance trusts
2. Charitable trusts
3. Honorary trusts
4. Totten trusts
5. Clifford trusts

Life Insurance Trusts. A **life insurance trust** is a type of irrevocable *inter vivos* trust in which the only asset contained in the trust is a life insurance policy. The settlor is generally the person whose life is insured. The settlor simply pays premium amounts to the trustee, who may be either an individual or the life insurance company itself. In the former case, the trustee's only duty (until the settlor's death) is to mail premium payments to the insurance company.

A life insurance trust may serve several useful purposes. In contrast to an ordinary life insurance policy, a life insurance trust may provide for deferred distribution—for example, to minor beneficiaries—upon the death of the person whose life is insured. Moreover, because the trust is irrevocable, the policy is not included either in the settlor-decedent's probate estate or tax estate. A life insurance trust can be particularly useful in the case of a large estate comprised primarily of *illiquid* assets such as real estate or business interests. The insurance proceeds provide liquidity for payment of debts and taxes without having to sell other assets and without increasing estate-tax liability (since the proceeds are not part of the settlor's tax estate).

A life insurance trust holds no advantages, other than those mentioned above, over an ordinary life insurance policy that either (1) names a trust as beneficiary or (2) is transferred to an *inter vivos* trust during the settlor's lifetime. Moreover, because the trust is irrevocable, the settlor cannot alter the plan for distribution of the proceeds; this drawback may pose a significant problem if circumstances change—for example, in the event of a subsequent divorce—and deserves careful consideration, regardless of the size of the individual's estate. Also, the tax rules for gifts made to irrevocable trusts are complex, and lawyer's fees and accountant's fees are likely to be substantial.

Charitable Trusts. Express trusts may be classified either as private or charitable. A private trust is created for the benefit of a definite and ascertainable beneficiary. By contrast, a **charitable trust** is created for indefinite and changing beneficiaries, so that the public or community as a whole is viewed as the beneficiary. A charitable trust must also be created for a charitable purpose; otherwise, the trust will fail for lack of a definite or ascertainable beneficiary. According to the Restatement (Second) of Trusts, charitable purposes include:

1. The relief of poverty
2. The advancement of education
3. The promotion of health

4. Governmental or municipal purposes
5. Other purposes the accomplishment of which is beneficial to the community

Charitable trusts are enforced by the state's attorney general on the public's behalf.

Perhaps the most important difference between charitable and private trusts is that charitable trusts are subject to the doctrine of *cy pres* (literally meaning ''as near as possible''), by which a court can substitute one charitable organization or group of recipients for a prior beneficiary when the prior beneficiary ceases to exist or ceases to be charitable in nature. The *cy pres* doctrine also applies where the directions to the trustee of a charitable trust become impracticable and frustrate the charitable purpose or where the stated purpose has become obsolete.

Honorary Trusts. An **honorary trust** is one that is created for some noncharitable purpose but does not directly benefit any human being. Common examples of honorary trusts include trusts created for the care of pets, for the erection of monuments, and for the maintenance of grave sites. Since an honorary trust has no direct beneficiary and therefore no one to enforce the trust, the trustee is generally on his or her ''honor'' to carry out the settlor's wishes.

Totten Trusts. A **Totten trust** is simply a bank account in which title is shown, for example, as ''Yuan Sheng, Trustee for Mei-Ling Sheng.'' On the death of the owner of the account (i.e., the trustee), the balance of the account automatically passes to the beneficiary and is not subject to probate. Thus, a Totten trust account is a type of revocable *inter vivos* trust. Totten trusts are also referred to as *savings bank trusts*. P.O.D. (payable-on-death) accounts, introduced in Chapter 4, are used more commonly today and serve the same purpose as Totten trusts, although a P.O.D. account is not actually a trust.

Clifford Trusts. A **Clifford trust**, also referred to as a *reversionary trust* or *short-term trust*, is a type of trust in which the settlor retains the right to possess again the property transferred in trust—that is, the settlor retains a reversionary interest—upon the occurrence of an event or the expiration of a period of time. Clifford trusts are named after the person who first created this type of trust and established its validity in the federal tax courts. Dr. Clifford wished to transfer income from certain assets *temporarily* to his children, to be taxed at their relatively low income-tax rates rather than at his rates. He established a trust whereby the property would *revert* back to him after ten years and one day. Initially, the tax laws allowed a settlor to shift income temporarily under this type of trust arrangement as long as the income interest was established for more than ten years or for the life of the beneficiary (or for the life of another whose life expectancy was greater than ten years). Unless the trusts met at least one of these requirements, the income from the property placed in trust was taxed to the settlor rather than to the income beneficiary.

After the Clifford case and the resulting tax legislation, the "Clifford trust" became a popular income-shifting device for higher-bracket taxpayers, particularly as a means of planning for a child's college education. However, the 1986 Tax Reform Act established more restrictive rules with respect to Clifford trusts; as a result, Clifford trusts are no longer attractive as estate-planning devices.

Trusts Arising by Operation of Law

While an express trust is produced by the actual "express" intention of the settlor, other types of trusts may be created without such intention and are said to arise *by operation of law*. Trusts arising by operation of law are not estate-planning devices but rather are remedial devices developed by the courts and used to settle legal disputes. Although such trusts are not of concern to the probate paralegal, the two most common such trusts—the *resulting trust* and the *constructive trust*—are nevertheless discussed briefly below.

Resulting Trusts. One example of a trust arising by operation of law is the **resulting trust**, in which an intent to create a trust, although not expressed, may be inferred from circumstances. For example, where a person conveys legal title to another intending to create an express trust, but the trust fails for lack of one or more elements necessary for the creation of a valid express trust, the law presumes that the settlor did not intend to confer a beneficial interest on the transferee, and a resulting trust will arise by operation of law, by which the transferee is deemed to hold the property in trust for the transferor and has a duty to reconvey the property to the transferor (or to his or her estate). Similarly, if property placed in an express trust is excessive for accomplishing the purpose of the trust, a resulting trust may arise, requiring the trustee to reconvey the excess property to the settlor. Also, in some states a resulting trust arises when one person pays the purchase price for property while title is taken in another's name, at least under certain circumstances.

Constructive Trusts. Another example of a trust arising by operation of law is the **constructive trust**, which arises where one person has fraudulently or otherwise wrongfully acquired legal title in property from another. The wrongdoer is said to hold the property in constructive trust for the original owner and is under a duty to reconvey it. Third parties who subsequently acquire title from the wrongdoer, with or without knowledge of the fraud or impropriety, might also be deemed to hold the property in trust for the original owner. Although a mere breach of promise generally does not give rise to a constructive trust, there are several exceptions to this rule, including a breach of promise concerning a will or inheritance.

DEVELOPING AN ESTATE PLAN

The foregoing materials have provided you with a general sense of the trust concept as well as some basic terminology. Before examining further how trusts are used by estate-planning lawyers, it is important to understand the estate-planning process both as a whole and from the lawyer's perspective. In developing a plan for disposition of a client's property upon death, the lawyer is guided by the following broad and often competing objectives:

■ Providing for distribution to the client's desired beneficiaries and in the manner and time desired by the client
■ Minimizing income-tax and death-tax liability, both at the federal and state levels
■ Minimizing delays and expenses associated with distribution at death

The estate-planning lawyer must also address certain concerns not directly related to the disposition of property at death, including:

■ Proper and continued care of the client and management of the client's assets in the event the client becomes incapacitated
■ Care and custody, upon incapacity or death, of the client's minor or adult dependents in accordance with the client's wishes

The client's own personal and family objectives must be considered in light of these broader objectives as the first step in the estate-planning process. The lawyer must then help the client to achieve his or her goals through the use of the various estate-planning devices and techniques available to the client. These objectives and means are examined in the following materials, with particular emphasis on the trust as an estate-planning tool.

Personal and Family Considerations

The estate-planning lawyer not only must implement the client's intention regarding the disposition of the estate but also must assist the client in formulating that intention by pointing out possibilities the client may not have considered. A variety of personal and family considerations should come to bear in developing a distribution plan that fully reflects the client's desires. A plan by which the entire estate passes outright to the surviving spouse fails to account for the possibility that the surviving spouse may remarry and leave all or a significant portion of the estate to people who are strangers to the deceased spouse. Accordingly, before settling on such a plan, the client should consider the likelihood of remarriage, the size of the estate, and the expected interests of others (such as children) that might be detrimentally affected. A distribution plan requiring an *equal* division of property among children may fail to account for their relative needs. One child may achieve financial security by marrying into a wealthy family, while another child struggles financially as a single parent with limited resources. On the other hand, if a particular devisee is financially irresponsible, a more sensible plan may call for a smaller relative distribution or for small periodic distributions to that devisee. Persons under mental or physical disabilities typically require special care that is generally quite costly. Such persons may qualify for government benefits and assistance such as Supplemental Security Income

(SSI) or Medicare, but only if their income and the value of their assets are sufficiently low. Not only might an inheritance disqualify the person from receiving this assistance, the government also might be entitled to seize the inheritance to offset benefits previously paid. This problem may be addressed either by excluding persons under permanent disabilities entirely from the distribution plan or by providing for distribution at the discretion of the executor or trustee. Children by prior marriages or relationships, as well as marriages in which the value of the estate of one or both spouses at the time the marriage began is substantial, also present special challenges to the estate planner.

 TAYLOR TRUST: Walter and Betty Taylor are both concerned about preserving their estates for their respective families, particularly since they have been married for only ten years and since they accumulated a significant portion of their respective assets prior to the marriage. Specifically, Betty wishes to ensure that her interest in her family's ranch passes to her blood relatives, while Walter desires to pass his most valuable asset—his general contracting business—down to his son David, who has helped his father with the business for many years. At the same time, however, Walter and Betty both wish to provide for the needs of the surviving spouse. You will learn shortly how trusts can be used to meet these conflicting objectives by providing for limited and successive enjoyment of their respective estates.

Uses and Limitations of Wills and Will Substitutes

From previous chapters, you should already have a thorough grasp of the procedural merits and drawbacks associated with nonprobate transfers (aside from *inter vivos* trusts) as well as with transfers under a will (as summarized in Table 9-1). No single estate-planning technique is appropriate in every situation, and rarely is one technique by itself adequate to address all of the needs of one particular person. If the primary objective is to avoid probate, an unmarried person with a very simple distribution plan—for example, a plan that gives the entire estate to one or two adult children or siblings—might use some combination of joint ownership, P.O.D. accounts, and life insurance to transfer the entire estate quickly and inexpensively, without resort to the court system. Although the joint-tenancy form of ownership deserves serious consideration where creditors are a primary concern, exclusive use of the joint-tenancy form of ownership as an estate-planning technique is unlikely to address all of the client's estate-planning objectives. Similarly, exclusive use of the tenancy-by-the-entirety form of co-ownership between spouses, although easy to implement and effective in avoiding probate upon the death of the first spouse, is unlikely to adequately address all of the client's objectives.

In many cases involving modest estates, a simple will or a will with a testamentary trust is recommended. If the primary concern is creditors or possible conflict among heirs and devisees, resort to the court system may be inevitable in any event, and subjecting the entire estate to probate might be

TABLE 9-1   USES AND LIMITATIONS OF ESTATE-PLANNING DEVICES

Device	Advantages	Disadvantages
Intestacy	■ No effort ■ No expense ■ Creditors' claims cut off in probate	■ Property distributed according to state law ■ Probate (unless informal probate, small-estate set aside or summary administration available) ■ Administrator appointed by court ■ Personal guardian selected by court
Simple will	■ Overcomes disadvantages of intestacy ■ Relatively low front-end cost ■ Cuts off creditors' claims	■ Probate (unless informal probate, small-estate set aside, or summary administration available)
Summary administration	■ Faster and less costly than probate	■ Court proceedings and paperwork generally require attorney's assistance ■ Available only in certain situations ■ Not available in all states
Community property form of ownership	■ No effort to implement ■ Avoids probate (with respect to portion passing to spouse) ■ Favorable tax consequences (stepped-up basis on both halves)	■ Restricted to ownership between spouses ■ Does not avoid probate with respect to portion not passing to surviving spouse ■ Court proceeding still required for portion passing to surviving spouse ■ Probate if simultaneous death of both spouses ■ May be inconsistent with overall will plan ■ Co-ownership between surviving spouse and decedent spouse's devisee(s) may create conflict ■ Possible stepped-down basis for depreciating property ■ Creditors of one spouse may reach both halves (under some circumstances) ■ May operate unfairly upon divorce
Tenancy by the entirety	■ Simple to implement ■ Avoids probate ■ Protects against unwanted transfer by other spouse (joint action required)	■ May be inconsistent with overall will plan ■ Restricted to ownership between spouses ■ Spouses must own equal interests (inflexible) ■ One spouse cannot transfer interest without other spouse's consent
Small estate set-aside	■ Avoids probate or other court proceedings ■ Tangible personal property quickly and easily distributed ■ Useful in conjunction with other probate avoidance techniques	■ Limited to small estates ■ Not available if real property is otherwise part of probate estate ■ Potential for fraud and abuse by heirs ■ Not available in all states
Joint tenancy	■ Avoids probate ■ Simple to create ■ Surviving joint tenant can immediately deal with decedent's interest	■ Other joint tenant(s) can transfer/transmute interest ■ May be inconsistent with overall will plan ■ Decedent joint tenant has no control over disposition of interest by surviving joint tenant(s)

Continued

TABLE 9-1   CONTINUED

Device	Advantages	Disadvantages
Joint tenancy (*continued*)	■ Decedent owner's creditors cannot reach surviving owners' interests ■ Available in all states	■ Possible lien against or forced sale of entire property to satisfy creditors of one joint tenant ■ Probate at death of surviving joint tenant ■ Probate if simultaneous death of joint tenants ■ Joint tenancy with nonspouse may create conflict ■ Adverse tax consequences
Totten trust or P.O.D. account	■ Avoids probate ■ Simple to create ■ Useful to make specific monetary gifts ■ Useful in conjunction with other probate avoidance techniques ■ Available in all states	■ May be inconsistent with overall will plan ■ Limited to accounts at financial institutions
Life insurance	■ Avoids probate (unless estate is beneficiary) ■ Provides liquidity for payment of debts, taxes, estate costs, etc. ■ Useful for young family to build estate and establish financial security ■ High return on investment ■ Available in all states	■ May be inconsistent with overall will plan ■ High front-end cost
Inter vivos (living) trust	■ Avoids probate ■ Avoids conservatorship of estate ■ Unified management ■ Continuity of management ■ Useful if professional management desired ■ Trustee's performance can be tested ■ Contest less likely than with will ■ Useful for deferring distribution ■ Useful for married couple to reduce/defer estate-tax liability	■ Initial expense and formalities ■ Client's psychological resistance to unfamiliar ideas ■ Separate records required ■ Effective only for assets transferred to trust ■ Reliable successor trustee required ■ Trustee fees ■ Trustee not monitored by court ■ Creditors' claims not cut off as in probate (except in some states)
Will with testamentary trust	■ Same advantages as simple will ■ Useful if professional management desired ■ Useful for deferring distribution ■ Useful for married couple to reduce/defer estate-tax liability	■ Lacks other advantages of *inter vivos* trust ■ Reliable trustee required ■ Trustee fees

Note: This table excludes *inter vivos* transfers (including gifts, sales, and transfers to irrevocable trusts) motivated by tax considerations in larger estates.

desirable for the protection of the decedent's interests against claims of interested persons. (In some states, though, including California, creditor-claim statutes are now applicable to decedents' trust estates as well as to probate estates.) Where death taxes and income taxes are of primary concern, as in the case of larger estates, particularly those of married persons, one or more trusts are almost invariably recommended. Testamentary trusts and *inter vivos* trusts may be employed with equal effectiveness for a variety of uses, while *inter vivos* trusts hold a number of additional advantages. The more common uses that the probate paralegal is likely to encounter in the context of family wealth transactions are addressed throughout the remaining materials in this chapter.

Deferring Distribution through the Use of Trusts

The most significant and perhaps the most obvious use of the trust is to defer distribution to one or more beneficiaries. Deferring distribution may serve one or more of the purposes discussed below.

Property Management. The estate-planning lawyer must address the possibility of the client's property passing to a person not sufficiently mature or competent to manage his or her inheritance in a responsible manner, such as a minor child of a predeceased beneficiary or an elderly beneficiary (such as a parent) who is prone to mismanagement or susceptible to undue influence. If the amount is sufficiently low, applicable law may permit another person, usually a parent or other legal guardian, simply to take possession of the property on behalf of the devisee. Applicable law may also provide for the establishment of a custodian account until the devisee attains a certain age (see Chapter 11). However, where the inheritance is substantial, a court-appointed financial guardian or conservator will be required (see Chapter 11) unless the decedent planned ahead and provided a trust for the devisee.

A trust is far more flexible than a guardianship or a custodian account. It affords the decedent a great deal of control as to how the property will be managed and applied for the benefit of the beneficiary as well as to when distributions occur. The settlor may allow the trustee as much or as little discretion as the settlor wishes regarding the management and distribution of the trust property. A certain amount of discretion should be allowed in order to accommodate unexpected changes in circumstances that may and frequently do occur. For example, the settlor may give the trustee the power to distribute income and principal to or for the benefit of the beneficiary for such purposes as the beneficiary's support, maintenance, and education until such time as outright distribution of the remaining trust estate is called for under the terms of the trust. The trust may call for outright distribution of the *entire* remaining trust estate in one lump sum or, more typically, in fractional amounts over a period of time—for example, one-third when the beneficiary attains the age of 21, one-third at age 30, and the remainder at age 40. Most estate planners agree that, unless a beneficiary is developmentally disabled or otherwise clearly incompetent to manage his or her own affairs, distributions of principal while the beneficiary is relatively young are preferable. However, trusts continuing for a beneficiary's entire lifetime are not unheard of and may be appropriate in certain situations, such as in large estates where the income from the trust might be sufficient to support the beneficiaries (also, revocable *inter vivos* trusts typically continue for the duration of the settlor-beneficiary's lifetime).

Successive and Limited Enjoyment. A trust is an effective means of providing for limited enjoyment of one beneficiary in order to preserve trust property for enjoyment by one or more successive beneficiaries. Perhaps the most common situation where this objective may be desirable involves the settlor's surviving spouse. The following will provision exemplifies a typical distribution plan under a testamentary trust:

> "Upon my death, if my wife Carmen survives me, I leave my entire estate in trust to my brother Scott for the benefit of Carmen during her lifetime. The trustee shall pay to or apply for the benefit of Carmen all income and as much principal from the trust as necessary, in the trustee's reasonable discretion, for Carmen's support, maintenance, and care. Upon Carmen's death, the trust shall terminate, and the trustee shall distribute the remaining trust estate to my issue, upon the principle of representation."

Establishing a trust for the surviving spouse addresses the problem of unwanted diversion of the decedent's property to strangers while at the same time providing for the spouse's continued financial support.

In very large estates, it may be preferable to retain the assets in trust, distributing only the income to the beneficiaries while allowing the beneficiaries to borrow from the trust for specified purposes, such as starting a business. Another situation where distribution of income only might be appropriate involves the newly married beneficiary, where the spending habits of the new spouse are not known. An alternative way to address this problem is by fractional distributions over time, on the theory that the longer the couple is married the less likely it is that they will divorce.

Concurrent Enjoyment. Outright distribution of the estate fails to address the possibility of unexpected future needs of particular beneficiaries. Where a trust is established in order to delay distribution to two or more children, it is generally recommended that distribution of principal to all children be delayed until the youngest child attains a certain age, such as age 25. Delaying distribution in this manner will ensure that all trust assets are available to meet unexpected needs of minor children (or grandchildren) such as expensive medical care. A trust calling for this type of plan is commonly referred to as a **family pot trust**, and the provisions that allow the trustee to distribute income and principal among the beneficiaries according to need are commonly referred to as "sprinkling" provisions. A family pot plan may not be necessary in the case of large estates, where both anticipated and unexpected financial needs are adequately met by each beneficiary's share.

TAYLOR TRUST: Walter and Betty Taylor have settled on a distribution plan in which one or more trusts will serve all three of the purposes discussed above. Under the plan, assuming that Walter dies first, his entire estate, except for certain items of tangible personal property and with the possible exception of his contracting business, will be retained in trust for the duration of Betty's lifetime. Until Betty's death, the income from the trust property will be paid to Betty; trust principal will also be available for Betty's support as well as to meet the needs of Walter's children and grandchildren (including college education for the grandchildren). The trustee will be given a certain amount of discretion as to distribution of principal among the beneficiaries. Upon Betty's subsequent death, the remaining trust property will be distributed outright to Walter's issue, except that any distribution to a grandchild will be kept in a separate trust and applied toward the grandchild's college education, at least for a period of time. A similar plan will control Betty's estate if she should predecease Walter. Later in this chapter, you will learn that Walter's estate will actually be allocated at his death between two different trusts for the purpose of carrying out this distribution plan while at the same time avoiding estate-tax liability (see *Estate Planning and Taxes; Estate-Tax Planning for Married Persons*).

Future Interests and the Rule Against Perpetuities

Where a beneficiary's right to possession and enjoyment of all or some portion of the subject property is deferred until some future time, the beneficiary is said to own a *future interest* in the property. If the beneficiary's eventual right to possession and enjoyment is not in doubt, then the beneficiary is said to have a *vested* interest, even though the beneficiary may not have a present right to possession or enjoyment (all present property rights are vested). By contrast, if a beneficiary's eventual right to possession and enjoyment depends upon the occurrence or nonoccurrence of some event, then the interest is said to be *contingent*, and the future interest does not vest until the contingency is removed. Future interests in real property may be created through the use of estates that are shorter in potential duration than a fee interest, such as a life estate or a tenancy for years (for example, "I give Blackacre to A for life, then to B."). Today, however, future interests are generally created through the use of trusts. Consider the following alternative trust provisions:

SCENARIO 1: *S's will states: "I leave my estate to T in trust for the benefit of A during A's lifetime, then upon A's death to B."*

SCENARIO 2: *S declares to T: "I hereby give this check for $50,000 to you in trust, income and principal to be applied for the benefit of A in your reasonable discretion during A's lifetime. Upon A's death, I instruct you to distribute the remainder to B if B survives A, otherwise to C."*

In both provisions, A has a present vested interest as beneficiary of the trust. In the first provision, B has a vested future interest, while in the second provision, B and C each hold a contingent future interest. The interests of B and C are also referred to as *remainder interests,* and B and C are said to be *remaindermen,* since they are entitled to whatever property is "remaining" at A's death.

By creating future interests, it would seem that a person could control the disposition of property indefinitely. However, the right to exercise "dead-hand control" of property is limited in most states by a rule of law referred to as the *Rule Against Perpetuities*, which establishes limits on the time within which a beneficiary's interest must vest. This rule of law can be very difficult and confusing to apply, even for experienced estate planners, and is not of vital concern to the probate paralegal. For their own protection and for the protection of their clients, estate-planning lawyers typically include *perpetuities-saving clauses* in their trust documents; such clauses provide for automatic termination of a trust at the time that a violation of the Rule would otherwise result.

Additional Uses of *Inter Vivos* Trusts

As discussed earlier, deferring distribution through the use of trusts protects the beneficiaries and allows successive, limited, and concurrent enjoyment of a decedent's estate. These objectives may be accomplished with equal postmortem effectiveness through the use of either testamentary or *inter vivos* trusts. However, *inter vivos* trusts have a number of additional advantages:

- At the decedent's death, as well as in the event of the settlor's incapacity in the case of a grantor trust, the successor trustee (generally named in trust instrument) may immediately assume the office and provide uninterrupted management of the trust assets.
- An *inter vivos* trust may be used to protect the settlor from his or her own wasteful spending habits or poor financial judgment incapacity.
- Property placed in trust during the decedent's lifetime is not subject to estate administration, and in contrast to testamentary trust provisions included in the decedent's will, *inter vivos* trust instruments need not be probated.
- Establishing a trust during one's lifetime allows the settlor to "test" the trust—that is, to determine whether the trust provisions adequately address the settlor's needs.
- It is more difficult to wage a successful challenge against an *inter vivos* trust than against a will; thus, the use of an *inter vivos* trust discourages challenges or contests from disappointed heirs.

An irrevocable *inter vivos* trust may serve additional purposes as well, as discussed later (see *Additional Considerations for Large Estates*). The advantages of using revocable *inter vivos* trusts are summarized in Table 9-1.

TAYLOR TRUST: Walter and Betty Taylor will be establishing an *inter vivos* trust at this time. During their joint lifetimes, they will serve as co-trustees, and each spouse will retain the sole right to revoke the trust as to his or her separate property. Joint action will be required to revoke the trust with respect to community property. In the event of Betty's incapacity, Walter will continue to serve as sole trustee, and the trust will become irrevocable as to Betty's property but will remain revocable as to Walter's property. In the event of Walter's incapacity, Walter's son David will serve as co-trustee along with Betty, and the trust will become irrevocable as to Walter's property while remaining revocable as to Betty's property. At the first spouse's death, the surviving spouse may continue to serve as trustee (although if Walter dies first, David and Betty will serve as co-trustees). Thus, the trust will provide for continued and uninterrupted management of all trust property as well as obviating the necessity for probate of all property properly placed in trust prior to the owner-spouse's death. (The proper procedures for placing property in trust are discussed in Chapter 10.)

Marital Property Agreements

A marital property agreement establishes the character of all or some portion of a married person's property as either community or separate. Marital property agreements are commonly used in community-property states in order to overcome the presumption that all property acquired during marriage is community property, although they are used in other states as well to alter the rights of a married person with respect to a spouse's property. The agreement may be as simple as a one-page document executed by both spouses in which the spouses declare *all* property they own to be either community property or separate property. Where a couple has been married for a long time while residing in a community-property state, it is a common practice by lawyers to incorporate a simple community-property agreement into the estate plan in order to dispel any doubt as to the nature of the spouses' property. A marital-property agreement may, on the other hand, be quite complex, particularly in the case of second marriages or where either one or both spouses came into the marriage with substantial assets. A complete estate plan for an unmarried client contemplating marriage might also include an agreement with the prospective spouse concerning the character of property already owned as well as property acquired during the marriage; a marital property agreement executed prior to marriage is referred to as a *premarital* or *prenuptial agreement.*

 TAYLOR TRUST: Recall from Paralegal Assignment 1 that, even though the Taylors have been married for only ten years, the value of community property is likely to be significant. Ms. Cargis has explained to the Taylors that this issue will have a significant impact on the disposition of their respective estates and has indicated to them what their options are. Walter and Betty have reached a relatively complex agreement, calling for certain assets (and all income therefrom) to remain separate property of the respective spouses while other assets (and all income therefrom) are treated as community property. For example, the agreement will make clear that Walter's rental property (and all income therefrom) is and will remain his separate property, while the property used as their residence is community property. Ms. Cargis will prepare a written marital property agreement that Walter and Betty will execute along with their other estate-planning documents.

Small Business Interests

Small-business interests require special consideration during the estate-planning process. In the absence of careful planning, problems involving *valuation, management,* or *liquidity* may arise after the owner's death (or incapacity), as discussed below.

The Problem of Valuation. Since a small business is a unique asset, determining its value is inherently problematic. After the owner's death, the Internal Revenue Service may question how the value used for death-tax and/or income-tax purposes was determined. Valuation of a small-business interest is also a potential area of dispute between the deceased owner's estate and other co-owners of the business (stockholders or partners), as well as the decedent's heirs, devisees, and creditors. Resolving such problems generally requires an expensive and time-consuming appraisal of the business as well as negotiation among the parties involved. If valuation problems cannot be resolved by these means, the parties may ultimately resort to litigation to settle the matter.

Valuation problems can be prevented in many cases through the use of a properly structured buy-sell agreement (in the case of a partnership) or stock-redemption agreement (in the case of a corporation), in which the price and terms for a sale or redemption upon death are predetermined. Providing contractually for postmortem value and disposition of the business interest prior to the owner's death makes a successful challenge by the IRS or by other persons interested in the deceased owner's estate far less likely. If co-owners cannot agree on a predetermined value, they might nevertheless agree to be bound to an appraisal made by an agreed-upon third party.

As a related matter, the value of certain small businesses for federal estate-tax purposes can be minimized through what are referred to as *estate-tax freeze* techniques, which involve the judicious use and timing of predeath transfers. Similar techniques may also be employed to permit payment of estate taxes in installments over a period of years rather than in one lump sum shortly after death. The tax rules in this area are complex and are best understood and applied only by experienced estate-planning attorneys and certified public accountants.

Continuity of Management. Another potential problem with postmortem disposition of small-business interests stems from the fact that the owner of the small-business interest is normally involved actively in managing and operating the business. Thus, upon the owner's death (or incapacity), unless immediate and effective steps are taken to provide for continued management or for sale of the business, the business may deteriorate, resulting in substantial loss to the estate and to the beneficiaries. Where the decedent devoted many years to establishing and building the business, it can be tragic to see the entire value of the business lost in a short period of time. Continuity of management may be provided for prior to death by a variety of means, including an *inter vivos* trust arrangement, the corporate form of ownership, or a properly structured partnership agreement. If these methods are not used, the appointment of a special administrator (see Chapter 5) may be necessary to protect and preserve the asset.

The Problem of Liquidity. Where a decedent's estate faces substantial tax liability or other debts, it may be necessary to sell a small-business interest to satisfy these claims, particularly where the business interest is the largest asset of a decedent's estate. An undesired sale of a small business may have a devastating effect on the decedent's family or other co-owners, who may have looked to the business for regular income as well as for a sense of identity and pride. Accordingly, as a preventive measure, adequate amounts of life insurance should be purchased to provide the liquidity necessary to meet all foreseeable tax obligations and debts so that a forced sale of the business will not be necessary.

PRACTICE TIP: Where an estate-planning client holds a small-business interest, additional duties are cast not only on the estate-planning lawyer but also on the paralegal, who may be asked to obtain, review, and summarize a variety of business-related documents, such as corporate bylaws (and amendments), partnership agreements (and amendments), financial statements, and tax returns. If the lawyer determines that a corporation should be formed to further the client's estate-planning objectives, the probate paralegal may be requested to assist in the incorporation process. In addition, if the lawyer determines that contractual agreements with co-owners are necessary to serve the estate-planning needs of the client, the lawyer and probate paralegal must assume a transactional and potentially adversarial posture for this purpose.

TAYLOR TRUST: Since Walter Taylor's general contracting business is his largest asset, special care must be taken to guard against the types of problems discussed above. Walter is sole owner of the business and wishes to leave the business entirely to his son David. Thus, there are no potential postmortem management or valuation conflicts with co-owners. However, the absence of an arms-length valuation agreement may pose a problem in the event of an estate-tax audit. Ms. Cargis has recommended to Walter that he obtain annual appraisals to support the eventual date-of-death valuation. The business is incorporated, and the shares of stock in the corporation will be placed in Walter's *inter vivos trust*. The trust will provide for the outright disposition of the business to David upon Walter's death, and David will serve as co-trustee (along with Betty) after Walter's death. Thus, continuity of management should not pose a problem, unless David predeceases Walter, in which event the trust instrument will direct the trustee to sell the business.

Walter already owns a life insurance policy on his own life; the proceeds are payable to Betty. However, there is no assurance that Betty will be willing to apply these proceeds for the payment of debts or taxes upon Walter's death in the event additional liquidity is required to prevent an unwanted sale of Walter's business. Thus, Ms. Cargis has recommended the use of a separate life insurance trust for this purpose. Under the terms of the life insurance trust, the proceeds will be paid upon Walter's death to the Walter and Betty Taylor Trust, rather than to a particular person such as Betty or David. The life insurance trust will be irrevocable, so the proceeds will not add to Walter's gross tax estate.

ESTATE PLANNING AND TAXES

Regardless of the size of an estate, a comprehensive estate plan often includes the strategic application of a variety of tax concepts to minimize both estate-tax liability and income-tax liability. Of particular significance for married persons are the tax-basis rules respecting transfers of community property to a spouse. In larger estates, additional planning techniques involving gifting may be useful to further reduce death taxes and income taxes.

Estate Planning and the "Tax Basis" Concept

Recall from Chapter 7 that all taxable *inter vivos* gifts are cumulated with the estate remaining at the time of death to determine tax liability under the federal unified transfer-tax system and that no transfer-tax liability is incurred unless and until cumulative taxable transfers exceed $600,000 in total value. Accordingly, persons with modest estates need not be concerned with federal transfer taxes. However, *inter vivos* gifts and postmortem transfers also carry income-tax consequences that must be addressed during the estate-planning process, regardless of the estate's value.

Income Taxes and the Concept of Tax Basis. Gifting decisions often turn on the concept of **tax basis** (hereafter referred to simply as *basis*), which refers to the consideration paid for an asset, decreased to account for such factors as depreciation and depletion, and increased to account for such factors as improvements made to the asset. Adjustments to the initial basis are most common in the case of real-property assets. Upon subsequent sale of the asset, if the amount realized from the sale exceeds the asset's adjusted basis, the resulting capital gain must be reported as income for tax purposes; conversely, if the amount realized from a subsequent sale is less than the adjusted basis, the resulting loss may be deducted from income for income-tax purposes.

A gift is *not* a taxable event under the income-tax laws. In the case of an *inter vivos* gift, the donee receives what is referred to as a **carryover basis**; that is, the donee's basis in the asset is the same as the donor's basis (Table 9-2A), except that the carryover basis cannot be greater than the asset's fair market value at the time of the gift (Table 9-2B). However, in the case of a gift resulting from death (an inheritance), the donee receives what is referred to as a **stepped-up basis** in the asset; that is, the donee's basis is the asset's fair market value at the time of the donor's death (Table 9-2C), although an alternate valuation date of six months after the date of death may be used instead for this purpose. The donee must take this new basis regardless of whether the asset has increased or decreased in value; thus, a "step down" in basis is also possible (Table 9-2D).

Tax Basis and Estate-Planning Strategies. These basis rules suggest several estate-planning strategies. If a person inheriting an asset turns around and sells that asset immediately, it is likely that little or no gain or loss will result from the sale, since the stepped-up basis is likely to be the same as the sale

TABLE 9-2   TAX BASIS—*INTER VIVOS* VS. POSTMORTEM TRANSFERS

A. *Inter vivos* gift of low-basis asset		B. *Inter vivos* gift of high-basis asset	
$100,000	X's basis	$100,000	X's basis
$150,000	FMV at time of gift	$80,000	FMV at time of gift
$100,000	Y's basis (*carryover*)	$80,000	Y's basis (*FMV*)
$150,000	Proceeds from sale by Y	$80,000	Proceeds from sale by Y
$50	Taxable gain on sale (*Y pays tax for realized appreciation instead of X*)	$0	Taxable gain/loss on sale (*no income-tax deduction for depreciation*)
C. Postmortem transfer of low-basis asset		**D. Postmortem transfer of high-basis asset**	
$100,000	X's basis	$100,000	X's basis
$175,000	FMV at X's death	$80,000	FMV at X's death
$175,000	Y's basis (*step up*)	$80,000	Y's basis (*step down*)
$175,000	Proceeds from sale by Y	$80,000	Proceeds from sale by Y
$0	Taxable gain on sale (*appreciation escapes capital gains tax*)	$0	Taxable gain/loss on sale (*no income-tax deduction for depreciation*)

Abbreviations: X, transferor; Y, transferee; FMV, fair market value.

amount. Thus, an asset having a low basis relative to its fair market value—that is, an asset that has appreciated in value or is likely to appreciate prior to the owner's death—should be held until death in order for the donee to receive a basis step up and avoid capital-gains tax liability. On the other hand, if an asset has depreciated in value since it was acquired, the owner should consider selling it in order to utilize the income-tax deduction for the loss. If the asset is transferred gratuitously (either during lifetime or at death), a potential income-tax deduction for depreciation will be lost. If the owner prefers to make an *inter vivos* gift of a high-basis asset, the donor should consider a youthful donee who is likely to hold the asset for potential long-term appreciation until his or her death.

Tax Basis and Community Property. Income-tax basis considerations play an important role in planning estates that include significant community-property interests. With respect to community property only, the federal income-tax laws provide for a stepped-up basis, upon the death of one spouse, in not only the deceased spouse's one-half interest but also in the surviving spouse's one-half interest, even though no transfer of the survivor's interest has occurred. This rule provides for equal income-tax treatment for married individuals residing in either community-property or separate-property states. The rule suggests that, between spouses, the community-property form is preferable to the joint-tenancy form of co-ownership, at least from an income-tax standpoint (see Figure 9-4). The rule also provides another advantage in holding low-basis community-property assets until the death of one spouse.

FIGURE 9-4   TAX BASIS—JOINT TENANCY VS. COMMUNITY PROPERTY

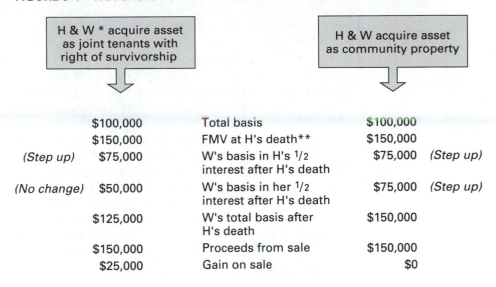

	H & W * acquire asset as joint tenants with right of survivorship		H & W acquire asset as community property
	$100,000	Total basis	$100,000
	$150,000	FMV at H's death**	$150,000
(Step up)	$75,000	W's basis in H's 1/2 interest after H's death	$75,000 (Step up)
(No change)	$50,000	W's basis in her 1/2 interest after H's death	$75,000 (Step up)
	$125,000	W's total basis after H's death	$150,000
	$150,000	Proceeds from sale	$150,000
	$25,000	Gain on sale	$0

* H, husband; W, wife.
** Assumes H dies first.

Estate-Tax Planning for Married Persons

Spouses with a combined estate significantly below $600,000 in value (accounting for taxable *inter vivos* gifts as well) need not be concerned with federal estate taxes. No estate-tax liability will be incurred at the death of either spouse, even where the first spouse to die leaves his or her entire estate to the surviving spouse. However, if the combined estate approaches $600,000 in total value, the estate-planning techniques discussed below should be considered in anticipation of the estate increasing in value.

The Marital Deduction. The unlimited marital deduction for gifts to a spouse, introduced in Chapter 7, suggests a variety of tax-planning techniques for spouses with combined estates exceeding $600,000 in value. As a starting point in this discussion, refer to Figure 9-5. Assume that the combined estate value is $800,000 and that the husband (H) dies first, leaving his entire estate outright to his wife (W) (either by will or by intestate succession). Regardless of whether H's share exceeds $600,000 in value, no estate tax need be incurred upon his death in light of the unlimited marital deduction. However, upon W's death, her estate will be subject to estate tax (Figure 9-5A). In this example, estate-tax liability at W's death might have been avoided if H had left part of his share to someone other than W—that is, "bypassing" W—thereby making use of all or part of H's $600,000 exemption equivalent (Figure 9-5B) as well as the marital deduction, if necessary (Figure 9-5C), to eliminate estate-tax liability at W's death.

Qualified Terminable Interest Property (QTIP). The distribution plans illustrated in Figure 9-5B and C may be further refined by placing the property transferred to W in trust for her benefit. However, unless W is given a sufficient degree of control over the trust, the transfer will not qualify for the marital deduction, because it will not be considered a transfer to W. If W is given the power to terminate the trust or otherwise to demand payment of the trust principal, then the transfer to the trust will clearly qualify for the marital deduction as a transfer to the surviving spouse. However, H loses control over the ultimate disposition of the property passing to W. This problem can be solved through the use of a special type of trust, referred to as a *QTIP* trust. The term *QTIP* is an acronym for **qualified terminable interest property** and is provided for under the provisions of the Internal Revenue Code. A QTIP trust may be used to provide for successive enjoyment of a decedent's estate while at the same time permitting the use of the marital deduction. In other words, although QTIP property does not pass outright to the surviving spouse, the property may be treated in this manner for the purpose of the marital deduction. The property is then included in the surviving spouse's gross tax estate. Thus, the estate tax is not avoided but is deferred through the use of a QTIP trust. In order for property to qualify for the marital deduction under the QTIP provisions of the Internal Revenue Code, the following requirements must be strictly met:

1. The surviving spouse is entitled for life to all of the income from the entire interest.
2. Such income is payable annually or at more frequent intervals.
3. The surviving spouse has the power, exercisable in favor of himself or herself (or his or her estate), to appoint the entire interest.
4. Such power is exercisable by the survivor alone and in all events (although it may be limited to exercise either during life or by will).
5. No part of the interest is subject to a power in any other person to appoint to anyone other than the surviving spouse.

Note that the surviving spouse's rights in QTIP property extend only to *income* and not to principal, and so the decedent spouse may retain control over the disposition of principal after the spouse's death.

A QTIP trust is one example of what is referred to more generally as a *marital deduction trust.* Under another form of marital deduction trust, referred to as a *lifetime income power-of-appointment trust,* the surviving spouse may be given a general power of appointment over the entire trust estate in addition to the same powers provided for under the QTIP provisions. This form of trust is not used as widely as the QTIP trust, however, since it fails to protect the decedent spouse's estate from diversion by the surviving spouse. In those instances where it is desirable to afford the surviving spouse some degree of control over the trust corpus (in addition to trust income), a QTIP trust that also grants to the spouse a *limited* power of appointment may be used. A third form of marital deduction trust, referred to as an *estate trust,* is

FIGURE 9-5 PRESERVING THE UNIFIED CREDIT AGAINST FEDERAL ESTATE TAX

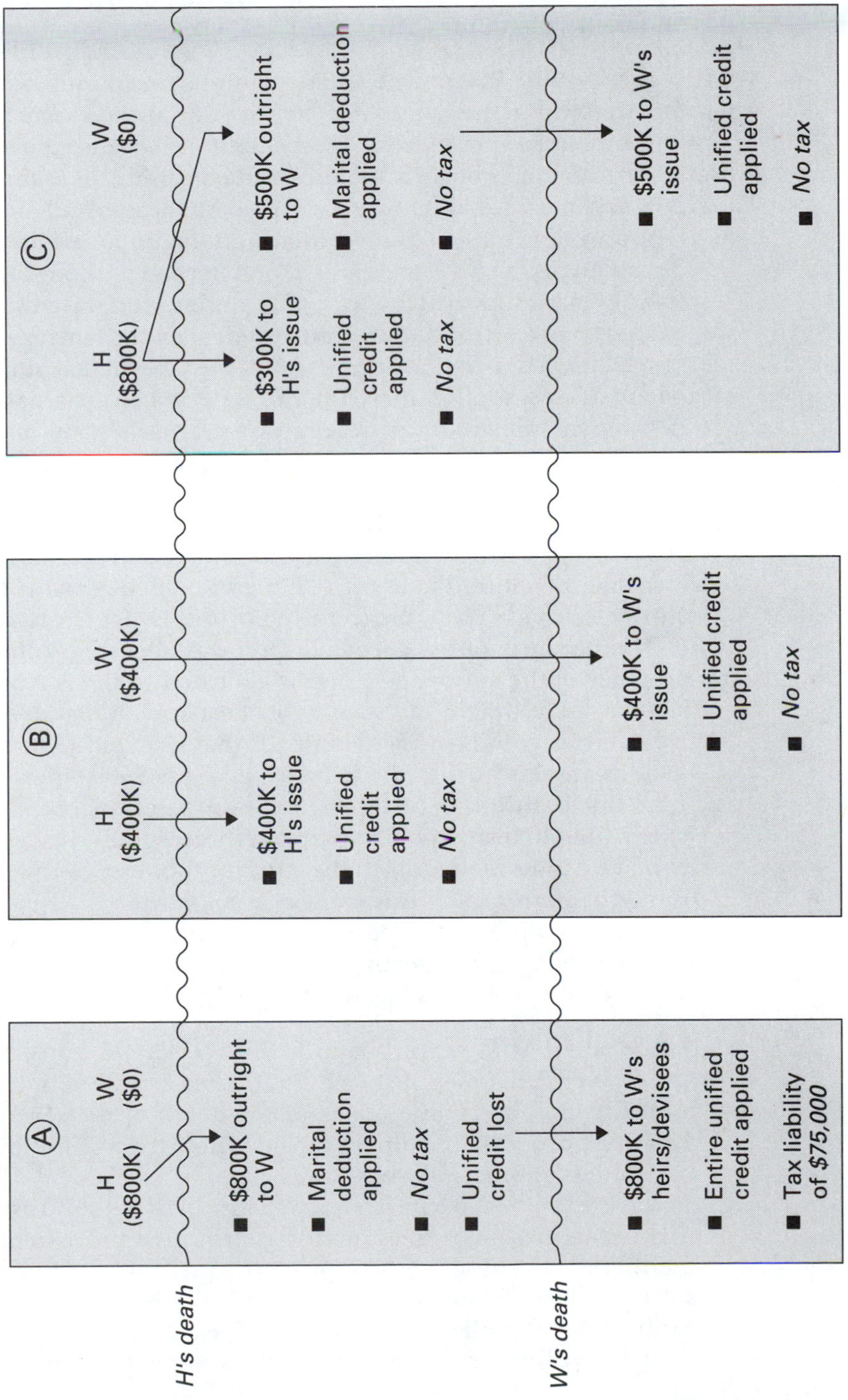

A

H's death

H ($800K) W ($0)

- $800K outright to W
- Marital deduction applied
- *No tax*
- Unified credit lost

W's death

- $800K to W's heirs/devisees
- Entire unified credit applied
- *Tax liability of $75,000*

B

H ($400K) W ($400K)

- $400K to H's issue
- Unified credit applied
- *No tax*

- $400K to W's issue
- Unified credit applied
- *No tax*

C

H ($800K) W ($0)

- $300K to H's issue
- Unified credit applied
- *No tax*

- $500K outright to W
- Marital deduction applied
- *No tax*

- $500K to W's issue
- Unified credit applied
- *No tax*

also allowed under the federal tax laws but is rarely used today, because it serves none of the nontax purposes of a QTIP trust.

"AB" and "ABC" Plans. The estate-planning techniques discussed above may be used with either a testamentary trust or an *inter vivos* trust. However, *inter vivos* trusts are preferred in most situations because they serve the additional purposes of probate avoidance and continuity of management in the event of incapacity. The most widely used such plan calls for the assets of both spouses to be placed, during their joint lifetimes, either in one trust or in separate trusts (a single trust is assumed hereafter). (See Figure 9-6.) This is generally accomplished by way of a declaration of trust in which the spouses serve as trustees and continue to deal with their respective assets in the same manner as before the trust was established. Until the death or incapacity of one spouse, the trust can be revoked or amended by either spouse as to his or her respective assets only, and the trust may be amended by agreement of both spouses.

Upon the death or incapacity of one spouse, if separate trusts were established initially, that trust becomes irrevocable; if a single trust was established at the outset, the trust assets are allocated to two separate trusts: (1) a survivor's trust (referred to as the "A" trust), which remains revocable, and (2) the decedent's bypass trust (referred to as the "B" trust), which is irrevocable. The property of the deceased spouse is allocated to the B trust, and the property of the surviving spouse is allocated to the A trust. This plan is particularly useful where the spouses' estates are comparable in value, as is common in community-property states. If the deceased spouse's share—that is, the amount allocated to the B trust—exceeds $600,000 in value, federal estate taxes will ordinarily be owing, since the assets placed in the B trust do not pass to the surviving spouse. To avoid this result, the excess amount may either be distributed outright to the surviving spouse, to the A trust, or to a QTIP trust (referred to in this context as a "C trust"). Under any of these three scenarios, the marital deduction is available to defer estate-tax liability until the second spouse's death. This distribution scheme serves a variety of important estate-planning objectives:

- Estate administration (probate) is unnecessary to transfer the trust estate of either spouse, because the trust is established during their joint lifetimes and continues until the death of the second spouse. However, property remaining outside the trust will not escape probate unless another will substitute is used.
- In the event of incapacity of either spouse, a successor trustee named in the trust instrument may immediately step in and assume management and control of the trust property, thereby avoiding the necessity of a court-appointed conservator for those assets.
- Both spouses' unified credit ($600,000 exemption equivalent) may be preserved by limiting the amount passing to the surviving spouse.

FIGURE 9-6   REVOCABLE TRUST WITH "ABC" PLAN

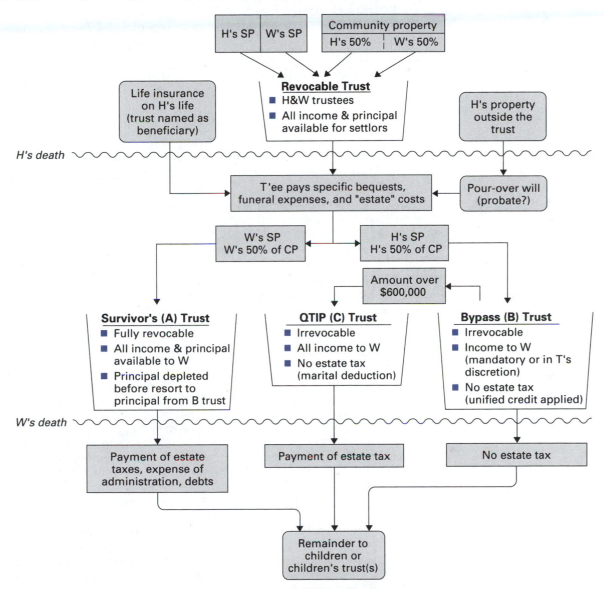

- If the combined estate of H and W is significantly under $1.2 million in value, the trust instrument may exclude a provision for a QTIP ("C") trust.
- The life insurance policy may be placed in trust instead; or the policy may designate W as beneficiary.
- H and W may establish separate *inter vivos* trusts instead.
- After H's death, if W revokes the Survivor's Trust (as to a portion or all of the property), the property may be subject to probate but will return to the trust under the terms of W's pour-over will (unless W revokes her pour-over will, in which event the property will pass under the terms of her new will or, if none, to W's intestate heirs).
- An "AB" or "ABC" plan may be implemented by a testamentary trust as well as an *inter vivos* trust.

Thus, a combined estate up to $1,200,000 in value can be transferred by the spouses without estate-tax liability.

Estate-tax liability for combined estates exceeding $1,200,000 can be deferred until the second spouse's death through the use of a QTIP provision.

All estate assets, whether in the A, B, or C trust, are available after the first spouse's death for the support and maintenance of the surviving spouse as primary income beneficiary.

Diversion of the deceased spouse's estate by the surviving spouse—for example, in the event of remarriage—may be prevented by retention of the deceased spouse's assets in an irrevocable trust (the B and C trusts) until after the second spouse's death.

FOCUS: *Inter vivos* and testamentary trusts may be used with equal effectiveness for the purpose of minimizing estate-tax liability. However, *inter vivos* trusts serve several additional purposes, including probate avoidance and continuity of asset management.

TAYLOR TRUST: If Walter Taylor were to die today, his net tax estate without the marital deduction would be valued at approximately $900,000 (this includes the proceeds from his life insurance policy). After a thorough discussion with Ms. Cargis about his alternatives, Walter has settled on a postmortem plan under which his business would pass outright to David, while Walter's remaining trust property will be allocated between a bypass trust and a QTIP trust. The amount allocated to the QTIP trust will be the minimum amount required to use Walter's entire unified credit; in other words, all but $600,000 of Walter's property will be allocated to the QTIP trust. Thus, the unified credit and the marital deduction will be used together to avoid any estate tax upon Walter's death (assuming he dies first).

With respect to Betty's plan, Betty's joint-tenancy interest in her family's ranch will remain outside the trust and pass to her surviving brothers and sisters (Betty will execute a power of attorney as part of her estate plan that gives one of her sisters the authority to deal with Betty's interest in the ranch if Betty should become incapacitated; see Chapter 11). Although the value of her remaining assets appears to be relatively low, it is important to keep in mind that she has acquired a considerable community-property interest in Walter's earnings during their ten years of marriage and will continue to do so in the future. Moreover, she expects a sizeable inheritance from her aunt within five or ten years. If Betty survives Walter, upon his death her interest in the trust property will be allocated to a survivor's trust that will be fully revocable by her; if she fails to arrange for a different distribution of the survivor's trust assets, they will pass at her death to Walter's issue in the same manner as the remaining assets in the bypass and QTIP trusts. The same basic allocation scheme will be put into effect in the event Betty predeceases Walter, although if Betty dies within the near future, it is unlikely that a QTIP trust will be required since the total value of Betty's trust property will probably be well below $600,000.

(For discussion of which assets to allocate to which trusts as well as the procedural, bookkeeping, and accounting requirements involved in establishing and administering these multiple trusts, see Chapter 10.)

Additional Considerations for Large Estates

In large estates, potential estate-tax liability may be significant despite the use of the planning techniques discussed up to this point. The use of an irrevocable *inter vivos* trust and/or an *inter vivos* gifting plan may help to limit the gross tax estate as well as to shift income to lower-bracket taxpayers, while charitable gifts may be used to reduce the taxable estate. A final concern with large estates is the generation-skipping transfer tax (GSTT), which can be avoided through proper planning.

Annual Gift-Tax Exclusion. One widely used method of reducing potential transfer-tax liability is the use of the $10,000 annual gift-tax exclusion per donee, as discussed in Chapter 7. By employing this method along with the concept of gift splitting, a married couple with three children and five grandchildren could reduce their combined taxable estate by $160,000 in any given year simply by each making a gift of $10,000 to each child and grandchild! Obviously, this type of gifting plan is called for only for estates that are potentially subject to transfer-tax liability and should be used only if the remaining assets are adequate to meet the donor's financial needs for the duration of his or her lifetime.

Income Shifting. Due to the progressive nature of income taxes both for individuals and for trusts and estates, aggregate income-tax liability in larger estates can be reduced by splitting income among taxpayers—for example, by giving an income-producing asset to a person in a lower marginal income-tax bracket. This technique is particularly useful in large estates where donors may make substantive gifts without jeopardizing their own financial security. However, the tax laws place certain restrictions on how much income can be shifted to minors under the age of 14. Under what is commonly referred to as the "kiddie tax," net *unearned* investment income (in excess of $1,000) of a child under 14 years of age is taxed at the parents' highest rate when this rate exceeds the child's income-tax rate. To report such income, the parent must file IRS Form 8615 (Tax for Children Under Age 14 Who Have Investment Income of More Than $1,000). The Clifford trust, discussed earlier in this chapter, was also widely used as an income-shifting device prior to the 1986 Tax Reform Act.

Freezing Asset Values through Irrevocable Transfers. *Inter vivos* gifts of appreciating property may be made, either outright or in trust, to minimize the size of the gross tax estate. Gifts are inherently irrevocable, since the donor relinquishes all ownership and control of the gifted property. For transfer-tax purposes, a gift is valued at the time it is made. Thus, the appreciation in the gifted property after the gift but prior to the donor's death will escape estate taxes. However, irrevocable transfers (whether outright or in trust) result in a carryover basis, not a stepped-up basis, for the transferee. Accordingly, lifetime gifts of appreciating property should be made cautiously with *both* income-tax and transfer-tax ramifications in mind.

Charitable Gifts. Charitable gifts should be considered to reduce the taxable estate. Gifts to qualifying charitable organizations may be made outright, either as testamentary or as *inter vivos* gifts. As an alternative, it may be desirable to make charitable gifts in trust. Income from the trust estate may be distributed to the settlor and to his or her surviving spouse and family without loss of the charitable deduction; however, the trust must be irrevocable, and the terms of the trusts must meet the strict requirements of the Internal Revenue Code. Also, the use of a trust permits greater flexibility in applying the trust property for charitable purposes.

Generation-Skipping Trusts. As noted in Chapter 7, a generation-skipping transfer tax, which is separate and distinct from an estate tax, will be owing for gratuitous transfers to donees such as grandchildren when the total of such transfers exceeds $1 million. A special generation-skipping trust may be included as part of an overall estate plan for a large estate, limiting the value of the trust assets to $1,000,000 and providing for the excess to be allocated to another trust, such as a QTIP trust or a charitable trust, instead.

POSTMORTEM PLANNING

Although one ordinarily thinks about estate planning as occurring prior to rather than after death, a variety of postmortem planning concerns, usually tax related, often arise, particularly in large estates where there is a surviving spouse and where trusts are involved. For example, if estate-tax liability upon the surviving spouse's death is anticipated, a gifting plan should be considered after the first spouse's death. A disclaimer of an inheritance may be appropriate to shift income or to avoid subjecting the disclaimed property to creditors of the heir or devisee. Also, where a testamentary or *inter vivos* trust calls for only a portion of the estate to be placed in trust or for the allocation of the estate among two or more trusts, the question of which assets should be allocated to which trust must be addressed (see Chapter 10). The spouse's right to an elective share must be considered (see Chapter 3). Finally, it may be desirable to subject all or some portion of the estate to probate even if otherwise unnecessary—for example, when all property may be disposed of by some form of summary administration or where most or all assets were transferred to an *inter vivos* trust. In a large estate, a probate estate as an additional taxpaying entity may reduce aggregate income-tax liability during the duration of estate administration. Estate administration may also be desirable in any event to limit the rights of creditors and protect the interests of the decedent.

10 THE PARALEGAL'S ROLE IN ESTATE PLANNING AND IN ESTABLISHING AND ADMINISTERING TRUSTS

Paralegal Assignment 10

A great deal of information about the Taylors is needed in order to develop and implement their estate plan. For this purpose, the Taylors have completed a comprehensive information form and have provided to the law firm a variety of personal records and documents. The legal documents necessary to implement the Taylors' estate plan must now be prepared and executed. Ms. Cargis has asked you to assist in this process. Once the Taylors' trust is established and funded, it must be administered in accordance with the terms of the trust, both during and after the Taylors' joint lifetimes. You will learn later in this chapter that once all or some portion of the trust becomes irrevocable, the successor trustee becomes accountable to the remainder beneficiaries and must begin reporting trust income to the state and federal tax authorities. Various accounting rules must be adhered to from this point forward, both for the beneficiaries' protection and for income-tax purposes. Finally, you will learn how and under what circumstances the trust may be revoked, modified, or terminated.

ESTATE PLANNING AND THE PARALEGAL

As in the area of estate administration, the estate-planning process is a team effort among the client, the lawyer, and the paralegal. Some decisions—for example, determining the form of title in which the client should hold a particular asset or which legal documents will best carry out the client's objectives—should be made by the lawyer. However, many other decisions—such as who should inherit the estate, who should make decisions for the client in the event of incapacity, and who should serve as personal representative—although often requiring clarification by the lawyer, should ultimately be made by the client. The paralegal's role in the estate-planning process, while important, is perhaps not as vital or extensive as in the "procedure-intensive" area of estate administration. Nevertheless, the paralegal serves several important roles in this process, including: (1) gathering and organizing personal, financial, and legal information about the client; (2) responding to routine questions from the client; and (3) assisting in the preparation, revision, and execution of the legal documents needed to implement the plan. The paralegal may also be required to keep abreast of changes in the law in order to update and revise various legal forms used by the law firm.

The Initial Contact

The law firm's initial contact with an estate-planning client is often through the paralegal. The paralegal must be prepared during this initial conversation, which generally takes place by telephone, to obtain some basic facts regarding the prospective client's personal, family, and financial situation in order to determine the complexity of the estate as well as the urgency of the prospective client's estate-planning needs. A brief single-page questionnaire that calls for the following information may suit this purpose:

- Name, age, address(es), and telephone number
- Marital status, former marriages, and number of children (by present as well as prior relationships)
- Place of domicile during current and any prior marriages
- Occupation and employer
- Estimated total value of real estate
- Estimated total value of personal property
- General state of health of all immediate family members
- Existing estate plan and lawyer who prepared the documents

An experienced paralegal who asks the appropriate questions can also pick up some very important clues during this initial contact. The initial contact may suggest undue influence, particularly if a family member or friend is calling on behalf of the client. If so, the paralegal might strongly suggest that the client come to the estate-planning interview alone; at a minimum, the paralegal should apprise the lawyer of the situation prior to the interview. On the other hand, the initial contact may reveal a high level of discomfort with the idea of establishing an estate plan, since it requires one to face the prospect of death. The client may be reluctant to consult a lawyer, possibly because of a negative prior experience or simply because of ignorance about what estate-planning lawyers do. In these situations, it may be desirable for a family member or friend to accompany the client to the interview to make sure that the client follows through. Prospective clients who are either married or soon to be married present a potential conflict of interest, and the paralegal should inquire further about the prospective clients' circumstances.

Many prospective clients will insist that they know what their estate-planning needs are and are simply calling around for the best price. Particularly common is the prospective client who insists on a living trust, although others will insist just as vehemently that all they need is a simple will. The paralegal must emphasize to every prospective client that proper estate planning is a complex process and that an in-depth interview with the attorney is necessary in order to assess the client's needs and the appropriate documents to meet those needs.

Gathering Information for the Interview

Under some circumstances, an immediate interview with the attorney may be appropriate—for example, if a death in the immediate family is impending or if the client is about to leave the country. Otherwise, prior to the estate-planning interview, the law firm should provide to the client some general informational materials to alert the client to the complexity of the estate-planning process as well as to stimulate the client's thinking about the various decisions that must be made during the process. The law firm should also provide an information form to the client to complete as fully as possible prior to the estate-planning interview (see Exhibits 1 and 2 in the Taylor file). The information form should be organized in such a manner that it can serve as a ready reference for the information necessary to make planning decisions and document decisions as well as to prepare estate-planning documents. The paralegal should *not* insist that the client prepare detailed financial statements for the estate-planning interview, because this might delay the interview and may even discourage the prospective client from following through with the law firm. However, if financial statements are already available, the client should bring them along to the interview.

Engaging the client in the process of gathering information serves three useful purposes. First, it forces the client to review his or her own personal papers, such as insurance policies, deeds, wills, and so forth, thereby becoming a more knowledgeable and active participant in the planning process. Second, it reduces the work load for the lawyer and for the paralegal, who must sort through, organize, and review the client's papers if the client has not already done so, thereby making for an unproductive estate-planning interview. Third, if the paralegal explains to the client that his or her participation in this respect will help to reduce the law firm's fees, the client is likely to be appreciative, which in turn will enhance the firm's relationship with the client.

A Client Information Form, along with various informational materials, may be provided in the form of an estate-planning package. The package might include some or perhaps all of the following items, depending upon the client's particular situation as determined by the initial contact with the paralegal:

- Client Information Form
- An overview of the estate-planning process
- An overview of the probate process, indicating its advantages and disadvantages, along with a table of statutory commissions and fees
- A list of will substitutes, indicating their uses and limitations
- A diagram of intestate succession
- A glossary of estate-planning terminology
- A summary of how a revocable living trust works, indicating its advantages and disadvantages
- A diagram illustrating the ''AB'' and ''ABC'' trust plans
- A list of estate-planning decisions such as choice of beneficiaries and choice of executor/trustee, along with factors affecting those decisions
- A federal transfer-tax rate schedule
- A schedule of income-tax rates for estates and trusts

 PRACTICE TIP: The cover letter for the estate-planning package should confirm the date and time of the estate-planning interview and should emphasize the importance of completing the Client Information Form as fully as possible prior to the interview. Many lawyers also incorporate a fee agreement into this letter, requesting the client's signature at the end of the letter to indicate agreement to the fee arrangement. This may be particularly important with spouses, who must agree at the outset to dual representation by the law firm.

The Estate-Planning Interview

An in-depth estate-planning interview is necessary to determine the client's objectives, to review the client's alternatives, and to settle on a plan. The paralegal's presence at this interview is generally not required but may be appropriate in some cases to help familiarize the paralegal with the client's circumstances and the estate plan. The client should be discouraged from bringing to the initial interview his or her personal papers, such as deeds, wills, tax statements, insurance and financial account statements, and so forth. Instead, the client should be encouraged to review these papers and documents prior to the interview and provide the requested information about the documents on the Client Information Form. It is important at the initial estate-planning interview to focus on the client's objectives and to help the client understand the process rather than sort through various legal and financial documents. The lawyer may ask the client to provide the documents to the paralegal as soon as possible after the interview. The paralegal may be requested to review the documents and to brief the attorney as appropriate. In particular, the paralegal may be asked to summarize the client's current will plan, if any, for the lawyer. After the lawyer has had an opportunity to review certain documents belonging to the client and to reflect on the client's situation and alternative courses of action, a second planning meeting with the client may be required in order to finalize the plan.

The Legal Documents

It is the lawyer's ultimate responsibility to ensure that all legal documents required to implement the estate plan are properly prepared and executed. However, the paralegal may provide invaluable assistance in this effort by proofreading the documents for errors, inconsistencies, and omissions prior to the lawyer's final review. The paralegal's training allows him or her to review the documents for *substantive* errors and omissions, not just typographical or grammatical errors. The paralegal must not take this task lightly; the lawyer may be too busy to read the documents word by word from beginning to end and will rely heavily on the paralegal's ability to spot possible problems and bring them to the lawyer's attention.

Estate-planning documents may be categorized in terms of their general function as follows:

1. Documents that provide for disposition of the client's property (wills, testamentary trusts, and *inter vivos* trusts)
2. Documents that merely transmute the form in which title in the client's property is held (marital-property agreements and certain types of deeds)
3. Documents that transfer title in the client's property to an *inter vivos* trust (deeds, assignments, stock and bond powers, etc.)
4. Documents that provide for the client's incapacity (powers of attorney, living wills, conservator nominations, and *inter vivos* trusts)

In most cases, documents from each of these four categories are required to implement a comprehensive estate plan. The materials below will focus on the *inter vivos* trust document as well as on the documents that transfer title to such trusts. Other legal documents listed above are treated in other chapters.

ESTABLISHING AND FUNDING *INTER VIVOS* TRUSTS

An estate plan that includes a revocable trust requires not only a written trust document but also certain other legal documents. Of particular concern to the paralegal are those documents that serve to transfer the settlors' assets to the trust. The plan may call for the transfer to the trust of most—if not substantially all—of the settlor's assets. Certain types of assets, however, should not be placed in trust, and certain others cannot be placed in trust.

Preparing and Executing the Legal Documents

In estate planning matters involving the use of trusts, the paralegal typically assists in the preparation and execution of not only trust instruments but also other documents that often accompany *inter vivos* trusts, including pour-over wills, trustee's certificates, abstracts of trust, and certain tax forms in the case of irrevocable trusts.

The Trust Instrument.   Express *inter vivos* trusts are created by a written trust document, also referred to as a *trust instrument* or *instrument of trust* (the term *trust*, unlike the term *will*, does not refer to a document but rather to a legal concept). Not unlike a will, a trust document may be fairly brief and concise or, at the other extreme, may be quite lengthy and complex. The length of a trust document depends upon its purpose as well as the writing style of the person drafting the document. Similar to wills, trust documents are typically organized under headings, or *articles*, and may include subheadings as well. A trust is generally given a name; the settlor's name is customarily used to identify the trust—for example, "The John Smith Trust" or "The Smith Family Trust."

As in the case of wills, many provisions included in a trust document are likely to be standard or "boiler-plate," particularly those relating to the powers of the trustee and to taxes. Once the law firm has developed its forms, preparing a trust document for a specific client is largely a matter of determining which form to use and which alternative and optional provisions to include in the document. Once the lawyer makes these decisions, the document may be generated easily by entering variable information into the computer. The lawyer may request the paralegal's assistance in developing trust forms as well as in revising and updating these forms to reflect changes in the law. As with wills, computer-generated trust forms provided by third-party vendors should be used with extreme caution and should be evaluated first by the lawyer for their integrity, flexibility, and comprehensiveness. A certain amount of customized drafting is likely to be required in any event, particularly for the dispositive provisions. The experienced probate paralegal may be asked to assist in drafting, although many lawyers prefer to either perform all necessary drafting themselves or delegate this responsibility to associate attorneys within the firm.

Inter vivos trusts need not meet the formal requirements for execution of wills. Certain formalities, however, should be observed if the validity of the trust is to be acknowledged by third parties, such as financial institutions and title companies. The signatures of the settlor(s) and trustee(s) are universally required and should be notarized. The settlor's signature signifies his or her intent to establish the trust, while the trustee's signature signifies his or her acceptance of the duties of the office of trustee. In the case of two or more settlors or co-trustees, the signature of each settlor and co-trustee is required. However, in the case of a declaration of trust, since the settlor is also the trustee, a single signature by the settlor-trustee is sufficient. The lawyer preparing the trust instrument and advising the settlor typically signs the instrument as well, so that third parties (banks, title companies, and so forth) will be less inclined to scrutinize the document and more ready to acknowledge its validity.

Schedule(s) of Trust Assets. A typical *inter vivos* trust document will refer to and incorporate by reference one or more attached schedules (commonly entitled *Schedule A*, etc.) that list the assets placed in the trust. For an unmarried settlor, a single Schedule A generally suffices. However, for married settlors, it may be appropriate to use three schedules, one for community property (Schedule A) and one for each spouse's separate property (Schedules B and C) (see Exhibit 3 in the Taylor file). It is important to keep in mind that such schedules merely provide a convenient means of recordkeeping. Listing an asset on a schedule does not automatically place it in trust. The reason for this is that such lists are unreliable from an evidentiary standpoint to show if and when a transfer was actually intended by the settlor. The proper procedures for placing various types of assets in trust is discussed a bit later (see *Funding* Inter Vivos *Trusts)*.

The Pour-Over Will. An *inter vivos* trust, if used as a means of disposing of substantially all of the settlor's estate, essentially serves as a substitute for a will. However, some of the settlor's property might remain outside of the trust at his or her death. This may be intentional in some instances and unintentional in others, as discussed later. Property remaining outside of the trust and not disposed of by some other means may be brought into the trust after the settlor's death to be administered and distributed in the same manner as all other trust assets. This is accomplished through the use of a **pour-over will** (Exhibit 4 in the Taylor file), so called because the property disposed of under its provisions is "poured over" to the trust upon the settlor's death. The pour-over will is a simple one- or two-page document; however, it must be executed in accordance with the same formal requirements for execution of other wills. A pour-over will may also provide its own distribution plan for certain assets remaining outside the trust, while pouring over other assets.

The Trustee Certificate. Third parties such as financial institutions and title companies are likely to require proof of the trustee's authority prior to dealing with the trustee. The trustee should provide to any party requesting such proof a certificate of his or her authority, a simple one-page document signed by the attorney and indicating the name of the trust, the date the trust was established, the settlor's name, and an affidavit by the attorney as to the trustee's authority (see Exhibit 5 in the Taylor file). Although this certificate is analogous in function to Letters Testamentary or Letters of Administration in a decedent's estate, it lacks the authoritative weight of a court order. As a result, some third parties may not accept a certificate of authority by itself as sufficient evidence of the trustee's authority and instead may insist that the trustee provide them either with a copy of the trust instrument or with an *abstract* of the trust instrument. The abstract should include the provisions relating to the establishment of the trust and the trustee's powers, as well as the signatory provisions, while excluding the dispositive provisions, which are a private matter and need not be examined in order to assess the validity of the trust and the authority of the trustee.

IRS Forms 56 and SS-4. As discussed later in this chapter, an irrevocable trust (but not a revocable trust) is considered a distinct taxable entity. Accordingly, just as in decedents' estates, the trustee of an irrevocable trust should inform the Internal Revenue Service of the fiduciary relationship by using IRS Form 56 (Notice of Fiduciary Relationship). The trustee must also obtain an Employer Identification Number (EIN) to use for filing tax returns as well as for establishing accounts at banks and other financial institutions. IRS Form SS-4 (Application for Employer Identification Number) is used for this purpose. Trustees of revocable trusts should submit Forms 56 and SS-4 to the IRS only in the event the trust becomes irrevocable.

Funding *Inter Vivos* Trusts

A trust operates only on the property that is properly placed in the trust. A trust instrument is, for all practical purposes, a worthless document, even though it may be eloquently drafted and include all of the required notarized signatures, if the property that the settlor intends to be controlled by the terms of the trust is not properly placed in the trust. Consider the typical *inter vivos* trust intended to serve as a unifying estate-planning device. Its effectiveness as such a device requires that substantially all of the settlor's assets ultimately be transferred to the trust. Most transfers are accomplished during the settlor's lifetime, although postmortem transfers to the trust are possible as well, by any of the following means: (1) under the terms of the settlor's pour-over will; (2) from another person, either by outright gift, under the terms of a will or trust, or by the exercise of a power of appointment; or (3) under an existing or after-acquired employee benefit plan, life insurance policy, or other contractual arrangement, in which the trust is designated as death beneficiary.

One of the paralegal's most important functions in the area of estate planning is to carry out the transfer of clients' assets to their *inter vivos* trusts. This responsibility involves the preparation of various documents of title, such as deeds and bills of sale, as well as involves interaction with various third parties, such as banks, stock transfer agents, and title companies. The specific procedural steps for transferring particular types of assets are discussed in the materials that follow.

Vesting Language. Estate planners commonly refer to property placed in trust as being "transferred to the trust." For the purpose of discussion, the materials in this chapter follow this common terminology. However, it is important to keep in mind that property "placed in trust" is actually transferred to the *trustee* and not to the trust. It is the trustee that assumes legal title in the trust property, not the trust itself. In other words, the property is "owned in trust" by the trustee. When an asset owned by the settlor is placed in trust, the document used to effect the transfer, such as a deed, stock power, or bill of sale, must indicate the name of the new owner—that is, how title should vest. The precise vesting language appropriate for the transfer depends on the type of property involved as well as the particular requirements of third parties, such as transfer agents or title companies. Generally speaking, however, vesting language should include the trustee's name, the name of the trust, and the date that the trust was initially established—for example: "Jane D. Doe, as trustee of the John Q. Smith Trust under instrument dated September 17, 1993." The same language should be used for the trustee's transactions, such as sales, purchases, loans, leases, and other contracts, with third parties. If the John Q. Smith Trust in the example above is later amended, the vesting language for subsequent transactions should indicate as follows: "Jane D. Doe, as trustee of the John Q. Smith Trust under instrument dated September 17, 1993, *as amended.*" The trustee's signature on legal documents, including checks, should be accompanied by the trustee's "short" title—for example, "Jane D. Doe, trustee."

FOCUS: An *inter vivos* trust operates only on property that has been properly placed in the trust. Merely listing an asset on a schedule is insufficient from an evidentiary standpoint for this purpose. The proper procedure for placing an asset in trust, as well as the proper vesting language to be used on documents of title, depends upon the type of asset involved as well as the particular requirements of certain third parties, such as transfer agents and title companies.

Initial Funding. One essential element of a trust is a transfer of an existing property interest to the trust at the time the settlor intends to create the trust. This formality should be strictly observed in all cases. One commonly used method of providing initial funding is to prepare a bill of sale for some item of tangible personal property owned by the settlor (other than a motor vehicle or other asset accompanied by a document of title). Executing a bill of sale at the same time that the trust is executed ensures that this initial funding requirement is met.

Real Property. The settlor must execute some form of deed in order to transfer a real-property interest (other than a security interest) to a trust (Figure 10-1). The transfer may also involve additional procedures as well.

Quitclaim Deeds, Grant Deeds, and Warranty Deeds To transfer an interest in real property other than a security interest (see *Deeds of Trust and Mortgages*), one of three types of deeds—a *quitclaim deed, grant deed,* or *warranty deed*—should be used. The legal effect of a **quitclaim deed** is to transfer whatever interest the transferor may have in the subject property interest, if any, without any guarantees or representations regarding the transferor's legal right to make the transfer—that is, without regard to whether the transferor has *marketable title.* On the other hand, a **grant deed** guarantees to the transferee that the transferor holds marketable title, except as specified in the deed. In some states, a grant deed is referred to instead as a **warranty deed**, while in other states the term *warranty deed* refers more particularly to a deed in which the grantor makes certain express promises about the title being transferred.

Quitclaim deeds are generally used for gratuitous transfers among family members, particularly for the purpose of adding joint tenants to the title.

FIGURE 10-1   TRANSFERRING REAL-PROPERTY INTERESTS TO AN *INTER VIVOS* TRUST

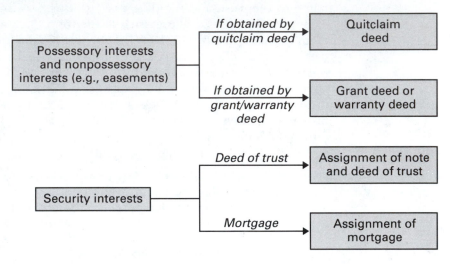

Although either a quitclaim deed or a grant deed/warranty deed may be used for gratuitous transfers to a trust, as a rule of thumb, if the settlor obtained title by way of a grant deed/warranty deed, then a grant deed/ warranty deed should be used to effect the transfer, while if the settlor obtained title by way of a quitclaim deed, then a quitclaim should be used. The information needed to prepare the deed to transfer the property to the trust may be obtained from the original deed transferring title to the settlor. The settlor's signature on the deed should be notarized, and the deed should be recorded in the office of the recorder in the county where the real property is located.

Property Insurance   Property-insurance policies covering the property placed in trust should be amended to reflect the change in ownership. This can be accomplished by way of a simple letter of instruction to the insurance company (see Exhibit 14 in the Taylor file).

Property Taxes   Transferring real property to a *revocable* trust has no effect on the value used to assess property taxes (tax base). However, the county assessor may require the settlor to complete a form verifying the nature of the transfer. Also, transferring the settlor's residence to a *revocable* trust will not result in termination of any homeowner's property-tax exemption. Again, however, the county assessor may require the settlor to complete a specific form to prevent such termination (or to re-establish the exemption if termination resulted).

Title Insurance   A transfer of real property to a trust might void the settlor's title-insurance policy. The paralegal should contact the title company to determine whether the transfer is permitted under the policy. If not, the title company can prepare an *amendatory endorsement* for the purpose of permitting the transfer.

Refinancing Some institutional lenders may refuse to provide refinancing while the property is in trust; in this event, the settlor must revoke the trust as to the specific property, obtain refinancing, and then transfer the asset back to the trust. To avoid the delay and expenses associated with this procedure, the settlor may wish to obtain refinancing prior to making the initial transfer to the trust.

Deeds of Trust and Mortgages. Some real-property interests merely serve to secure a debt owed by another, as where an individual obtains a loan to finance the purchase of property or to transform the equity in property already owned into cash. The most commonly used instruments for financing the purchases of real estate are the *deed of trust* (or *trust deed*), and the *mortgage.* These two types of instruments serve a similar purpose, even though their underlying legal theories differ somewhat, and every state provides for either one or the other as a means of establishing an interest in real property to secure a debt. A **deed of trust** serves to transfer a *legal* interest in the property to a trustee (grantee) until the borrower (grantor) has paid off the debt to the lender (beneficiary). However, the trustee has no powers unless the borrower defaults on the loan or violates one of the other promises in the trust deed, in which event the trustee may sell the property and pay the lender back from the sale proceeds. If and when the borrower pays the lender the entire amount of the debt, the trustee transfers its legal interest, evidenced by the deed of trust, to the borrower. A **mortgage** is a contract by which the borrower (referred to as the *mortgagor*), pledges property to another (referred to as the *mortgagee*) as security in order to obtain a loan. Although a mortgage serves essentially the same function as a deed of trust and promissory note, its legal underpinnings are somewhat different. By using a mortgage deed, the lender (grantee) is actually placing a *lien* against the property, thereby obtaining an equitable interest in the property.

A deed of trust and underlying promissory note may be transferred to the trust through the use of a simple one-page *assignment of note and deed of trust.* A mortgage holder (lender) may transfer the mortgage to an *inter vivos* trust through the use of a simple one-page *assignment of mortgage.* Since a deed of trust or mortgage establishes an interest in real property, the assignment should be recorded in the same manner as a deed.

 TAYLOR TRUST: The Taylors own three separate real-property interests that will be placed in trust. Walter purchased the property on which he built his current residence shortly after he married Betty, obtaining title in his name alone from the seller by grant deed. Accordingly, Walter will place this property in trust through the use of a grant deed (see Exhibit 10 in the Taylor file). However, Walter and Betty have agreed (under the terms of their marital property agreement) that the true character of the property is community and that Walter will transfer title to himself and Betty as community property through the use of a quitclaim deed (see Exhibit 9 in the Taylor file). This additional step will provide additional support for a full step up in tax basis upon the death of the first spouse.

Walter acquired a second property, which he uses as rental property, from his father by quitclaim deed before his father's death. Walter and Betty have agreed that this property (and all income therefrom) is Walter's separate property. A quitclaim deed will be used to transfer this asset to the trust.

Walter had rented a third property, acquired prior to his marriage to Betty, to his son David for several years, and last year David purchased the property as his residence. To assist David in the purchase, Walter loaned $20,000 to David for his down payment, taking back a trust deed in the property to secure the loan. The trust deed and underlying note will be assigned to the trust (see Exhibit 11 in the Taylor file). Walter and Betty have agreed that this asset is Walter's separate property.

Stocks and Bonds. Publicly traded stocks and bonds must be reregistered in the trustee's name. This is accomplished in the same manner as for transfers by a personal representative of a decedent's estate—the settlor must provide to the issuer's transfer agent the original bond or stock certificate, along with a stock or bond power and transmittal letter. Either the law firm or a stockbroker may assist the settlor in this matter. However, a stockbroker is likely to insist on opening a new account in the trustee's name, possibly requiring an additional fee.

Accounts at Financial Institutions. To transfer accounts at banks and other financial institutions, or to transfer treasury bills, mutual-fund shares, or money-market accounts, a simple letter of transfer is often adequate. However, some institutions provide their own specific form for this purpose. If a transmittal letter is sufficient, a single letter may be used for several accounts at the same institution. Both the settlor and the trustee should sign the letter, and their signatures should be notarized. In the case of a grantor trust, the settlor should sign the letter twice, once as settlor and once as trustee.

 PRACTICE TIP: The transmittal letter should indicate the account number as well as the settlor's Social Security number as the tax identification number for the account. For a joint account owned by a married couple, either spouse's Social Security number may be used. If the settlor plans to perform these transfers independently, the paralegal may wish to provide to the settlor several standard letters, leaving a blank space for the account type and number. The client may then follow up on this matter independently.

 TAYLOR TRUST: Walter and Betty Taylor each have a money-market account that will be placed in trust through the use of a transmittal letter. Walter has placed additional savings into a retirement account for self-employed persons, called a Keogh account. This account will not be placed in trust, however, since the transfer would be deemed an early distribution and would result in a penalty (see *Assets That Cannot or Should Not Be Owned in Trust*).

Tangible Personal Property. Tangible personal effects, such as furniture, clothing, and so forth, that are not accompanied by any document evidencing ownership may be transferred to an *inter vivos* trust through the use of either an *assignment* or a *bill of sale* (although its name may suggest that its use is limited to sales, a bill of sale can be used to document gratuitous transfers as well) (a bill of sale for the transfer of Walter's coin collection to the trust is included in the Taylor file as Exhibit 13). If probate avoidance is a primary concern, the total value of personal effects may be sufficiently low that transfer to the trust is unnecessary. As noted earlier, many lawyers prefer to dispose of personal effects (except those of significant value) under the terms of a pour-over will. Since ownership in motor vehicles is evidenced by a certificate of title, a simple assignment or bill of sale is not sufficient. The settlor must complete and sign the specific form required by the state bureau of motor vehicles.

Safe-Deposit Boxes. Transferring a safe-deposit box to a trust is not effective to transfer the contents of the box. However, it is generally recommended that all boxes be transferred so that, after the settlor's incapacity or death, the successor trustee can gain access to the box. The transfer is accomplished simply by completing a new file card provided by the bank.

Small-Business Interests. Whether a small-business interest can and should be placed in trust depends on whether the business is organized as a corporation, a sole proprietorship, or a partnership. The procedures for proper transfer also depend on this distinction.

Sole Proprietorships An unincorporated business owned entirely by one person is referred to as a *sole proprietorship*. This type of business is not recognized as a legal entity distinct from its owner. Accordingly, ownership in the "business" as a distinct asset cannot be transferred, either to a trustee or to anyone else. Instead, the *assets* of the business must be transferred. To place a sole proprietorship in trust, then, the settlor must execute a bill of sale that lists all the business's assets (see *Tangible Personal Property*).

Partnership Interests An unincorporated business owned by two or more persons (or entities) is referred to as a *partnership*. A partnership may be either a *general partnership* or a *limited partnership*. In a general partnership, each partner remains personally liable for claims of third parties against the partnership, while in a limited partnership, only the general partners remain personally liable; the limited partners may be viewed more like shareholders of a corporation in that their risk of loss is limited to their investment. In fact, a limited partnership, like a corporation, must register with the Department of Corporations in the state where the business is organized before issuing shares to its investors.

A general partnership interest may be placed in trust only if the transfer is permitted under the terms of the partnership agreement or if the partners otherwise consent to the transfer. Limited partners' interests, on the other hand, are freely transferrable without the approval of the general partner(s). A transfer of either a limited or general partnership interest is accomplished through the use of a simple one-page assignment. In either case, the transfer should be indicated in the partnership's records.

PRACTICE TIP: When a limited partnership interest is placed in trust, the paralegal should inform the general partner(s) of the transfer and request the general partner(s) to (1) record the transfer in the partnership books and (2) report the transfer to the Department of Corporations (in the state where the limited partnership is registered). General partners of limited partnerships are notoriously remiss in doing so; accordingly, the paralegal should follow up on this matter to ensure that these steps are taken.

Shares of Stock in Small Corporations A "small" corporation is one where shares of stock may be offered and sold without registration with the state or federal government. In order to transfer shares of stock in a small corporation to a trust, a simple one-page assignment should be prepared for the settlor's signature. Additionally, the corporation must reissue the shares in the name of the trustee. However, the bylaws of the corporation may require other owners to consent to ownership in trust. Under the laws of most states, professional corporations formed for practitioners such as doctors and lawyers can be owned only by individuals and not in trust or by an entity such as another corporation.

Under certain circumstances, a small corporation may qualify for favorable income-tax treatment under Subchapter "S" of the Internal Revenue Code. The corporation must affirmatively elect to be treated as an "S corporation." An electing corporation is limited to one class of stock and to 35 or fewer shareholders. Also, each shareholder must be either an individual, an estate, or a trust (corporations and partnerships cannot be shareholders of an S corporation), and a shareholder-trust must have no more than one current beneficiary. Where shares of an S corporation are placed in a revocable trust, the settlor is generally the sole beneficiary, and the corporation will continue to receive favorable income-tax treatment. However, at the settlor's death, the corporation is likely to lose its status as an S corporation if the stock is allocated to a bypass trust. A QTIP trust, however, qualifies as an S corporation shareholder, since the surviving spouse is the sole beneficiary.

 TAYLOR TRUST: Walter Taylor's general contracting business is organized as a qualifying Subchapter S corporation, and Walter is the sole shareholder. The business is Walter's most valuable single asset and must be placed in trust in order to avoid probate. A one-page Stock Assignment Separate from Certificate, signed by Walter, will be used to effect the transfer (see Exhibit 12 in the Taylor file). The corporation will then reissue Walter's shares in his name as trustee. If another attorney assisted Walter in forming the corporation and with other corporate business, it may be appropriate for that attorney to assist in reissuing the stock. Walter intends to pass the entire value of the business down to his son David. Allocation to either the bypass trust or QTIP trust would defeat this objective. Accordingly, the trust instrument directs the trustee to distribute the shares of stock in the corporation outright to David upon Walter's death or, if David fails to survive his father, to sell the business.

Assets Located in Another State. If the settlor wishes to place assets located in another state into a trust, the trust must comply with the laws of the other state in order for the transfer to be effective. There are several possible ways to address this issue. The first is to either research the trust laws of the other state or retain a lawyer in the other state to review the trust instrument, then amend the document as required. The second alternative is to prepare an additional trust document solely for the asset(s) in the other state, naming the primary trust as beneficiary at the settlor's death. The third alternative is to simply dispose of the asset(s) and either deposit the proceeds in an account located in the settlor's state or use the proceeds to acquire an asset located in that state. Finally, if the property is moveable, it can simply be relocated.

Assets That Cannot or Should Not Be Owned in Trust. Many third parties will not accept "personal" checks from a trustee. Thus, placing a checking account into a revocable trust defeats the purpose of the account. The settlor must make sure, however, that the balance in the account remains sufficiently low to avoid probate by transferring excess amounts promptly to a savings account or money-market account that has been placed in trust.

Rights to benefits under contractual arrangements such as annuities, pension plans, IRAs, Keoghs, and other employee benefit and retirement plans should not be transferred to an *inter vivos* trust. Under most such arrangements, a transfer is deemed a distribution and may result in cancellation or a penalty; moreover, most plans simply prohibit such a transfer. Instead, the settlor should consider designating the trust as death beneficiary.

Certain types of corporate stock cannot be owned in trust. The federal tax laws prohibit a trust from owning stock *options* as well as stock issued by public offering for the purpose of starting up a corporation (referred to as § 1244 stock). In addition, as noted earlier, shares of stock in S corporations may be owned only by certain trusts, and professional corporations cannot be owned in trust in any event (see *Small-Business Interests*).

Another type of asset that cannot be owned in trust is a homestead. A homestead, as distinguished from a probate homestead (see Chapter 3), establishes certain rights of the owner of property used as a principal residence as against the owner's creditors. Homestead interests are equitable in nature and cannot be owned by a trustee, except where the owner of the homestead is also the trustee (as in a typical revocable trust).

Finally, ownership in trust of club memberships (country clubs, tennis clubs, and the like) may be prohibited either under the terms of the club's bylaws or by statute.

 TAYLOR TRUST: A portion of Walter's savings is invested in mutual funds in the form of a Keogh account. The death beneficiary currently named on the account is Walter's son David. To avoid penalties for premature distribution, the account will remain outside the trust, and Walter will designate the trust as death beneficiary by obtaining and completing the appropriate form supplied by the mutual-fund company.

TRUST ADMINISTRATION

The extent of the law firm's involvement in administration of the trust depends upon the circumstances. The lawyer or law firm might be serving as trustee. This is particularly common where an individual having first priority as successor trustee prefers not to take on the responsibility. In this event, the paralegal typically assumes the ongoing role of bookkeeper. Otherwise, the law firm plays a more limited role during the administration of a trust, advising the trustee on an *ad hoc* basis regarding the trustee's powers and fiduciary duties—for example, whether a transaction or distribution is proper under the terms of the trust—as well as representing the trustee in disputes with the beneficiaries or with third parties. While such matters are generally only of tangential concern to the probate paralegal, the well-informed probate paralegal should nevertheless understand the fundamental powers and duties of the trustee as well as the rights of beneficiaries. Moreover, certain matters commonly arising during the administration of trusts do call for the paralegal's assistance. The probate paralegal may be requested to assist in the preparation of regular accounting as well as tax returns, to address various procedural postmortem concerns in the case of *inter vivos* trusts, and to prepare trust amendments and amended trusts.

Powers of the Trustee

Powers may be conferred upon a trustee by the express terms of the trust as well as by the terms of a statute or court decree. In addition, a trustee may exercise those powers that are necessary or appropriate to carry out the purposes of the trust and that are not forbidden by the terms of the trust. Co-trustees must exercise their powers jointly by *unanimous* agreement and are not permitted to allocate functions among themselves, unless the terms of the trust permit otherwise. Any action by fewer than all co-trustees is voidable by the beneficiaries. Most powers conferred upon a trustee are *discretionary* in nature; that is, the trustee may exercise the power as appropriate in his or her judgment. Other powers, however, may be *mandatory* in that the trustee is required to exercise the power—for example, a directive by the trust to pay taxes or to make certain distributions.

Duties of the Trustee

By accepting the responsibilities of the trustee's office, the trustee becomes a fiduciary and must meet extremely high standards in administering the trust property, regardless of his or her level of compensation for providing such services. However, standards to which the trustee is held may depend upon the trustee's level of sophistication. The trustee's specific duties are discussed below.

Duty to Exercise Due Care. In administering the trust, the trustee must exercise a degree of care, skill, and prudence that would be exercised by a *reasonably prudent person in managing his or her own property.* Reasonable care requires a certain level of effort and attention, reasonable skill requires a certain level of capability and competency, and reasonable prudence requires a certain level of caution and conservatism. Even where the trust provisions give the trustee absolute or uncontrolled discretion, the trustee is still required to meet this standard as well as to act in good faith. As a general rule, the courts will not second guess a *business judgment* by the trustee, regardless of the consequences of the decision. However, the court will intervene where the trustee has completely failed to exercise his or her judgment with regard to a discretionary power.

Duty to Preserve Trust Property and Make It Productive. While a personal representative must be concerned merely with preserving and protecting an estate, a trustee must also make the trust property productive by investing it. At the same time, however, the trustee must not engage in speculation. Failure to invest trust funds prudently *and* profitably may result in the trustee's personal liability for loss to the trust estate. Although the trustee may seek investment advice and assistance from others, the trustee cannot escape personal liability by relying on the advice of "experts" or by delegating the investment function to any other person.

Duty of Loyalty. The trustee owes his or her *sole* loyalty to the beneficiaries of the trust, and this duty extends *equally* to all beneficiaries. This may pose a dilemma where the trust provides for successive enjoyment—for example, where income from the trust is payable to a surviving spouse for life, after which the remaining corpus is to be distributed to the settlor's children. Income-producing assets may not appreciate to the same extent as a nonincome-producing asset; thus, the interests of the income beneficiary and the remaindermen are in conflict. A well-drafted trust instrument may avert this dilemma—for example, by identifying the income beneficiary as the "primary beneficiary."

Aside from accepting fees for serving as trustee, the trustee cannot profit personally from the trust or otherwise take personal advantage from his or her position as trustee. However, the trustee is entitled to additional compensation for extraordinary services as well as for services provided to the trust in some other capacity—for example, legal services. Unless expressly authorized by the terms of the trust, the trustee is prohibited from entering into any transactions, such as sales of property and loans, with the trust. This prohibition against self-dealing applies to the trustee's spouse as well. Self-dealing is prohibited regardless of the trustee's intentions or the resulting benefit to the trust. The beneficiaries may respond to a prohibited transaction in one of three ways: (1) any beneficiary may *set aside* the transaction; (2) the beneficiaries may *recover any profit* by the trustee resulting from the transaction; or (3) the beneficiaries may *affirm* the transaction (which generally occurs where the trust has benefited from the transaction).

Duty to Keep Trust Assets Separate. The trustee has a duty to keep the trust assets separate from his or her own personal assets and to maintain separate and complete records. In the event of a loss of trust property, the trustee may be held personally liable to the beneficiaries for the loss where the trust assets were not separated from the trustee's own assets, regardless of whether commingling assets contributed to the loss. All trust assets must be titled in the trustee's name *as trustee* for the specific trust rather than in the trustee's name personally.

Fiduciary Accounting under the Revised Uniform Principal and Income Act. Where the settlor is also the trustee and sole beneficiary, as in the case of a typical revocable living trust during the settlor's lifetime, no duty to others is owed; since the trust is still revocable, the remainder beneficiaries merely have an expectation rather than a property interest. Accordingly, no trust accounting is required in this situation, and no separate records or books are required, except that the settlor-trustee should maintain a current list of the trust assets. However, when a trust becomes irrevocable, the trustee must thereafter provide an account to the beneficiaries (including the settlor, if the settlor is a beneficiary) on a periodic basis (most trust instruments require accounting on an annual or more frequent basis). The trustee also has a duty to account and furnish information to a beneficiary upon request.

Trust accounting can be quite complex, involving special rules for allocation of receipts and expenditures to either income or principal. Proper allocation is very important for the purpose of income taxation as well as to determine the respective rights of the beneficiaries in cases of successive enjoyment. The character of certain receipts or expenditures may pose allocation problems. As a general rule, while income from trust assets is credited to income, assets themselves are credited to principal. However, the character of some types of receipts—particularly, corporate distributions—may be unclear. Also, certain expenses may be incurred to protect both income and principal. With respect to trust income, additional issues arise regarding the apportionment of income accrued but not yet received at the outset of as well as at the end of an income-beneficiary's term.

Most states have attempted to resolve allocation problems through legislation. Approximately one-third of the states adopted the original Uniform Principal and Income Act (UPIA), which was approved in 1931, although most of these states modified its provisions significantly because it left many problems unresolved. The Revised Uniform Principal and Income Act, approved in 1962, is more comprehensive than the original Act and has also been adopted in approximately one-third of the states. The UPIA applies not only to trusts but also to decedent's estates, although decedent's estates involve the additional accounting problems of interest and increase, as discussed in Chapter 8.

Section 4 of the Revised UPIA provides for the apportionment of receipts, while Section 13 addresses problems of allocating expenditures (see Figure 10-2). The expenditures listed in Section 13(a) are charged against income, while all others are charged against principal. The UPIA allocation scheme is summarized in Table 10-1. In examining Table 10-1, note that, under the Revised UPIA, corporate distributions, if made in the form of ordinary dividends, as well as distributions of either cash or shares of stock where the corporation gives a stockholder an option to receive a distribution either in cash or in stock, are allocable to income. However, distributions in the form of a stock split or stock dividends, as well as distribution in total or partial liquidation, are allocable to principal. Also, although capital gains are generally allocated to principal, a portion of the net proceeds from the sale of any part of principal that has not produced an average net income of at least 1% per year for more than a year (referred to as "unproductive property") is treated as delayed income to which the income beneficiary is entitled.

FIGURE 10-2   REVISED UNIFORM PRINCIPAL AND INCOME ACT

Section 4   [When Right to Income Arises; Apportionment of Income]

(a) An income beneficiary is entitled to income from the date specified in the trust instrument, or, if none is specified, from the date an asset becomes subject to the trust. In the case of an asset becoming subject to a trust by reason of a will, it becomes subject to the trust as of the date of the death of the testator even though there is an intervening period of administration of the testator's estate.

(b) In the administration of a decedent's estate or an asset becoming subject to a trust by reason of a will
   (1) receipts due but not paid at the death of the testator are principal;
   (2) receipts in the form of periodic payments (other than corporate distributions to stockholders), including rent, interest, or annuities, not due at the date of death of the testator shall be treated as accruing from day to day. That portion of the receipt accruing before the date of death is principal, and the balance is income.

(c) In all other cases, any receipt from an income producing asset is income even though the receipt was earned or accrued in whole or in part before the date when the asset became subject to the trust.

(d) On termination of an income interest, the income beneficiary whose interest is terminated, or his estate, is entitled to
   (1) income undistributed on the date of termination;
   (2) income due but not paid to the trustee on the date of termination;
   (3) income in the form of periodic payments (other than corporate distributions to stockholders), including rent, interest, or annuities, not due on the date of termination, accrued from day to day.

(e) Corporate distributions to stockholders shall be treated as due on the day fixed by the corporation for determination of stockholders of record entitled to distribution or, if no date is fixed, on the date of declaration of the distribution by the corporation.

Continued

FIGURE 10-2   CONTINUED

Section 13   [Charges Against Income and Principal]

(a) The following charges shall be made against income:

(1) ordinary expenses incurred in connection with the administration, management, or preservation of the trust property, including regular recurring taxes assessed against any portion of the principal, water rates, premiums on insurance taken upon the interests of the income beneficiary, remainderman, or trustee, interest paid by the trustee, and ordinary repairs;

(2) a reasonable allowance for depreciation on property subject to depreciation under generally accepted accounting principles, but no allowance shall be made for depreciation of that portion of any real property used by a beneficiary as a residence or for depreciation of any property held by the trustee on the effective date of this Act for which the trustee is not then making an allowance for depreciation;

(3) one-half of court costs, attorney's fees, and other fees on periodic judicial accounting, unless the court directs otherwise;

(4) court costs, attorney's fees, and other fees on other accounting or judicial proceedings if the matter primarily concerns the income beneficiary, unless the court directs otherwise;

(5) one-half of the trustee's regular compensation, whether based on a percentage of principal or income, and all expenses reasonably incurred for current management of principal and application of income;

(6) any tax levied upon receipts defined as income under this Act or the trust instrument and payable by the trustee.

TAYLOR TRUST: If either Walter or Betty should become incapacitated, the trust will become irrevocable as to the incapacitated spouse's property. The successor trustee will at this time be accountable to the remainder beneficiaries and must maintain complete and careful records conforming to the allocation rules discussed above. However, the trust need not be split into separate trusts at that time; third parties will still deal with the trustee(s) of the "Walter and Betty Taylor Trust" rather than Walter's trust or Betty's trust (see *Administration of* Inter Vivos *Trusts by Successor Trustees).*

Payment of Taxes. The trustee has a duty to report trust income and to pay all taxes that may be owed by the trust. The trustee is personally liable for interest or penalties owing as a result of a breach of this duty. The tax consequences of placing property in trust depend primarily on whether the trust is revocable or irrevocable (see Table 10-2). A *revocable* trust is not treated as a distinct taxable entity apart from its settlor; the settlor's power to revoke the trust is tantamount to ownership. For the same reason, the transfer of property by the settlor to a revocable trust is not a taxable event for gift-tax purposes. All income from a revocable trust is taxable to the settlor and is

TABLE 10-1　ALLOCATING FIDUCIARY INCOME AND EXPENDITURES*

Income	Allocated to Income Beneficiary? (*Inter Vivos* Trusts)	Allocated to Income Beneficiary? (Decedent's Estates and Testamentary Trusts)
Interest Rent Annuities	Yes, if income is actually received during income beneficiary's term	No, if due at date of testator's death; otherwise, only amount accrued during income beneficiary's term
Ordinary dividends	Yes, if date determined by corporation (or date of declaration of distribution) is during income beneficiary's term	Same
Stock dividends Stock splits	No, unless shareholders can choose to receive in the form of either stock or cash	Same
Capital gains	No, except for portion of gain from sale of underproductive property	Same

Expense	Income Beneficiary	Corpus
Repairs Maintenance	Ordinary and necessary	Extraordinary repairs
Improvements	No	Yes
Depreciation	Trustee may set aside reasonable allowance (depreciation reserve), except for property used as a residence by a beneficiary	No
Mortgages	Interest payments	Payments of principal
Taxes Insurance premiums	Yes	No, except for special property assessments resulting in permanent improvements
Court costs Attorney's fees Compensation to trustee	50% or as directed by court	50% or as directed by court (but 100% of legal fees incurred to establish trust)

*Under Revised Uniform Principal and Income Act; information provided in this table is not comprehensive; these rules apply only if controlling instrument or state law does not specify otherwise.

TABLE 10-2   TAXATION OF TRUSTS

| Type of Trust | Tax Consequences | | |
	Settlor	Trustee	Beneficiary
Revocable	■ Taxed on income ■ No gift for gift-tax purposes ■ Trust property included in gross tax estate	■ Not taxed on income ■ No Form 1041 required	■ Taxed on distributions of income ■ Receives carryover basis in trust principal*
Irrevocable *inter vivos*	■ Not taxed on income** ■ Gift for gift-tax purposes (i.e., included in gross tax estate but valued at time of *inter vivos* transfer)	■ Must report all income (Form 1041) ■ Must provide Schedule K-1 to beneficiaries to whom current income is distributed ■ Taxed on retained income ■ Receives carryover basis in trust property*	■ Taxed on distributions of income ■ Receives carryover basis in trust principal*
Testamentary trust	■ Trust property included in gross tax estate	■ Same as irrevocable *inter vivos* trust except that trust receives stepped-up (or stepped-down) basis in trust property	■ Same as irrevocable *inter vivos* trust except that beneficiary receives stepped-up (or stepped-down) basis in trust property

*If settlor retains a reversionary interest, trust income may be taxable to settlor under tax rules relating to reversionary (Clifford) trusts.
**Limited to fair market value at time of gift.

reported on the settlor's individual tax return. All property remaining in a revocable trust at the settlor's death is included in the settlor's gross tax estate for estate-tax purposes.

In contrast, an *irrevocable* trust is treated under the tax laws as a distinct taxable entity, and a transfer by the settlor to such a trust does constitute a gift for gift-tax purposes. The trustee receives a carryover basis in the property. All current income distributed to a beneficiary is taxed to the beneficiary, not to the trustee, at his or her individual income tax rates. All current income retained by the trustee (undistributed) is taxed once to the trustee at the same rates that apply to decedents' estates, then accumulated to principal, so that it is not taxed again as income when it is eventually distributed. Upon receipt of principal during the settlor's lifetime, a beneficiary receives a carryover basis in the property distributed. Upon receipt of principal after the settlor's death, however, the beneficiary receives a stepped-up (or stepped-down) basis in the property.

IRS Form 1041 The trustee is responsible for filing state and federal income-tax returns to report trust income and for paying the tax. The trustee must report *all* trust income, even if the trust is taxed on only a portion of the income. At the federal level, IRS Form 1041 (U.S. Fiduciary Tax Return) is used for this purpose. The trustee may choose to report on either a calendar year or fiscal year. Tax payments are properly chargeable equally to income and principal (see *Trust Accounting under the Revised UPIA*).

IRS Form 1041S A simplified federal tax form—IRS Form 1041S (U.S. Fiduciary Income Tax Return for Nontaxable Simple Trusts)—may be used in lieu of Form 1041 where all income from the irrevocable trust is passed through to the *settlor*, who reports the income on his or her individual income-tax return. This would occur where the settlor of a grantor trust has become incapacitated, as well as after the first spouse's death where all income is passed through to the surviving spouse-settlor. The settlor-beneficiary's Social Security number may be used on Form 1041S. Form 1041S serves essentially as an information return, since it is used only where no income tax is owed by the trust.

Schedule K-1 If income was distributed during the tax year, the trustee must attach to Form 1041 a separate Schedule K-1 (Beneficiary's Share of Income, Deductions, Credits, etc.) for each distributee to show who received the distribution from the trust. The trustee must also provide a copy of Schedule K-1 to the beneficiary.

FOCUS: An irrevocable trust (or a revocable trust that has become irrevocable) is treated under the tax laws as a distinct taxable entity. The trustee must file a fiduciary income-tax return (IRS Form 1041) to report *all* income from trust property. The trustee is taxed, however, only on current income retained in trust, while the beneficiaries must report and pay tax on all current income distributed to them.

Administration of *Inter Vivos* Trusts by Successor Trustees

Upon establishing a typical revocable *inter vivos* trust, the settlor, as trustee and sole current beneficiary, may continue to deal with the trust property as his or her own. Since the settlor may revoke the trust and is the only current recipient of the benefits of the trust, remainder beneficiaries merely hold expectations rather than property interests at this point, just as devisees under the terms of a will have no enforceable rights during the testator's lifetime. Accordingly, during this time the settlor-trustee owes no fiduciary duty to any other person. The only administrative concerns of the settlor-trustee during this time are to (1) make sure that title in the trust assets is properly held by the settlor as trustee, (2) make sure that all proceeds from the sale of a trust asset are promptly placed in trust, and (3) maintain a current schedule of trust assets.

Incapacity of the Settlor. Upon the incapacity or death of the settlor, because the settlor no longer has the legal capacity to revoke the trust, the trust becomes irrevocable. A successor trustee may step in and immediately assume management and control of the trust property. The successor trustee is generally designated in the trust instrument (typically a spouse in the case of a married couple). An incapacitated settlor typically continues to be the sole present beneficiary. However, since the trust is now irrevocable, the successor trustee is also accountable to the remainder beneficiaries. Moreover, when the trust becomes irrevocable, it is considered a distinct taxable entity, and the successor trustee must report income from the trust to the federal and state taxing authorities. In the case of a single trust established by a married couple, the trust would become irrevocable as to the incapacitated spouse's property only, and only that portion would be treated separately for income-tax purposes. Although such a trust is likely to include an "AB" or "ABC" allocation plan, separate trusts are generally not called for until the death of one of the spouses. Also, until the death of the settlor (or until the death of both spouses in the case of a trust established by a married couple), all trust income continues to "pass through" the trust to the settlor(s) and is reported on the settlor's individual income-tax return.

Immediate Concerns upon the Settlor's Death. The death of a person whose assets have been held in an *inter vivos* trust presents a common situation in the area of trust administration with which the probate paralegal may expect to be involved. Most settlors name a family member or friend, rather than a professional fiduciary such as a bank or trust company, as successor trustee, just as when nominating an executor in a will. Even a relatively sophisticated individual trustee is not likely to be aware of the administrative duties required of the successor trustee. Even where the trust serves to avoid probate and calls simply for outright distribution at the settlor's death, the successor trustee's job is far from simple.

A variety of postmortem concerns must be addressed in any event, including:

1. Obtaining a federal tax identification number (EIN) to use in identifying all trust accounts and assets and on tax returns
2. Obtaining certified copies of the death certificate
3. Paying the decedent's debts
4. Determining the extent of the decedent's estate both inside and outside the trust
5. Valuing the decedent's assets for the purpose of estate-tax liability
6. Determining tax liability and filing tax returns (state and federal income-tax and estate-tax returns)
7. Arranging for payment of benefits and proceeds under life insurance policies, pension plans, and other contractual arrangements

Trusts that call for the continuation of the trust after the settlor's death may raise additional concerns, such as:

1. Proper procedures for establishing separate trusts
2. Allocation of the decedent's debts and taxes among trusts

3. Allocation of income and principal among beneficiaries
4. Allocation of the trust assets among multiple trusts (for example, if the trust includes an "AB" or "ABC" plan or if the plan provides for separate trusts for each beneficiary)

Although ease of administration is often professed as one of the chief advantages of using an *inter vivos* trust instead of a will, the actual experiences of successor trustees generally do not support this claim. Individual trustees who attempt to administer *inter vivos* trusts without the assistance of a certified public accountant or probate lawyer almost invariably, albeit inadvertently, violate the terms of the trust in one or more ways. Errors in allocation generally benefit one beneficiary at the expense of another, while other errors may operate to the equal detriment of all beneficiaries. Perhaps the most costly errors involve trusts that include an "AB" or "ABC" plan, originally established for the primary purpose of avoiding estate taxes. Where the trustee neglects to file separate income-tax returns for a bypass and QTIP trust, or where the trustee fails to allocate income from each trust according to the terms of the instrument, the Internal Revenue Service is unlikely to acknowledge the existence of separate trusts. Such mistakes may result in substantial tax liability, and the trustee may be liable for payment of interest on the tax and for penalties as well. The successor trustee (usually a member of the settlor's family) may be seeking assistance from the lawyer after a significant problem has surfaced. If so, the paralegal may be asked to collect and review the trustee's records, books, account statements, and tax returns in order to determine the source or extent of an allocation error and to reconstruct the records to reflect the proper state of affairs.

 PRACTICE TIP: Estate-planning lawyers are partially at fault for many of the problems that successor trustees get themselves into. Too many lawyers fail to educate the estate-planning client about postmortem trust administration. The paralegal can help to solve this problem by asking the person designated as successor trustee to be present when the trust instrument is executed and to discuss postmortem procedures with the lawyer and/or the paralegal at that time. The paralegal should also develop a standard follow-up letter for trust clients that includes postmortem instructions; the paralegal should instruct the trust client to keep a copy of the letter with the trust instrument and other important papers, to review the instructions with the successor trustee, and to inform the successor trustee to contact the law firm promptly upon the client's incapacity or death.

Allocation of Assets among Trusts. Allocation of trust assets among two or more trusts is a simple procedural matter that may be performed by the trustee or by the paralegal. A simple written allocation schedule indicating each trust by name and indicating the assets allocated to the trust is sufficient to effect an allocation. The schedule should indicate the value of each asset and, for noncash assets, how the value was determined (for example, by two appraisals from real-estate agents). It is unnecessary for title in the assets to be changed to reflect the allocation. If the trustee subsequently wishes to exchange assets between trusts, each exchange should be recorded in the asset allocation schedule and signed by the trustee.

Although bookkeeping is a straightforward matter, allocation *decisions* are generally based on a variety of factors requiring the lawyer's judgment and knowledge. As noted earlier in this chapter, the trustee owes a duty of loyalty equally to all beneficiaries. When the trust calls for division of the trust estate into two or more trusts, the allocation must be fair to all beneficiaries in light of the terms of the trust instrument. It would be a breach of fiduciary duty, for example, for the trustee to allocate appreciating assets to one trust while allocating depreciating assets to another with the intention of favoring one beneficiary over another, unless called for under the trust instrument. Estate-tax and income-tax considerations also enter into allocation decisions. In allocating assets pursuant to an ''AB'' or ''ABC'' plan, appreciating or ''growth'' assets are generally allocated to bypass trusts because the appreciation will escape estate taxation at the death of the second spouse, while income-producing assets are generally allocated to a marital deduction trust such as a QTIP trust in order to provide current income to the surviving spouse while at the same time minimizing estate taxes on the spouse's death. However, the trustee should also consider the beneficiaries' relative income-tax brackets.

Transfers of Beneficial Interests

Unless otherwise restricted by statute or by the terms of the trust, a trust beneficiary is free to assign his or her equitable interest in a trust to another. However, if the trust estate consists of real property, the assignment must be in writing. The transferee takes the interest subject to all conditions and limitations that would have applied but for the assignment. An *involuntary* assignment of a beneficial interest may occur in the case of a financially insolvent beneficiary; except as otherwise provided by statute or validly restricted by the terms of the trust, the debtor-beneficiary's creditors may satisfy their debts by reaching the beneficial interest through appropriate civil proceedings. However, unless the beneficiary-debtor is sole beneficiary and can presently demand conveyance of the trust property, the creditor may reach only the interest of the beneficiary and not the trust property itself. The usual remedy of the creditor is either to require the trustee to pay the beneficiary's income to the creditor until the debt is satisfied or to force a sale of the beneficial interest and have the proceeds applied to the creditor's claim.

Spendthrift Trusts. In most states, a settlor may legally restrict transfers of beneficial interests through the use of a **spendthrift trust**. A spendthrift trust is any trust that includes a special ''spendthrift provision'' prohibiting the beneficiary from transferring his or her interest voluntarily. The trust may also, and generally does, prohibit involuntary transfers (see Taylor file, Exhibit 3). However, a spendthrift provision restricting involuntary transfers but not voluntary transfers violates public policy and is invalid (although the other provisions of the trust generally remain valid). A spendthrift provision does not apply to income or principal once it has been paid to the beneficiary. After distribution, the property is no longer protected by the spendthrift provision and is subject to the claims of creditors. Spendthrift provisions do not apply to a beneficiary who is also the settlor; otherwise, persons could easily avoid their creditors by transferring legal title in their property to another while retaining the right to income from the property.

Support Trusts. A **support trust** is any trust that by its terms requires the trustee to distribute only as much income or principal as is necessary for the beneficiary's support. The beneficiary of a support trust is not entitled to payments of either income or principal. The beneficial interest is not assignable, either voluntarily or involuntarily, because it is viewed as personal to the beneficiary, and no one but the beneficiary can enjoy it.

Forfeiture. A forfeiture provision calls for either the accumulation of income or payment of income to another in the event that the beneficiary becomes bankrupt or insolvent. Forfeiture provisions have been consistently upheld by the courts and may be used effectively to protect against involuntary transfers.

Discretionary Trusts. A **discretionary trust** is any trust that allows the trustee discretion whether to distribute or withhold payments of income or principal to a beneficiary. Because the beneficiary has no right to payments that can be enforced against the trustee, the beneficiary's creditors cannot reach the income or principal until the trustee exercises his or her discretion and makes a payment. However, the trustee's discretion must relate to the beneficiary's right to income and/or principal, not just to the time and manner of payment.

Disclaimers. Just as a devisee in a decedent's estate may disclaim an inheritance, a beneficiary may disclaim an interest in a trust. However, the disclaimer must be made within a reasonable time after the interest vests in the beneficiary. For beneficial interests that vest upon the settlor's death, a valid disclaimer must be made within nine months thereafter. Disclaimers are often motivated by income-tax considerations. However, a disclaimer may also be made as a legitimate measure of protection against creditors.

Revocation, Modification, and Termination of Trusts

In most states, a trust is irrevocable by the settlor unless the power to revoke is reserved expressly by the settlor; in other states, a trust is revocable unless made irrevocable by the terms of the trust instrument. The trust may be revoked by any instrument showing the settlor's intent. A simple letter of instruction to the trustee will suffice, unless the trust instrument provides for more specific requirements. However, an *inter vivos* trust cannot be revoked through the use of a will unless expressly authorized by the trust. In the case of a grantor trust, the settlor-trustee may also revoke the trust by simply removing the trust property from it. As trustee, the settlor might simply dispose of the trust property and deposit the proceeds in a personal account. If the settlor-trustee does not wish to dispose of the property, the trust can be revoked by reconveyance. For example, if a quitclaim deed was used to place the property in trust, another quitclaim deed may be used to remove it. This method can be used to revoke the trust as to all or any portion of the trust estate. The power to revoke a trust includes the power to amend or modify the trust. An amendment to a trust is analogous to a codicil in form and substance, except that the formal requirements for execution of wills do not apply. Major changes and modifications may call for an *amended trust* to replace the original one.

A trust is terminated when the duration of the trust as specified by the settlor has expired or when the purposes of the trust have been accomplished. At this time, the trustee is required to promptly wind up the trust's affairs and to distribute the remaining trust property to the beneficiaries. If the trustee is given discretion to terminate the trust, such discretion must be exercised reasonably in light of the purposes of the trust. Under some circumstances, a trust may be terminated prematurely or modified by agreement of the beneficiaries. In most states, however, *all* beneficiaries must consent (minor and unborn beneficiaries may be represented by a guardian *ad litem* for this purpose). Also, modification or termination must not interfere with a *material purpose* of the trust, unless the settlor joins the beneficiaries in requesting termination. A trust may be terminated by court order where the trust purposes are accomplished early or where the trust purposes become illegal or impossible to carry out. A well-drafted trust will permit the trustee to terminate the trust prematurely if circumstances have changed so that continuation of the trust would undermine its purposes, as well as if the expenses of administration outweigh the benefits of continuing the trust. A court may also authorize or direct a trustee to deviate from the administrative terms of a trust if compliance with the terms of the trust would interfere with the accomplishment of the trust purposes and the settlor did not know or anticipate the new circumstances. However, changed circumstances cannot be used to change the beneficial rights of the beneficiaries.

Paralegal Assignment 10

Recall that your current assignment as probate paralegal involves the preparation and execution of all legal documents required to transfer the Taylors' assets to their newly established trust. The legal documents required to transfer the appropriate assets to their trust are included in the Taylor file as referenced throughout Chapter 10.

11 PROTECTIVE PROCEEDINGS AND PLANNING FOR INCAPACITY

In the Taylor matter, Walter and Betty are concerned not only with the post-mortem disposition of their respective estates but also with the consequences in the event either of them becomes incapacitated to the extent of being no longer capable of self-care or management of property and business affairs. Their *inter vivos* trust will provide some measure of protection in the event of incapacity. However, Ms. Cargis has pointed out to them that additional legal documents may provide further protection, and she has asked you to prepare and assist the Taylors in executing these documents according to the information obtained during her interview with the Taylors. These topics are addressed later in the chapter, while the first portion of the chapter examines the various court proceedings that serve to protect the interests of incapacitated persons and minors. It is impossible to discuss all of the variations that exist among the jurisdictions with respect to protective proceedings, so the provisions of the U.P.C. will be highlighted as a point of reference.

PROTECTION OF PERSONS UNDER DISABILITY AND MINORS

The first main section of this chapter deals with court proceedings and alternative procedures intended to ensure that the *personal* needs—food,

277

clothing, shelter, medical care, and so forth—of a disabled individual or minor are met. Proceedings for the protection of *estates* of persons under disability and minors are examined later in the chapter.

Guardianships

A **guardianship** is an arrangement under which legal authority and responsibility for the care, custody, and control of a person, referred to as the **ward**, is conferred upon another person (or upon an organization), referred to as a **guardian**, by court appointment or by parental or spousal nomination. Under the U.P.C., a person under the age of 21 for whom a guardian has been appointed *solely* because of minority (rather than due to incapacity) is referred to more specifically as a *minor ward*. A guardian's primary authority and responsibility extends to the person of the ward and not to the ward's property or financial and business affairs. A **guardian** *ad litem* is a special type of guardian appointed by the court to represent and defend a minor or incompetent person only for a court proceeding (the term *ad litem* means "for the suit" or "for the purposes of the law suit"). In some states, the term *guardianship* is given a somewhat different meaning, referring instead to a protective proceeding for a *minor*, either for the minor's care, custody, and control ("guardianship of the person") or for the estate of the minor ("guardianship of the estate"), while protective proceedings for incapacitated adults and their estates are referred to as *conservatorships* (see Table 11-1).

Guardianship proceedings are similar in many respects to proceedings for decedents' estates (see Figure 11-1 for a summary of guardianship pro-

TABLE 11-1 PARTIES TO PROTECTIVE PROCEEDINGS—TERMINOLOGY

	Protection of Persons under Disability and Minors		Protection of Estates of Persons under Disability and Minors	
	Legal Representative	Protected Person	Legal Representative	Protected Person
U.P.C.	Guardian	Ward *or* minor ward (for minor not under other disability)	Conservator	Protected person
Florida	Personal guardian *or* guardian of the person	Ward	Guardian of property (*also* financial guardian *or* guardian of estate)	Ward
California Minors	Guardian of the person	Ward	Guardian of the estate	Ward
Disabled Adults	Conservator of the person	Conservatee	Conservator of the estate	Conservatee

ceedings). However, because the underlying purpose of a guardianship proceeding is to protect a *living person* rather than the *estate* of a *decedent*, many
significant differences exist, including the following:

■ In proceedings to establish a guardianship, the court must first be
satisfied that the person to be protected is sufficiently incapacitated
(except for disability resulting solely from a person's minority).

FIGURE 11-1 GUARDIANSHIP/CONSERVATORSHIP PROCEEDINGS

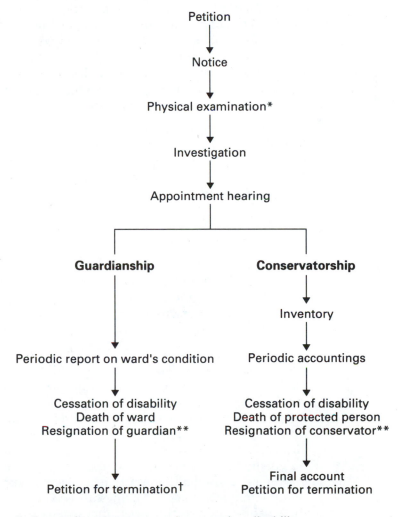

* Except for minors not under any other disability.
** Court will appoint successor if court accepts resignation and
disability has not ceased.
† Except upon death of ward or attainment of majority of minor
not under any other disability.

- In proceedings to establish a guardianship, an investigation and report by the local government's social service agency is required.
- In contrast to proceedings for the appointment of a personal representative, where the court may not require a hearing if all of the paperwork is in order and no objections have been filed, a hearing in open court for the appointment of a guardian is required.
- The proposed ward is entitled in most cases to notice of the appointment proceedings (as well as of all subsequent proceedings) and is entitled to be present at the hearing.
- The class of persons considered to be ''interested'' and thus entitled to notice of guardianship proceedings is more narrowly defined than in decedents' estates.
- Guardianship proceedings, unlike those for decedents' estates, are continuing in nature, terminating only upon the ward's death or cessation of disability or incapacity.

The paralegal's role in guardianship proceedings is similar to that for formal proceedings involving decedents' estates. Where the law firm is representing the person petitioning for the appointment of a guardian, the paralegal assists in a variety of matters, including the following:

1. Collecting information needed to prepare the petition
2. Ensuring that all notice requirements have been met
3. Preparing and filing the petition to establish the guardianship
4. Correcting all errors and deficiencies in the petition and accompanying documents

If the law firm represents the guardian after appointment, the paralegal typically prepares the guardian's reports (as required by the court or requested by other persons interested in the welfare of the ward) and prepares petitions for court approval of compensation for the guardian as well as for the law firm.

Appointment Proceedings. The proposed ward (including minors as well as adults) or any person interested in the welfare of the proposed ward may petition the court for the appointment of a guardian (U.P.C. §§ 5-206[a], 303[a]). The proper venue for initiating guardianship proceedings is the place where the proposed ward resides or is present or, in the case of an alleged incapacitated person admitted to an institution pursuant to a court order, the place where that court is located (U.P.C. §§ 5-205, 302). In the case of a proposed minor ward, the court may appoint an attorney to represent the minor in the proceedings if the court deems it necessary to protect the minor's interests. However, the proposed minor ward is not otherwise entitled to legal representation (U.P.C. § 5-206[d]). In the case of an alleged incapacitated person, unless the proposed ward is represented by legal counsel, the court must appoint an attorney to represent the proposed ward in the proceeding (U.P.C. § 5-303[b]). Court-appointed legal counsel may serve as guardian *ad litem* if appropriate, while further interim protection may involve the *ex parte* appointment of a *temporary guardian* pending a hearing to establish a more permanent arrangement.

Determining the Guardian The court may appoint as guardian for a minor any person whose appointment would be in the best interest of the minor. If the minor is 14 or more years of age and has nominated a guardian, the court will appoint that person unless it finds the appointment contrary to the best interest of the minor (U.P.C. § 5-207). Any qualified person may be appointed guardian of an incapacitated person. Unless lack of qualification or other good cause dictates the contrary, the court shall appoint a guardian of an incapacitated person in accordance with the incapacitated person's most recent nomination in a durable power of attorney (U.P.C. § 5-303[a], [b]) (see *Planning for Incapacity*).

In the absence of a nomination by the incapacitated person, the following are entitled to consideration for appointment in the order listed:

1. The spouse of the incapacitated person or a person nominated by will of a deceased spouse or by other writing signed by the spouse and attested by at least two witnesses
2. An adult child of the incapacitated person
3. A parent of the incapacitated person, or a person nominated by will of a deceased parent or by other writing signed by a parent and attested by at least two witnesses
4. Any relative of the incapacitated person with whom the person has resided for more than six months prior to the filing of the petition
5. A person nominated by the person who is caring for or paying for the care of the incapacitated person (U.P.C. § 5-305[c])

With respect to persons having equal priority, the court shall select the one it deems best qualified to serve. Also, the court, acting in the best interest of the incapacitated person, may pass over a person having priority and appoint a person having a lower priority or no priority (U.P.C. § 5-305[d]). The petition to establish a guardianship may, but need not, request that a particular person be appointed as guardian. The U.P.C. neither expressly permits nor prohibits appointment of joint guardians. If no person listed above is available and willing to serve as guardian, the court may appoint a *public guardian* or private charitable organization to serve.

Notice Requirements In the case of a proposed minor ward, the petitioner must provide notice of the hearing to (1) the minor if the minor is at least 14 years of age and is not the petitioner; (2) any person alleged to have had the principal care and custody of the minor during the 60 days preceding the filing of the petition; and (3) any living parent of the minor; notices may be given personally or by mail (U.P.C. § 5-206[b]). In the case of an alleged incapacitated person, the petitioner must provide notice to the following persons:

1. The proposed ward and spouse (if any), or (if none) adult children, or (if none) parents

2. Any person who is serving as guardian or conservator or who has the care and custody of the proposed ward
3. In case no other person is notified, at least one of the nearest adult relatives, if any can be found
4. Any other person as directed by the court (U.P.C. § 5-304[a])

In the case of an alleged incapacitated person, notice must be provided personally to the proposed ward, and other persons entitled to notice must also be served personally if the person to be notified can be found within the state (U.P.C. § 5-304[c]). The alleged incapacitated person may not waive notice (U.P.C. § 5-304[d]). In all other cases, notice must be provided at the same time and in the same manner as required in formal proceedings to establish decedents' estates (U.P.C. §§ 5-206[b], 304[c]).

FOCUS: In the case of a proposed *minor ward*, the petitioner must provide notice of the appointment hearing to the minor if the minor is at least 14 years of age and is not the petitioner; under the U.P.C., notice to the proposed minor ward may be provided either personally or by mail. In the case of an alleged incapacitated person, notice must be provided personally to the proposed ward, who may not waive notice.

Investigation and Determination of Incapacity Except for guardianships established for the protection of a person solely because the person is a minor, before appointing a guardian, the court must first be satisfied that the person to be protected is sufficiently incapacitated. The U.P.C. defines *incapacitated person* as "any person who is impaired by reason of mental illness, mental deficiency, physical illness or disability, advanced age, chronic use of drugs, chronic intoxication, or other cause (except minority) to the extent of lacking sufficient understanding or capacity to make or communicate responsible decisions" (U.P.C. § 5-103). A physician or other qualified person appointed by the court must examine the proposed ward and submit a written report to the court. An investigation and report by the local government's social service agency will also be required. The investigator will interview the proposed ward, noting his or her present physical condition and living environment as well as visiting the place where it is proposed that the ward will be detained or reside after appointment of the guardian. The investigator will also interview the person who filed the petition as well as the proposed guardian. The court may also require one or more additional investigative reports by a public or charitable agency (U.P.C. § 5-303[c]).

The Court Hearing In contrast to proceedings for the appointment of a personal representative, where the court may not require a hearing if all of the paperwork is in order and no objections have been filed, a hearing in open court for the appointment of a guardian is required in any event. Any other person interested in the welfare of the proposed ward may appear in the proceedings, either at or prior to the hearing (U.P.C. §§ 5-205, 303[d]). The court will generally insist that the proposed guardian be present at the hearing to attest to the satisfaction of the judge that he or she is willing and able to assume the responsibilities as guardian; appearance by the attorney alone is not sufficient. If the proposed ward is an adult, he or she is entitled to be present at the court hearing (U.P.C. § 5-303[c]). In order to ensure that this right is protected, the court generally insists on the proposed ward's presence at the hearing, regardless of physical or mental condition, except upon affidavit by the personal physician that the proposed ward's presence would pose a significant health risk. The court will order the appointment if satisfied that the interests of the proposed ward would best be served thereby; otherwise, the court may either dismiss the proceedings or make any other order that it deems appropriate (U.P.C. §§ 5-206[c], 306[b]). The court will issue letters of guardianship to the guardian as evidence of his or her authority.

Establishing a Guardianship without Court Proceedings. Guardianships are generally established through formal appointment proceedings, although the U.P.C. permits a person to act as guardian by parental or spousal nomination in lieu of court appointment (see §§ 5-202, 301). Nomination may be made only by the spouse of an incapacitated adult or by the parent of an unmarried incapacitated person or minor. The nomination must be in writing and must be attested by two competent witnesses; a postmortem nomination can be included in a will. Upon the death (or incapacity) of the spouse or parent, the nominee can establish the guardianship simply by filing his or her acceptance with the court where the disabled person resides or, in the case of nomination by will, with the court where the will is probated. The clerk will then issue letters to the guardian as evidence of his or her authority; the letters will indicate that appointment was other than by court order. The appointee must provide written notification of the appointment to the ward as well as to any adult currently caring for the disabled person, although either the ward (if over the age of 14) or the current caregiver may terminate the appointment by filing a written objection with the court within 30 days after receiving notice of the appointment (U.P.C. §§ 5-203, 301[d]).

Powers and Duties of a Guardian. U.P.C. §§ 5-209 and 309 govern the general powers and duties of a guardian. Once the court issues letters of guardianship, the guardian has the power to take custody of the person of the ward and to establish the ward's place of abode, except if inconsistent with a court order relating to the detention or commitment of the ward. The guardian has the power to consent to medical or other professional care or treatment and to consent to the ward's marriage or adoption. The guardian is empowered to receive money for the support of the ward if the money is payable to either the ward or the ward's parent(s), guardian, or custodian under the terms of any statute, insurance policy, conservatorship, trust, device, custodianship, or other private contract. Also, if no conservator for the estate of the ward has been established, the guardian may take appropriate action to compel the performance by any person with a duty to support the ward. In some states, a guardian may be granted additional powers to institutionalize the protected person against his or her will where the person is gravely disabled and is dangerous to himself or herself or to others.

The court may limit the guardian's powers to the extent that they fail to serve the best interest of the ward; in the case of a minor ward, any such limitations are generally imposed for the purpose of developing the ward's self-reliance. The extent of the guardian's powers are determined by statute, subject to any limitations and restrictions imposed by the court. Any such limitations or restrictions must be indicated on the letters.

A guardian has not only the power but also the duty to assume care, custody, and control of the ward. In the case of a minor ward, a guardian generally has the same responsibilities as a parent for the support, care, and education of the ward, except that the guardian is not personally liable for the ward's expenses and is not personally liable to third parties for acts of the ward merely by reason of the relationship. The guardian is under a legal duty to become acquainted with the ward and to maintain sufficient personal contact with the ward to know of the ward's capabilities, limitations, needs, health, and so forth. To a limited extent, a guardian's duties may extend to the minor's property as well. The guardian must take reasonable care of the ward's personal effects; must apply any available money of the ward to the ward's current needs for support, care, and education; and must conserve any excess money of the ward for the ward's future needs, unless another person has been appointed as fiduciary for the ward's *estate*, in which event the minor's personal guardian must pay over to the fiduciary all money not required to meet the ward's current needs.

Post-Appointment Proceedings. By accepting appointment, a guardian submits personally to the continuing jurisdiction of the court in any proceeding relating to the guardianship (U.P.C. §§ 5-208, 307). The guardian must report to the court the condition of the ward and the ward's estate that has been subject the guardian's possession and control, as ordered by the court or on petition of any person interested in the ward's welfare. Also, on its own ruling, the court may require a report or regular periodic reports (U.P.C. §§ 5-209[b][5], 309). In all post-appointment court proceedings, written notice must be provided to the ward, to the guardian, and to any other person as ordered by the court. Personal service is generally not required in post-appointment proceedings (U.P.C. §§ 5-208, 307). The court at the place where the ward resides has concurrent jurisdiction with the court in which the guardian's acceptance was filed over all proceedings relating to the guardianship. If not the same court, jurisdiction can then be transferred if the court at the place where the ward resides determines, after consulting with the other court, that this would be in the best interest of the ward (U.P.C. §§ 5-211, 312). A guardian is entitled to reasonable compensation for his or her services and to reimbursement for expenses incurred to provide necessities, such as food, clothing, and shelter, to the ward. However, unless payment or reimbursement is by a court-appointed fiduciary for the ward's estate, the court must first approve any such compensation or reimbursement (U.P.C. §§ 5-209[d], 309).

Termination of Guardianships. U.P.C. §§ 5-210 and 310 govern termination of guardianships. A guardianship terminates automatically upon the ward's death or, in the case of a minor ward only, upon adoption or marriage of the ward. A guardianship also terminates upon the guardian's removal or resignation, although in the latter case, the guardian's resignation must first be approved by the court. A petition for removal or resignation may, but need not, include a request to appoint a successor guardian. In any event, the court must appoint another guardian (unless the ward is no longer under disability). A guardianship also terminates upon cessation of disability or incapacity. Except in the case of a minor ward, where disability ends automatically when the ward attains the age of majority, cessation of disability or incapacity must be proved to the court before the guardian can be discharged. Any person interested in the ward's welfare may petition the court for removal of the guardian or for termination of the guardianship. The ward, if at least 14 years of age, may also petition for removal of the guardian or termination of the guardianship (U.P.C. §§ 5-212, 311).

Substitutes for Guardianship Proceedings

A formal guardianship arrangement is only necessary where no other means is available and adequate to protect the interests of the person to be protected. First, guardianship proceedings for minors are generally not required where there is a natural or adoptive parent who is willing and fit to care for the child; a parent has the legal authority and responsibility for the care, custody, and control of a minor child without court order. For adult children, however, the status of parent (natural or adoptive) is insufficient in itself to confer authority over the care, control, and custody of an incapacitated person. Similarly, the spouse of an incapacitated person or minor does not have such authority due solely to the marital relationship. Second, for incapacitated adults, certain planning devices are available to allow another person to make decisions on behalf of the incapacitated person with respect to health care, as long as the planning device is executed prior to incapacity (see *Planning for Incapacity*). Third, state law may provide for an abbreviated court proceeding to confer on one person the authority to consent to particular medical treatment on behalf of an incapacitated person. Finally, in the case of a minor not under other disability and without parent, a court-appointed conservator of the estate of the minor may exercise the same powers as a guardian unless and until a guardian is appointed (U.P.C. § 5-423). All of the various methods for protection of incapacitated persons and minors are summarized in Figure 11-2.

FIGURE 11-2   PROTECTION OF INCAPACITATED PERSONS AND MINORS

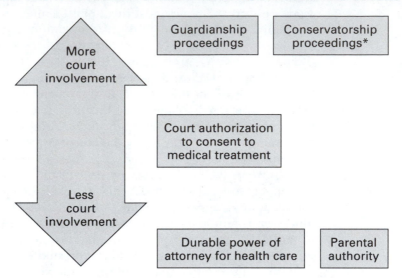

* In the case of a minor without parent, a conservator also has the authority of a guardian unless a guardian has been appointed.

PROTECTION OF ESTATES OF PERSONS UNDER DISABILITY AND MINORS

While the preceding materials in this chapter dealt with legal procedures intended to ensure that the *personal* needs of a disabled individual or minor are met, the following materials pertain to proceedings for the protection of *estates*—assets, financial and legal affairs, and so forth—of persons under disability and minors. As you examine these materials, bear in mind that in the typical case where the individual requires both types of protection, a single court proceeding for both purposes is generally used.

Conservatorships

Many adults are unable to manage their own property and handle their own financial and business affairs effectively for such reasons as mental illness or deficiency, physical illness or disability, chronic use of drugs or alcohol, confinement, or disappearance. If there is property that may be wasted or dissipated unless property management is provided, or if money is needed for the support, care, and welfare of the person or those entitled to the person's support, it may be necessary through formal court proceedings to confer authority on another to act on the disabled person's behalf in protection of these interests. Similar protection may also be required for a minor, regardless of other disability. The total value of property that a minor may legally own is severely limited in every state by statute (generally to no more than a few thousand dollars). Also, with certain exceptions, minors lack the legal capacity to enter into binding contracts. Generally speaking, a parent (either natural or adoptive) may handle a child's financial and business affairs on the child's behalf without court authorization. However, where there is no parent or where the parent has abandoned the child or is unfit to manage the child's affairs, some other person must be given the legal authority to do so. Whether or not a guardian has been appointed, a court proceeding may be required to protect the property or handle the financial and business affairs of a minor or of a disabled adult if protection and management cannot otherwise be provided—for example, by parental authority, by a guardian, by a trustee under the terms of a trust, or by a custodian (see *Substitutes for Conservatorship Proceedings*).

In many cases, it is appropriate to confer authority over all of the protected person's business and financial affairs on a continuing basis by establishing a conservatorship. A **conservatorship** is an arrangement under which one person (or organization), referred to as a **conservator**, has been given by the court the legal authority over and responsibility for management of another person's property or financial and business affairs—that is, the estate of another person (see Figure 11-1 on page 279 for a summary of conservatorship proceedings). The person whose estate is protected is commonly referred to as a *conservatee*, although the U.P.C. uses the term *protected person* in the context of conservatorships as well as in the context of other more limited protective proceedings (see *Substitutes for Conservatorship Proceedings*). In some states, the term *conservatorship* is given a somewhat different meaning, referring instead to a protective proceeding for an incapacitated *adult*, either for the adult's care, custody, and control ("conservatorship of the person") or for the estate of the adult ("conservatorship of the estate"), while protective proceedings for minors and their estates are referred to as *guardianships* (see Table 11-1).

Appointment Proceedings. Conservatorship proceedings may be initiated by the person to be protected or by any person who is interested in the estate, affairs, or welfare of the person to be protected, including a parent, guardian, custodian, or any person who would be adversely affected by lack of effective management of the person's property and business affairs (including a creditor of the person to be protected) (U.P.C. § 5-404[a]). The proper venue in which to initiate conservatorship proceedings is either the place where the person to be protected resides (whether or not a guardian has been appointed in another place) or any place where the person's property is located (U.P.C. § 5-403).

The Petition The petition for appointment of a conservator must set forth:
1. The interest of the petitioner
2. The name, age, residence, and address of the person to be protected
3. The name and address of the guardian, if any
4. The name and address of the nearest relative known to the petitioner

5. A general statement of the property of the person to be protected with an estimate of the value thereof
6. Any compensation, insurance, pension, or allowance to which the person to be protected is entitled
7. The reason why appointment of a conservator is necessary
8. If the appointment of a conservator is requested, the name and address of the person whose appointment is sought and the basis of the claim to priority for appointment (U.P.C. § 5-404[b])

A complete inventory is not required at this time. Also, the petition may, but need not, request that a particular person be appointed as conservator.

Determining the Conservator The following persons are entitled to consideration for appointment as conservator in the order listed:

1. A conservator, guardian of property, or similar fiduciary appointed or recognized by an appropriate court of any other jurisdiction in which the protected person resides
2. An individual or corporation nominated by the protected person 14 or more years of age and of sufficient mental capacity to make an intelligent choice
3. The spouse of the protected person
4. An adult child of the protected person
5. A parent of the protected person, or a person nominated by the will of a deceased parent
6. Any relative of the protected person who has resided with the protected person for more than 6 months before the filing of the petition
7. A person nominated by one who is caring for or paying benefits to the protected person

However, the court may pass over a person having priority if the court deems that appointment of a person having lower priority would be in the best interest of the protected person. With respect to persons having equal priority, the court shall select the one it deems best qualified to serve (U.P.C. § 5-409).

Notice, Investigation, and Interim Protection Notice requirements, both for the initial appointment proceedings and for subsequent proceedings, are similar to those for guardianships, except that if the person to be protected has disappeared or is otherwise situated so as to make personal service of notice impracticable, notice to the person may be given by publication (U.P.C. § 5-405). The court may require that the person to be protected be examined by a physician and may order an investigation and report similar to that required in guardianship proceedings (U.P.C. § 5-406[b]). While a petition is pending and after preliminary hearing and without notice to others, the court may preserve and apply the property of the person to be protected as may be required for the support of the person to be protected or dependent of the person to be protected (U.P.C. § 5-407[b][1]). Interim protection may involve the *ex parte* appointment of a *temporary conservator* pending the court hearing to establish a more permanent arrangement.

The Court Hearing As in guardianship proceedings, the person to be protected is entitled to representation by legal counsel and is entitled to be personally present at the appointment hearing (U.P.C. § 5-406[d]). The court will generally insist on the presence at the hearing of the person to be protected, unless the person has disappeared or a physician has determined that the person's presence would pose a significant health risk. If the court determines that a basis exists for appointment of a conservator, the court will order that Letters of Conservatorship be issued. At the hearing or any time thereafter, the court may place limitations on the conservator's powers for the purpose of instilling self-reliance in the person to be protected; any such limitations should be indicated on the Letters of Conservatorship. The court may require a conservator to furnish a bond in the amount of the aggregate capital value of the property of the estate (except for the value of any real property that the conservator lacks power to sell or convey without court authorization and funds deposited under arrangements requiring a court order for their removal) plus one year's estimated income (U.P.C. § 5-411).

PRACTICE TIP: All of the information needed to file the petition for appointment of a conservator should be obtained during the first interview with the client. The paralegal may perform all or part of this function, although it is clearly the lawyer's responsibility to determine (1) whether a conservatorship is necessary or desirable; (2) who should file the petition and who should serve as conservator; and (3) whether the matter is urgent enough to warrant the appointment of a temporary conservator. Assuming that the law firm is representing the petitioner and/or the proposed conservator, the client should also be provided with some informational materials regarding the powers and duties of a conservator (some jurisdictions require that the conservator read an approved informational packet before Letters of Conservatorship can be issued).

Powers, Duties, and Liabilities of a Conservator. The appointment of a conservator vests in the conservator title as trustee to all property subject to the conservatorship, and letters of conservatorship are evidence of transfer of the assets to the conservator (U.P.C. § 5-419). A conservator may be granted broad or narrow powers, depending upon those powers requested and upon the court's exercise of its discretion in conferring powers (U.P.C. § 5-425). Generally speaking, however, a conservator has all of the powers conferred by law on a trustee as well as any additional powers conferred upon conservators under state law regarding the management of the protected person's estate and the application of income from the estate (U.P.C. § 5-423[a]). In addition, a conservator of the estate of an unmarried minor (under the age of 18 years), as to whom no one has parental rights, has the duties and powers of a guardian of a minor until the minor attains the age of majority or marries, although the parental rights conferred on a conservator do not preclude appointment of a guardian (U.P.C. § 5-423). The court may limit the conservator's powers to the extent desirable to foster self-reliance in the protected person. Except as limited by court order, a conservator may perform all reasonable administrative acts in efforts to accomplish the purpose of the appointment without obtaining court authorization or confirmation (see U.P.C. §§ 5-423, 424).

Once appointed, a conservator acts as a fiduciary and must observe the standards of care and prohibition against self-dealing applicable to trustees (U.P.C. § 5-416). This duty involves not only preserving the conservatorship estate but also making the property productive. All property subject to the conservatorship must be applied for the benefit of the protected person or the person's dependents. The conservator cannot be held personally liable on a contract properly entered into unless the conservator fails to reveal the representative capacity and identify the estate in the contract (U.P.C. § 5-428[a]). The conservator is personally liable for obligations of the estate or for torts committed in the course of administration only if personally at fault (U.P.C. § 5-428[b]).

Within 90 days after appointment, the conservator must file with the court a complete inventory of the estate subject to the conservatorship, providing a copy to the protected person (if the protected person is at least 14 years old and has sufficient mental capacity to understand the arrangement) and to any guardian or parent with whom the protected person resides (U.P.C. § 5-417). The conservator must maintain records of the administration and provide the same to any interested person upon request. The conservator must also provide an accounting to the court on an annual or more frequent basis, unless the court directs otherwise, as well as provide a final account upon termination of the conservatorship (U.P.C. § 5-418).

Post-Appointment Proceedings. Any person interested in the welfare of the person for whom a conservator has been appointed may file a petition in the appointing court for an order:

1. Requiring bond or collateral or additional bond or collateral, or reducing bond
2. Requiring an accounting for the administration of the trust
3. Directing distribution
4. Removing the conservator and appointing a temporary or successor conservator
5. Granting other appropriate relief (U.P.C. § 5-415[a])

A conservator may also petition the appointing court for instructions concerning fiduciary responsibility (U.P.C. § 5-415[b]). The court may remove a conservator for good cause, upon notice and hearing, or accept the resignation of a conservator. Upon the conservator's death, resignation, or removal, the court may appoint another conservator (U.P.C. § 5-414). Written notice of hearing on a petition for an order subsequent to appointment of a conservator must be given to the protected person, any conservator of the protected person's estate, and any other person as ordered by the court (U.P.C. § 5-405[b]).

Termination of Conservatorships. The protected person, conservator, or any other interested person may petition the court to terminate the conservatorship. A protected person seeking termination is entitled to the same rights and procedures as in an original proceeding for a protective order. The conservator must submit a final account at the time termination is sought. Upon termination, title to assets of the estate passes to the formerly protected person or to successors. If the court approves the account, the order of termination must provide for expenses of administration and direct the conservator to execute appropriate instruments to evidence the transfer (U.P.C. § 5-429).

A conservator's responsibilities extend beyond the death of the protected person. The conservator must continue to protect and preserve the estate until another fiduciary is appointed. The conservator must also deliver to the court for safekeeping any will of the deceased protected person that has come into the conservator's possession and inform the named executor of the delivery. Although under no duty to do so, the conservator may apply to the court to exercise the powers and duties of a personal representative if no other person has done so within a certain period of time after the death of the protected person (U.P.C. § 5-424[e]).

Substitutes for Conservatorship Proceedings

Many incapacitated adults as well as most minors do not require the measure of protection afforded by formal conservatorship proceedings. These proceedings are only necessary where no other means are available and adequate to protect the estate of the person. Such means include

1. Custodian accounts
2. The authority of a guardian
3. Abbreviated court proceedings for single transactions
4. Various estate-planning devices

All of these methods for protection of the estate are summarized in Figure 11-3 and discussed in the following materials.

Custodian Accounts. In most states, transfers of property to minors may be made to another person for the benefit of the minor through the use of a special type of account referred to as a **custodian account**. A custodian account is like a trust in that the person receiving the property on the minor's behalf (the custodian) is under a fiduciary duty similar to that of a trustee and may deal with the custodial property in much the same way as a trustee. However, a custodian account does not provide the same degree of flexibility as a trust, since nearly all of the terms of a custodial arrangement are determined by statute rather than by private agreement. Many states have adopted the Uniform Transfers to Minors Act (UTMA), formerly called the Uniform Gifts to Minors Act. Under the UTMA, only one person may act as a custodian, and a transfer to a custodian may be made for only one minor per account. A custodian account must terminate upon the minor's attainment of 18 years of age, unless the nominating instrument specifies a later time; in

FIGURE 11-3   PROTECTION OF ESTATES OF INCAPACITATED PERSONS AND MINORS

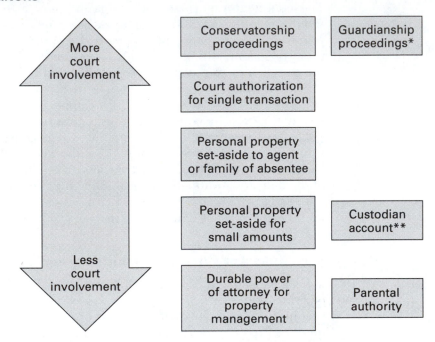

* A guardian also has authority over estate of ward unless conservator appointed.

** Fiduciary must obtain court approval for transfers to custodian exceeding $10,000 in value.

any event, however, the account must terminate no later than upon the minor's attainment of 25 years of age.

Under the UTMA, any person having the right to designate the recipient of property transferable upon the occurrence of a future event may revocably nominate a custodian to receive the property for a minor beneficiary upon the occurrence of the event by naming the custodian followed in substance by the words: "as custodian for [name of minor] under the [name of state] Uniform Transfers to Minors Act"; or, if the time for transfer to the minor is to be delayed beyond the age of 18, by the words: "as custodian for [name of minor] until age [age for delivery of property to the minor] under the [name of state] Uniform Transfers to Minors Act." The nomination may also name one or more substitute custodians to whom the property must be transferred, in the order named, if the first nominated custodian dies before the transfer or is unable, declines, or is ineligible to serve. The nomination may be made in a will, a trust, a deed, an instrument exercising a power of appointment, or in a writing designating a beneficiary of contractual rights that is registered with or delivered to the obligor of the contractual rights.

The UTMA also permits *present* transfers of property by irrevocable (*inter vivos*) gift to a custodian for the benefit of a minor as well as by declaration in which the owner of property continues to own the property but as custodian for the benefit of a minor (similar to a declaration of trust). A personal representative, trustee, or conservator may make an irrevocable transfer to another adult or to a trust company as custodian for the benefit of a minor if the fiduciary considers the transfer to be in the best interest of the minor and if the transfer is not prohibited by or inconsistent with provisions of the applicable will, trust agreement, or other governing instrument. However, if the transfer exceeds $10,000 in value, it must first be authorized by the court.

 TAYLOR TRUST: Ms. Cargis has included a provision in the Taylors' trust instrument giving the trustee broad discretion to select the payee of any trust principal or income to which a minor beneficiary would otherwise be entitled. The provision explicitly authorizes but does not require the trustee to make such payments to a custodian under the Uniform Transfers to Minors Act (see Exhibit 3 in the Taylor file).

 PARKER ESTATE: Recall from Chapter 8 that Susan Burns's newborn daughter Tracy was entitled to the one-third portion of Irene Parker's residuary estate that her father, John Parker, would have received had he survived Irene. Under the UTMA, Sharon may distribute Tracy's share to Susan Burns (Tracy's mother) as custodian for Tracy until Tracy attains the age of 18. Irene's attested will authorized the personal representative to make distributions to a custodian. However, even without the provision, the distribution to Susan Burns as custodian for Tracy would be permitted, since it is not prohibited by or inconsistent with the will.

Also recall that after Fred Parker's death, Irene changed the designated beneficiary of her life insurance policy from her husband Fred to her granddaughter Cindy Madson. The proceeds of the policy ($50,000) were not included in Irene's probate estate. On the life insurance company's form, Irene nominated Sharon as custodian to receive the proceeds on Cindy's behalf. Thus, the proceeds can be placed in a custodian account until Cindy attains the age of 18. Had Irene failed to nominate a custodian (which is unlikely, since the insurance company would probably have required such a nomination), it may have been necessary either to establish a conservatorship or to petition the court for authorization to hold the funds in a blocked account, since the amount involved is too large to permit Sharon to receive the funds directly without some protective measures for Cindy (see *Single Transactions and Other Special Situations*).

Authority of a Guardian over the Ward's Property. If a court has appointed a legal guardian for the minor or disabled person, the guardian may handle the person's property and financial and business affairs if the amounts involved are sufficiently low that the acts are more in the nature of providing for the person's current personal welfare than providing for business or financial management. However, it is important to keep in mind that a guardian's primary authority and responsibility concerns the ward's *person* rather than his or her property or financial and business affairs. While the guardian may take control of the ward's personal effects and receive money for the purpose of providing for the ward's current needs, further control over the ward's estate may require the appointment of a conservator.

Single Transactions and Other Special Situations. If formal conservatorship proceedings were required for every minor and incompetent adult entitled to an inheritance or device from a decedent's estate, the court system would quickly become overburdened. Thus, all states provide by statute for alternative procedures. Under one common statutory provision, inheritances and devices sufficiently low in value (e.g., under $2,000) may be released by the personal representative to a parent, legal guardian, or other adult caregiver upon receipt of a signed affidavit from the recipient that the property will be given to or applied for the benefit of the minor or incapacitated person; the personal representative then files the affidavit with the court. For pecuniary inheritances and testamentary devices of more significant value, a petition to the probate court for deposit of the funds in a blocked account is a widely used alternative. The funds must remain in the blocked account until further court order. This method may be used even where a conservator has been appointed, in which case the funds placed in the blocked account may or may not become part of the conservatorship estate. In the case of a missing person entitled to an inheritance or testamentary gift of personal property, state law may allow the absentee's agent or a family member to receive the personal property on petition to the court and notice to interested persons. A subsequent accounting may be required after the status of the missing person has been determined.

Aside from gifts, inheritances, and testamentary devices to incapacitated persons and minors, state law may permit the court to authorize, direct, or ratify a particular transaction, such as a contract for sale of property, a lease, or a loan agreement, without appointing a conservator, if the transaction is necessary or desirable to meet the foreseeable needs of the person requiring protection or if the court otherwise determines that the transaction would be in the best interest of the person (see, e.g., U.P.C. § 5-408). A married person may be permitted to engage in a transaction involving the community property of a disabled spouse without first being appointed by the court as conservator through a similar proceeding, although continual management of both halves of the community estate requires that either the spouse or another person be appointed as conservator.

 PARKER ESTATE: Recall from Chapter 8 that Cindy and Deborah Madson are entitled under the terms of Irene's holographic codicil to the contents (jewelry) of Irene's safe. The value of the jewelry was appraised at only $500. Sharon Madson, as the parent of Cindy and Deborah, executed an appropriate affidavit and filed it (as personal representative) with the court. However, this affidavit procedure is not available for distribution of Tracy Burns's one-third share of Irene's residuary estate to Tracy's mother Susan because the amount of this share is too large.

Estate-Planning Devices. As discussed in Chapter 9, by establishing an *inter vivos* trust while still legally competent, an individual may provide for continuity of property management, but only with respect to property properly placed in trust. Joint-tenancy bank accounts may also be used to avoid conservatorship proceedings, but only with respect to the particular account. Another widely used planning device that serves as a conservatorship substitute is the durable power of attorney, which will be discussed shortly.

PLANNING FOR INCAPACITY

Planning for one's incapacity is arguably more important than planning for disposition of one's property after death. Although improper planning for postmortem transfers may result in undue delays, expenses, and taxes, the consequences of inadequate planning for incapacity may be far more devastating. Formal protective proceedings can be humiliating and degrading for the individual as well as for the family. Moreover, unlike probate proceedings for a decedent's estate, protective proceedings must continue until the individual either regains competency or dies, resulting not only in a continual administrative burden on the family but also in a continual financial drain on the incapacitated person's estate (or on the family, if the estate is inadequate) as attorney's fees and fiduciary fees accumulate. Additionally, because of the emotional and financial stress on the family, bitter and divisive disputes may arise concerning the proper care of the incapacitated person. Finally, and perhaps most devastating of all, health care providers may be obligated to sustain the person's life artificially in the absence of proper planning, against the wishes of the family as well as the probable wishes of the incapacitated person.

Three primary means are used by estate-planning lawyers to provide for continued management of a client's estate in the event of incapacity. One means is an *inter vivos* trust in which the individual, while he or she is still legally competent to execute a trust instrument, designates a successor trustee to step in and provide continued management of the trust estate in the event of the settlor's incapacity. However, an *inter vivos* trust alone may not obviate the necessity of protective proceedings, since the trustee has authority only over those assets properly placed in trust. For other property, continuity of management can be accomplished with another device referred to as a *durable power of attorney for property management*. Third, if for any reason these other means fail to prevent conservatorship proceedings, the client's wishes as to who should be appointed by the court as a conservator should be expressed in writing, either in a separate instrument, referred to as a *nomination of conservator*, or by an express provision in a durable power of attorney for property management.

Three primary means are used to confer authority to make decisions relating to the personal welfare of an incapacitated person. The first is the *durable power of attorney for health care*. The second is a *nomination of guardian* (either a separate writing or included in a durable power of attorney for health care). The third means is a document commonly referred to as a *living will*, by which an individual expresses his or her wishes regarding the use of artificial means to sustain his or her life.

Durable Powers of Attorney

A **power of attorney** is a written instrument by which one person, as *principal*, appoints another person as an *agent*, conferring upon the agent the authority to perform certain specified acts or types of acts on behalf of the principal. The agent, referred to as an *attorney in fact*, may use the power of attorney as evidence of his or her authority. A power of attorney establishes a principal-agent relationship in which the rights and duties of the parties are governed generally by the law of agency. A power of attorney may be either *general, limited,* or *specific* in nature (or some combination of these). A general power authorizes the agent to act with respect to any and all matters on the principal's behalf. By contrast, a limited power confers authority over only certain matters, while a special power places limits on the agent's discretion, authorizing the agent to act on behalf of the principal only on certain terms. A power of attorney may be general in nature although special with respect to certain assets, or it may be both limited and special in nature. Except under certain circumstances, a principal may amend or revoke a power of attorney at any time.

Powers of attorney are useful in a variety of situations. A person who plans an extended trip out of the country might confer a general power of appointment of a family member to handle all of the person's financial and legal affairs during his or her absence. Perhaps this same person owns a house that is for sale; in that event, the person might wish to set the minimum price or other terms that the agent would be authorized to accept by conferring a special power with respect to the sale but a general power with respect to all other matters. Suppose instead that all that is required in the person's absence is the continued management of one particular investment property; in this case, a limited power would be appropriate. However, in a conventional employment relationship, it is generally not necessary for the employer (principal) to confer a power of attorney upon an employee (agent), since the employee's authority is defined by an employment agreement and is generally apparent to third parties.

Generally speaking, a power of attorney terminates automatically upon the incapacity of the principal. However, by including appropriate language in the instrument, the principal can create a power of attorney that either continues to be effective during incapacity or that actually becomes effective at and not until the time the principal becomes incapacitated. A power of attorney that is effective during the principal's incapacity is referred to as a **durable power of attorney**. If it does not take effect until incapacity of the principal, the power may be referred to more particularly as a *springing* durable power of attorney. In any event, however, a valid durable power must be executed before the principal becomes incapacitated (a conservator, guardian, or similar fiduciary cannot execute a durable power on behalf of the ward or protected person). Two distinct types of durable powers are used in estate planning: (1) the durable power of attorney for property management, and (2) the durable power of attorney for health care. Statutes authorizing the former type are typically found in the state's probate code (see, e.g., U.P.C. § 5-501, *et seq.*), although the durable power for health care is generally provided in the health code or similar code (the U.P.C. does not provide specifically for the durable power for health care).

FOCUS: An ordinary power of attorney confers authority on the agent to act on behalf of the principal only while the principal is legally competent. In contrast, a *durable* power of attorney gives the agent the right to act on the principal's behalf during the principal's incapacity and, in the case of a *springing* durable power of attorney, not until that time.

Durable Powers of Attorney for Property Management. The durable power of attorney for property management is also commonly referred to as either a *financial* durable power of attorney or a *general* durable power of attorney (an imprecise use of the term *general*). A durable power of attorney for property management not only serves to avoid a conservatorship of the estate in the event of incapacity, it can also be used along with an *inter vivos* trust to avoid probate; in the event the settlor becomes incapacitated before placing his or her property in the trust and is near death, the attorney in fact may immediately step in and complete the transfers. Appointment of a conservator may take several weeks or more, and the settlor may die in the meantime before the transfers can be made.

All states provide for the durable power of attorney for property management. Although the laws are not uniform in this area, many states have adopted the Uniform Durable Power of Attorney Act, which has been included in the Uniform Probate Code (U.P.C. § 5-501, *et seq.*). Under the U.P.C., a valid durable power of attorney may be created only by a writing showing the intent of the principal that the authority conferred shall be exercisable notwithstanding the principal's subsequent disability or incapacity (U.P.C. § 5-501). Under the U.P.C., unless the instrument states otherwise, a durable power of attorney remains effective notwithstanding the lapse of time since its execution (U.P.C. § 5-502). Some statutes, however, limit the time period after execution within which the power may be exercised, although the period is tolled during incapacity.

A principal may revoke or amend a durable power of attorney at any time, except during periods of incapacity. Under the U.P.C., upon the principal's disability or incapacity, an attorney in fact is accountable to any court-appointed conservator or guardian of the principal's estate, who in turn has the same power to revoke or amend the power of attorney for property management as the principal would have had but for the incapacity (U.P.C. § 5-503[a]). Under the common law of agency, an agent's authority terminates automatically upon the death of the principal. Under the U.P.C., however, the death of the principal who has executed a written power of attorney, durable or otherwise, does not revoke or terminate the agency as to the attorney in fact or other person, who, without actual knowledge of the death of the principal, acts in good faith under the power (U.P.C. § 5-504[a]).

The estate-planning client should consult with the attorney in order to determine the desired scope and extent of the powers to be granted by the durable power of attorney for property management. A general power as to the principal's entire estate is appropriate in many cases, particularly where the power is conferred upon a spouse. Estate-planning lawyers generally advise clients not to withhold any powers, but rather to allow the agent as much discretion as possible; withholding powers may serve to defeat the purpose of the instrument as an effective planning device for incapacity. The client should then sign his or her initials to each deleted item. The client must also decide who to designate as attorney in fact. In some states, the attorney in fact must be one individual person, while other states allow co-agents. Although a minor may act as attorney in fact, this is generally not recommended, since a minor lacks the legal competency to execute many legal documents. At least one or two successive agents should be designated. It is generally recommended that the same person named as executor and/or trustee is also named as attorney in fact and that successors be designated similarly in order to unify management of the principal's estate. No persons other than those designated may act as attorney in fact under the instrument.

Durable Powers of Attorney for Health Care. The durable power of attorney for health care gives the agent authority to consent, to refuse to consent, or to withdraw consent to any care treatment, service, or procedure to maintain, diagnose, or treat a physical or mental condition, and to receive and to consent to the release of medical information, subject to any limitations included in the document. However, state law may prohibit an agent from authorizing commitment to or placement in a mental health treatment facility, convulsive treatment, psychosurgery, sterilization, or abortion. The agent has no authority as long as the principal is able to give informed consent, and no treatment may be given to the principal under the agent's authorization over the principal's objection. A court can take away the agent's power if the agent authorizes anything that is illegal, acts contrary to the principal's known desires, or does anything that is clearly contrary to the principal's best interests. The principal may revoke the agent's authority by notifying the agent or the treating doctor, hospital, or other health care provider of the revocation, either orally or in writing.

A durable power of attorney for health care may also be used to nominate a guardian, although the health-care agent need not be the same person as the guardian, since a court-appointed guardian does not serve the same function as the health-care agent. While the guardian is empowered to make general decisions about how the personal needs of the individual may best be met, this power does not extend to important life-or-death decisions regarding medical treatment. Only the durable power of attorney for health care can confer such authority,

A durable power of attorney for health care may also be used to control how bodily remains should be handled after death, at least to the extent permitted under state health and safety laws. An individual may use the durable power of attorney for heath care to

1. Consent to examination of his or her body after death to determine the cause of death
2. Give the agent the power to authorize an autopsy (or to withhold such authorization)
3. Direct the disposition of his or her remains after death, or authorize the agent to so direct
4. Donate body parts for therapeutic, educational, or scientific purposes, or for transplant

Since the durable power of attorney for health care is such a powerful document, the individual must carefully and reflectively consider the extent of the powers to be granted, particularly those involving the use of life-sustaining medical equipment, as well as the choice of health-care agent. These decisions are highly personal, reflecting the individual's religious and philosophical beliefs. The lawyer and the paralegal must both be very careful not to direct or influence the client in any manner. After consulting the lawyer as to the purpose of the legal document and various decisions to be made, the client should discuss this matter with close family members as well as his or her physician(s) before making any final decisions. The client should also talk to prospective agents to determine whether they would be willing to serve.

The health-care agent must be one individual person; co-agents are not permitted. At least one or two successive agents should be designated, and no persons other than those designated may act as agent. The health-care agent and attorney in fact for property management need not be the same person. In choosing a health-care agent, an individual should consider (1) whether the person is sufficiently mature to make life-and-death decisions in a rational and responsible manner; (2) whether the person will be readily accessible in the event of a medical emergency; and (3) how closely the person's own philosophy regarding life-and-death issues reflects the individual's own beliefs. Minors cannot serve as health-care agents. Also, state law may prohibit certain persons, such as the treating health-care provider, an employee of the treating health-care provider, or the operator of a board and care home, from acting as health-care agent (unless the person is also a family member).

Preparing the Documents. A comprehensive estate plan should include both a durable power of attorney for property management and a durable power of attorney for health care. The client's existing durable powers of attorney, if any, should be thoroughly reviewed and updated if necessary. An existing durable power of attorney may require updating for a variety of reasons, including the following:

1. The durable power of attorney may have terminated or may terminate in the near future because of lapse of time.
2. The durable power of attorney may have been valid in the state where it was executed but invalid in this state.
3. The client may wish to limit or expand the powers conferred by the instrument.
4. The client may wish to change one or more of the designated agents, either because they are no longer available or for some other reason.

To update an existing power, a new instrument should be prepared and executed to replace the existing one. The new instrument should expressly revoke all prior ones. It is not recommended that the existing instrument be revised, either on its face or by some sort of written amendment, since unauthorized alteration may be suspected.

Once the client has made final decisions about the desired provisions and terms of the durable powers of attorney, the instruments can be prepared. Some lawyers prefer to use a single document for both health-care and property management, while others prefer to use separate documents. Many states provide a statutory form for a durable power of attorney for property management. A statutory durable power of attorney has the same advantages and disadvantages as those of a statutory will (see Chapter 2). The form is simple to prepare, and compliance with the statutory form ensures the instrument's validity, thereby facilitating recognition of the instrument by third parties. On the other hand, a statutory form is inflexible in its provisions. Whether the lawyer chooses to adopt the statutory form depends primarily, of course, upon the desired provisions. Although preprinted statutory forms are widely available at office supply stores in those states that provide for their use, the law firm should not use preprinted forms but rather should produce its own statutory form with the firm's letterhead. It is essential that a durable power of attorney for health care be readily recognized and accepted by treating health-care providers, because medical emergencies often demand immediate decisions. State and local health-care organizations have recently begun developing and distributing their own standard durable power of attorney forms for this purpose. The law firm should consider using these forms once they gain broad acceptance and recognition among local health-care professionals.

 PRACTICE TIP: If the agent needs to deal with the principal's real property, it may be necessary to record the instrument at that time. Thus, the law firm's durable power of attorney forms should leave an appropriate space at the top for recording information. Also, instead of typing the name of the attorney in fact and of the successors, many lawyers prefer that the client print or write this information in blank spaces provided on the form and initial each entry. This procedure provides strong evidence that the principal intended to designate the persons indicated as agents. As a related procedural matter, lawyers generally prefer to use durable power forms that include an exhaustive list of all possible types of powers (and property, in the case of a durable power for property management). The lawyer may then review each item on the list with the client, crossing out particular items as desired by the client.

Executing and Processing the Documents. Durable powers of attorney are generally executed at the same time as other estate-planning documents. Certain formalities are required for execution of durable powers of attorney. In some states, the principal's signature must be notarized, while in other states witnesses may be used as a substitute for acknowledgment. If the principal resides in a board and care home, a valid durable power of attorney for health care may also require the signature of a patient advocate. The client should be instructed to keep the original durable power of attorney in the same place as the client's other estate-planning documents. Since time is of the essence in a medical emergency, the client should provide a copy of the durable power of attorney for health care to: (1) each designated agent; (2) the client's personal physician(s); and (3) the local hospital to which the client would most likely be admitted in the event of a medical emergency. These parties should be informed whenever the client executes a new durable power of attorney or otherwise revokes the existing one.

Nomination of Guardian/Conservator

In the event that a trust and durable powers of attorney fail to provide for the continued care of an individual or for continued management of the individual's estate in the event of incapacity, guardianship and/or conservatorship proceedings may be necessary in order to protect the individual's interests. While still legally competent, the individual may nominate another person to act as guardian or conservator in the event such proceedings are necessary through the use of a simple written nomination. The nomination may be made in a separate writing, which should either be notarized or witnessed (the U.P.C. requires attestation by two witnesses). Alternatively, a nomination of conservator may be included in a financial durable power of attorney, while a nomination of guardian may be included in a durable power of attorney for health care.

Living Wills

A **living will** or *living will declaration* is a written document by which an individual can express his or her wishes concerning the use of artificial means, as well as forced nutrition (food) and hydration (water), to sustain his or her life in the event of a "terminal condition." A *terminal condition* is caused by injury, disease, or illness from which there can be no recovery and which makes death imminent within a reasonable degree of medical certainty. The term *living will* is a misnomer, because the document is not a testamentary instrument and serves no dispositive purpose; accordingly, the living will is also commonly and more accurately referred to as a *directive to physician*.

In the 1980s, the courts slowly began to recognize an individual's right to die or to "pull the plug" and to protect physicians from liability for acting in good faith under direction by the individual with a terminal condition. Despite continued opposition by various pro-life groups, the validity of the living will has been upheld in nearly all states. The withholding or withdrawing of life-prolonging procedures pursuant to a living will or a durable power permits the natural process of dying to occur. This situation must be distinguished from mercy killing, euthanasia, or physician-assisted suicide, which involve an affirmative or deliberate act or omission on the part of the physician to end life other than to permit the natural process of dying. Physician-assisted suicide may constitute a tortious or criminal act, although the law in this area is currently being tested in both the state and federal courts.

Legal Effect. The living will does not serve to affirmatively order the attending physician to discontinue artificial life support but rather preserves the right of the terminally ill individual to so instruct the physician at the time that artificial life support is being used. However, the individual may be in a comatose state or otherwise unable to instruct the physician to terminate life support at that time. In that event, in many states no other person (with the common exception of the individual's spouse) may instruct the physician on behalf of the terminally ill spouse pursuant to the living will. Thus, under this common statutory scheme, if there is no spouse, or if both spouses are involved in a common accident and are unable to act on each other's behalf, the living will by itself will be insufficient to serve its purpose. Accordingly, any person concerned about preserving his or her right to die should execute *both* a living will and a durable power of attorney for health care. By executing both documents while still legally competent and before the onset of a terminal illness, the individual can best ensure that his or her wishes will be carried out. Although the attending physician is generally protected by statute from liability when acting in good faith pursuant to the terms of a durable power of attorney for health care or a living will, the physician is far more likely to honor the terms of a living will when it is accompanied by a durable power of attorney for health care and when the designated agent concurs that artificial life support should be terminated.

Departing somewhat from the rules discussed above, some states (e.g., Florida) have enacted statutes allowing certain other persons to instruct the attending physician respecting life-sustaining measures *without* a living will *or* durable power of attorney for health care, at least where witnesses are present at the time of the consultation between the physician and the person directing the physician. Even under this type of statute, however, the use of a living will and durable power are universally recommended as the best means of ensuring that the individual's wishes will be carried out.

Execution, Validity, and Revocation. A valid living will may be executed either prior to or after notification of the terminal condition, as long as the maker is not incapacitated. However, in many states, if an individual wishes to execute a living will after learning that he or she has a terminal condition but prior to incapacity, a sufficient time period—for example, five days—must elapse after notification before the individual can execute a valid living will. The reason for this is that the emotional trauma may initially impair the individual's judgment. In nearly all states, a valid living will expires automatically after a certain period of time—for example, after five years—has elapsed since its execution, unless it is signed and dated again before the document expires. Just as with durable powers of attorney, however, the time limitation is extended by any period of incapacity. Also, the legislative trend is away from expiration due solely to lapse of time. A living will is invalid anytime during pregnancy.

Although statutory forms for living wills are not required in any state, some states provide a suggested form, and certain language may be required by statute, as in the case of a durable power of attorney. In some states, a valid living will must be notarized, while other states allow the use of witnesses in lieu of acknowledgment. Living wills may be revoked either by a signed and dated writing, by physical act (tearing, cancellation, etc.), or by an oral expression of intent to revoke made to the attending physician.

PRACTICE TIP: Where both living wills and durable powers of attorney for health care are authorized, they may be combined as a single document. This approach enables the attending physician to refer to a single document to determine both the individual's wishes and the agent's authority to carry out those wishes (see Figure 11-4). If a suggested form is provided by statute, it is recommended that this form be used, at least to the extent that it fully and accurately expresses the individual's wishes. Once the living will is executed, the client should be instructed to keep the original document and to provide copies to his or her personal physician and to each agent designated in the client's power of attorney for health care. The law firm should provide to the client a wallet-sized card stating that the individual has executed these documents and listing the names and telephone numbers of the individual's physician, attorney, and health-care agents. As the expiration date of a living will approaches, the law firm's tickler system should provide a reminder to send an appropriate notice to the client.

FIGURE 11-4   DURABLE POWER OF ATTORNEY FOR HEALTH CARE—STATEMENT OF DESIRE CONCERNING MEDICAL TREATMENT

I do not want my life to be prolonged and I do not want life-sustaining treatment to be provided or continued: (i) if I am in an irreversible coma or persistent vegetative state; (ii) if I am terminally ill and the application of life-sustaining procedures would serve only to artificially delay the moment of my death; or (iii) under any other circumstances where the burdens of treatment outweigh the expected benefits. I want my agent to consider the relief of suffering and the quality as well as the extent of the possible extension of my life in making decisions concerning life-sustaining treatment.

Paralegal Assignment 11

Recall that Ms. Cargis has asked you to prepare and assist the Taylors in executing the documents necessary to provide for their incapacity. Walter and Betty Taylor will each execute a durable power of attorney for property management and for health care (see the Taylor file, Exhibits 6 and 7, respectively). The former will include a nomination of conservator, while the latter will include a directive to physician (living will) and a nomination of conservator of the person (under applicable law, the term *conservator* rather than *guardian* is used in referring to the person caring for the personal welfare of an incapacitated person who is an adult). Both forms will be notarized, and the originals are to be retained by the client, while copies are provided to the Taylors' personal physician and the agents designated in the powers. Wallet cards will be prepared and provided to both Walter and Betty. Under applicable law, the durable power for property management does not expire because of lapse of time, but the durable power for health care terminates seven years after its execution. Accordingly, you should indicate in the firm's tickler system to contact the Taylors when the expiration approaches.

12 PROFESSIONAL RESPONSIBILITY AND THE PROBATE PARALEGAL

The subject of professional responsibility is the final topic in this text but is by no means the least important. The materials in this chapter assume that the student has already had some exposure, by way of an introductory course in the paralegal profession, to the subject of professional responsibility. Accordingly, it should suffice here merely to reiterate a few fundamentals before examining the particular ethical problems that the probate paralegal is likely to encounter at the workplace.

The standards of professional conduct to which lawyers are held are governed in each state by ethical guidelines and rules patterned after the Model Code of Professional Responsibility ("Code" hereafter) and Model Rules of Professional Conduct ("Rules" hereafter), both developed by the American Bar Association (ABA). The Code is comprised of 12 canons, each of which is accompanied by a series of ethical considerations (EC) and disciplinary rules (DR). Although by their terms the Code and Rules apply only to lawyers, and *not* their employees, the Rules make clear that it is the lawyer's additional responsibility to make reasonable efforts to ensure that the conduct of all employees under his or her supervision adhere to the same standards (see Rule 5.3, Figure 12-1).

Although enforceable disciplinary rules for paralegals have not yet been established, two national paralegal organizations—the National Association of Legal Assistants (NALA) and the National Federation of Paralegal Associations (NFPA)—have each developed a model set of guidelines for the paralegal profession which, in many respects, mirror those developed by the

FIGURE 12-1   PROFESSIONAL RESPONSIBILITY AND THE PARALEGAL

ABA MODEL RULES OF PROFESSIONAL CONDUCT

Rule 5.3   Responsibilities Regarding Nonlawyer Assistants
With respect to a nonlawyer employed or retained by or associated with a lawyer:
(a) a partner in a law firm shall make reasonable efforts to ensure that the firm has in effect measures giving reasonable assurance that the person's conduct is compatible with the professional obligations of the lawyer;
(b) a lawyer having direct supervisory authority over the nonlawyer shall make reasonable efforts to ensure that the person's conduct is compatible with the professional obligations of the lawyer; and
(c) a lawyer shall be responsible for conduct of such a person that would be a violation of the rules of professional conduct if engaged in by a lawyer if: (1) the lawyer orders or, with the knowledge of the specific conduct, ratifies the conduct involved; or (2) the lawyer is a partner in the law firm in which the person is employed, or has direct supervisory authority over the person, and knows of the conduct at a time when its consequences can be avoided or mitigated but fails to take reasonable remedial actions.

CODE COMPARISON: There is no direct counterpart to this Rule in the Model Code of Professional Responsibility. [Disciplinary Rule] 4-101(D) provides that "A lawyer shall exercise reasonable care to prevent his employees, associates, and others whose services are utilized by him from disclosing or using confidences or secrets of a client. . . ." DR 7-107(J) provides that "a lawyer shall exercise reasonable care to prevent his employees and associates from making an extrajudicial statement that he would be prohibited from making under DR 7-107."

NALA CODE OF ETHICS AND PROFESSIONAL RESPONSIBILITY

Canon 12 A legal assistant is governed by the American Bar Association Code of Professional Responsibility.

NALA MODEL STANDARD AND GUIDELINES FOR UTILIZATION OF LEGAL ASSISTANTS

Guidelines . . . Legal assistants should . . . (3) [u]nderstand the attorney's Code of Professional Responsibility and these guidelines in order to avoid any action which would involve the attorney in a violation of that Code, or give the appearance of professional impropriety.

ABA for lawyers. In fact, the NALA imposes upon the paralegal the same standards of professional responsibility as those imposed on lawyers under the ABA Code, as well as requires the paralegal to be familiar with the provisions of the ABA Code (see Figure 12-1).

UNAUTHORIZED PRACTICE OF LAW

Canon 3 of the Code establishes that a lawyer should assist in preventing the unauthorized practice of law. The appropriate parameters of the probate paralegal's responsibilities, authority, and judgment have already been addressed throughout Chapters 1 through 11 as they relate to specific tasks. However, a few fundamental points are worth reiterating. First, only an experienced paralegal should endeavor to assist in drafting estate-planning documents such as wills and trusts, and any drafting by the paralegal *must* be reviewed by the lawyer before the documents are executed or otherwise given legal effect. In fact, many estate-planning lawyers insist upon either drafting all documents themselves or enlisting the assistance of associate attorneys, but not paralegals, for this purpose. Second, the probate paralegal must be extremely careful not to make any independent legal judgments or to advise clients in matters requiring legal judgment. This caveat is probably most pertinent in the area of estate planning, where the paralegal is called upon on a daily basis to respond to routine questions by clients regarding their estate plan and to clarify for clients certain information or advice imparted by the attorney.

CONFLICTS OF INTEREST

Conflicts of interest and the lawyer's duty to exercise his or her independent professional judgment on behalf of the client are governed by Canon 5 of the Code and by Rules 1.7, 1.8, and 1.9 (see Figure 12-2). Conflicts of interest fall into two broad categories. The first includes situations where the interests of one client (or prospective client) conflict with those of another

FIGURE 12-2   CONFLICTS OF INTEREST

ABA CODE OF PROFESSIONAL RESPONSIBILITY

Canon 5 A lawyer should exercise independent professional judgment on behalf of a client.

Ethical Consideration 5-16 In those instances in which a lawyer is justified in representing two or more clients having differing interests, it is nevertheless essential that each client be given the opportunity to evaluate his need for representation free of any potential conflict and to obtain other counsel if he so desires. Thus before a lawyer may represent multiple clients, he should explain fully to each client the implications of the common representation and should accept or continue employment only if the clients consent. If there are present other circumstances that might cause any of the multiple clients to question the undivided loyalty of the lawyer, he should also advise all of the clients of those circumstances.

Ethical Consideration 5-17 Typically recurring situations involving potentially differing interests are those in which a lawyer is asked to represent . . . beneficiaries of the estate of a decedent. Whether the lawyer can fairly and adequately protect the interests of multiple clients in these and similar situations depends upon an analysis of each case. In certain circumstances, there may exist little chance of the judgment of the lawyer being adversely affected by the slight possibility that the interests will become actually differing; in other circumstances, the chance of adverse effect upon his judgment is not likely.

Continued

FIGURE 12-2   CONTINUED

ABA MODEL RULES OF PROFESSIONAL CONDUCT

Rule 1.7   Conflict of Interest: General Rule

(a) A lawyer shall not represent a client if the representation of that client will be directly adverse to another client, unless: (1) the lawyer reasonably believes the representation will not adversely affect the relationship with the other client; and (2) each client consents after consultation.

(b) A lawyer shall not represent a client if the representation of that client may be materially limited by the lawyer's responsibilities to another client or to a third person, or by the lawyer's own interests, unless: (1) the lawyer reasonably believes the representation will not adversely affect the relationship with the other client; and (2) the client consents after consultation. When representation of multiple clients in a single matter is undertaken, the consultation shall include explanation of the implications of the common representation and the advantages and risks involved.

Rule 1.8   Conflict of Interest: Prohibited Transactions

. . . (c) A lawyer shall not prepare an instrument giving the lawyer or a person related to the lawyer as parent, child, sibling, or spouse any substantial gift from a client, including a testamentary gift, except where the client is related to the donee.

COMMENT: . . . A lawyer may accept a gift from a client, ... If effectuation of a substantial gift requires preparing a legal instrument such as a will or conveyance, however, the client should have the detached advice that another lawyer can provide.

Rule 1.9   Conflict of Interest: Former Client

A lawyer who has formerly represented a client in a matter shall not thereafter: (a) represent another person in the same or a substantially related matter in which that person's interests are materially adverse to the interest of the former client unless the former client consents after consultation; . . .

Rule 1.14   Client Under a Disability (Official Comment)

COMMENT: . . . If the lawyer represents the guardian as distinct from the ward, and is aware that the guardian is acting adversely to the ward's interest, the lawyer may have an obligation to prevent or rectify the guardian's misconduct.

client (or prospective client). For the probate law firm, the most common example of this type of conflict involves dual representation of spouses in estate planning. The second broad category relates to matters in which the *personal* interests of the lawyer, paralegal, or other member of the law firm conflict with those of the client—for example, where the lawyer (or paralegal) is also a beneficiary of a client's estate. Any potential or actual conflict of interest of which the paralegal is aware should be brought to the lawyer's attention. In many cases, the law firm may continue representation despite the conflict by full disclosure of the potential conflict and consent of all parties whose interests might be affected. In other cases, the conflict may preclude representation by the law firm.

Dual Representation of Spouses in Estate Planning

Estate planning for spouses is typically a joint venture, and in many—perhaps in most—cases, the interests of the spouses are not in conflict. Consider the typical scenario involving a married couple in their fifties or beyond whose lengthy marriage is the only one for both spouses and whose property was accumulated almost entirely during the marriage. It is likely in this situation that the spouses will have similar wishes regarding the disposition of their estate. In other situations, however, conflicts are much more likely. Even in the scenario described above, the potential for conflict exists.

Perhaps the most common conflict involves children of one spouse that are not also children of the other spouse. The spouses may have quite different ideas as to what portion of the estate should pass to these children or, in the case of a trust, whether and on what terms trust income and principal should be available for these children. A wide disparity in wealth or age of the spouses may also result in conflict. The more wealthy spouse may be inclined, contrary to the wishes of the other spouse, to leave a portion of his or her property to certain blood relatives (e.g., parents or siblings), even if the other spouse survives the more wealthy spouse. Similarly, a spouse who is significantly older than the other spouse may be reluctant to leave the bulk of his or her property (either outright or in trust) to a young spouse who is likely to enter into another relationship after the older spouse's death. Finally, an *inter vivos* trust that provides for the creation of a bypass trust and one or more marital deduction trusts (i.e., an "AB" or "ABC" plan) at the first spouse's death may present a conflict of interest where the surviving spouse serves as successor trustee. In administrative matters such as the distribution of income and principal, the determination of asset values and allocations among trusts, and the payment of administrative expenses, the surviving spouse has numerous opportunities to administer the trust in his or her favor at the expense of the remainder beneficiaries.

Dual representation of clients (including spouses) whose interests are potentially adverse is not prohibited. However, whether or not it appears that an actual conflict of interest between the spouses exists, prior to providing any legal services for both spouses, the law firm should obtain a written agreement from both spouses to the law firm's dual representation. Unless both spouses so agree, the law firm should not counsel both spouses (see EC 5-16; Rule 1.7; Figure 12-2).

 PRACTICE TIP: The areas of potential conflict listed above are readily apparent and are properly addressed by the attorney during the planning process rather than by the paralegal. Other conflicts, however, may not be so apparent. Understandably, the spouses may be reluctant to voice their disagreements during the estate-planning interview. The paralegal can assist in this matter by looking out at all times for any friction or tension between spouses. The paralegal should pay careful attention to the statements and general behavior of both spouses. Telephone calls by one spouse to the law firm may be particularly revealing, and the paralegal should be sure to make written notes of any comments made during a conversation that might suggest a potential conflict. The paralegal should also be careful not to succumb to pressure from a dominant spouse who claims to speak on the other spouse's behalf, especially if there is any possibility at all that the other spouse's interests may be adversely affected by the dominant spouse's request or instruction.

 TAYLOR TRUST: In the Taylor matter, recall from Chapter 10 that a legal services agreement was provided to the Taylors for their review as part of the estate-planning package (mailed to the Taylors prior to the initial meeting with Ms. Cargis). This agreement includes a dual-representation provision (see Exhibit 16 in the Taylor file). Also, recall from Chapter 9 that there are several areas in which Walter's interests and Betty's interests are not entirely in accord. For example, Walter wishes his business to pass to his son David, while Betty wishes her interest in her family's ranch to pass to her surviving brothers and sisters. Also, although Walter wishes to make adequate and continued provision for Betty during her lifetime, he is concerned that his grandchildren receive a college education. As you discovered in Chapter 9, a variety of estate-planning techniques may be employed to address these issues. By confronting the estate-planning process as a cooperative effort, Walter and Betty were able to implement a thoughtful plan in respect of each other's wishes without separate legal counsel. As a precautionary measure, during the estate-planning interview, Ms. Cargis explained each potential area of conflict as the issues arose, reminded the Taylors that they could seek separate counsel, and made written notes of the Taylors' reactions, discussion, and opinions about each area of potential conflict. As the Taylors arrived at mutually agreeable solutions to each problem, Ms. Cargis made a written note of their agreement.

Beneficial Interests and the Law Firm

The problem of the lawyer (or an employee of the lawyer) as beneficiary of the client's estate may arise in the context of either estate planning or decedents' estates. In the area of estate planning, the issue may be one of undue influence or conflict of interest, or possibly both. Consider the following example in light of Rule 1.8 (Figure 12-2).

EXAMPLE: *During Danita's estate-planning interview with Stephen (a lawyer), Danita asks Stephen if he knows of any worthy local charities to which she might give a portion of her estate. Stephen suggests a particular charitable organization, and Danita follows Stephen's recommendation. Stephen fails to disclose to Danita that he is a paid officer and member of the board of directors of the charitable organization. **Result:** Stephen's action is a form of self-dealing that would probably be considered a conflict of interest, even though Stephen does not clearly benefit from the devise, at least not directly. Danita's heirs might also raise the issues of undue influence and fraud.*

With respect to decedents' estates, a lawyer does not necessarily violate his or her professional responsibility by representing more than one beneficiary (see EC 5-17; Figure 12-2). Nor is it considered a conflict of interest for a lawyer who is a beneficiary of an estate (or whose employee is a beneficiary) to represent the personal representative of the estate, even though many aspects of estate administration—for example, valuation of assets, handling creditors' claims, and preparing tax returns—affect the amount of the distribution to the lawyer-beneficiary or paralegal-beneficiary (see Rule 1.7(b); Figure 12-2). However, where a beneficiary (of an estate or trust) is a present client of the law firm, the law firm must ordinarily decline to represent the estate or trustee (at least where the beneficiary and fiduciary are not the same person), since the interests of these parties is inherently adverse. Also, certain conflicts arising during the course of administration may require withdrawal or other appropriate action.

EXAMPLE: *Peter is a paralegal employed by Ai-lien (a lawyer). Peter is a devisee under the terms of Olga's will. Ai-lien has been retained to represent the executor of Olga's estate. During the course of administration, the validity of the will is contested by an intestate heir who is excluded from distribution under the terms of the will. Peter's intestate share of the estate would greatly exceed his share under the terms of the will.* **Result:** *Assuming the law firm's appropriate posture is to defend the validity of the will, Peter's interests have become adverse to those of the estate.*

In the foregoing example, whether the law firm should withdraw its representation of the estate altogether is not certain. Perhaps the lawyer could agree that Peter (the paralegal) will have no involvement as a paralegal with Olga's estate. Would this adequately address the conflict? Perhaps a more viable solution might be for the law firm to assume a neutral posture as to the will's validity and advise the personal representative to retain other counsel for the purpose of defending the will contest. Finally, would the conflict be more critical if it were Ai-lien (the lawyer) rather than Peter (the paralegal) whose interest in the estate would be affected by the outcome of the will contest? Despite this type of conflict, the law firm may nevertheless engage in representation upon the written consent of all parties whose interests are affected.

An additional problem involves the personal representative who is also a beneficiary of the estate. Ordinarily, there is no conflict of interest. However, if these two interests should become adverse, the law firm is obligated to the client in his or her capacity as personal representative, not as beneficiary. Consider the following scenario:

EXAMPLE: *Gilberto and Ramon, who are brothers, are involved in a common automobile accident in which Gilberto is clearly at fault. Gilberto is killed and Ramon suffers serious injuries resulting in physical debilitation. Gilberto leaves an estate of substantial value. Ramon is serving as personal representative of the estate and is one of three residuary beneficiaries under the terms of Gilberto's will. Although Ramon's health-insurance plan covers most of his actual medical expenses relating to the injury, he is also considering a personal-injury law suit against Gilberto's estate.*

In this scenario, although it is clear enough that Ramon must retain other legal counsel to represent him in his law suit against the estate, what is the appropriate posture of the law firm representing Ramon as personal representative? Is the law firm obligated to defend the estate against the personal financial interests of its client? This dilemma cannot be solved by the law firm's withdrawing its representation, because the law firm's successor will face the same problem. In this situation, it is likely that Ramon will have to either refrain from filing the law suit or resign as personal representative. Indeed, if Ramon pursues the civil action and does not voluntarily resign as personal representative, other persons interested in Gilberto's estate may (and in all likelihood would) petition the court to remove Ramon from office.

 PARKER ESTATE: In the Parker matter, recall the uncertainty regarding the effect of Irene Parker's holographic codicil on the distribution of the estate. Ms. Cargis filed a "Petition to Determine Persons Entitled to Distribution of Estate," in which she took a position favoring Sharon as devisee. Did this position constitute a conflict of interest, since the law firm was also representing Sharon as personal representative? A similar issue arises with respect to Sharon's creditor claim for reimbursement of funeral expenses. In both instances, there is no conflict, because Sharon's interests as a beneficiary or creditor, while adverse to other beneficiaries, are not adverse to the estate.

Conflicts of Interest in Protective Proceedings

Protective proceedings typically involve several different parties in interest, including the following:

1. The petitioner seeking to establish the guardianship, conservatorship, or other protective measure
2. The person appointed as guardian or conservator
3. The person to be protected
4. Any other person interested in the welfare of the protected person or, in the case of a conservatorship, in the estate of the protected person (including creditors)

The interests of all of these parties are potentially adverse to one another, at least to the extent that the different parties are involved, and the law firm must generally limit its representation accordingly. However, the law firm's representation of a court-appointed guardian or conservator (or similar legal representative) presents a special situation. In representing the legal representative, the law firm actually owes its duty of loyalty to the protected person, since the representative is merely acting in his or her fiduciary capacity on behalf of the protected person. Accordingly, while the protected person and the representative may both hold the status of "client," the interests of the protected person are paramount. Where the interests of the personal representative become adverse to those of the protected person, or if the representative proposes a course of action that the lawyer believes is not in the best interests of the protected person, the law firm may be required to advise against the proposed action or employ other measures necessary for what the lawyer reasonably believes to be the best interests of the protected person, even though such measures may be adverse to the interests of the representative (see Rule 1.14, Comment; Figure 12-7). The law firm's special obligations to a client under disability will be examined in more detail later in this chapter.

The law firm may also face a conflict where a legal representative has not yet been appointed by the court. Particularly problematic is the situation where the person to be protected is a present client of the law firm. Consider the following scenario:

SCENARIO: *Edwin is a long-standing client of the law firm. One day the paralegal receives a telephone call from Edwin's son Barry, who indicates that his aging father's state of mind is faltering and that it may be necessary to appoint a conservator. Two days later, at the paralegal's request, Barry brings Edwin into the law office to discuss the matter with the lawyer. Edwin strongly objects to the idea of establishing a conservatorship, insisting that he can manage his own affairs. Based on her observations of Edwin during the meeting, the lawyer believes that Edwin is legally competent to manage his own affairs.*

In the foregoing scenario, Edwin's clear objection to the initiation of protective proceedings may prohibit the law firm from assisting Barry in initiating conservatorship proceedings as well as from representing Barry as conservator of his father's estate. In fact, given Edwin's long-standing relationship with the law firm, it may be appropriate for the law firm to represent Edwin in opposing the appointment of a conservator. The law firm's appropriate response may have been less clear under other circumstances. For instance, what if Barry were also a present client of the law firm? What if the lawyer agreed with Barry that Edwin is legally incompetent? Would it not be consistent with Edwin's interests for the law firm to provide whatever measure of protection the lawyer believes in good faith to be necessary for the protection of Edwin's estate, even if this involves initiating conservatorship proceedings against Edwin's wishes? Is there some obligation that overrides the conflict-of-interest rule? Consider this question in light of EC 7-11 and Rule 1.14 (Figure 12-7), as well as in light of the discussion later in this chapter respecting the limitations of the law firm's duty of zealous representation.

The Lawyer or Paralegal as Fiduciary

As a general rule, it is not considered a conflict of interest for the lawyer to serve as both lawyer for a fiduciary and as fiduciary, whether personal representative, trustee, conservator, or guardian. The only inherent conflict-of-interest issue involves attorney fees, since the interest of the lawyer in being compensated is adverse to the interest of the estate in preserving and protecting the estate's assets. This issue is addressed adequately by statutory requirements for court approval of fees and by notice requirements, at least with respect to court-supervised proceedings. However, in the case of the *inter vivos* trust, where no court supervision is required, the risk of abusing the powers of the fiduciary office is far greater. The terms of the trust may require periodic accountings to the beneficiaries and/or approval by the beneficiaries of all payment of fiduciary fees; otherwise, since the trust is a private arrangement, it is up to the beneficiaries to enforce their equitable title through appropriate civil action.

 FOCUS: Where the lawyer (or employee or associate of the lawyer) is a beneficiary or personal representative of a decedent's estate, the law firm may nevertheless provide representation of the personal representative, unless the resulting conflict of interest impairs the lawyer's ability to exercise his or her independent professional judgment on behalf of the estate.

CONFIDENTIALITY AND THE ATTORNEY-CLIENT PRIVILEGE

Because of the inherent nature of the field of estate planning and probate, the probate paralegal becomes privy to very personal and private client information. The professional responsibility of the lawyer and the paralegal to protect and preserve the client's confidences and secrets (see Figure 12-3) requires that the paralegal refrain under all circumstances from discussing clients' affairs with friends, relatives, or other office personnel. This duty of confidentiality operates hand-in-hand with a fundamental rule of evidence referred to as the *attorney-client privilege*, under which confidential communications between a client and lawyer (as well as the lawyer's employees, including the paralegal) are protected from disclosure. The rule facilitates effective legal representation by allowing free and unhindered communication between the client and lawyer. Both oral and written communications are protected under the rule. The person claiming the privilege has the burden of proving that the communication is protected by the rule. The "attorney-client privilege" rule of evidence is more narrow in terms of what types of information are protected from disclosure than is the duty of confidentiality imposed by Canon 4 of the Code. Thus, even where it is doubtful that a client communication is privileged, the law firm may nevertheless be obligated to preserve its confidentiality unless and until disclosure is compelled in a court proceeding.

The "Client"

The attorney-client privilege applies only to communications by the *client*. In the case of a legally incompetent person, however, the privilege applies to confidential communications by the incompetent as well as by the person consulting the lawyer on behalf of the incompetent. The privilege applies to communications by clients and by *prospective* clients. When and whether the law firm actually enters into an employment agreement with the "client" is not important. Any confidential consultation with the lawyer (or employee of the lawyer) in his or her professional capacity is protected.

EXAMPLE: *Vonnie, who is neither a present nor former client, contacts the law firm's probate paralegal by telephone to discuss her family situation and to inquire whether the law firm can assist her. The next day, the probate para-*

FIGURE 12-3   CONFIDENTIALITY AND THE ATTORNEY-CLIENT PRIVILEGE

ABA CODE OF PROFESSIONAL RESPONSIBILITY

Canon 4   A lawyer should preserve the confidences and secrets of a client.

Ethical Consideration 4-3   Unless the client directs otherwise, it is not improper for a lawyer to give limited information from his files to an outside agency necessary for statistical, bookkeeping, accounting, data processing, banking, printing, or other legitimate purposes, provided he exercises due care in the selection of the agency and warns the agency that the information must be kept confidential.

ABA MODEL RULES OF PROFESSIONAL CONDUCT

Rule 1.6   Confidentiality of Information
  (a) A lawyer shall not reveal information relating to representation of a client unless the client consents after consultation, except for disclosures that are impliedly authorized in order to carry out the representation. . . .

NFPA AFFIRMATION OF RESPONSIBILITY

IV. Client Confidences   A paralegal shall preserve client confidences and privileged communications. DISCUSSION: Confidential information and privileged communications are a vital part of the attorney, paralegal and client relationship. The importance of preserving confidential and privileged information is understood to be an uncompromising obligation of every paralegal.

NALA CODE OF ETHICS AND PROFESSIONAL RESPONSIBILITY

Canon 7   A legal assistant must protect the confidences of a client, and it shall be unethical for a legal assistant to violate any statute now in effect or hereafter to be enacted controlling privileged communication.

*legal receives a telephone call from Vonnie's son, Carmine (who is neither a present nor former client). Carmine learned that his mother had contacted the law firm and wishes to find out what his mother's intentions are. **Result:** The communication by Vonnie was made to the paralegal in his or her professional capacity; even though Vonnie is not yet a client of the law firm, the communication is privileged. Accordingly, the paralegal has a professional obligation to preserve the confidentiality of the communication (see Figure 12-3).*

In the foregoing example, what if Carmine requested the law firm to represent him in opposition to his mother's attempt to modify the terms of a trust with respect to which Vonnie is the trustee and Carmine is a beneficiary? Should the law firm decline engagement with Carmine in light of Vonnie's confidential communication to the paralegal? Is the law firm precluded from representing either party at this point?

Holder of the Privilege

The purpose of the attorney-client privilege is to protect the client; accordingly, as a general rule, only the client, and not the attorney or any other person, holds the privilege. In the field of probate law, however, the "client" is often unable, as a result of disability or death, to invoke the privilege. A court-appointed fiduciary such as a guardian, conservator, or personal representative of a decedent's estate is deemed to hold the privilege on behalf of the protected person or decedent.

EXAMPLE: *As the result of a sudden stroke, Jim becomes unable to manage his own business affairs. At the time of the stroke, Jim was involved in a variety of business ventures and was a party to two different pending law suits. Jim's brother Gib wishes the law firm to assist him in securing his appointment as conservator of Jim's estate. The law firm agrees, and Gib is appointed. After Gib's appointment, in order to assist Gib in handling Jim's affairs, the lawyer conducts several interviews with Jim at his home to attempt to solicit certain information from him that may be helpful in the litigation.* **Result:** *The communications by Jim to the lawyer are confidential and protected by the attorney-client privilege. Gib holds the privilege and may assert it on Jim's behalf.*

In the preceding example, assume instead that Jim died as a result of his stroke, that Gib was named as successor trustee under the terms of Jim's *inter vivos* trust, and that at Jim's death no probate is required because substantially all of his assets were placed in trust. Can Gib invoke the privilege on Jim's behalf? Most courts would hold that since Gib is acting as a fiduciary and serving essentially the same function as a personal representative, he may invoke the privilege on his brother's behalf; it might be necessary, however, to obtain a court order clearly establishing that right before it is exercised, and in any event this preventative course of action is recommended. An alternative course of action in this case would be to establish a probate estate, even though not required under applicable statute, for the purpose of clearly establishing the privilege through the appointment of a personal representative.

Persons claiming an interest in a deceased client's estate cannot invoke the privilege with respect to a communication relevant to the disposition of the estate. The rationale for this is that the deceased client probably would have wanted all issues and disputes regarding the disposition of the estate to be resolved and therefore would have wanted any communications that would facilitate his or her desired disposition to be disclosed.

"Confidential" Communications and Third Parties

To be protected under the rule of attorney-client privilege, the client must intend the communication to be confidential. Generally speaking, where a third party (other than an employee of the lawyer) is present at the time of the communication, then the communication is not considered confidential, unless the presence of the third party is necessary for the communication. The problem of unwanted disclosure to third parties is particularly common in estate planning and protective proceedings, where it is not uncommon for a relative, friend, doctor, or nurse, to be present during a meeting between the lawyer (or paralegal) and the client. Estate-planning clients who are spouses generally expect to meet with the lawyer (and paralegal) together during the estate-planning process. A request that one spouse leave the room while particular topics are addressed may cause undesired tension between the spouses and undermine the cooperative estate-planning effort. The usual solution to this problem is a dual-representation agreement that includes a provision stating that the lawyer (or paralegal) may reveal all information affecting both spouses to each of them, thereby releasing the lawyer (and paralegal) from the ethical duty to protect the confidences of one spouse from the other. Even where the spouses have agreed to dual representation on such terms, the spouses may nevertheless agree informally between themselves that particular information communicated to the lawyer (or paralegal) be kept secret from the other spouse. In any event, if the spouses will not agree to dual representation on these terms, the law firm should withdraw from engagement with one or both spouses.

PRACTICE TIP: As noted earlier, the lawyer, paralegal, and other employees of the lawyer have an ethical duty to protect their clients' confidences so that the attorney-client privilege can be effectively invoked if necessary (see Figure 12-3). Toward this end, the lawyer and the lawyer's employees should adhere to the following office policies and procedures:

- Where no third party is present, it should be assumed that *every* communication by the client is intended by the client to be confidential.
- Written communication to potentially adverse persons should be made by the lawyer rather than by the paralegal or other nonlawyer employee, although the paralegal may assist in this matter either by preparing the letter for the lawyer's approval and signature or by reminding the lawyer to draft an appropriate letter. In any event, caution and discretion should be exercised in all disclosures to interested persons other than the personal representative, since they are potentially adverse parties. When there is any doubt as to whether certain information may be disclosed to another person, the paralegal should refrain from providing the information and discuss the matter with the lawyer first.
- Where any third party is present, the lawyer (or employee) should suggest that the third party leave the room, explaining respectfully the law firm's duty of confidentiality. If the *client* insists on the third party's presence, the lawyer (or employee) should make a handwritten note of this fact as well as make complete handwritten notes of the discussion, including who is present and all comments and suggestions made by the third party during the discussion.
- The lawyer (or employee) should refrain from discussing any information of a potentially confidential nature outside of the office.

■ As a general policy, a nonlawyer employee should not provide any document to any person other than the client—including the client's spouse or a close family member of the client—without first consulting the lawyer. However, the experienced paralegal may be competent to determine independently whether the information or document requested may be provided without jeopardizing the client's confidence (see EC 4-3; Figure 12-3).

FOCUS: The paralegal should assume that the estate-planning client considers every communication to the law firm secret and made in complete confidence. The paralegal must make reasonable efforts to preserve the client's confidences and secrets by exercising discretion during conversations with the client where any third party (except for the lawyer or certain associates or employees of the lawyer) is present.

Written Instruments Affecting Interests in Property

Despite the important function that the attorney-client privilege plays in the legal system, the right is not an absolute one, so a variety of exceptions exists. One exception that is highly relevant to the probate paralegal involves communications by the client suggesting an intent or plan to engage in a crime or fraudulent activity. Another exception to the attorney-client privilege that is of particular relevance to the probate paralegal involves written instruments—e.g., deeds, wills, codicils, trusts, powers of appointment, and so forth—executed by a client and purporting to affect an interest in property. After the client's death, no privilege exists with respect to communications by the client that are relevant to the client's intent with regard to the instrument. In other words, if a communication is relevant to the instrument's validity (i.e., to prove or disprove legal capacity, fraud, undue influence, or mistake), interpretation, or construction, the communication is not protected.

EXAMPLE: *Rosemary, the widow of Felix's deceased brother, accompanies Felix to an estate-planning interview with the law firm. Immediately after executing his will at the law firm's office, Felix meets briefly with the probate paralegal to review the instructions for the handling and safekeeping of various legal documents prepared by the law firm. During this meeting, Felix mentions casually to the paralegal: "I'm glad this matter is finally taken care of. My sister-in-law, Rosemary, has been twisting my arm to get this done for some time." After Felix's death, the validity of the will, which provides for Felix's entire estate to pass to Rosemary, is contested by Felix's intestate heirs. Result: Felix's remark may be relevant to the issue of the will's validity, since it suggests possible undue influence or duress. Accordingly, the communication by Felix to the paralegal is not protected by the privilege, and disclosure may be compelled during the proceedings involving the will contest.*

This exception is fully applicable to communications to the lawyer who drafted the instrument as well as to the lawyer (or paralegal) who serves as a witness to the execution of the instrument.

CLIENT COMMUNICATIONS

The law firm has a professional obligation to keep the client reasonably informed about the status of the client's matter and to explain a matter to the extent reasonably necessary to permit the client to make informed decisions regarding the representation, except where fully informing the client according to this standard may be impracticable (see Rule 1.4 and Comment; Figure 12-4). One of the most common general complaints about lawyers is that they often fail to maintain adequate communication with clients. Dissatisfaction of this sort is all too common in the context of decedents' estates. As noted in Chapter 5, it is important for the lawyer or paralegal to explain the probate process to the personal representative as well as to other appropriate family members, indicating the potential problems and delays that might be anticipated. In addition, however, a regularly scheduled (weekly or biweekly) telephone call by the paralegal to the personal representative is also recommended. The personal representative may be reluctant to call the law firm to discuss what the personal representative perceives to be trivial questions or minor problems. Frequent and regular contact may serve to identify potential problems or delays before additional delay or expense to the estate results. Moreover, regular client contact enhances the lawyer-client relationship, and a satisfied client will refer others to the law firm. The law firm should also consider periodic written communication to appropriate family members (in addition to notices that may be required by statute) for the purpose of keeping them apprised of developments and progress. Regular communication gives the family members a strong impression, and accurately so, that the administration is moving forward and that the law firm is making a concerted effort for the benefit of all concerned. However, as noted earlier, the paralegal must exercise extreme caution in providing information to potentially adverse third parties.

DILIGENCE AND COMPETENCY

The law firm has a professional responsibility to exercise reasonable diligence in all matters entrusted to it (see Rule 1-3; Figure 12-5). Undue delay in preparing an estate plan or settling an estate, as well as failure to discharge all of its duties to the client, may constitute a breach of this responsibility, as discussed below.

Diligence and the Scope of the Law Firm's Employment

The rules of professional responsibility require the law firm under certain circumstances to assist a client in matters related either directly or indirectly to the matter at hand. However, the firm's professional obligation to send reminders and updates to estate-planning clients is less certain under the Model Rules and Model Code.

Duty to Assist the Client in Related Matters. In any field of law, including the areas of estate planning and probate, the scope of the law firm's repre-

FIGURE 12-4 CLIENT COMMUNICATIONS

ABA MODEL RULES OF PROFESSIONAL CONDUCT

Rule 1.4 Communication

(a) A lawyer shall keep a client reasonably informed about the status of a matter and promptly comply with reasonable requests for information.

(b) A lawyer shall explain a matter to the extent reasonably necessary to permit the client to make informed decisions regarding the representation.

COMMENT: . . . Ordinarily, the information to be provided is that appropriate for a client who is a comprehending and responsible adult. However, fully informing the client according to this standard may be impracticable, for example, where the client is a child or suffers from mental disability. . . . In some circumstances, a lawyer may be justified in delaying transmission of information when the client would be likely to react imprudently to an immediate communication. Thus, a lawyer might withhold a psychiatric diagnosis of a client when the examining psychiatrist indicates that disclosure would harm the client.

sentation should be clearly defined under the terms of an employment agreement. Without a clear agreement, the law firm may be risking professional discipline and/or liability (generally based upon negligence) for not fully discharging its professional obligation to the client. For the probate law firm, this problem takes on particular significance in certain areas. Consider the following questions that may arise in the absence of an express agreement:

- When assisting in the preparation and execution of a probate-avoidance trust, is the law firm also obligated to assist in the transfers of property to the trust? Durable powers of attorney? A living will?
- During the administration of a decedent's estate, does the law firm representing the personal representative have a duty to assist in matters relating to the decedent's nonprobate property as well, at least where the personal representative is also the distributee of the nonprobate property?
- In representing a personal representative, does the law firm have a duty to determine whether the personal representative must file an estate, gift, income, or other tax return on behalf of the decedent?
- In representing a personal representative, does the law firm have a duty to defend law suits against the decedent or the estate? If the law firm is not competent in this area, is there an obligation to assist the personal representative in obtaining competent counsel for this purpose?

The answers to these questions depend largely, of course, upon the particular circumstances involved. The scope of the law firm's obligation in any

FIGURE 12-5   COMPETENCE AND DILIGENCE

ABA CODE OF PROFESSIONAL RESPONSIBILITY

Canon 6   A lawyer should represent a client competently.

ABA MODEL RULES OF PROFESSIONAL CONDUCT

Rule 1.1   Competence
A lawyer shall provide competent representation to a client. Competent representation requires the legal knowledge, skill, thoroughness and preparation reasonably necessary for the representation.

Rule 1.3   Diligence
A lawyer shall act with reasonable diligence and promptness in representing a client. COMMENT: . . . Perhaps no professional shortcoming is more widely resented than procrastination. A client's interests often can be adversely affected by the passage of time or the change of condition; in extreme instances, as when a lawyer overlooks a statute of limitations, the client's legal position may be destroyed. Even when the client's interests are not affected in substance, however, unreasonable delay can cause a client needless anxiety and undermine confidence in the lawyer's trustworthiness.

Rule 1.16   Declining or Terminating Representation (Official Comment)
COMMENT: A lawyer should not accept representation in a matter unless it can be performed competently, promptly, without improper conflict of interest and to completion.

NFPA AFFIRMATION OF RESPONSIBILITY

III. Competence and Integrity   A paralegal shall maintain a high level of competence and shall contribute to the integrity of the paralegal profession. DISCUSSION: The integrity of the paralegal profession is predicated upon individual competence. Professional competence is each paralegal's responsibility and is achieved through continuing education, awareness of developments in the field of law and aspiring to the highest standards of personal performance.

NALA CODE OF ETHICS AND PROFESSIONAL RESPONSIBILITY

Canon 9   A legal assistant shall work continually to maintain integrity and high degree of competency throughout the legal profession.

Canon 10   A legal assistant shall strive for perfection through education in order to better assist the legal profession in fulfilling its duty of making legal services available to clients and the public.

given situation might very well be determinable under the law of contracts rather than by a rule of professional responsibility. Nevertheless, each state has responded individually (by administrative decision or opinion, disciplinary rule, or ethical guideline) to these and similar issues in terms of professional obligation. The probate paralegal should be familiar with the position adopted by the bar association in his or her own jurisdiction, since there is by no means complete consensus among the states on these issues.

 PARKER ESTATE: In the Parker matter, recall that Sharon indicated to Ms. Cargis that she intends to prepare and file a fiduciary income-tax return for the estate without the law firm's assistance. Is the law firm thereby released from any obligation respecting fiduciary taxes? Probably so, although for the law firm's protection it is important to confirm in writing all statements made by the client releasing the law firm from any duties with which it might have otherwise been charged.

Reminders and Updates for Estate-Planning Clients. The estate-planning process rarely ends after an initial plan is established. Subsequent review of the estate plan may be desirable for a variety of reasons:

- An estate-planning document that was valid when executed may later become invalid—for example, if:
    1. Under applicable law, the document has become invalid due solely to the passage of time (automatic expiration is particularly likely in the case of durable powers of attorney).
    2. The document was valid when executed but has become invalid due to a change in the law (although this is unlikely, since legislators typically limit applicability of new legislation to instruments executed after the effective date of the new law).
    3. The client moves to a different jurisdiction that does not recognize the validity of a particular document because of its present form or the manner in which it was executed.
    4. Without the assistance of a lawyer, the client attempts to modify a document, either on its face or by another instrument, with an unintended result.

- Review of the client's estate plan might be appropriate due to a change in the client's personal and/or family circumstances—for example:
    1. The death of the person selected by the client as fiduciary or agent (e.g., executor, guardian, conservator, attorney in fact, or successor trustee)
    2. A change in the client's marital status (i.e., marriage, divorce, separation, or death of the client's spouse)
    3. A change in the client's health (e.g., deteriorating mental competency or change in physical health, especially the onset of a terminal illness)

4. Changes relating to the client's heirs or beneficiaries (e.g., death, birth, marriage, divorce, adoption, relationship with the client)

■ Review of an estate plan may be appropriate due to a change in the client's financial, legal, or business circumstances—for example:

1. A significant increase (or, less significantly, decrease) in the value of the client's personal wealth (e.g., due to inheritance or gift, uninsured illness or other catastrophe, personal injury award, or divorce settlement)
2. A change in employment affecting death benefits for the client's surviving spouse or dependents
3. Acquisition of property located in a different state
4. Retirement
5. Acquisition or termination of a business interest

■ Review of an estate plan may be appropriate because of changes in the law—particularly, changes in the tax laws.

At the time an estate plan is established, either the lawyer or the paralegal should explain to the client the various circumstances that may call for review of the plan and urge the client to contact the firm promptly in the event of any such changes (preferably, in anticipation of such an event). A written letter listing the events indicated above should also be provided to the client at this time.

Aside from instructing the client at the time the plan is established, what is the law firm's professional responsibility to inform the client by letter of any changes in the law that may affect the client's estate plan or to remind the client by letter when the expiration of a document such as a durable power of attorney approaches? Aside from the issue of the law firm's professional obligation, it is certainly to the law firm's business advantage to maintain periodic contact with the client. The client is more likely to contact the law firm again to review the estate plan and to make the necessary changes. Continued contact enhances the lawyer-client relationship, thereby minimizing disputes over past and future services; moreover, a satisfied client is more likely to refer others to the law firm. Although it is unlikely that the lawyer can be disciplined professionally or held liable for failure to follow up on such matters, the law firm should nevertheless develop and consistently employ a tickler system for the purpose of alerting clients of all important dates and deadlines affecting their estate plan. In addition, in order to ensure that the firm is not bound by any such obligation, an appropriate limitation on the scope of the law firm's services should be included in the employment agreement.

 TAYLOR TRUST: Recall that the Taylors' durable powers of attorney are valid and enforceable only for seven years after execution (except that any periods of incapacity extend the period). Either the paralegal or other employee will include this data in the firm's tickler system to ensure that a reminder letter is mailed to the Taylors three to six months prior to expiration of these documents. Also, key data regarding the Taylors and their estate plan will be entered into the firm's database so that the Taylors will be included in a list of clients to be informed of changes in the law that may affect them.

Avoiding Undue Delays

An unreasonable delay in handling any client matter, whether a probate or estate-planning matter, may subject the lawyer to professional discipline, as discussed below.

Delay in Establishing an Estate Plan. If an individual approaches the law firm for estate-planning assistance, but it is too late to establish a plan—for example, where the individual is seeking assistance for a parent who is no longer legally competent—then the law firm is obviously not at fault for any damage resulting from the family's failure to establish a plan sooner. In other situations, however, whether the standard of diligence has been met may not be so clear. Consider the following scenario:

EXAMPLE: During their initial meeting with the lawyer and paralegal, a married couple indicate that they plan to leave for an extended trip abroad in one week. Their estate is sufficient in size that an inter vivos *trust with an "AB" or "ABC" plan is advisable. Their estate is also complex, and the lawyer wishes to obtain numerous documents from the clients and examine them before establishing a plan.*

If the law firm agrees to assist in this matter, what efforts must the law firm make to put into place the desired plan before the trip? What if the couple were leaving the following day instead of the following week? If there is insufficient time to prepare all of the documents to put into place the desired plan, but a simple will and testamentary trust can be prepared and executed right away, is the law firm obligated to assist in establishing a "temporary" plan? By failing to take the time generally required to obtain and examine the client's personal, legal, and financial documents, to discuss all of the options with the client, and to reflect prior to making important decisions, the lawyer runs the risk of oversight or error in judgment in developing the plan. At the same time, having agreed to assist the clients, the law firm's best efforts to assist them in achieving their estate-planning objectives are required, even though sufficient time may not be available to establish the best possible plan. The law firm may, of course, decline engagement where it appears that circumstances would prevent the exercise of due diligence. Otherwise, the lawyer should be sure to address any potential problem of this sort in a carefully drafted legal services agreement. For example, if there is insufficient time to establish a comprehensive plan, the client's written consent to a more "temporary plan" should be obtained.

As a related problem, assume as in the foregoing example that the law firm assists in establishing an *inter vivos* trust for a client who plans to leave shortly for an extended trip. Further assume that there is insufficient time to effect all of the desired transfers to the trust prior to the trip. A pour-over will is crucial, of course, in this situation. However, as discussed in Chapters 9 and 10, for the purpose of avoiding probate, an *inter vivos* trust is useful only to the extent that it is funded prior to the settlor's death. Accordingly, unless a summary procedure is available under applicable law as an alternative to probate, the trust will not serve one of its chief purposes. One possible solution to this problem would be for the client to sign certain documents, such as deeds, bills of sale, and so forth, in blank before the trip while the law firm actually prepares the document later. Is this solution acceptable from an ethical viewpoint?

Delay in Settling Decedents' Estates. The prompt settlement and distribution of a decedent's estate is in the best interest of all parties involved (including the law firm, since a significant portion of its fees may be paid only upon approval by the court of the final account). What circumstances, however, would constitute a failure on the part of the law firm to fulfill its professional obligation in this area? Generally speaking, any expense or damage to the estate or to the estate's beneficiaries resulting from avoidable delay or lack of diligence by the law firm indicates a breach of duty. Consider the following scenarios, any of which may potentially constitute a breach of the law firm's duty of due diligence:

SCENARIO 1: The law firm agrees to prepare and file the federal and state death-tax returns and the fiduciary income-tax return(s) for the estate, but overlooks a filing deadline; as a result, interest and/or penalties are imposed for late payment and filing.

SCENARIO 2: Promptly after the decedent's death, the personal representative provides an accurate list of the decedent's creditors to the law firm. The firm delays in providing written notice to these creditors, and a certain creditor whose claim would have been cut off had the firm provided prompt notice files a valid claim.

SCENARIO 3: Because of the law firm's failure to inquire about assets of the decedent located out of state, a particular asset is not discovered until after the estate is closed, and the estate must be reopened at additional expense to the decedent's heirs.

While a comprehensive letter of instruction to the personal representative at the outset of administration will provide a large measure of protection in the event that the personal representative fails in his or her fiduciary duties, a letter of instruction will not shield the law firm from liability in the event of its own negligence in representing or advising the personal representative.

Other forms of negligence, while not damaging the estate or the beneficiaries as directly or significantly, may nevertheless result in minor delays, additional paperwork for the law firm, and general inconvenience. An undue delay in proceeding toward settlement and distribution may necessitate the filing of an interim account. Errors or oversights in preparing or filing court documents, if not identified in time and promptly corrected, may result in postponement of a court hearing. The costs of the law firm's own negligence should not be passed on to the decedent's heirs but should be borne by the law firm. To avoid such costs, the law firm should consistently employ the policies and practices discussed in the materials that follow.

Competency and the Probate Paralegal

While it is fundamental that a paralegal may not perform tasks that constitute the practice of law, the probate paralegal should also be careful to engage only in those functions for which he or she is competent, regardless of whether the task is one that generally may be performed by a nonlawyer (see NFPA Affirm. of Resp. III; NALA Code, Canon 9; Figure 12-5). Toward this end, the probate paralegal must recognize the limits of his or her own expertise and seek supervision and assistance from others in matters exceeding those limits. Particular areas, such as preparing tax returns and drafting complex provisions for wills and trusts, should be left to the experienced probate paralegal unless adequate instruction and supervision can be provided by the lawyer or by a more experienced paralegal.

Above and beyond these basic imperatives, the probate paralegal should strive not only for competency but for excellence as well in performing his or her job duties and in service to the client, in the following ways:

- The paralegal should consistently strive to produce work products of the highest possible quality. Under the pressure of time to meet a deadline, it is far preferable to seek assistance in producing a final draft of a document or other work product than to cut corners, which often results in a substandard product that reflects poorly not just on the paralegal but on the entire law firm.

- The paralegal should stay abreast of all current developments in the field through regular review of appropriate professional periodicals and journals, as well as by participating in continuing-education programs sponsored by local bar associations and paralegal associations (NFPA Affirm. of Resp. III, Discussion; NALA Code, Canon 10; see Figure 12-5).

- The paralegal should devote as much time as possible on the job to those tasks which he or she is uniquely qualified to perform as a paralegal. An effective and profitable law firm is one where each member of the team functions at his or her highest level of competency, at least to the extent that is practicable. The lawyer should not perform those functions that can be competently performed by the paralegal or other nonlawyer employee. Similarly, the paralegal should delegate to clerical employees those tasks that do not require the specialized training or expertise of a paralegal. At the probate law office, effective delegation of duties often calls as well for the assistance of outside experts, including accountants, appraisers, and stockbrokers, where such experts can perform a particular task more efficiently and at lower cost to the client

Organizing and Processing Workflow

Perhaps the most significant contribution that the probate paralegal can make to the overall quality of service—in terms of both diligence and competence—to the client is in developing and streamlining procedures for processing estate-planning and probate matters.

Developing a Filing System for an Estate. Because of the large volume of paperwork involved in the administration of a typical decedent's estate, developing and maintaining an effective filing system is crucial. Once court proceedings are initiated, the volume of documents in the law firm's files increases quickly and dramatically. Locating documents and assimilating information from the files can easily become a time-consuming chore unless an effective system is employed on a consistent basis by all personnel handling the files. The use of multiple files for each individual estate is highly recommended. Each of the following separate files should be established for any estate, even relatively simple ones:

- A primary or *master* file containing the following documents:
    1. Master checklist (at the top of the file)
    2. Probate questionnaire
    3. Preliminary inventory
    4. Legal-services agreement

- A subfile for *financial* documents of the decedent, such as insurance policies, deeds, leases, stock certificates (including a document index or checklist at the top of the file)
- A subfile for the decedent's *personal* documents (birth certificate, death certificate, adoption papers, naturalization papers, marriage certificate, wills, codicils, trusts, powers of attorney, premarital and postmarital agreements, agreements and court orders for marital dissolution, and so forth)
- A subfile for all documents included in the *court file* (and only those documents)
- A subfile for *correspondence and notes* (including notes from telephone conversations)

For more complex estates, the probate law firm should also consider using the following separate files as applicable:

- A subfile for each of the decedent's *business interests* in general partnerships, sole proprietorships, and small corporations
- A subfile for each *special court proceeding* relating to the estate (will contests, confirmation of sales, petitions for instructions, petitions to determine heirship, etc.)

■   A subfile for any *matter requiring special attention*, including such matters as complex transactions, litigation, and disputed creditors' claims
■   A subfile for *ancillary administration*, if the domiciliary personal representative is also acting as ancillary representative
■   A subfile for *estate- and gift-tax returns* (and related information)

In addition to facilitating organization of documents, the use of subfiles also allows one person to refer to one part of the file while other persons are using other portions of the file. The more subfiles that are used, the less likely it is that one person will have to wait until another is finished with a file.

Master Checklist. A ''master checklist'' allows the paralegal to monitor the progress of an estate or of an estate-planning project at a glance. The checklist provides the following information:

1.   What tasks must be performed
2.   When each task must or should be performed
3.   Whose job it is to perform each task
4.   Whether and when each task has been completed

The paralegal should develop a master checklist for each of the following areas:

1.   Probate
2.   Protective proceedings
3.   Estate planning (*inter vivos* trusts)
4.   Estate planning (wills)

The lawyer, not the paralegal, must determine which master checklist is appropriate and which of the tasks appearing on the checklist must be accomplished. With this information, the paralegal may determine when and by whom each task should be performed, and follow up on each task to ensure that it is performed in a timely manner, as well as revise and update the checklist as required.

Calendar and Tickler Systems. Decedents' estate administration requires strict adherence to a variety of deadlines. At a minimum, the law firm should maintain a calendar system that conforms to the requirements of the firm's professional-liability insurance carrier. Failure to use a calendar system is generally considered a breach of professional obligation as well. The paralegal should determine and record not only on the master checklist but also on an estate calendar (working together with the firm's docket clerk, if any) all relevant deadlines that may be determined based upon date of death, date of appointment of the personal representative, and date of notice to creditors by publication. Additionally, the firm should develop and consistently employ an effective tickler system in order to monitor deadlines and to ensure that the estate progresses as quickly as possible toward settlement and final distribution.

PRACTICE TIP: It is strongly recommended that the law firm use a computer program in its calendaring and tickler system. Programs designed specifically for this purpose are reasonably priced and readily available. Although the use of computer applications for these functions is not yet mandated by rules of professional responsibility, it is becoming increasingly common for professional-liability insurance carriers to require the use of a computerized calendar system.

THE LIMITS OF ZEALOUS REPRESENTATION

Both the estate-planning and probate areas provide innumerable opportunities for fraud and other "overzealous" misconduct by the law firm on behalf of the client, as discussed in the following materials.

Estate Planning and the Client's Creditors

Estate planning often involves the *inter vivos* transfer of one or more assets by the client to another person, and there are of course a variety of legitimate tax and nontax reasons for such transfers, as discussed in previous chapters. However, how should the law firm respond to the estate-planning client who indicates that he or she wishes to transfer assets to another for the purpose of protecting the assets from the client's creditors? Consider this question in light of Rule 1.2, Rule 1.6 (Comment), and Rule 1.16 (see Figure 12-6), all of which suggest that if a conveyance is indeed fraudulent in nature, and the lawyer (or paralegal) is aware or should be aware of this fact, the lawyer may be exposed to professional liability if the law firm assists in or otherwise advises the client to make the transfer.

It is important to keep in mind that a transfer is not fraudulent merely because it might be disadvantageous to a creditor. If there are legitimate other reasons for the transfer—for example, providing financial assistance for a child or parent, income shifting, estate-tax planning, and so forth—then the transfer will probably not be viewed as fraudulent. When, then, is a proposed course of action considered a fraud against the client's creditors? Under the Uniform Fraudulent Transfer Act (UFTA) and similar statutes adopted by most states, a conveyance is fraudulent: (1) as to creditors if, without regard to actual intent, the conveyance is made without fair consideration, and the person will thereby be rendered insolvent; (2) as to both present and future creditors, if the conveyance is made with actual intent to hinder, delay, or defraud either present or future creditors; or (3) as to both present and future creditors, if the person making the conveyance intends or believes he or she will incur debts beyond his or her ability to pay as they mature (Uniform Fraudulent Transfers Act, §§ 4, 6, and 7).

 PRACTICE TIP: The UFTA suggests that the law firm should make a concerted effort to determine the client's financial solvency if a substantial irrevocable *inter vivos* transfer is being considered, particularly where the client has expressed a concern about creditors. Specifically, the client should be asked to provide the law firm with financial statements (balance sheets and income statements) for at least the last three years. The financial statements should be

FIGURE 12-6   ZEALOUS REPRESENTATION AND PROBLEM OF FRAUD

ABA MODEL RULES OF PROFESSIONAL CONDUCT

Rule 1.2   Scope of Representation

. . . (d) A lawyer shall not counsel a client to engage, or assist a client, in conduct that the lawyer knows is criminal or fraudulent, but a lawyer may discuss the legal consequences of any proposed course of conduct with a client and may counsel or assist a client to make a good faith effort to determine the validity, scope, meaning or application of the law.

(e) When a lawyer knows that a client expects assistance not permitted by the rules of professional conduct or other law, the lawyer shall consult with the client regarding the relevant limitations on the lawyer's conduct.

COMMENT: . . . When the client's course of action has already begun and is continuing, the lawyer's responsibility is especially delicate. The lawyer is not permitted to reveal the client's wrongdoing, except where permitted by RULE 1.6 ["Confidentiality of Information"]. However, the lawyer is required to avoid furthering the purpose, for example, by suggesting how it might be concealed. A lawyer may not continue assisting a client in conduct that the lawyer originally supposes is legally proper but then discovers is criminal or fraudulent. Withdrawal from the representation, therefore, may be required.

Rule 1.6   Confidentiality of Information

. . . COMMENT: . . . [T]o the extent a lawyer is required or permitted to disclose a client's purposes, the client will be inhibited from revealing facts which would enable the lawyer to counsel against a wrongful course of action. The public is better protected if full and open communication by the client is encouraged than if it is inhibited.

Several situations must be distinguished. First, the lawyer may not counsel or assist a client in conduct that is criminal or fraudulent. . . .

The lawyer's exercise of discretion requires consideration of such factors as the nature of the lawyer's relationship with the client and with those who might be injured by the client, the lawyer's own involvement in the transaction and factors that may extenuate the conduct in question. Where practical, the lawyer should seek to persuade the client to take suitable action. In any case, a disclosure adverse to the client's interest should be no greater than the lawyer reasonably believes necessary to the purpose. . . .

Rule 1.16   Declining or Terminating Representation

. . . (b) . . . [A] lawyer may withdraw from representing a client if . . . (2) the client has used the lawyer's services to perpetrate a crime or fraud; (3) a client insists upon pursuing an objective that the lawyer considers repugnant or imprudent;. . . .

analyzed by a certified public accountant who should determine independently the solvency of the client. The law firm (and accountant) may justifiably rely on the information supplied by the client without further investigation to determine their accuracy or truthfulness.

Fraud in the Settlement of Decedents' Estates

The area of decedents' estates provides innumerable opportunities for fraudulent activity. For example, the personal representative might propose to overvalue or undervalue an asset for the purpose of defrauding beneficiaries, the taxing authorities, or creditors; or a relative of a decedent might propose a fraudulent conveyance in order to avoid probate. The paralegal should become familiar with as many common ploys as possible, and whenever a client suggests a fraudulent or criminal course of conduct, the paralegal should promptly bring the matter to the lawyer's attention. To preserve the attorney-client privilege, however, the paralegal should not make any determinations about whether any particular communication is excepted from the privilege without first seeking instructions on the matter from the lawyer (see Rule 1.6; Figure 12-6).

Zealous Representation and Persons under Disability

Any mental or physical condition of a client that renders the client incapable of making a considered judgment on his or her own behalf casts additional responsibilities on the lawyer. Where a legal representative has been appointed, the lawyer must look to the representative for decisions that are normally made by the client. If no legal representative has been appointed for a client who is under disability, the lawyer should attempt to maintain a normal attorney-client relationship and obtain all possible aid from the client, at least to the extent that the client is capable of understanding the matter in question and communicating with the lawyer (EC 7-11; Rule 1.4[a] and Comment; see Figure 12-7). In addition, depending upon the circumstances, the lawyer might be required to make certain decisions on behalf of the client as *de facto* guardian and/or to seek the appointment of a legal representative (EC 7-11; Rule 1.4[b] and Comment [see Figure 12-7]). Such actions may be taken against the wishes of the disabled client if, in the lawyer's independent professional judgment, the actions are necessary to protect the client's interests. Conversely, as noted earlier in this chapter, where the law firm represents the legal representative as distinct from the protected person, the lawyer may be required to take certain measures in protection of the protected person against the wishes of the legal representative.

One of the most common ethical issues confronting the estate-planning lawyer involves the determination of legal competency. Is it the lawyer's responsibility to judge whether an estate-planning client whose state of mind has reportedly been faltering—for example, where the client has been exhibiting symptoms of Alzheimer's disease—has the "testamentary capacity" (as defined in Chapter 2) to execute a valid will? If so, what steps must the law firm take to make such a determination? If the lawyer does determine that the client has sufficient mental capacity to execute a valid will, on what basis should the lawyer determine whether the client has the higher level of competency required to execute other legal documents such as a deed, *inter vivos* trust, durable power of attorney, living will, or nomination of

FIGURE 12-7   ZEALOUS REPRESENTATION AND PERSONS UNDER DISABILITY

ABA CODE OF PROFESSIONAL RESPONSIBILITY

Ethical Consideration 7-11   Any mental or physical condition of a client that renders him incapable of making a considered judgment on his own behalf casts additional responsibilities upon his lawyer. Where an incompetent is acting through a guardian or other legal representative, a lawyer must look to such representative for those decisions which are normally the prerogative of the client to make. If a client under disability has no representative, his lawyer may be compelled in court proceedings to make decisions on behalf of the client. If the client is capable of understanding the matter in question or of contributing to the advancement of his interests, regardless of whether he is legally disqualified from performing certain acts, the lawyer should obtain from him all possible aid. If the disability of a client and the lack of a legal representative compel the lawyer to make decisions for his client, the lawyer should consider all circumstances then prevailing and act with care to safeguard and advance the interests of his client. But obviously a lawyer cannot perform any act or make any decision which the law requires his client to perform or make, either acting for himself if competent, or by a duly constituted representative if legally incompetent.

ABA MODEL RULES OF PROFESSIONAL CONDUCT

Rule 1.14   Client Under a Disability
   (a) When a client's ability to make adequately considered decisions in connection with the representation is impaired, whether because of minority, mental disability or for some other reason, the lawyer shall, as far as reasonably possible, maintain a normal client-lawyer relationship with the client.
   (b) A lawyer may seek the appointment of a guardian or take other protective action with respect to a client, only when the lawyer reasonably believes that the client cannot adequately act in the client's own interest.

COMMENT: . . . The fact that a client suffers a disability does not diminish the lawyer's obligation to treat the client with attention and respect. If the person has no guardian or legal representative, the lawyer often must act as de facto guardian. Even if the person does have a legal representative, the lawyer should as far as possible accord the represented person the status of client, particularly in maintaining communication.
   If a legal representative has already been appointed for the client, the lawyer should ordinarily look to the representative for decisions on behalf of the client. If a legal representative has not been appointed, the lawyer should see to such an appointment where it would serve the client's best interests. Thus, if a disabled client has substantial property that should be sold for the client's benefit, effective completion of the transaction ordinarily requires appointment of a legal representative. In many circumstances, however, appointment of a legal representative may be expensive or traumatic for the client. Evaluation of these considerations is a matter of professional judgment on the lawyer's part.

guardian/conservator? Where a close judgment call is required, on which side should the lawyer err?

Adding to the dilemma is the fact that if the lawyer proceeds as if the client is competent when in fact the client is not competent, as a practical matter, not only is there no resulting harm, this course of action may very well serve the best interests of the client's family. Consider the following scenario:

SCENARIO: *Sam is near death after an unexpected and massive stroke, and his testamentary capacity is questionable. Sam's two children, who are both competent adults, have asked the lawyer what can and should be done in the way of estate planning before Sam's death. Sam has a large estate but has no will. Under the applicable law of intestate succession, Sam's entire intestate estate will pass to his widow; given the present size of the estate, substantial estate taxes would be owed after the widow's death.*

In this scenario, it seems to be in the family's interest for Sam to execute a will that includes a testamentary trust calling for a bypass and marital deduction trust (an "AB" plan). Should the lawyer assist in this plan? Consider this dilemma in light of Rule 1.2 and 1.6 (see Figure 12-6) as well as EC 7-11 (see Figure 12-7), any of which might prohibit the lawyer from assisting Sam in executing the will.

 PRACTICE TIP: Where the extent of a mental disability varies from time to time, the lawyer might legitimately serve the client's interest by persuading the client to execute certain legal documents during a period of relative lucidity. In any event, the paralegal can assist the lawyer in determining the legal competency of an individual by conversing with the person, by attentive observation of the person's demeanor, by soliciting comments from relatives and friends about the person's recent behavior, and by contacting the person's physician. Indeed, the law firm is obligated to do so where legal competency is in question. If a reasonably diligent inquiry is made and complete written records of observations, discussions, and other evidence are maintained and evaluated, the lawyer's good-faith judgment will meet his or her professional responsibility.

GLOSSARY

Abatement   In the context of distribution of an estate, the reduction of a distributee's share to pay a claim against the estate. Under the U.P.C., unless otherwise specified in the decedent's will, claims should be satisfied by resorting first to the decedent's intestate property; after intestate property is exhausted, gifts under the decedent's will are *abated* in the following order: (1) residuary devises; (2) general devises; and (3) specific devises.

Ademption by extinction   Revocation by extinction of a specific gift in a testator's will. A specific gift is *adeemed* (i.e., revoked) if the property is not part of the testator's estate at the time of death, and the donee is not entitled to any property in lieu of that particular property. In many states, ademption by extinction may be avoided if it can be inferred from the circumstances that, at the time the property was disposed of, the testator did not intend the gift to adeem.

Ademption by satisfaction   Revocation of a gift under a will where the gift is satisfied either in whole or in part by an *inter vivos* transfer from the testator to the devisee subsequent to (but not prior to) execution of the will. The testator must intend that the transfer serve as satisfaction of the gift, and many states require written evidence of such intent, either in the will, by a contemporaneous writing signed by the testator, or by written acknowledgment by the devisee.

Administrator (of an estate)   The legal representative of a decedent's estate. If named in the decedent's will, the administrator is referred to more specifically as the *executor*. In some states, an administrator of the estate or an executor is referred to instead as the *personal representative* of the estate. (See **executor**, **personal representative**.)

Administrator C.T.A. (*cum testamento annexo*)   A personal representative who was not nominated to serve as representative in the decedent's valid, probated will; also referred to as an *administrator with will annexed*.

Administrator D.B.N. (*de bonis non*)   Literally meaning "administrator of goods not administered," a term used in many states to refer to a successor representative.

Advancement   An *inter vivos* gift (that is, a gift made by a person during his or her lifetime) made with the intention that the gift is to be applied toward the donee's eventual inheritance from the person. An *inter vivos* gift will be treated as an advancement only in the case of total intestacy.

Affidavit of Domicile   Also referred to as an *affidavit of residence,* a notarized document provided to a stock transfer agent for the purpose of determining the state of residence of the decedent. States that impose their own inheritance or death taxes require this information prior to allowing the transfer of securities of corporations organized in the state.

Affinity, relationship by   Family relationship by marriage rather than by blood.

Ancillary administration   Estate administration in a foreign state—that is, in a state other than that of the decedent's domicile. Ancillary administration is required to administer all of the decedent's property located in a foreign state.

Antilapse statute   A statute providing for a gift that otherwise would lapse to pass to the devisee's issue. Antilapse statutes in some states apply only where the decedent was related by blood (either by blood or marriage in some states) to the predeceased devisee. (See **lapse**.)

Ascendant   A lineal ancestor of another person; for example, a parent, grandparent, and so forth up through preceding generations; also referred to as *lineal ascendant*.

Attestation clause   A provision in an attested will immediately before the witnesses' signatures that recites the facts of the will's execution. The provision establishes a rebuttable presumption as to these facts.

Attested will   A witnessed will.

Beneficiary   In the law of trusts, a person entitled to some benefit under the terms of a trust. The beneficiary is said to hold *equitable title* in the trust property; that is, the beneficiary has an equitable interest in the property and has a right to enforce the trust against the trustee. A person entitled to all or some portion of income from a trust estate is referred to more specifically as an *income beneficiary*. The term *beneficiary* is also used more broadly to refer to a person entitled to receive all or some portion of a decedent's estate under the terms of a will.

Bequeath   Originally, to give personal property by will to another; now synonymous with devise.

Bequest   Originally, a gift by will of personal property (see **legacy**); now synonymous with **devise**.

Carryover basis   An income-tax basis that is carried over from a transferor of property to a transferee so that the transferee's basis in the asset is the same as the transferor's basis. The donee of an *inter vivos* gift of property takes a carryover basis in the property, except that the carryover basis cannot be greater than the asset's fair market value at the time of the gift. (See **tax basis**; compare **stepped-up basis**.)

Charitable trust   A trust created for indefinite and changing beneficiaries and for a charitable purpose; the public or community as a whole is viewed as the beneficiary whose rights are enforced by the state attorney general.

Civil-law method   A method of determining next of kin for the purpose of intestate succession; under this method, all claimants related to the decedent in the lowest degree share in the decedent's estate as next of kin. (Compare **modified civil-law method**.)

Clifford trust   A grantor trust whereby the grantor (settlor) retains the right to possess again the property transferred in trust—that is, the settlor retains a reversionary interest—upon the occurrence of an event or the expiration of a period of time; unless the requirements of the federal tax laws are met, the income from the property placed in trust will continue to be taxed to the settlor.

Codicil   A testamentary instrument executed subsequent to the execution of a valid will; codicils must be executed with the same formalities required for the execution of wills.

Collateral (relative)   A person who is related through common ancestry to another but is neither a lineal ascendant nor a descendant of the other person; for example, an aunt, nephew, or cousin. (Compare **ascendant**, **descendant**.)

Common-law state   See **separate-property state.**

Community property   A form of ownership in real or personal property between a husband and wife. Each spouse owns an undivided one-half interest in every item of community property. Generally, all property acquired during marriage, including all income produced from such property, is community property of the spouses. Eight states—Arizona, California, Idaho, Louisiana, Nevada, New Mexico, Texas, and Washington—have adopted a community-property system and are referred to in this context as community-property states.

Community-property state   See **community property**.

Concurrent ownership   Co-ownership in property. There are four distinct and mutually exclusive forms of concurrent ownership: (1) joint tenancy, (2) tenancy in common, (3) tenancy by the entirety, and (4) community property. (Compare **ownership in severalty**.)

Consanguinity, relationship by   Relationship by blood.

Conservator   See **conservatorship**.

Conservatorship   An arrangement under which one person (or organization), referred to as a *conservator*, has been given by the court the legal authority over and responsibility for management of another person's property and financial and business affairs—that is, the estate of another person. The person whose estate is protected is typically referred to as a *conservatee*, although the U.P.C. uses the term *protected person* in the context of conservatorships as well as in the context of other more limited protective proceedings. In some states, the term *conservatorship* is given a somewhat different meaning, referring instead to a protective proceeding for an incapacitated *adult*, either for the adult's care, custody, and control ("conservatorship of the person") or for the estate of the adult ("conservatorship of the estate"), while protective proceedings for minors and their estates are referred to as *guardianships*. (See **guardianships**.)

Constructive trust   A trust arising by operation of law where one person has fraudulently or otherwise wrongfully acquired legal title in property from another; the wrongdoer is said to hold the property in constructive trust for the original owner and is under a duty to reconvey it. Moreover, third parties who subsequently acquire title from the wrongdoer, with or without knowledge of the fraud or impropriety, might also be deemed to hold the property in trust for the original owner. The constructive trust is not an estate-planning device but rather a remedial device developed by the courts and used to settle legal disputes.

Custodian account   A special type of account established under the Uniform Transfers to Minors Act in which the owner of the account, referred to as the *custodian,* is under a fiduciary duty to hold property for another person until the person attains a certain age. If the legal document, such as a will or trust, creating the custodian account fails to specify an age for termination of the account, the custodian account terminates when the beneficiary attains the age of 18; otherwise, the document may call for the property to be held by the custodian until the beneficiary attains the age of 25.

Cy pres   Literally meaning "as near as possible," a legal doctrine by which a court can substitute one charitable organization or group of recipients for a prior beneficiary when the prior beneficiary ceases to exist or ceases to be charitable in nature. The *cy pres* doctrine also applies where the directions to the trustee of a charitable trust become impracticable and frustrate the charitable purpose or where the stated purpose has become obsolete. (See **charitable trust**.)

Decedent   A deceased person.

Decedent's estate administration   A court proceeding by which the will (if any) is proved, a personal representative is appointed by the court, the decedent's assets are inventoried, debts and final expenses are paid, and the distribution plan is approved by the court. The purpose of these proceedings is to (1) protect the decedent's heirs from fraud and embezzlement, (2) ensure that local, state, and federal taxes are paid, and (3) protect creditors of the decedent.

Declaration of trust   A declaration by the owner of property during his or her lifetime that he or she holds the property (as trustee) henceforth for the benefit of another; an express trust is thereby created without transfer of legal title in the property by the settlor to another. A trust created by declaration of trust is referred to under the federal tax laws as a *grantor trust.* (See **express trust, grantor trust**.)

Deed of trust   Also referred to as a *trust deed,* a commonly used instrument for financing the purchase of real estate; a deed of trust serves to transfer a *legal* interest in the property to a trustee (grantee) until the borrower (grantor) has paid off the debt to the lender (beneficiary). However, the trustee has no powers unless the borrower defaults on the loan or violates one of the other promises in the trust deed, in which event the trustee may sell the property and pay the lender back from the sale proceeds. If and when the borrower pays the lender the entire amount of the debt, the trustee transfers its legal interest, evidenced by the deed of trust, to the borrower.

Degree of kinship   The proximity of a relationship between two family members, as determined by the total number of steps, one for each generation, from one person up to the nearest common ancestor, then counting the number of steps down from the common ancestor to the other person.

Demonstrative gift   A gift in a will that is payable first from particular property of the estate and then out of the general assets of the estate if the particular property is insufficient to satisfy the gift. A demonstrative gift is actually a particular type of general gift. The distinction between a general and a demonstrative gift comes into play in the context of abatement—as long as the particular fund or property identified in the will is available to satisfy a demonstrative gift, the gift is not subject to abatement along with other general gifts. (Compare **general gift**, **specific gift**.)

Descendant   A person's offspring, including a child, grandchild, and so forth down through subsequent generations; also referred to as *lineal descendant* or *issue*.

Devise   *Verb:* originally, to give real property by will to another; now synonymous with **bequeath**; *noun:* originally, a gift by will of real property; now synonymous with **bequest**.

Devisee   Originally, person to whom real property was given under a will; now a beneficiary of a gift of any kind under a will. (See **bequest**.)

Discretionary trust   Any trust that allows the trustee discretion whether to distribute or withhold payments of income or principal to the beneficiary. Since the beneficiary has no right to payments that can be enforced against the trustee, the beneficiary's creditors cannot reach the income or principal until the trustee exercises his or her discretion and makes a payment.

Domiciliary administration   Estate administration in the place where the decedent was domiciled at the time of his or her death. All of the decedent's assets located in the state where the decedent was domiciled at the time of his or her death are subject to domiciliary administration (except for assets that can be transferred outside of probate).

Dower and curtesy   Rights at common law of the surviving spouse (*dower* in the case of a widow and *curtesy* in the case of a widower) to a life estate in one-third of all real property of the decedent acquired during the marriage, regardless of the decedent's will, and free from all creditors' claims or conveyances made by the decedent without the spouse's consent.

Durable power of attorney   A power of attorney that continues to be effective during the principal's disability or incapacity. A valid durable power of attorney must be executed while the principal is legally competent. If it does not take effect until incapacity of the principal, the power may be referred to more particularly as a *springing* durable power of attorney. Two distinct types of durable powers are used in estate planning: (1) the durable power of attorney for property management, and (2) the durable power of attorney for health care.

Escheat   Passage of intestate property to the state or some agency or subdivision thereof.

Estate   Generally, all assets and financial legal rights and obligations attributable to an individual (either living or deceased). The term *probate estate* refers to that portion of an individual's estate that is subject to, and passes through, formal probate proceedings. The term *trust estate* refers to all assets and financial legal rights and obligations transferred to or otherwise held in a trust by a trustee. (For *estate* as defined for estate-tax purposes, see **tax estate**.)

Estate planning   The process of developing a plan for building and preserving a person's estate during one's lifetime—particularly by providing for continued management of a person's property in the event of incapacity—and for transferring the estate at the person's death, all in a manner consistent with the person's wishes and at minimum expense and delay.

Executor   The individual or corporation nominated in a will to collect and inventory the decedent's assets, pay outstanding debts and taxes of the decedent, and distribute the decedent's remaining estate to the beneficiaries. The term *executrix* traditionally refers to a female executor, although the term *executor* is used today for both genders. The term *administrator* is used to refer to a court-appointed representative of a decedent's estate where the decedent died without a valid will. An administrator with the will annexed is appointed by the court to represent the decedent's estate where the decedent failed to appoint an executor in the will or where the named executor is unable or unwilling to so serve. *Personal representative* is a more general term referring to any of the above.

Exoneration, doctrine of   With respect to the distribution of a testate estate, a doctrine under which a devisee entitled to particular property is freed from an obligation such as a lien or encumbrance (e.g., a mortgage) on that property for which the decedent was personally liable. If the devisee is exonerated, the obligation must instead be paid from other assets of the estate (at least to the extent possible).

Exordium clause   An introductory provision or clause in a will; exordium clauses included in lawyer-prepared wills typically establish the testator's present testamentary intent and revoke all prior wills and codicils.

Express trust   A trust created at the express and intended direction of the owner of property (*settlor*). An express trust may be created either by a transfer of property from the settlor to another person as trustee (either during the settlor's lifetime or by testamentary disposition in the settlor's will) or by a *declaration of trust* whereby the settlor declares that he or she holds the property (as trustee) henceforth for the benefit of another.

Family pot trust   A trust under the terms of which distribution of principal to multiple beneficiaries is delayed, typically until the youngest beneficiary (usually a child or grandchild of the settlor) attains a particular age, thereby ensuring that all trust assets are available to meet unexpected needs of any beneficiary.

Fiduciary   A person charged with the duty of trust on behalf of another; administrators of decedents' estates, guardians, conservators, and trustees are fiduciaries and owe a *fiduciary duty*—that is, a duty of honesty and loyalty—to those whose interests they represent.

Formal proceedings   Under the U.P.C., an estate proceeding involving a "petition" to the court, a court hearing (adjudication), and prior notice of the hearing. (Compare **informal proceeding**, **supervised administration**.)

Fraud in the execution   Also referred to as "fraud *in factum*," an intentional misrepresentation to the testator by another person as to the nature or contents of the will, relied upon by the testator in executing the will.

Fraud *in factum*   See **fraud in the execution**.

Fraud in the inducement   An intentional misrepresentation to the testator by another person as to facts other than the nature of contents of the will that motivate the testator to make the will or to make a particular gift in the will.

General gift   A gift in a will of a general economic benefit, payable out of the general assets of the estate. In contrast to a specific gift, a general gift does not entitle the donee to any particular thing. The most prevalent example of a general gift is a *pecuniary* gift—i.e., a gift of a particular sum of money. (Compare **demonstrative gift**, **specific gift**.)

Generation-skipping transfer tax (GSTT)   A federal tax levied on significant wealth (more than $1 million) that is transferred to the decedent's grandchildren (or to subsequent generations). The purpose of the GSTT is to offset the delay in the second estate tax where the decedent's estate plan calls for the estate to "skip" the first generation, since the decedent's children are likely to die before the grandchildren. The GSTT is levied in addition to the federal estate tax and is reported on the same form (IRS Form 706). The GSTT applies not only to direct skips but also to *indirect* skips—for example, where the property is left in trust for the benefit of a child's lifetime and, upon the child's death, is transferred to the grandchildren.

Grant deed   A form of deed that guarantees to the transferee that the transferor holds marketable title, except as specified in the deed. Grant deeds are used for sales and exchanges of real-property interests as well as for transfers without consideration to trusts. (Compare **quitclaim deed**; **warranty deed**.)

Grantor trust   A term used in the federal tax laws to refer to an express trust created during the settlor's lifetime without transfer of legal title in the property to another party. A grantor trust is created by *declaration of trust*, whereby the owner of property declares that he or she holds the property (as trustee) henceforth for the benefit of another. (See **express trust**, **declaration of trust**.)

Gross estate   For the purpose of federal estate taxation, all property owned by the decedent at the time of death. The gross estate is referred to more specifically as the *gross tax estate*. The gross estate includes *all* property owned by the decedent at the time of death, regardless of whether the property is subject to probate.

Guardian   See **guardianship**.

Guardian *ad litem*   A special type of guardian appointed by the court to represent and defend a minor or incompetent person in a court proceeding (the term *ad litem* means "for the suit" or "for the purposes of the law suit").

Guardianship   An arrangement under which legal authority and responsibility for the care, custody, and control of a person, referred to as the *ward*, is conferred upon another person (or upon an organization), referred as a *guardian*, by court appointment or by parental or spousal nomination. Under the U.P.C., a person under the age of 21 for whom a guardian has been appointed *solely* because of minority (rather than due to incapacity) is referred to more specifically as a *minor ward*. A guardian's primary authority and responsibility extend to the person of the ward and not to the ward's property or financial and business affairs. In some states, the term *guardianship* is given a somewhat different meaning, referring instead to a protective proceeding for a *minor*, either for the minor's care, custody, and control ("guardianship of the person") or for the estate of the adult ("guardianship of the estate"), while protective proceedings for incapacitated adults and their estates are referred to as *conservatorships*. (See **conservatorships**.)

Heir   A person entitled to receive part or all of a decedent's estate in the event of the decedent's intestate death. The identity of a person's heirs is determined by the state's laws of intestate succession.

Holographic will   A will that is in the testator's handwriting.

Honorary trust   A trust created for some noncharitable purpose—for example, for care of pets or grave sites—but without a beneficiary. The trustee is on his or her "honor" to carry out the settlor's wishes, since there is no beneficiary to enforce the trust.

Incorporation by reference   A legal doctrine by which a separate writing in existence at the time a will is executed is made part of the will by reference in the will to the writing.

Independent significance   A legal doctrine by which a will may dispose of property by reference to documents, facts, or events that may have sufficient significance apart from their impact on the will.

Informal proceeding   Under the U.P.C., either a testacy or appointment proceeding involving a verified ''application'' to a nonjudicial officer of the court, referred to in the U.P.C. as the *Registrar,* who may either ''accept'' or ''deny'' the application. Informal proceedings may be used in combination with *formal proceedings* so that any question relating to the estate may be resolved by court adjudication without necessarily subjecting the estate to the necessity of judicial orders for other questions. (Compare **formal proceedings**, **supervised administration**.)

Interested witness   A witness to a will who stands to benefit under the provisions of the will.

Inter vivos   Among or between the living.

Inter vivos **trust**   Also called a living trust, a trust document that is created and put into effect during the settlor's lifetime. (Compare **testamentary trust**.)

Intestate   (1) To die without a valid will. (2) Describing a decedent who has died without a valid will. *Noun:* **intestacy**. *Antonym:* **testate**.

Intestate succession   Referring to entitlement in a decedent's property not disposed of by a valid will or other method of transfer.

Irrevocable trust   A trust that, once created, cannot be revoked by the settlor; an irrevocable trust, once established, forever terminates the settlor's rights with respect to the trust property, unless the settlor retains a reversionary interest in the property. Testamentary trusts are inherently irrevocable, although an *inter vivos* trust may be either revocable or irrevocable. (Compare **revocable trust**.)

Issue   See **descendant**.

Joint tenancy   A form of co-ownership, joint tenancy is property ownership by two or more persons in which all owners share ownership equally and in an undivided manner. Each and every joint tenant has a ''right of survivorship''—that is, when a joint tenant dies, his or her interest in the property automatically passes to the surviving joint tenant(s), regardless of whether the deceased joint tenant indicated otherwise in his or her will. Unless joint tenants agree otherwise, any joint tenant may transfer a joint-tenancy interest during his or her lifetime (either to another joint tenant or to another party). (Compare **tenancy-in-common**.)

Joint will   A single will executed by two or more persons and intended to serve as the will of each.

Jurisdiction   The power and authority of a court to hear and decide certain types of legal matters; in matters relating to decedent's estates, trusts, and protective proceedings, jurisdiction lies with a court that is referred to in most states as the *probate court*. (Compare **venue**.)

Lapse   With respect to the law of wills, describing the situation where a gift fails because the devisee predeceased the testator. An alternative disposition may be made by the will to avoid lapse. Otherwise, in the absence of an antilapse statute, the gift passes to the residuary devisee (or to the remaining members of the class in the case of a *class gift*, or to the intestate heirs if the will fails to indicate a residuary beneficiary or if the lapsed gift is a residuary gift). (See **antilapse statute**.)

Legacy   A gift by will of personal property. (See **bequest**.)

Legatee   A person to whom personal property is given under the terms of a will.

Letters of Administration   A formal instrument issued by the court authorizing a person to serve as personal representative of the decedent's probate estate. In some states, *Letters Testamentary* are issued instead if the personal representative was nominated in the decedent's probated will, while in other states *Letters of Administration* are issued in all cases. (Compare **Letters Testamentary**.)

Letters Testamentary   A formal instrument issued by the court authorizing a person nominated in the decedent's probated will to serve as personal representative of the decedent's probate estate. Courts in some states do not issue Letters Testamentary but rather issue *Letters of Administration* in all cases. (Compare **Letters of Administration**.)

Life insurance trust   A type of irrevocable *inter vivos* trust in which the only asset contained in the trust is a life insurance policy. The proceeds are not subject to probate, and because the trust is irrevocable, the proceeds are not included in the settlor-decedent's taxable estate.

Living will   Also referred to as a *directive to physician*, a written document by which an individual expresses his or her wishes concerning the use of artificial means to sustain his or her life in the event of a terminal illness.

Marital deduction   An unlimited deduction from taxable *inter vivos* gifts and from a decedent's gross tax estate for all property passing to the decedent's surviving spouse. As a result of the marital deduction, in most situations where there is a surviving spouse to whom a large portion of the estate passes, no estate tax will be owing upon the death of the first spouse. As a general rule, the marital deduction is available only for property passing outright to the surviving spouse; if the spouse is not given complete control over the use, enjoyment, and disposition of the property, the marital deduction cannot be used. However, the tax law provides certain exceptions to this rule where the property is placed in trust for the use and benefit of the surviving spouse until his or her death.

Marital property   Property owned concurrently by a husband and wife as either community property or in the form of tenancy by the entirety.

Mistake in the execution   A mistake on the part of the testator as to the nature or contents of the executed instrument.

Mistake in the inducement   A mistake on the part of the testator as to certain facts other than the nature of contents of the will that motivates the testator to make the will or to include a particular provision in the will.

Modified civil-law method   A method of determining next of kin for the purpose of intestate succession; under this method, all claimants related to the decedent in the lowest degree share in the decedent's estate as next of kin, unless claimants are related to the decedent most closely through different ancestors, in which event the claimants who are related through nearer ancestors take as next of kin to the exclusion of all others. (Compare **civil-law method**.)

Mortgage   A contract by which the borrower (referred to as the *mortgagor*) pledges property to another (referred to as the *mortgagee*) as security in order to obtain a loan. By using a mortgage deed, the lender (grantee) is actually placing a *lien* against the property, thereby obtaining an equitable interest in the property. (Compare **deed of trust**.)

Mutual wills   Also referred to as *reciprocal wills*, two or more wills each executed by a different person that contain substantially similar provisions; these wills are commonly used by two spouses.

Next of kin   The surviving relative or relatives of a decedent most closely related to the decedent, as determined by the civil-law method or by the modified civil-law method. (See **degree of kinship**, **civil-law method**, **modified civil-law method**.)

No-contest clause   A special provision included in a will for the purpose of discouraging will contests; any contesting devisee forfeits his or her inheritance if a no-contest clause is included in the will, but if the contestant defeats the will, the clause is also defeated. Although no-contest clauses are made expressly enforceable by statute in most states, some states refuse to recognize their validity.

Nuncupative will   An oral will made by a person in peril of death; where authorized, a nuncupative will may dispose of limited amounts of personal property.

Omnibus clause   A request in the petition for final distribution of a decedent's estate that after-discovered property be distributed to specified persons, such as the residuary beneficiary or a trustee of a testamentary trust. An omnibus clause avoids the necessity of reopening the estate in the event of newly discovered property.

Ownership in severalty   Sole and absolute ownership in property, more commonly referred to as individual ownership.

Partial intestacy   Referring to the situation in which a person has died failing to dispose of only a portion of his property by will or other method of transfer.

Per capita   Equally (literally, "by the head"), as in an equal division of an estate among heirs or beneficiaries.

Per capita **with right of representation**   A method of distributing a decedent's estate among surviving issue that combines the common-law principle of representation with the *per capita* approach. Under this method, the estate is distributed according to the principle of representation unless all takers are related to the decedent in the same degree, in which event the estate is distributed *per capita*.

Personal representative   A general term describing the person in charge of the collection, management, and distribution of a decedent's estate. (See **administrator [of an estate], executor**.)

Per stirpes   By representation (literally, "by the root"), as in the distribution of a decedent's estate. (See **principle of representation**.)

P.O.D. (payable on death) account   See **Totten trust account**.

Pour-over will   A simple one- or two-page will under the terms of which property remaining outside of an *inter vivos* trust and not disposed of by some other means is distributed at the testator's death to the trust to be administered and distributed in the same manner as all other trust assets. A pour-over will must be executed in accordance with the same formal requirements for execution of other wills.

Power of appointment   A power conferred by one person, either by deed or by will, on another person to select the person(s) entitled to receive and enjoy particular property and/or income from the property. A *general* power of appointment authorizes the holder to select any person, including himself or herself, as the recipient, whereas a *limited* power does not (a limited power may place additional restrictions on the holder's authority as well). A general power of appointment is fully subject to federal estate taxation.

Power of attorney   A written instrument by which one person, as principal, appoints another person as an agent, conferring upon the agent the authority to perform certain specified acts or types of acts on behalf of the principal. The agent, referred to as an *attorney in fact*, may use the power of attorney as evidence of his or her authority.

Present testamentary intent   Intention by a testator to make a particular instrument his or her will at the time he or she signs it.

Pretermitted heir   Literally meaning "forgotten heir," an heir of the decedent inadvertently omitted from the decedent's will and excluded under the will from sharing in the decedent's estate; pretermitted-heir statutes entitle a pretermitted spouse or child of the decedent to an intestate share of the decedent's estate, but only under certain circumstances.

Principle of representation   A common-law principle governing the distribution of property among issue of a descendant. Under this principle, the estate is divided into as many shares as there are children of the decedent still alive and deceased children of the decedent who left issue surviving the decedent; each living child takes his or her share, while the issue of a predeceased child share by the same principle. (Compare **per capita**.)

Probate   In its strictest meaning, this term refers to the proving of the authenticity and validity of a decedent's will. However, the term has assumed a much broader popular meaning and is now commonly used to describe the court proceeding by which the will (if any) is proved, a personal representative is appointed by the court, the decedent's assets are inventoried, debts and final expenses are paid, and the distribution plan is approved by the court. The purpose of probate proceedings is to (1) protect the decedent's heirs from fraud and embezzlement, (2) ensure that local, state, and federal taxes are paid, and (3) protect creditors of the decedent.

Probate bond   A promise to pay in the event of a breach of trust by the personal representative—for example, if the personal representative fraudulently uses estate assets for his or her personal benefit. The promisor is usually a corporation and is referred to as a *surety*.

Probate homestead   Referring to the right of a decedent's surviving spouse and minor children to continued ownership and possession of property owned by the decedent and used as their residence. Probate-homestead property is exempt from all claims against the decedent or the decedent's estate; typically, protection for the decedent's children terminates when the child reaches the age of majority, while protection for the spouse terminates upon his or her death.

Publication   In the law of wills, a testator's declaration to the witnesses, at the time the testator signs the will, that the instrument is his or her will; the U.P.C. uses the term *acknowledgment* instead.

Qualified domestic trust (QDT)   Under the federal tax laws, any trust: (1) that requires at least one trustee to be either an individual who is a citizen of the United States or a domestic corporation; (2) that requires that no distribution of corpus from the trust can be made unless such a trustee has the right to withhold from the distribution the tax imposed on the QDT; (3) that meets the requirements of any applicable regulations; and (4) for which the executor has made an election on the estate-tax return of the decedent. For federal estate-tax purposes, the marital deduction is generally not allowed if the surviving spouse is not a citizen of the United States, unless the property passes to such a surviving spouse in a QDT or if such property is transferred or irrevocably assigned to a QDT before the estate-tax return is filed.

Qualified terminable interest property   Also referred to by the acronym *QTIP*, a term used in the Internal Revenue Code referring to property that, although not transferred outright to the transferor's spouse, nevertheless qualifies for the marital deduction for gift- and estate-tax purposes, thereby escaping death taxes upon the transferor's death. QTIP property is created with the use of a *QTIP trust*; the rights of the surviving spouse as beneficiary under a QTIP must meet the strict technical requirements of the QTIP provisions of the Internal Revenue Code. (See **marital deduction**.)

Quasi-community property   Property acquired during marriage outside of a community-property state which, if the spouses lived in a community-property state at the time, would be characterized as community property; quasi-community property is treated as community property at death or divorce. Only two states, California and Idaho, have adopted the quasi-community property concept.

Quitclaim deed   A form of deed used to transfer whatever interest the transferor may have in the subject property interest, if any, without any guarantees or representations regarding the transferor's legal right to make the transfer—that is, without regard to whether the transferor has *marketable title*. Quitclaim deeds are generally used for gratuitous transfers among family members and for transfers to revocable trusts. (Compare **grant deed**.)

Reciprocal wills   See **mutual wills**.

Registrar   A term used in the U.P.C. to refer to an officer of the court who receives, reviews, and evaluates applications and other documents submitted to the court in estate proceedings. In the case of informal and summary estate proceedings, the Registrar's decision has the same authoritative weight as that of a judge, although the Registrar has no discretionary powers.

Republication by codicil   A legal doctrine by which a codicil and a will to which the codicil refers are treated as a single testamentary instrument executed at the date of the codicil or of the last codicil; the will is deemed to be republished and reexecuted along with the codicil, so that the will is made to speak as of the date of the codicil.

Residuary gift   A gift in a will of what remains of the testator's property after payment of debts, expenses, and taxes as well as after satisfying all specific, general, and demonstrative gifts. A residuary gift is created by a *residuary clause* for the purpose of avoiding partial intestacy.

Resulting trust   A trust arising by operation of law in which an intent to create a trust, although not expressed, may be inferred from circumstances; for example, where a person conveys legal title to another intending to create an express trust, but the trust fails for lack of one or more elements necessary for the creation of a valid express trust, the transferee may be deemed to hold the property in trust for the transferor and has a duty to reconvey the property to the transferor (or to his or her estate). The resulting trust is not an estate-planning device but rather a remedial device developed by the courts and used to settle legal disputes.

Revocable trust   Commonly referred to as a *revocable living trust,* a type of express trust created by a settlor during his or her lifetime; the settlor retains the power to revoke the trust and take back ownership of the trust property. (Compare **irrevocable trust**.)

Separate property   Any property owned by a person other than as community property or in the form of tenancy by the entirety.

Separate-property state   In the context of marital property, a state that has not adopted a community-property system of property ownership between spouses; also referred to as common-law state. (Compare **community-property state**.)

Settlor   The creator of a trust, also called the *grantor* or *trustor.*

Soldiers' and sailors' wills   Oral wills made by enlisted members of the armed forces while on active duty.

Special administrator   A person appointed by the court to serve temporarily as administrator of a decedent's estate until the appointment of the personal representative; a special administrator may be required where a delay in appointing the personal representative is likely and where urgent action is required to protect or preserve the decedent's estate in the meantime.

Specific gift   A gift in a will of a particular item of property distinct from all other property in the testator's estate. In order for a gift to be characterized as a specific gift, the testator must intend the donee to receive a particular thing, and only that thing. (Compare **demonstrative gift**, **general gift**.)

Spendthrift trust   Any trust that includes a special provision (spendthrift provision) prohibiting the beneficiary from transferring his or her interest voluntarily. The trust may also, and generally does, prohibit involuntary transfers. However, a spendthrift provision restricting involuntary transfers but not voluntary transfers violates public policy and is invalid (although the other provisions of the trust generally remain valid).

Statutory commission   Also referred to as a *statutory fee,* a commission computed as a percentage of the value of the estate and serving as compensation to the personal representative and to the estate's attorney for ordinary services—that is, for those services performed in the regular course of administration. Under a typical commission schedule, statutory fees as a percentage of the estate's value decrease as the value of the estate increases.

Statutory fee   See **statutory commission**.

Statutory will   A will in a form prescribed by statute; where authorized, statutory wills are conclusively valid as to form.

Stepped-up basis   An increase in the income-tax basis of property upon transfer. The most common situation in which a step up in basis will occur is when a decedent dies owning appreciated property; the estate or heir acquires a basis in the property equal to the fair market value on the date of death (or alternate valuation date if available and elected). Accordingly, an heir or devisee will receive a ''stepped-down'' basis instead if the value of the property has depreciated between the time it was acquired and the owner's death. (See **tax basis**; compare **carryover basis**.)

Stock or bond power   A special power of attorney authorizing the transfer of publicly traded securities (stocks and bonds). A stock or bond power must be executed by a person having the authority to sign on behalf of the decedent (e.g., the personal representative).

Supervised administration   A system of estate administration under the U.P.C. in which the administration of the estate is treated as a single continuous formal proceeding to secure complete administration and settlement under the continuing authority of the court.

Support trust   Any trust that by its terms requires the trustee to distribute only as much income or principal as necessary for the beneficiary's support. The beneficiary of a support trust is not entitled to payments of either income or principal. A beneficial interest in a support trust is not assignable, either voluntarily or involuntarily.

Tax basis   Also referred to as *income-tax basis* or *basis*, a tax term referring to the consideration paid for an asset, decreased to account for such factors as depreciation and depletion, and increased to account for such factors as improvements made to the asset.

Tenancy by the entirety   A form of concurrent property ownership shared by two spouses. This form is provided for only in a minority of common-law states. Under this form, each spouse owns an undivided one-half interest in the property, and neither spouse can transfer an interest without consent of the other spouse. At the death of a spouse, the deceased spouse's interest passes to the surviving spouse. (Compare **community property**.)

Tenancy-in-common   A type of co-ownership, tenancy-in-common is a form of property ownership by two or more persons in which, unlike joint tenancy, the co-owners have no right of survivorship. Tenants-in-common may own property in unequal proportions and may freely transfer their respective interests either during their lifetime or by will. A husband and wife may hold property as tenants-in-common, and their respective interests will be characterized as separate rather than community property, as long as the document of title clearly indicates so. (Compare **joint tenancy**.)

Testament   A will.

Testamentary capacity   The mental capacity of a person to execute a valid will; testamentary capacity requires that the maker of the will be of legal age (generally 18) and of sound mind—that is, that the person know what property he or she owns and whom he or she wants to benefit from the will.

Testamentary trust   A trust that is established by the will of a decedent; a testamentary trust cannot come into being until after the decedent's death because a will has no legal effect until the death of the decedent.

Testator   The person making and executing a will. *Adjective:* **testate**.

Testimonium clause   A written declaration by a witness to a will, made under penalty of perjury (although not made or signed before a notary public), as to the facts surrounding the execution of the will. A testimonium clause provides a substitute for in-court testimony, thereby obviating the need to locate witnesses in the event the validity of the will is challenged when offered for probate. (Compare **attestation clause**, **self-proved will**.)

Totten trust account   A form of savings or checking account in which the balance remaining in the account at the owner's death is payable to a beneficiary named by the account owner; distribution of the funds to the beneficiary is not subject to probate. *P.O.D. (payable on death) accounts*, which are more commonly used today, have the same effect as Totten trust accounts.

Trust   A fiduciary relationship with respect to property, subjecting the person by whom the title to the property is held to equitable duties to deal with the property for the benefit of another person, which arises as a result of a manifestation of an intention to create it. A trust may be established by a trust agreement executed during the settlor's lifetime or may arise after the death of a testator (or, in the case of a *constructive trust*, by operation of law). All trusts involve three essential parties: (1) the settlor, who transfers title in certain property to a trustee; (2) the trustee, who is given legal title to the property; and (3) a beneficiary, who is entitled to the benefits of the trust (according to its provisions). The trust is enforceable only by its beneficiaries, whose rights arise from what the law calls their *equitable title*. The settlor retains no rights over property transferred to the trust and cannot control the trustee's acts (except in the case of a revocable trust or where the settlor is also trustee and/or beneficiary). A property interest must be transferred to the trust in order for the trust to be valid; trust property is also called the *corpus* or *res*.

Trust administration   The process of managing and distributing the property placed in trust.

Trustee   A party who obtains legal title to property from another and is legally obligated as a fiduciary to manage and distribute the property for the benefit of a third party.

Trustor   See **settlor**.

Undue influence   In the context of execution of wills, mental or physical coercion by a person against a testator impinging upon the testator's freedom and resulting in the wishes of that person being substituted for those of the testator.

Uniform Probate Code   A model statutory scheme developed by legal scholars intended both as a guide for state legislatures and as a reflection of current law in the United States in the areas of wills, trusts, and decedents' estate administration.

Uniform Testamentary Additions to Trusts Act   A broadly drafted statute, which has been adopted in many states, permitting the pour-over of estate assets to an *inter vivos* trust as amended at the time of the testator's death.

Universal succession   Summary distribution of a decedent's estate under the U.P.C., in which, if certain requirements are met, a decedent's estate that otherwise would be subject to either formal or informal administration may be distributed without administration to the heirs or devisees, who are referred to under these provisions as *universal successors.* There are no limitations as to the value of an estate that may be distributed to universal successors under the U.P.C.

Venue   Place or location for the occurrence of an event; within the context of legal procedure, the proper location (e.g., state, county, or city) for legal proceedings in a court of law. (Compare **jurisdiction**.)

Ward   A person for whom a guardian has been appointed. (See **guardianship**.)

Warranty deed   A deed in which the grantor makes certain express promises about the title being transferred; in some states, however, this term is used synonymously with the term *grant deed*, which holds a somewhat different meaning. (See **grant deed**; compare **quitclaim deed**.)

Will   A legal document by which a person states his or her binding intentions regarding the disposition of his or her property upon death; a will has no legal effect until the maker's death, and therefore the maker is free to modify or revoke a will in any way prior to death. (For specific types of wills, see, e.g., **holographic will**, **attested will**.)

Will contest   A proceeding in probate challenging the validity of a will or a part thereof; a will contest may be based upon any of the following grounds: (1) lack of due execution; (2) revocation of the will; (3) lack of testamentary capacity; (4) undue influence (including duress and menace); (5) fraud; or (6) mistake.

INDEX